THE BOOK OF SELF CREATION

THE BOOK OF SELF CREATION

Shadow Tree Series
Volume 1

Jacobus G. Swart

THE SANGREAL SODALITY PRESS
Johannesburg, Gauteng, South Africa

First edition, 2009
Second edition, 2011

Published by The Sangreal Sodality Press
74 Twelfth Street
Parkmore 2196
Gauteng
South Africa
Email: jacobsang@gmail.com

Copyright © 2009 Jacobus G. Swart

All rights reserved. No part of this publication may be reproduced or transmitted in any form or by any means, electronic or mechanical, including photocopy, without permission in writing from the publisher. Reviewers who wish to quote brief passages in connection with a review written for inclusion in a magazine, newspaper or broadcast need not request permission.

ISBN 978-0-620-42884-2

Dedicated to Gidon Fainman

"Unbreakable are links of love which faith and friendship forge among all souls discerning one another by the Light within them. Welcome indeed are they that enter with entitlement our closest circles of companionship."

—William G. Gray (*The Sangreal Sacrament*)

Contents

Introduction i

1. *Kabbalah*: Facts & Fiction 1
    A. Introduction 1
    B. The Rise of *Kabbalah* 14
    C. Ten and not Nine, Ten and not Eleven 56
    D. Right, Left and Centre 90

2. From "Nothing" to "Something" 103
    A. *Ain Sof:* "The Eternal No-Thing" 103
    B. "Three-Acting-Together-As-One" 114
    C. Space, Time and Events 119
    D. Fate, Destiny and Free Will 127

3. The Triple Soul & Shadow Bodies 139
    A. Introduction 139
    B. The Three Selves 142
    C. Shadow Bodies 154
    D. The Mantle of Righteousness 157

4. Magical Empowerment 163
    A. Introduction 163
    B. Discovering the *Nefesh* 165
    C. Self-Exorcism 181
    D. The Rite of *Noten Kavod* (Giving Respect) ... 186

5. The Science of Breath 189
    A. *Avir:* Universal Life-Force 189
    B. The Mother Breath 193
    C. The Complete Breath 195
    D. Advanced Breathing Programme 196
    E. Taking on the Name 204

6. Invoking Divine Power 215
    A. Introduction 215
    B. Invocation of Subtle Energy 221
    C. Practising the Presence: Spontaneous Dance ... 227
    D. Exercising the Spirit Body 228
    E. Creating Your Own Reality 229
    F. Directing *Ruchaniyut:* Spiritual Force 245

7. Four in the Heavens, Four on the Earth 253
    A. Introduction 253
    B. Identification with the Elements 256
    C. Breathing the Elements 258
    D. Amplification of the Elements 260
    E. Balancing with the Elements 262
    F. Projecting the Elements 263
    G. Mastering the Universal Element 266
    H. *Arba Ruchot:* The Four Winds (Directions) 269

8. The Five-fold Path 289
    A. *Kavvanah:* Attitude or Focussed Awareness 289
    B. *Devekut:* Divine Union 299
    C. *Hishtavut:* Equanimity 310
    D. *Hitbodedut:* "Aloneness" or Meditation 313
    E. *Ru'ach ha-Kodesh:* Universal Consciousness 346

9. *Maggidim:* Spirit Messengers 351
    A. Introduction 351
    B. Contacting a *Maggid* 360
    C. The Power of Positive Feeling 361
    D. *Otiot:* Hebrew Letters as Archetypes 369
    E. *Shemot:* Words of Power 379

10. Ascending in Light 395
    A. Introduction 395
    B. The Procedures of Light 398
    C. *Lekaven Tiferet:* Acknowledging Beauty 402
    D. Tracing the *Bet* 404

References & Bibliography 423

Illustrations
    Cover Illustration .... N. Vueden
    Page 68 .... Tree of Life
    Page 130 .... Star of David
    Page 151 .... Triads of the Tree of Life
    Page 153 .... Scale of Beauty, Mercy & Severity
    Page 211 .... The Body & the Tetragrammaton
    Page 253 .... Circled Hexagram
    Page 254 .... The Four Elements
    Page 280 .... Cosmic Cross
    Page 281 .... Signing the Cosmic Cross
    Page 303 .... The Bow—*Keshet*
    Page 406 .... Circle of Zodiacal Correspondences
    Page 414 .... Interlocking Circles
    Page 414 .... Body of Light

Hebrew Transliteration

There are transliterations of Hebrew words and phrases throughout this work. In this regard I have employed the following method:

The Hebrew vowels are pronounced:

> "a" — like "a" in "f**a**ther";
> "e" — like the "e" in "l**e**t" or the way the English pronounce the word "**A**ir" without enunciating the "r";
> "i" — like the "ee" in "s**ee**k";
> "o" — like the "o" in "n**o**t" or the longer "au" in "n**au**ght"; or again like the sound of the word "**Awe**";
> "u" — like the "oo" in "m**oo**d";
> "uh" — like the "u" in "h**u**rt" or the "ea" in "h**ea**rd";
> "ai" — like the letter "y" in "m**y**" or "igh" in "h**igh**" or like the sound of the word "**eye**"; and
> "ei" — like the "ay" in "h**ay**."

The remaining consonants are as written, except for:

> "ch" which is pronounced like the guttural "ch" in the Scottish "Lo**ch**" or the equivalent in the German "I**ch**," and "tz" which sounds like the "tz" in "Ri**tz**" or like the "ts" in "hear**ts**."

In most cases an apostrophe (') indicates a glottal stop or a small break to separate sections of a word or create a double syllable, etc. For example, I often hear people speak of *Daat* (Knowledge), sounding one long "*ah*" between the "*D*" and the concluding "*T*." The correct pronunciation is however *Da'at*, the apostrophe indicating that the term comprises actually two syllables, "*dah*" and "*aht*." In this word a quick glottal stop separates the one syllable from the other.

One further rule is that the accent in Hebrew is more often than not placed on the last syllable of the word. Of course there are numerous instances which disprove this rule, but it applies almost throughout Hebrew incantations, e.g. those to be found in Merkavistic literature.

"A Palace is made with many windows facing east and west... ... .

INTRODUCTION

A fellow Companion of the Western Inner Way asked what turned out to be a most difficult question for me to answer. He queried the readership I meant to target with this book. The truth of the matter is that I simply did not contemplate only certain individuals or select groups reading this text, or even that any readers may find the terminology employed throughout this work somewhat difficult to understand. So for whom is this book written? For all who seek God within and who would prefer to steer the course of their lives in a personal manner. In this regard, this book is not written exclusively for "rationalists," since reason is not the primary instrument at our disposal on the road to self-discovery and self-creation. However, neither is it intended specifically for "sensationalists." Physical sensation is equally not the ultimate basis of our "Inner Knowledge" and "Spiritual Growth." We cannot reject feeling and rest on thinking alone. Thus I am calling on both the "rational" and "emotional" aspects of the reader, and am addressing those who will "think" and "feel" with me in this discourse, since this study lies between mind and body, both pushing the "I" towards a greater realisation of "God within."

The material shared in this book might appear most odd and farfetched to the average reader. However, after many years of practical employment of the teachings and techniques addressed here, I can assure you that this book comprises no fanciful notions. Besides employing these doctrines and practices to expand my consciousness and to evolve spiritually, I have used this information to consciously create my daily physical circumstances, and avert life threatening conditions.

So I am asking you to hear me out, and then make up your mind as to the verity of these teachings. I will not only impart the theory, but will share related techniques as well. The latter can be easily and comfortably worked, the only danger being the "fears" you may have "bought into" regarding possible detrimental effects on your body, mind, soul and spirit. Such fears are easily alleviated when one aligns oneself with the "Divine Intention" *inside* oneself. In this regard, my late mentor gave me the following advice years ago, and I have found it of inestimable value. Prior to studying any Kabbalistic material, one should sit for a few seconds in a restful, peaceful manner with eyes shut, and meditate on these words:

> "Open my eyes so that I may perceive the wonders of Your teaching."

Whisper this phrase repeatedly, and allow yourself to "feel" the meaning of the words you are uttering. Do not go on a mental trip, i.e. trying to explain the meaning of the phrase you are contemplating. Simply repeat the words and allow yourself to sense their meaning by experiencing what they "feel like" inside you. Continue with this for a while, then read the section you wish to study. It is often a good idea to read a section in its entirety, without trying to perceive the meaning within it, then to pause for a few seconds, and only afterwards attempting to understand the meaning of what was written. In this way you might start implementing an important teaching of *Kabbalah* within yourself, the one which enjoins us to unite two "worlds"—the "Inner" and the "Outer." By allowing yourself to develop a "feeling appreciation" of what you are reading, you learn to surrender to the words. You open yourself, abandon the "me," and purge arrogance and bias. You simply try to sense within your being what is being portrayed in the specific section you are reading. This action halts the expansion of your ego, and increases your chances of obtaining "True Knowledge."

There are always two sides to imparting a teaching. Firstly there is its transmission to the recipient. Secondly, the recipient must be a container capable of receiving the "higher mysteries hidden in the spaces" as it were, since words alone cannot express these teachings. They must be experienced directly. The act of surrendering to the words of a teaching, of sensing their meaning within your soul, is the first step in the direction of encountering the teaching in the most direct sense possible. Teachings, generally understood as esoteric or mystical in all traditions, are mostly written down nowadays, and available to all and sundry for personal perusal. It must however be made quite clear, that though you may read information on *Kabbalah*, Magic and related traditions from printed pages, what turns these teachings into such enigmas is the very fact that their true perception hinges on the condition of your "Self," your real "Inner Being" or Spirit.

By starting with this method of sensing the meaning of these texts through a "feeling appreciation" rather than a "thinking" one, you move in the direction of what is called *Devekut*, "Divine Union," a process we will discuss more fully later in this first volume. For now it is enough to know that it refers to you aiming to achieve a "Sacred Union" with God inside yourself. This ultimately enables you to gain true knowledge acquired from encountering the "sacred" within your own being.

Now, both Kabbalists and Ritual Magicians are inclined to portray those persisting within mainstream religions, to be spiritually poor, yet it is not necessary to be a "mystic" to be a Kabbalist or a Ceremonial Magician, for that matter, since many of those who pursue the study of these subjects, are not particularly mystically minded at all. They may have no practical experience of the unique metaphorical systems of these traditions, and maybe calling themselves "Kabbalists" might be wrong. Nevertheless, they are fellow voyagers in the realms of "Divine Revelation," who might be contributing as much to the survival of these traditions as a practising Kabbalist does.

Of course, it is the one working with both the theoretical and the practical aspects of these traditions, literally acting as a conduit directing the Divine Force-flow into mundane existence, who is able to *live* the real meaning of *Kabbalah* and Ritual Magic. In this regard, I am truly fortunate to have had the opportunity of studying and working for a period of about fourteen years with William G. Gray, the astute English occultist who approached both *Kabbalah* and the Western Mystery Tradition with basic "common sense." It is to him that I owe the spiritual sensibilities incorporated in my own life.

However, regarding the subject of study, you will eventually notice that when you say "I understand," you really only understand your own interpretation of what is said or written, i.e. the contents of your own mind. Your understanding depends on *your* abilities to perceive, and *your* mental and emotional states at the time of reading anything, will play a major role in how you perceive or understand the subject matter at hand. It is thus of utmost importance to read paragraphs and chapters from as many angles possible. Since your mental and emotional stances changes throughout the day, you will understand anything you read in various ways, such comprehension being always in harmony with mood and mind-set. Remember you will always look at the world through "'me'-coloured glasses." Thus, when you read something while in an angry frame of mind, you will understand what you read in an "angry" way. I can assure you that if you are in a "sexy mood," quite innocent material can turn into amazing pornography! It is because of this very factor, that you will gain the greatest benefit from spiritual literature, when you can encounter this material from as many perspectives, i.e. moods and mind-sets, as possible.

In my estimation the important principle in "learning" any teaching is the "fetching out" factor, the surfacing from inside yourself that which is there already. Books may bring out objective conscious recognition of it on normal focal levels, but that is all they will do. We suppose we are "pushing knowledge into people" by means of books and external instruction. In point of fact, how much are we fetching out of them by stimulating their imagination with meaningful symbology which evokes the right responses from them? We are certainly not isolated little "islands," as many would have it. Each of us is greatly impacted upon by those we meet in our lives. In fact, you and those you encounter are sometimes going to be disturbed to your very depths by what you will bring out of one another.

However, what we should be doing is guide the currents of consciousness which circulate through the "Ocean of Awareness" we all share, so that everyone benefits because of the modulations we made. In one way it is like a flow of pure energy. Each separate mind that uses it, is processing it in some way which will affect other minds accepting it. We live in a "sea" of each other's thoughts, and in this regard I have been impacted upon in the most meaningful manner imaginable. My life is constantly enriched by the "waves" my Spiritual Companions are making in this vast ocean of consciousness. In fact, this book is the product of what they managed to fetch out of me, hence I need to offer my most heartfelt thanks to Gloria, my mistress, my wife, my source of inspiration, the love of my life, who taught me that one is never too old to have a happy childhood; to William G. Gray, my beloved Father-Brother in the Blessed Blood, whose firm dedication to clarity and common sense, have helped me to expand my consciousness in absolutely the most meaningful way; to Norma Cosani, Gidon Fainman, John Jones, Geraldine Talbot, Marq and Penny Smith, Francois le Roux and Gerhard Muller, my intimate Companions in Temple *Lux Occidentis in Extensio* of the Sangreal Sodality in South Africa, whose kindness and compassion are beyond measure, and who taught me what companionship is all about; to Marcus Claridge and Hamish Gilbert, my Companions in the *Lux in Quercus* Temple in Britain, whose thoughtfulness and appreciation of this book have spurred me on to greater action; to Tünde Gelenscér and Bence Bodnar, my magical Companions in Budapest, who kept insisting that this text be brought into print; to Vilmosh Bodnar, my godson, who is contributing so enormously to the sparkle in my life; to all those Companions on our internet forums, "whose Names are known unto Omniscience alone," and whose inspired queries have greatly influenced the contents of this book.

I would like to offer my special gratitude to Norma Cosani, Marq Smith, Geraldine Talbot and Gerhardus Muller who took time of their busy daily schedules to read this book, offer advice, rectify spelling, advise on grammar, and who did not hesitate to "call me to duty" when it came to unravelling what appeared ambiguous and obscure.

I now leave this book in your care, and pray you will gain maximum benefit from working these teachings and techniques.

Jacobus Swart
Johannesburg
March 2009

. ...and within the windows are cut glass, and each piece of glass is its own unique colour... ... .

Chapter 1
KABBALAH: FACTS & FICTION

A. Introduction

There has been a lot of bickering about what *Kabbalah* is and what it is not. Opinions have ranged from those who insist that *Kabbalah* is exclusively Jewish to those who would have the most foreign elements included in this tradition. I have no contention with the claim that traditional *Kabbalah* is entirely Jewish in origin. However, I am equally aware that *Kabbalah* did not remain Jewish throughout the centuries of its existence, and that it diversified into what could be termed "cross-cultural factions," e.g. *"Jewish Kabbalah," "Christian Kabbalah"* and *"Hermetic Kabbalah."* While these factions can certainly be perceived to be separate entities, all of them are based on fundamental doctrines developed in traditional *Kabbalah*.

I fully accept that much diversification has been going on regarding the fundamental teachings of this tradition, especially over the last century. However, having closely investigated such "doctrinal variances," it is absolutely clear that this wonderful tradition would become meaningless when its fundamental principles are compromised. In other words, principle Kabbalistic teachings and rudimentary reasoning cannot simply be altered in accordance with some personal whim. Hence it is necessary to understand the central, vital core teachings behind this Tradition, before adjusting parameters in alignment with personal perceptions. One simply can no longer speak of *Kabbalah* when the supposedly stable primary symbols and doctrines of this tradition have been sacrificed in the fray. Such has been the case in a lot of works written in the name of *Kabbalah*, and which have little or no relation to the Tradition.

There are those who would hard-sell absolutely anything and call it *"Hermetic Qabalah."* As indicated, traditional *Kabbalah* is a Jewish tradition. *Christian* and *Hermetic Kabbalah* are clearly offshoots of traditional Jewish *Kabbalah*. However, during the latter half of the 20th century, especially with the birth of the internet, we find *Kabbalah* being linked not only to the outrageous, but to the depraved. One of the most ridiculous of this genre I have encountered is termed "*Typhonian Kabbalah*."

As an individual who likes to avail himself of all "perspectives" when it comes to a tradition to which I have devoted the major portion of my life, I was naturally intrigued when I chanced upon claims of "Typhonian" associations with *Kabbalah*. I read several works dealing with this subject matter, amongst others those written by Kenneth Grant.[1] I slogged through this trash in the hope of finding at least one fragment which might have some validity, instead of pertaining to the "mysterious sensationalist" type of occult literature, or being part of the "I-was-flogged-by-fiend" genre. What I found is that this literature panders to the gullibility of those who have a penchant for the grotesque and "slimy green things".....or of any other colour provided the sliminess is left intact.

The "demonic" features particularly prominently in the writings of Kenneth Grant *et al*, and this subject is equally addressed in *Kabbalah*. In fact, since the earliest beginnings of *Kabbalah*, the *mekubalim* have debated and written on the "*Sitra Achra*," the "Left Side" considered to be the realm of the demonic, *Klippot* (demonic shards), all manner of possession, spirit impregnations, the magical invocation of a variety of "spirit entity"—including those considered demonic, even the "intermarriage" with demons, etc.[2] I have perused many primary Kabbalistic texts dealing with this topic whenever and wherever I could acquire them, and while some of them are quite weird, nowhere did I find any Kabbalist buying into anything like the dribble put forth in these eccentric "Typhonian" fantasies of Kenneth Grant *et al*.

Naturally I vigorously combat this rubbish, and have no qualms identifying and publically exposing such nasty elements found invading literature purporting to be authentic *Kabbalah*. However, I should make it absolutely clear that this does not mean that I oppose "comparative studies" between Kabbalistic teachings and those of other spiritual traditions.

As a case in point, consider for example the oriental doctrine of the "*Chakras*." There have been several studies relating this system to the Kabbalistic Tree of Life.[3] There is fundamentally no problem doing such a comparative inquiry and deriving a lot of meaning from it. However, it would be wrong to consider the *Chakras* to be part of official Kabbalistic doctrine, especially when *Kabbalah* does not acknowledge any link to this oriental system whatsoever, and when no similar comparative application of the Tree of Life exists within Kabbalistic doctrine.

From primary Kabbalistic perspectives the Tree of Life is a "universal symbol." It was not initially developed to describe so called "energy centres" on the human anatomy, hence it is incorrect to assume the *Chakras* and the Tree of Life to be portraying the same spiritual reality. It is far too easy to come up with all sorts of odds and sods, claiming such to be official *Kabbalah*. This has been done much too often, with some or other "expert" making the most outrageous claims in the name of "*Kabbalah*."

I certainly do not object to a study of a fundamental Kabbalistic teaching related in a meaningful manner to an oriental or any other system for that matter. There are many "external" concepts and teachings studied in conjunction with the Kabbalistic Tree of Life, e.g. the mentioned *Chakras*, *Runes*, *I Ching*, *Tarot*, etc. However, what should be made clear is, that while everyone is fully entitled to come up with as many personal interpretations of the Tree of Life as he or she wishes, such readings should not be construed official Kabbalistic doctrine.

In this regard, what is important is that we understand what comprises Kabbalistic teaching, then investigate those "external factors" which might enhance our appreciation of a glyph like the Kabbalistic Tree of Life, which might bring a greater understanding of ourselves and our world, and which might broaden our horizons on all levels. At the same time, we need to also keep in mind that "comparative study" does not turn the "external elements" into the official doctrine of the tradition those elements are being compared with. As an analogy, comparing Hindu teachings and archetypes to ideas found in Christianity will not turn those into official Christian doctrine, or, vice versa, transform Christian teachings into official Hinduism.

On the other hand, when one considers the opposite side of the spectrum, i.e. *"Traditional Kabbalah,"* one finds that the expression *"authentic Kabbalah"* is used mainly to indicate exclusivist approaches to this tradition. For example, most *Chassidim* would consider *Kabbalah* to begin and end with Isaac Luria. In fact, when one mentions the word *"Kabbalah"* in mainstream Judaic circles, the conversation is automatically steered towards *"Lurianic Kabbalah."*

While there are some who might include selected doctrines from earlier schools, equally "authentic" teachings are conspicuously absent. It appears absurd to me that material and teachings which scholars, committed to the serious study of this Tradition, openly recognise and acknowledge as *Kabbalah*, should be rejected out of hand by "exclusivist" and "elitist" mainstream religious factions, even more so when the rejected material was written by Jews marching to a drumbeat at variance with that of "mainstream Judaism," e.g. by "Reform" or "Reconstructionist" Rabbis."

Considering this situation, I suppose one could then understand why the orthodox faction of "mainstream Judaism" rejected the *"Christian Kabbalah"* and Hermetic varieties out of hand as "inauthentic," this despite the fact that it was "authentic Rabbis," teaching "authentic *Kabbalah*," who actually imparted much of the doctrines considered "inauthentic" to their Christian compatriots, e.g in Renaissance Italy, etc.

Of course, we must also consider the strong emphasis placed on magical practices in *Hermetic Kabbalah*, and the tradition is supposed to have nothing in common with something so "debased" as "Magic" and the "occult." Supposedly no genuine Rabbi (a term which the "extreme right" would say describes only a *Chassid*) would associate with such detestable and heretical practices, which some call "Magic" and others *Kabbalah Ma'asit* (*Practical Kabbalah*).

Getting somewhat hot under the collar on occasion, I tended to confront those who made these claims head on. Eventually I realised that no amount of reasoning would vary the views of those who would blindly stick to their guns, even when their claims did not make sense in the face of all prevailing evidence. Besides, I have also learned that the teeth of foolish argument tears at everything until nothing is left.

So, why should I bother raising this topic here? I believe questioning the validity of certain claims regarding Jewish Mysticism and *Kabbalah* can only benefit those individuals who are willing to look at verifiable hard evidence, and who might be genuinely interested in getting clarity on a subject of great importance to those who are seriously pursuing these mysteries. As far as I am concerned, I will not be bullied into submission by anyone making all kinds of claims with nothing but highly selective quotes from a supposedly "Holy Book" to support their assertions. I have found that in such cases the preferred approach has been to deliberately sideline any evidence which might proof opposing opinions, obscure facts by restricting investigation, and to drown out voices of dissent with noisy rhetoric about "heretics."

My late mentor, William G. Gray, told me the best way to approach the Tradition is to query everything. In other words, one has to become a "living question mark," so to speak. So let us ask some questions, and try to arrive at some reasonable answers after having weighed the evidence most carefully.

A. Did the *Kabbalah* commence with Moses or with Adam as some would have it? When did it really start? Was there a Jewish mystical tradition prior to its inception?

B. Does the *Kabbalah* represent a uniform body of beliefs, which remained intact from its inception to this day, or does it comprise many diverse teachings which flourished at different times over the centuries of its development? By the same token one might ask whether a Kabbalist like Abraham Abulafia or Eleazar of Worms were familiar with the fundamental principals shared in the doctrines of Isaac Luria or Moses Chaim Luzzatto? Did Kabbalists espouse the same ideas down the centuries? Also, did Kabbalists living in the same era always agree with each other? Were *all* the teachings of this Tradition accepted by *all* Kabbalists at *all* times?

C. Were Kabbalists allowed to introduce "new" perspectives, and develop different concepts over the centuries of the existence of this Tradition? Who decided whether such innovations were "legitimate" or not? Is it possible for us to discover and develop new perspectives regarding this

Tradition today? What would be the criteria in this regard, especially in terms of restrictions?

D. Was the rule about one having to be 40 years old before one was allowed to investigate *Kabbalah*, strictly applied at all times? Were there "genuine" Kabbalists who commenced their studies of the Tradition while still in their teens? Were there major contributors within this Tradition, who died before they were forty years old? Why should they have been allowed to pursue their studies of Jewish Mysticism at such a young age, while others were restricted? Who set the criteria, or were rules adjusted in harmony with a religious mind-set of a specific era?

E. Who passed the Tradition to Christian clerics during the Renaissance? Were they orthodox Rabbis, and did their action constitute a betrayal of their religion? Were there any rules restricting these Rabbis from passing the teachings of *Kabbalah* to gentiles?

F. Did any orthodox Jewish Kabbalist ever indulge in practices pertaining to magic? Were magical practices part and parcel of the Kabbalistic tradition, and how much of it has survived fairly intact today? Have we got any evidence of such practices, perhaps described by practitioners who were themselves orthodox Jewish Kabbalists? Did these Kabbalists draw a distinction between their magic and their normal way of worship? What other "occult" teachings, i.e. various forms of divination, etc., were part and parcel of the Tradition?

G. Are all aspects of the Tradition, e.g. angels, demons, all Divine Names, etc., derived from strictly Jewish sources? Were there any "pagan" or foreign influences which entered the fray, and which were developed further in *Kabbalah* or in mainstream Judaism for that matter? Why is *Kabbalah* called neo-Platonism, in contrast to the Aristotelean views of mainstream Judaism?

H. Were the orthodoxy always fully accepting of Kabbalists and their teachings? Were there periods of serious conflict amongst mainstream orthodox Rabbis and those who accepted the teachings of *Kabbalah*? Were some of those Kabbalists, who are today accepted by all as major thinkers and contributors to the development of Kabbalistic concepts, once called "heretics," excommunicated by the religious authorities, and their works destroyed by those very authorities whose descendants shower them today with honour and legitimacy?

I. Probably the strongest protest against the non-Jewish forms of *Kabbalah* today derive from the ultra-orthodox *Chassidim*. However, were not these very religionists themselves once branded "heretics" by the orthodoxy? While claiming to be the true inheritors of *Kabbalah*, were the magical practices they so deny as having any standing within the ranks of real *Kabbalah*, once part and parcel of their own belief system? How legitimate were these practices, some of which might have been perceived as quite radical by antagonistic religious authorities? What happened to these teachings and practices? Is it once again a case of nobody being as conservative as an ageing radical?

As you have noticed, I have already briefly touched upon one or two of the queries raised, and while I am unable to answer all these questions in this work, I am hoping to address at least some of them. Since this book deals in a large measure with practices considered "occult," I thought we should forthwith address the question of possible associations between *Kabbalah* and the occult.

I am floored every time I read a "proclaimed" (self or otherwise) expert passing judgment on Kabbalistic works with "astute observations" like "a good study despite the inclusion of uncalled for **occult elements** in a serious investigation into Kabbalistic doctrines" (said about Leo Schaya's "*Universal Meaning of the Kabbalah*").[4] After having repeatedly encountered this kind of reaction to numerous Kabbalistic studies, I thought I would ascertain exactly what these "occult elements" are supposed to be. This turned out to be an extremely difficult task, since the word "Occult," like the term "Gnostic," has become a popular buzzword representing virtually anything personal sentiments wish it to be.

Having quizzed a host of individuals regarding their understanding of what they think "the occult" or "occultism" was all about, and some having been greatly suspicious of the "hidden agenda" behind my query, I ended up with a most confusing list of what is considered "occult" by both the general public as well as by those who claim to have "informed insight," the latter often hinting vaguely at having acquired their sagacity straight from the horse's mouth.

Here are ten brief extracts from this extensive list on what could be considered "occult." The phrasing of some of the responses are often so amusing, I thought the direct quotes might bring a smile to your face :

1.   Astrology and related "astral arts." To Astrology many joined numerology and "analysis of one's birth date," the latter being considered different from "numerology" by some.
2.   Palmistry, graphology (handwriting analysis), "checking the moles on one's body" and "looking at one's liver to find out what the weather would be like tomorrow." Since the latter two responses were so amusing, I could not resist quoting them verbatim. Included here is the practice of "reading faces," and other related divinatory activities pertaining to one's personal anatomy.
3.   Freemasonry, Rosicrucianism, etc., and literally every organization—whether involved in esoteric studies or not—whose meetings are held in private or considered clandestine, are all considered "occult." Even if their meetings were open to the public and their practices common knowledge, it is believed they were still meeting in "secret" and were working "hidden rituals which we do not know."

    On inquiring how these respondents could have such direct information regarding these hidden details, they often turned offensive.
4.   UFO's and the Egyptian pyramids, which some maintained are linked to "crop circles in England," and according to others to "South America," and again according to still others to a large hole in the North Pole (some having a suspicion that such a hole also exists in the South Pole and elsewhere, e.g. a special mountain somewhere in the USA),

Kabbalah: Facts & Fiction / 9

which leads to a powerful, sinister anti-Christian world in the centre of the Earth. This is but a brief summary of a voluminous list comprising even more outrageous related responses.

5. All forms of Divinations, e.g. Tarot, I Ching, Dream Interpretations, etc., far too numerous to list here in full.

6. "Wearing charms on your wrists"! At the time I thought the respondent might not object to one wearing these around one's ankles, but suspecting that the objection is to wearing "lucky charms" in general, I did not bother to question any further. As it is, there were many who thought "charms," "horseshoes," "amulets, "talismans," etc., to be positively diabolical since they "interfere with the work of God."

   I meant to ask how these objects meddled with "the work of the Almighty," but since the fanaticism of many of the respondents would have deemed me one of the "fallen ones doomed to eternal damnation," I thought further probing would be a waste of time.

7. Spiritualism, "travelling in the air with the help of demons," "making oneself invisible," and "calling up the dead which is called 'necromancy' which is calling up demons for nasty purposes." In this case, the passionate look and excitement of the respondent conjured up images in my mind of demons fornicating with humans blissfully heaving under the furious onslaught, though I cannot be sure that this is what the respondent had in mind.

8. Crystals and stones, "herbs used for occult reasons"—heaven knows what the respondent was talking about. Be that as it may, the most amusing response here must certainly be "Kissing stones and the rings of the bishops and the Mafia"! This response reduced me to fits of laughter!

9. "Doing black rituals with blood taken from the stabbed vagina of a virgin".....*OY!*.....and all forms of ritual magic and witchcraft, which include "praying to angels and demons." Here I wanted to remind the respondent, who informed me that he was a most committed Roman Catholic, that his own religion called on the aid of "angels and saints."

Be that as it may, one respondent queried whether I knew that David Copperfield and David Blaine have actually "sold their soles (sic!) to the Devil and that the public does not know that they are working REAL magic"? The same individual added apologetically that there is of course no such thing as "real magic." Well.....did the mentioned individuals work "real magic" or not? Since I did not pursue the topic with the respondent, there is no conclusive answer forthcoming.

10. My compilation of what the general public considers to be "occult" comprises over 2,000 different and, in many instances, unique responses. I certainly do not intend presenting you with the full enumeration, but I thought I would conclude this very condensed summary of my survey with a tenth "unique" response (10 being the "lucky number" as it corresponds to the ten "*Sefirot*" which might turn out to be fortuitous for me!)

This response is especially interesting as it derived from a "reborn Christian" who maintained the Roman Catholic church is practising "black magic all the time" by changing the wine in the communion chalice into the literal "blood of Jesus" and then drinking it. He added some thoughts regarding the "Virgin Mary" whom he said "is not the mother of Jesus but a pagan goddess of sacrifice who demands the blood of the Christian god which is the blackest side of occultism!"

Where have we heard that one before? Haven't Jews been accused of ritually sacrificing Christian children in order to drink their blood during Passover dinners, etc., and this despite the fact that religious Jews do not actually eat or drink blood at all, such actions being strictly forbidden by Jewish religious laws?

My survey concluded with the realisation that there is not an absolutely clear or exact definition of "the Occult." An etymological dictionary, which we might at least consider somewhat reputable, defines the term:

"**Occult:** from Latin *occult-(tum)* past participle of *occulere* 'to cover up, conceal' *oc–* & base *kel–* etc., 'to hide,' and seen in *celare*, 'to hide." 1. Hidden, secret, esoteric. 2. Specifically supernatural, mystic, magical: *occult sciences*; also as noun *the Occult.....*
Occultism: Theory of, and belief in supernatural, occult (unknown) forces and powers; study or practice of occult sciences and arts....."[5]

If I take these definitions at face value, then I am obliged to concede that all religious worship and all spiritual activities fall in the "occultism" category! On the other hand, since most of the items listed above have actually lost their earlier "hidden" status, and are now openly shared in the gutter press, i.e. journals and daily newspapers around the globe, it is somewhat odd to continue considering these topics "occult" from their erstwhile "clandestine status" perspective. In fact, as indicated earlier, the word "occult" is used loosely as a reference to any spiritual activity viewed with disapproval, or with approval by those who, like myself, define themselves "occultists." While there are amongst the latter several of the "sensationalist" variety, there are equally many who are most seriously aligned with the Western Mystery Tradition as a whole.

So how about *Kabbalah* and "the Occult"? At one stage *Kabbalah* was considered "occult," because it was a "hidden tradition" accessed by relatively few committed students and serious investigators. Considering the items earlier listed "occult," most of them are present in what is called "*Jewish Kabbalah*" or what I prefer to term "*Traditional Kabbalah*." For example:

1. Both astrology and numerology comprise major portions of Kabbalistic doctrine, and a large quantity of primary information is devoted to this topic both within mainstream Judaic texts and mystical writings.[6]
2. Palmistry (*Chochmat ha-Yad*) and studying the face (*Chochmat ha-Partzuf*), including examining the "moles" on the body, were practised by Kabbalists.[7]

    We might also note that the Holy Ari, read the faces of those he encountered,[8] but I must admit that none I am aware of were actually investigating the "livers" of their

3. As to the possibility that there might have been organizations or schools considered "occult," i.e. hidden or clandestine, amongst Kabbalists, there were indeed many Kabbalistic schools down the centuries who kept their teachings hidden from all but a very restricted membership. *Kabbalah* was for a long time, and in many instances still is, an exclusive esoteric tradition within the ranks of the larger community, and while the existence of such schools were common knowledge, their doctrines were secret and available to the mentioned very select few. What is more, they worked special ritualistic practices unknown to those outside their closest circles of companionship.

4. UFO's, Egyptian Pyramids and "crop circles" do not play a part in *Kabbalah*, even though some years back an acquaintance arranged for a "crop circle Tree of Life" to be constructed for her. Neither do "holes in the poles" feature in Kabbalistic doctrines. Probably the only "Inner World" Kabbalists might be interested in, is the "the World to Come."

5. As far as all sorts of divinations are concerned, there are very many in *Kabbalah*, including the mentioned "dream interpretations" discussed.[9] Consulting a variety of oracles (*Goralot*) is also not a strange pursuit amongst Kabbalists.[10]

6. Wearing special "charms," "amulets" or "talismans" was not a strange phenomenon in Kabbalistic circles, which included some of the greatest masters writing "*Kameot*" amongst their ranks. These *kameot* range in purpose from protection during childbirth to the promotion of physical health and the invocation of financial success, etc. There is an enormous literature, penned by "authentic" Kabbalists, in existence on this very topic.[11]

Regarding *kameot*, there are some who are of the opinion that they have been replaced by modern medication, e.g. pills. There are however many within this tradition, myself included, who prefer to employ *kameot* "with understanding" rather than taking pills "without understanding." It should also be noted that not all "*Kameot*" and "*Segulot*"(Magical Remedies [Spiritual Treasures])[12] are of the "pill taking" variety, and that the principles underlying "*Kameot*" are quite different from the mind-set behind taking pills.

7. Contacting the "spirits of the dead" is equally not a foreign custom amongst Kabbalists, who to this very day indulge in prostrating themselves on the graves of departed saints and chanting special incantations, in order to establish a link between the "soul" of the departed and themselves. Here we might also consider the topic of "*Maggidim*," a term used in reference to anything from living lay preachers to "spirit messengers," some of whom are spirits of the deceased.[13] In fact, this is what an "*Ibbur*,"[14] the beneficial "impregnation" of a living human by a deceased soul, is all about, which should be carefully distinguished from a "*dibbuk*" which pertains to malevolent possession.

As far as the earlier statement regarding "travelling through the air with the help of demons" is concerned, we might note "*kefitzat ha-derech*,"[15] magical travel from one destination to another, which involved the use of what is termed the "air of demons." When it comes to the use of techniques to create "invisibility," we again have several instances of these being employed in "*Practical Kabbalah*." Consider for example the great Shalom Sharabi, who is reported to have made his way to the Wailing Wall every night at midnight to pray. At the time the terrain of the Wailing Wall was prohibited to Jews, but this did not deter the remarkable 18th century Kabbalist from employing a special method to range himself invisible to the guards.

8. While I have certainly not seen Kabbalists kissing the rings, or the butts for that matter, of some highly esteemed noble or notorious personality, I have certainly perused writings describing the benefits derived from the use of certain minerals, plants, and other substances for a variety of special purposes.[16]

9. Again *Kabbalah* is no stranger to activities classified in the "ceremonial magic" genre. There are numerous rituals, incantationary uses of Divine Names, angelic invocations,

etc. to be found in the primary magical texts of *"Practical Kabbalah."*[17]

It is worth noting that the practitioners of all the related primary works, some of which are listed in the bibliography of this book, were all Rabbis, greatly esteemed in their communities. So, having established that most of what is generally considered "occult" was flourishing in the very heart of Jewish mysticism, I am even more baffled by claims denying any primary connection between *Kabbalah* and "the Occult."

Now, we will look at the origins and development of *Kabbalah*.

B. The Rise of *Kabbalah*

I find it somewhat difficult to understand how, in the face of all available evidence to the contrary, the ultra-orthodox Jewish faction could continue having us believe that *Kabbalah* represents a uniform, coherent body of mystical teachings which God gave to Moses (some say Adam), from whom it was passed intact down the ages from one chosen rabbinical authority to another. I suspect this claim has something to do with a most problematic issue to be found in spiritual traditions, one that needs to be faced fairly and squarely, especially as it negatively impacts the world of religion like a plague.

I am referring to the general tendency to consider traditions labeled "ancient" to be "good," and the view that anything contemporary cannot compare with the "Wisdom of the Ancients." I suppose in another couple of thousand years what is written today will be similarly categorized. However, plain common sense would tell one that just as much rubbish was written in ancient days as we find in our times, and equally profound and inspired material is penned today as in ancient writings.

Also, what is the difference between a tradition said to have been given by God to Adam, or one inspired by God in the 13th century and transmitted through Moses de Leon, the supposed author/editor of the *Sefer ha-Zohar* (*The Book of Splendour*)? Absolutely nothing, except that those who wrote in the Middle Ages were having the same problems we are facing in our own times. They were battling fellow religionists unwilling to give credence to anything not authored by some or other venerated ancient authority, i.e. at least one recognised as such by tradition, legend, or both. We similarly have to deal with the inevitable "one-up-man-ship" of the "Wisdom of the Ages" and infallibility of the "Sages of those Ages," whether history tells us otherwise or not. Equally, whether one recognises this as a prodigious load of baloney or not, this dreadful situation forced serious thinkers, who would have liked their personal output to be taken seriously, to attribute their own writings to some or other religious personality with a legendary reputation. This kind of thing is still happening in our day, believe it or not!

As far as the history of *Kabbalah* is concerned, we are faced with a battle raging between fundamentalist religionists not willing to concede the validity of serious historical research, especially when such investigation has proven conclusively that the tradition called "*Kabbalah*" indeed started in the Middle Ages. It would seem they think that if they have to admit the validity of verifiable facts, this would minimize the authenticity of the tradition. Since I do not care whether a tradition is two thousand years, two hundred years or two years old, this makes absolutely no sense to me at all. It is surely the teaching that is important, and how meaningful it is to us *NOW*. The issue is clearly again the "older-is-better-virus" which appears to be at work here, and it is high time somebody does something about that.

The history of *Kabbalah* involves a multitude of personalities and texts, and traces a tortuous path in the development of its many, even divergent concepts. The word "*Kabbalah*" did not originally refer to the mystical tradition which we now call by that name. In fact, the term was previously used to describe the traditions which were passed down orally from one generation to the next, until they finally found written expression in the *Mishnah*, the two versions of the *Talmud*, etc. These texts do not in any way refer to a mystical tradition called "*Kabbalah*," nor to one which purportedly started with Moses, nor, for that matter, was passed on to the mythical Adam by the Almighty in person.

Of course, the large body of Jewish mysticism is certainly much older than *Kabbalah*, incorporating the earlier Merkavistic traditions, Jewish Gnostic teachings, etc., but contrary to popular opinion maintaining *Kabbalah* to be an ancient tradition, the origins of which are lost in the mists of time, there is no evidence that there was a Jewish mystical tradition of *that name* prior to the 12th century, when the early Kabbalists put pen to paper in southern France, specifically Provence, and wrote the early works of this Tradition. Basically then, the mystical tradition called "*Kabbalah*" has been in existence for about 900 years only. Many surprised readers will probably wonder how early Jewish Mysticism, which existed for more than a millennium prior to the 12th century, fits into the picture and why it is not considered "*Kabbalah*."

There is no doubt the origins of *Kabbalah* can be traced to earlier Jewish mystical traditions, many elements of which can be found in Kabbalistic thinking. There are however a number of folk who make much more exotic claims regarding the origins of this mystical tradition, e.g. the teachings of *Kabbalah* were stolen from Ancient Egypt, etc. Such notions are fictitious and show an ignorance of the history of Jewish mysticism, from its earliest inception in the visions of Ezekiel to its modern expressions in our times. In fact, *Kabbalah* evolved out of the earlier mystical tradition known as *Ma'aseh Merkavah* (Work of the Chariot)[18] which, as indicated, is based on the visions of Ezekiel.

The Merkavistic tradition was considered extremely sacred, and the attainment of the *Merkavah* (Divine Chariot) was connected with what was called "a Descent of Fire from Heaven," said to encompass the aspirant and leading to phenomenal emotional and ecstatic experiences. Their teachings can be found in a number of sacred texts describing the "mystical ascent" into celestial dimensions termed "Heavenly Palaces," e.g. *Hechalot Rabbati* ([*Pirke Hechalot*] Greater Palaces); *Hechalot Zutarti* (Lesser Palaces); *Ma'aseh Merkavah* (The Work of the Chariot); *Sefer Hechalot* (3 Enoch*)*; etc.[19]

I have closely examined works like the *Hechalot Rabbati*, which is still not available to a general readership in a complete English translation. Curiously enough, the portions which have not been included in the published translations are in my estimation the most important ones, as they comprise the actual "hymns" and "incantations" used by the "Merkavist" as he "journeyed" through the various celestial dimensions (Palaces), and called on the "presence" of the "Prince of the Face," etc. Yet, closer scrutiny soon makes it very apparent that one simply cannot translate these vital portions of the text, since they comprise essential linguistic properties which are plainly lost in translation. In fact, it would seem that the actual meanings of the words in these "incantations" are almost of secondary value to the hypnotic rhythm, rhyme, and alliteration used throughout Merkavistic incantations.

Here is such an incantation. The Hebrew text has been transliterated into "Latin" letters for easy vocalization by those unfamiliar with the Hebrew alphabet. To read and experience the powerful use of rhythm and sound in this incantation, sound the words aloud and as fast as you can, while surrendering yourself to their impact, i.e. attempt to *feel what the words feel like*, rather than trying to "think" them in terms of meanings. Generally the accent is on the second syllable of the words, except in the case of the concluding words, specifically *Erech, Chesed* and *Emet*.

*Atah Hu **A**don : ha-**B**aruch : ha-**G**ibor : ha-**D**agul : ha-**H**adur : ha-**V**atik : ha-**Z**akai : he-**Ch**asin : ha-**T**ahor : hay-**Y**ashar : ha-**K**abir : ha-**L**avuv : ha-**M**echayeh : ha-**N**echmad : ha-**S**od : he-**A**neiv : ha-**P**odeh : ha-**Tz**ach : ha-**K**adosh : ha-**R**achman : ha-**Sh**omer : ha-**T**omech : Erech Apayim v'rav-Chesed v'Emet.*

The author is voicing ecstatic exclamations about the divine qualities of the Almighty, and, as you can see from the bold capitals, employed every letter of the Hebrew alphabet in chronological order. Of course, these words can be translated, but the intended impact of the sounds in the original invocation would be lost. This example is a minor one amongst the great hymns and incantations to be found throughout Hechalotic literature.

Now, considering the modern misappropriation of the celebrated mystical symbols derived from the prophetic visions of the prophet Ezekiel, I believe greater clarification would be in order. We might as well commence with the "*Merkabah/Merkavah*" question, since this appears to be a rather problematic issue, especially amongst would-be "new-age" mystics. The question is basically pronunciation, which in this case pertains to the Hebrew letter "*Bet*," being one of the double letters each of which has two pronunciations. In the current instance, the letter is pronounced either as a "*B*" or a "*V*," and in the word in question the pronunciation is "*MerkaVAH*" (accent on the last syllable). This term refers to a "chariot," as in "the chariot of the king" (*Merkavet ha-Melech*), etc. A "rider" or "charioteer" is called "*Rakav*" in Hebrew, which, as you can see, becomes a "chariot" with the addition of the "*Mem*" (*M*) prefix.

Much has been made of the concept of the *Merkavah* in recent years, with some totally outlandish, crazy, and very personal claims made as far as the vision of the prophet Ezekiel is concerned. Most of these are pure fantasy comprising a pseudo-mystical, pseudo-scientific and materialistic spirituality, or perhaps better—a kind of spirituality in which "life" in the "Kingdom of Spirit" is as time–space–event bound and finite, as this material realm we are currently occupying in the lower reaches of manifestation.

Some of the worst drivel dished out, pertains to individuals asserting that they have personally stood in front of the throne of God, having arrived there in a "*Merkaba*" which is asserted to be a spaceship piloted by "Lord Michael"—the archangel no less—and his cosmonaut "hosts." One claim regarding such a supposed sojourn, maintains the Divine One personally engraved the Ten Commandments on the claimant's buttocks! Later this was adjusted to be the "back" and not the "backside" of the individual in question. That people should buy this kind of trash without question and the use of common sense, is quite beyond my comprehension.

In confronting this hogwash head on, I have been told that I do not acknowledge "direct divine revelation," the sacred truths revealed in vision to those who have a hotline to God, and that I am working with archaic ideas. As it is, I most firmly believe in direct revelation, but I always question visionary experiences, since *ALL* such visions are heavily saturated with the personality of the one who is experiencing them. By that I do not mean that there is not a measure of truth in a vision, but before one can arrive at that kernel of truth, one has to get rid of the crust of dross comprising the memories, expectations and personally coloured interpretations of the visionary.

As noted, many have dreamed up all sorts of novel notions regarding "spaceships" and "space beings" associated with the *Merkavah* of Ezekiel, claims which probably would have made the good old prophet turn in his grave, and left him most perturbed and in a state of total confusion regarding the sanity of his interpreters. It is absolutely certain that the concept of the "*Merkavah*" and the teachings of "*Kabbalah*," have never at any time pertained to spaceships or space beings coming to save the "chosen few" from this "doomed planet," as some noisy pseudo-messiahs, employing a highly decorative pseudo-scientific oratory style, would have us believe. Each time I chance upon this trash on the internet, I am reminded of the author who made the trenchant remark regarding "the intense egotism of those who count the world well lost if only their own little souls survive death forever."[20]

As far as the mentioned spaceships and their presently "earthbound" cronies are concerned, I dare say that if a "cosmic being" desired to contact us, he/she/it certainly would not need the use of a spaceship to do so. In a state of expanded consciousness, which we term an "open state," anyone and anything can be reached instantaneously, especially since in the "Eternal Now" there is no distance whatsoever. Besides, the world of manifestation is purely a reflection of what we are within ourselves, hence I have successfully lived this realisation through those very teachings some have called archaic and outdated.

What I find surprising is that, despite the enormous amount of information available today, it would seem the contemporary mystery mongers and exotic "exponents" of "lost books of the *Merkavah*," are totally oblivious of the primary Merkavistic texts in existence, ignorant of the magnificent recovery of *these* "lost books" and the outstanding research which has been done on this material over the past century.[21]

Also, the fact that a number of centuries passed between the decline of "Merkavism" and the rise of *Kabbalah*, is often overlooked. In this period, from about the 9th to the 12th century, Jewish mystical activities were somewhat sparse and sporadic. In the late 12th and early 13th century *Kabbalah* sort of burst forth, as it were, in quite a frantic manner in Germany amongst the *Chassidei Ashkenaz* (the German Pietists), in the south of France, Provence, in the circle of Isaac the Blind, and in Spain, e.g. the famed Gerona School.

These mystics were known as *"Mekubalim"* (sing. *Mekubal*). However, as far as I know this appellation was not employed within the company of the 13th century *Iyyun* circle. Instead, I noticed more oblique references like *"Chachmei ha-Kabbalah"* (the wise sages of the *Kabbalah*) in the writings of this circle of contemplative mystics.[22] However, the word *"Mekubalim"* was definitely used in the 13th century.

In modern-day Israel a clear distinction is drawn between the Hebrew term *"Mekubal"* and the English word "Kabbalist," the Hebrew term being used in reference to the more authentic mystics, while the latter is understood to refer to—in the words of a fellow Companion—"the less serious new age types." I can imagine that for scholars writing in languages other than Hebrew, it will soon be very difficult to find suitable terms to distinguish between serious "Kabbalists," and those who adopted the title for nothing better than sickly sweet sentiments, or, worse still, to hard-sell plain water, cosmetics, candles, etc., in a manner which would imply these products to have special "talismanic properties"! I wonder how the mystics of other religions, i.e. the Sufis, would respond if this were to happen in their domain of spirit? Imagine "Sufi water," "Sufi candles," etc. It is truly sad to see our great Tradition being sullied by this low, nauseating commercialism!

Now, *Kabbalah* is certainly the most important descendant of Merkavism. However, for the survival of those teachings, practices, and documents which had an enormous impact on this *Kabbalah*, we owe an enormous amount to a truly remarkable family. We would have been sadly impoverished today had it not been for the tireless efforts of members of this incredible family, who collected everything mystical they could lay their hands on. I am referring to the Kalonymus clan, originally from Lucca in Italy, whose members were not only very prominent in the Jewish world over the centuries, but some of whom contributed to the early *Kabbalah*, firstly by sharing and developing those esoteric traditions which have been passed orally along their family lines for many generations, and secondly by writing these teachings down for the first time.

The story of how this family came to be the inheritors of the secret mystical teachings of Judaism, is a complex one filled with facts and fiction. Tradition has it that in the 9th century a certain Abu Aaron Ben Samuel ha-Nasi brought the secret Jewish mystical teachings from Baghdad to Italy, where he taught these mysteries to members of the Kalonymus family. We know that Abu Aharon taught in southern Italy, and that his teachings strongly impacted there on his other protégées, the Amittai family of Oria. While this family remained in Italy, it is also well established that the Kalonymus family emigrated from Italy and resettled along the Rhine, hence they carried Jewish mystical traditions to Germany. Eleazar of Worms, a member of this family, described this transmission in his book *"Secrets of the Prayers"* (*Sodot ha-Tefillah*). The translation is by Ivan G. Marcus, who is an expert on the 13th century German Pietists:

"They received the esoteric traditions about the arrangement of the prayers as well as the other esoteric traditions, rabbi from rabbi, all the way back to Abu Aaron, the son of R. Samuel the Prince (*ha-Nasi*) who had left Babylonia because of a certain incident and he was therefore required to travel all over the world (as a penance). He came to the land of Lombardy, to a certain city called Lucca. There he found our Rabbi Moses who composed the liturgical poem 'emat nora'otecha,' and he transmitted to him all of his esoteric traditions. This is R. Moses bar Kalonimos, son of R. Meshullum bar R. Kalonimos bar R. Judah. (Now R. Moses) was the first who emigrated from Lombardy, he and his sons, R. Kalonimos and R. Yequtiel, and his relative R. Itiel, as well as the rest of the people who counted. All of them were taken from Lombardy by King Charles who resettled them in Mainz. There they grew to prodigious numbers until 1096 when the Lord visited His wrath upon the holy communities, then were we all destroyed, utterly destroyed, except for a few of our relatives who survived including R. Kalonimos the Elder. He transmitted (the esoteric traditions)—as we have written —to R. Eleazar Chazan of Speyer. R. Eleazar Chazan transmitted them to R. Samuel the Pietist and R. Samuel the Pietist transmitted them to R. Judah the Pietist. And from him did I, the insignificant one (*ha-katan*) receive the esoteric traditions about the prayers as well as the other traditions....."[23]

Eleazar of Worms did not tell us what the "certain incident" was that "required" Abu Aaron "to travel all over the world," but we are told in the *"Chronicle of Ahimaaz"*[24] that a lion had killed and ate the donkey which turned the mill of Aaron's father. Apparently Abu forced the lion to take up the task usually assigned to the ass. When his father saw what his son had done to the "king of the beasts," he was so incensed that he exiled Aaron. Fact or fiction? Well, we simply do not know. What is certain is that there are many legends about this "master of all secret mysteries," as he was called by his followers and successors.

One tale relates how, during his travels, he encountered a young man who was an outstanding prayer leader, but noticing that this individual refrained from making any reference to God in his prayers, it dawned on Aaron that the youngster was actually not alive in the normal sense of the word, that he was in fact "living dead" as it were. He ascertained that the young man must have died, and was somehow being kept alive artificially. He then determined that what kept the individual alive was the insertion of the Ineffable Name into the flesh of his right arm. It is said that Abu Aaron removed the name by cutting it out of the arm of the youth, who was immediately reduced to dust.

The details of this saga have many parallels with the magical "*Golem*" making traditions, the methods of construction of which were held by the 13th century *Chassidei Ashkenaz* (German Pietists), and are particularly explained in the writings of Eleazer of Worms. Who is to say that these Pietists, whose most prominent members were from the Kalonymus clan, did not actually receive these teachings from Aaron of Baghdad himself?

Again we have major difficulties here distinguishing between what is fact and what is fiction. Rationalists would say that the "supernatural" details are fictional, and that we must view these in the light of what we know is the truth as far as reality is concerned, but that kind of approach would fly straight into the face of those of us who have had our own fair share of so called "supernatural" encounters, and know that these have knocked a crack in our understanding of reality. Anyway, we can conclude the saga of Aaron of Baghdad with the reference that he apparently acted as a judge in the Jewish community in Lucca, and that he was immortalized as "the master of all secret mysteries."

Eleazar of Worms informed us that members of the Kalonymos family were "taken from Lombardy by King Charles who resettled them in Mainz." Supposing this "King Charles" to be Charlemagne, some modern scholars maintained this account to be fictitious, comprising purely propaganda aimed at further aggrandizing the esteemed family, for whom a higher status was being claimed in the community, etc. Ivan Marcus states categorically: "Why was it R. Eleazar of Worms who transmitted this legend? The passage was framed in a propagandistic way on several counts. It was not about German Jewry as a whole, but about R. Eleazar's family, and he presented himself as the continuation of a chain of tradition, that was authentic because it derived from an ancient Jewish source of authority (R. Samuel the Prince) and from Charlemagne, the emperor of the Franks and the Romans in the West.

To be sure, R. Eleazar may simply be telling the truth as he knew it when he reported that his teacher, R. Judah the Pietist, had taught him the esoteric traditions he had learned from his father, R. Samuel the Pietist. As R. Eleazar mentions elsewhere, the son to whom he had transmitted the secret traditions had died, and he wrote down the formerly esoteric traditions because he had no one to whom he could transmit them."[25]

I am certainly grateful to Rabbi Eleazar for writing down the mysteries, and as far as the hereditary claims are concerned, I can only say that my old mentor taught me that what I perceive from anything I read, is always in exact accordance with my attitude, i.e. my mental and emotional stance during the reading. Hence I read Ivan Marcus' indictment of Eleazar's claims, and then reread the Rabbi's statements. I paused a day, then, when I was in a different frame of mind, reread Eleazar's claims. In all instances, the manner in which I perceived the Rabbi's intentions was entirely based on my own mental and emotional stance at the time, and not on what the good Rabbi actually said. In fact, every perception I have in this regard is entirely my own, which has nothing to do with the Rabbi's stance one way or the other.

I asked myself, what it would be like if I were the inheritor of a tradition which was passed along a family line for some generations, and felt the need to impart this truthfully? Would I express it any differently to the way Rabbi Eleazar said it, and were his words truly aimed at the aggrandisement of his family? Well, we cannot know what was in the Rabbi's mind at the time, hence one's reactions are once again purely one's own subjective responses in harmony with one's own attitude, approach and stance. Hence, we can either accept or reject what Eleazar said, but we cannot speak for him.

Is the claim that the Kalonymus family were brought to Germany by "King Charles" true or false? This has been a subject of some contention. If the claim is false, we can simply dismiss it. However if the claim is true, we might ask which "King Charles" are they talking about? Is it Charlemagne or perhaps another German monarch? We noted that Eleazar of Worms maintained that the mystical teachings were brought to Germany when "King Charles" invited the Kalonymus family to resettle in Mainz. Some scholars, while accepting the transfer of the mystical tradition from Italy to Germany via the Kalonymus family, dismissed the King Charles (Charlemagne) resettlement claims altogether, viewing these as fictitious propaganda. Other scholars in turn argue that the "King Charles" reference does not pertain to Charlemagne (800–814) as was commonly believed, but to his grandson Charles the Bald (875–877).

There is however another interesting connection between a German King and a member of the Kalonymus family, which might pertain to the saga of the transmission of the mysteries from Italy to Germany. Dates might be problematic, but there is a parallel between this story and the saga of the "King Charles" invitation. History tells us that during one of his battles in Sicily, the life of Otto II, the 10th century German Emperor, was saved by a Kalonymus. It would appear that subsequently the Emperor invited this member of the Kalonymus clan and his family to settle in Germany, where they rose to great distinction in Mayence. However, until new evidence is discovered to settle the debate once and for all, we shall never know why members of the Kalonymus family settled in Germany.[26]

Now, while the teachings of Abu Aharon played a prominent role in the thought of the German Pietists, it would be wrong to consider Abu Aharon as central to the rise of *Kabbalah*. Gershom Scholem succinctly summarized the saga noting that "The ideas of the Merkabah and the *Shi'ur Komah* were already known in France at the beginning of the ninth century, as witnessed by the attacks on them by Agobard, bishop of Lyons."[27] In fact, according to the available evidence, it would seem that from the 9th century onwards a number of mystical streams merged in Germany and the south of France. These were ultimately expressed in a new way in the writings of the early Kabbalists, such as the *Sefer ha-Bahir* (*The Book of Brilliance*) which appeared in Provence in the 13th century.[28]

Naturally it would be impossible to trace the entire history and development of *Kabbalah* in this compendium. Besides, there are a number of excellent works dealing specifically with the history of *Kabbalah*.[29] I believe the following condensed overview will offer a concise insight into the development of this vast tradition. While it is by no means a complete presentation, it lists the core concepts specifically important in different periods, and who the main characters were who played major roles in the development of *Kabbalah*.

1. **Twelfth and Early Thirteenth Centuries: The German Pietists, the South of France and the *Iyyun* (Contemplative) Circle.**
    Luminaries:
    a. David ben Yehudah of Regensburg (Yehudah ha-Chassid)
    b. Eleazar ben Judah ben Kalonymus of Worms (Eleazar of Germiza [Rokeach])
    c. Moses ben Jacob of Coucy
    d. Isaac the Blind
    e. *Iyyun* Circle
    Texts:
    a. *Sefer Chassidim* (*Book of the Pious*) [Yehudah ha-Chassid][30]
    b. *Perush al Sefer Yetzirah* (*Commentary to Sefer Yetzirah*) [Eleazer of Germiza][31]
    c. *Sodey Razaya* (*Secret of Secrets*) [Eleazer of Worms][32]
    e. *The Books of Contemplation* [*Iyyun* Mystics][33]
    f. *Sefer ha-Bahir* (*The Book of Brilliance*)[34]

This is probably the most complex era in the development of *Kabbalah*, especially since the topics addressed by the *Chassidei Ashkenaz* (German Pietists) and others, e.g. the *Iyyun* circle, cover a vast domain of esoteric doctrines and occult practices. Attempting to discuss these in the few pages allotted in this book to each of the listed periods would inevitably turn out to be most ineffectual. Thus I have elected to present a very slight introduction to the mystics of this period, as well as to the curious antics they got up to.

The German Pietists developed several doctrines derived from Merkavistic thought. Of these we might focus especially on the doctrine of the ten *Sefirot*, since it became central to *Kabbalah*. The origins of this doctrine can be found in the speculations on the emanation of ten Divine powers in the pre-*Kabbalah* Jewish Mysticism (Merkavism). It was these speculations, based on Gnostic thought and Neoplatonism, that eventually crystalized into the doctrine of the ten *Sefirot* in the writings of the early Kabbalists, e.g. in the *Sefer ha-Bahir* and the works of the *Iyyun* circle.

In the period preceding the writing of the *Sefer ha-Bahir* the names and positions of the emanated powers, which ultimately developed into the scheme of the ten *Sefirot,* were not yet settled or fully agreed upon by the Merkavah mystics. We know the early mystics did refer to ten powers, or "sayings" (*ma'amarot*) through which the world came into being. In fact, already in the *Pirke Rabbi Eliezer* (*Chapters of Rabbi Eliezer the Great*), an 8th century Midrash,[35] these are divided into three higher and seven lower "attributes" (*middot*), but the three supreme attributes were then understood to be: "Wisdom," "Understanding" and "Knowledge." These were chosen because they appear together, in that order, in several Biblical verses, e.g. *Proverbs 3:19–20*; *Proverbs 24:3*; *I Kings 7:14*; *Exodus 31:3*; etc.

It was only later that *Keter Elyon* (Supreme Crown) came to be seen as part of the powers in the scheme of Divine Emanation. Even in the writings of Eleazar of Worms, the term *Keter Elyon*, though appearing many times throughout his works, was never used as a reference to the first *Sefirah*. In fact, it would seem that the first time "Supreme Crown" was used in direct reference to the first sphere on the Tree of Life, was in the *Sefer ha-Bahir*, a work which appears to have been compiled by someone in the School of Isaac the Blind in Provence. Again, this compilation was done from many, even Gnostic, sources. It has been pointed out that Rabbi Isaac the Blind, who himself might have been the author of the *Sefer ha-Bahir*, was the first mystic to devote his entire life-work to mysticism, and his many disciples disseminated his teachings in Southern France and in Spain. It was his initial input that stimulated the development of contemplative Kabbalism amongst the 13th century Spanish Kabbalists.

Now, for all its references to and discussions of the *Sefirot*, the order of these "Divine Emanations" were not yet settled in the *Sefer ha-Bahir*. For its further development, one needs to look at the writings of the mentioned *Iyyun* Circle. Well known amongst these is the *Sefer ha-Iyyun*,[36] but there are a number of short texts in which many novel deliberations were introduced regarding the *Sefirot* and the thirty-two "Paths of Wisdom." Even here the order of the emanation of the *Sefirot* varied a lot, and opinions differed a lot amongst the members of this circle of mystics. It was really in the school of the Gerona Kabbalists, in the second half of the 13th century, that the doctrine of the Ten *Sefirot* began to take on a uniform pattern, and was finally presented in the *Sefer ha-Zohar* of Rabbi Moses de Leon of Guadalajara, in the form we are accustomed to.

Of course, I have literally just touched here and there on the origins and development of the doctrine of the ten *Sefirot*, with brief references to time and place, and have given only the slightest hints at some of the individuals involved, without actually going into greater detail in terms of the various formats of the *Sefirot* as presented by the many different characters in the early centuries of its development. This topic is much too big to address here, however it was discussed in great detail by the great scholars of the last century, e.g. Gershom Scholem,[37] etc.

Now, the German Pietists and the *Iyyun Circle* of mystics held several exotic notions regarding the mystery of creation and the realm of spirit. Amongst these is the notion of three "Hidden Splendours" termed "*Tzachtzachot*."[38] The source of the concept is the mystical speculations of the "*Chassidei Ashkenaz*," regarding the emanation of the ten *Sefirot*, comprising the Kabbalistic Tree of Life, out of *Ain Sof* (the Eternal No-Thing).

The early Kabbalists were particularly perplexed by the fact that while there are ten *Sefirot*, there were traditionally the so-called "thirteen attributes" of God, and they were wondering whether any connection existed between the *Sefirot*, and these "attributes." In a *"responsa"* attributed to the famous rabbi Hai Gaon, there are references to "three forces" which were understood to be the foundation of the "ten," hence they thought the "thirteen attributes" should be divided into "ten" and "three," respectively pertaining to the ten *Sefirot* and three "primordial forces."

The basic premise behind the doctrine of the "Hidden splendours," is the concept that *Ain Sof* (the Eternal No-Thing) is hidden and has therefore no active participation in the emanation process. In fact, the early Kabbalists maintained that there are intermediary stages between the unmanifest and the manifest, between the "Eternal No-Thing" (*Ain Sof*) and the ten *Sefirot*. In the 13th century some considered these stages to comprise ten "higher *Sefirot*" considered to be the "roots" of the regular ten *Sefirot*. Others, specifically those from the *Iyyun* Circle, thought this intermediary stage to be "three roots concealed in the depths of *Ain Sof*" which they termed *"tzachtzachot,"* and which were understood to be three unattainably hidden lights. They were called respectively:

1. *Or Penimi Kadmon* ("internal primordial light");
2. *Or Tzach* ("ultra-transparent light"); and
3. *Or Metzuchtzach* ("clear light").

Again, it would be impossible to address this topic, or any of the many interesting Kabbalistic notions deriving from this particular era, in greater detail here, but I would like to focus attention briefly on the practical spiritual techniques taught by these incredibly versatile mystics. Besides expanding on the doctrines of the earlier Merkavists, the *Chassidei Ashkenaz* considered "magic" to be a most exalted form of worship. While they remained attached to the very deep roots of mainstream religion as manifested in their times, they also studied *and practised* the magical notions of *"Practical Kabbalah."* They are reported to have been great masters of "creation magic," i.e. creating an artificial anthropoid, a *Golem*,[39] based on the "magical usage" of ideas found in the *Sefer Yetzirah* (Book of Creation), a work stemming from the earlier Merkavistic traditions.[40]

Interestingly enough, those mystics who were keen on creating an homunculus, maintained that while they were able to construct and animate such a being, they were unable to give it actual life in the sense of providing it with a *Neshamah*, consciousness, or reasoning ability, which they called "the power of speech." They indicated that in the primordial act of creation man was made in the "Image of God," hence we have articulate consciousness, but, whilst in imitation of our Creator we are able to construct an anthropoid in our image, we are unable to provide it with a living soul.

Amongst those who openly practised what we now term "Ritual Magic," is the towering figure of Eleazer of Worms, who was a member of the community of the German Pietists in the early years of the 13th century. The techniques he used for making a *Golem* have survived to this day, and much of his writing ended up in the famous compendium of "*Practical Kabbalah*" called the *Sefer Raziel*.[41]

2. **Thirteenth Century:** *Ecstatic Kabbalah.*
   Luminaries:
   a. Abraham ben Samuel Abulafia
   b. Joseph Gikatilla
   c. Isaac ben Samuel of Acco

   Texts:
   a. *Chayei ha-Olam ha-Ba* (*Life in the World to Come*) [Abraham Abulafia][42]
   b. *Or ha-Sechel* (*Light of the Intellect*) [Abraham Abulafia][42]
   c. *Chayei Nefesh* (*Life of the Soul*) [Abraham Abulafia][42]
   d. *Otzar ha-Chayim* (*Treasury of Life*) [Isaac of Acco)[43]
   e. *Sha'arei Orah* (*The Gates of Light*) [Joseph Gikatilla][44]

By now you have probably realised that, contrary to what might be expected, Kabbalistic doctrines were not actually all that uniform down the centuries. One of the main reason for this is that Kabbalists are generally highly individualistic, and have been approaching the tradition from many differing personal angles. The "speculative" Kabbalists opposed the "practical" Kabbalists and *vice versa*. For the sake of their very survival in their communities, some chose to work and study the tradition in absolute secrecy, and their esoteric leanings were only discovered after the demise of their mortal bodies.

Some, like Abraham Abulafia, became excommunicated outcasts, with a ban imposed on their works so powerfully, that these remained unpublished for centuries, and only read in secrecy by those who were able to get hold of copies of handwritten manuscripts. Others, like Moses Chaim Luzzatto, soon discovered that when it became known that they were studying and sharing Kabbalistic ideas, it could mean the public burning of their writings, as well as being coerced on the pain of possible excommunication, to sign a document of agreement never to pursue such topics again.

One should also remember that Kabbalists were often most complex characters. Take Abraham Abulafia as a case in point. He saw himself both as the "Messiah" and as a most serious sinner. The latter resulted from the enormous guilt he suffered because of his sexual proclivities. He complained that "for fifteen years, the Satan was at my right hand to mislead me."[45] He used the Kabbalistic technique of *Gematria* to show that the Hebrew word *Shatan* (שטן) has the same numerical value as the terms *Zera Lavan* (זרע לבן) meaning "white seed," and *Diabolos* (דיאבולוש) which is actually a Latin word for the Devil. He connected the word *Diabolos* to *Duo Bolos* (two balls). In this case "Satan" was his tendencies towards masturbation, which left him filled with ideas of his body, being "defiled with seed," deserving death since it committed murder, so to speak. It certainly shows what you can get out of Kabbalistic techniques.....if you force the issue!

Of course, in Judaism masturbation is considered a most terrible sin. The reasons given are that it is infertile sex, while those more mystically minded amongst them claim it to be objectionable because of the sexual fantasies invoked during masturbation, which distract the mind of the Kabbalist from using his mental faculties for "higher purposes" in higher spiritual realms." However, Rabbi Nachman of Bratzlav, an eighteenth century Kabbalist, maintained he discovered a method of rectifying the damage caused spiritually through masturbation.

However, officially masturbation and "nocturnal emissions" are still considered "polluting experiences" of the worst kind, and, as one individual said "The seed must not go into the earth, but must go into the womb, because on the Last Day *Lillit* would collect this spilled semen and turn it into demons." Actually some legends claim that *Lillit*, a female demon and first wife of Adam, is all the time changing spilled semen into demons, who would haunt the soul of the guilty party after death. This checks back to the Talmudic legend that *Lillit* lurks around for shed seed, stealing it with the intention of creating these little demons, in order to torture mankind. In theory man, shedding his seed outside its proper place, would populate the "spirit world with devils!" I am just wondering what most people are going to see in that "panoramic view" of one's life one is supposed to get after death?

Be that as it may, with Abraham Abulafia we saw the rise of what could be termed the "*Yoga* of *Kabbalah*," as well as the beginnings of "*Ecstatic Kabbalah*," the latter being an exact term used by scholars in reference to the teachings of this school of prophetic mysticism which included a number of Spanish Kabbalists, e.g. Abraham Abulafia, Joseph Gikatilla, Isaac of Acre, Moses Narboni, etc.

Abulafia, who did not care for the system of the ten *Sefirot* and did not feature it in his teachings, developed a unique system of kabbalistic procedures akin to "*mantra Yoga*," all distinctly designed to focus the mind during meditation. Such activities are already addressed in some detail in the writings of Eleazer of Worms, but were greatly enhanced and expanded by Abulafia who specialized in Kabbalistic "mantric meditations," so to speak. Currently the most famous of these techniques is the one quoted in his "*Or ha-Sechel*."[46] Basically the technique comprises the vocalizing of the individual letters of the Ineffable Name (*YHVH*) conjoined with single letters of the Hebrew alphabet, all uttered with specific vowels used in a special order. Though not exactly the same technique, you will find one such technique discussed in Chapter 8 in the section titled "*Yichudim: Aligning with Cosmic Forces*."

32 / *The Shadow Tree: The Book of Self Creation*

3. **Thirteenth to Fifteenth Centuries: The Spanish Schools until the Great Expulsion of 1492.**
   Luminaries:
       a. Moses ben Shem Tov de Leon
       b. Azriel ben Menachem of Gerona
       c. Moshe ben Nachman Girondi (Nachmanides)
   Texts:
       a. *Sefer ha-Zohar* (*The Book of Splendour*)[47]
       b. *Shekel ha-Kodesh* (*The Holy Coin*) [Moses de Leon][48]
       b. *Sha'ar ha-Kavvanah* (*The Gate of Kavvanah* [Focussed attention]) [Azriel of Gerona][49]
       c. *Pitron Chalamot* (*The Interpretation of Dreams*) [Solomon Almoli][50]

This is the era in which the *Sefer ha-Zohar* (The Book of Splendour), considered the "Bible" of *Kabbalah*, saw the light of day in Guadalajara, Spain. Until fairly recently it was more or less the general consensus amongst twentieth-century scholars that Moses de Leon was the sole author of the *Sefer ha-Zohar*, however, some contemporary scholars have recently forwarded the idea that the enormous body of this work comprised several layers of texts penned by a number of different authors. Moses de Leon could be considered a contributor amongst this set. So, while the origin of the *Zohar* was until recently conveniently placed at the door of Moses de Leon, this matter has become one of great confusion. Some scholars still concede that portions of the *Zohar* may indeed have been authored by Moses de Leon, but the general notion is that the work as a whole comprises a compilation of writings by a number of authors.

    In recent years we have witnessed a major resurfacing of interest in the *Zohar*, especially since the appearance of Daniel Matt's superb translation of the Aramaic text known as the "*Pritzker edition*." However, while I believe this revival of interest in this enigmatic text is a good thing, the idiosyncratic language of the *Zohar* has led to many weird interpretations of the text. In this regard it should be noted that when one attempts to interpret sections of the *Zohar*, it is important to know that while it is interesting and exciting to find all manner of free and spontaneous associations, draw conclusions which may or may not tie in with the ideas expressed in this enigmatic text, or make inferences in harmony with personally espoused notions regarding certain mystical teachings, one should always keep in mind that such activities are, more likely than not, wholly out of context in terms of what the author of that Zoharic portion was actually addressing in his employment of a unique and specialized symbolical language. Hence it is important that, before one may seek a more profound appreciation of the "hidden meanings" within any verse, one should first attempt to establish context, then try to comprehend the special symbology used in the text in terms of the actual tradition it represents.

Now, the *Zohar* can be considered a *Midrash* (a biblical commentary), and several sections within it are titled such. The text follows the same pattern of division of biblical books used in *midrashim*. The text is in fact a commentary on the Hebrew Bible, hence in perusing a specific sector of this work, it is important to know which section of the Bible it is actually addressing. Ascertaining this establishes the necessary context, which, as said, is required prior to reading the complex symbolical language used by the author. It also facilitates the process of unravelling the "sources" used by the author of the *Zohar*.

In fact, close scrutinising of the *Zohar* by various scholars has revealed the "principal sources" behind the *Zohar* to have been a whole range of Jewish sacred writings and biblical commentaries, e.g. the *Talmud Bavli* (Babylonian Talmud); *Pirke d'Rabbi Eliezer*; the *Pesiktot*; the *Midrash Rabba*; the *Targumim*;the *Midrash to Psalms*; Rashi's Bible and Talmud commentaries, etc. Furthermore, it appears many of the concepts expressed in the *Zohar*, were derived directly from thirteenth century Kabbalistic thought, e.g. the writings of Nachmanides, Azriel of Gerona, Ezra ben Solomon of Gerona, and others, especially from the mystical teachings disseminated in the schools of Spanish Kabbalism. Studying the writings of these authors also expedites easier comprehension of Zoharic symbolism. Amongst these, special attention should be paid to the writings of Josef Gikatilla, since these play a significant role in the *Zohar*, in which several core ideas were drawn from the works of this Kabbalist.

4. Fifteenth, Sixteenth and Seventeenth Centuries: *Kabbalah* and Christianity in Renaissance Italy.
Luminaries:
1. Jewish
    a. Judah Messer Leon
    b. Yochanan Allemano
    c. Abraham Yagel
    d. Judah Abravanel
    e. Isaac Abravanel
    f. Judah Muscato
    g. Mordechai Dato
    h. Joseph Solomon Delmedigo
    i. Menachem Azariah de Fano
2. Christian
    a. Giovanni Pico della Mirandola
    b. Johannes Reuchlin of Pforzheim
    c. Henry Cornelius Agrippa von Nettesheim
    d. Giordano Bruno
    e. Franciscus Mercurius van Helmunt
    f. Guillaume Postel
    g. Athanasius Kircher

Texts:
1. *Traditional Kabbalah*
    a. *Collectanaea* [Yochanan Alemanno][51]
    b. *Sefer Eilim* (Book of Palm Trees) [Joseph Solomon Delmedigo][52]
    c. *Gilgulei Neshamot* (Reincarnation of Souls) [Azariah de Fano][53]
    d. *Sefer Kanfei Yonah* (*The Book of the Wings of a Dove*) [Azariah de Fano][53]
    e. *Sefer Asarah Ma'amarot* (*The Book of Ten Sayings*)[Azariah de Fano][53]
2. *Christian Kabbalah*
    a. *Kabbalistic Conclusions* [Pico della Mirandola][54]
    b. *De Arte Cabalistica* (*On the Art of the Kabbalah*) [Johannes Reuchlin][55]
    c. *Oedipus Aegyptiacus* [Athanasius Kircher][56]

The Renaissance represents a period in which Jewish and Christian scholars freely intermingled, discussing *Kabbalah* quite openly, often with the support of the Italian nobility and even the Church itself. In this regard Moshe Idel, wrote "In Italy of the Renaissance period, Jewish thought developed in a manner unprecedented in earlier stages of Jewish intellectual history. Several of the most creative personalities in Jewish culture were in communication with leading spokesmen of Renaissance thought. This phenomenon is unique: Greek, Arabic and Christian philosophy developed in the absence of any significant oral connection with Jewish culture. Before the Renaissance, Jewish thought exercised no decisive influence upon the major representatives of gentile thought. In those instances where a certain Jewish influence may be detected, that influence originated from a written rather than an oral source. In the Renaissance period, on the other hand, a considerable number of Christian thinkers took instruction from Jews.....The Christians themselves initiated these contacts.....Not only did the gentiles want instruction in Hebrew; they also wanted to gain access to wider areas of Jewish thought, and particularly to the *Kabbalah*."[57]

It is generally accepted that Pico della Mirandola is the "father" of *Christian Kabbalah*. He learned much of the tradition from Yochanan Allemano, his Jewish teacher and friend. It is thought Mirandola's famous "*Kabbalistic Conclusions*" marks the very start of *Christian Kabbalah*, however it is worth noting that the Christian version of this tradition did not originate with him exclusively. While Mirandola is one of the sources of the *Christian Kabbalah*, and certainly the most important one at that, there were other contributors, specifically the christological works of two Jewish converts, e.g. Paulus de Heredia and Abner of Burgos, each writing a work on *Christian Kabbalah*, respectively *Galei Rezaya* and *Eggeret ha-Sodot*, which they deceptively claimed to have been written by certain Talmudic *tannaim*.[58] Other works of a similar nature were composed in Spain, and were doing the rounds in Italy during the 15th century.

It was in the "Platonic Academy" founded by Pico della Mirandola, which flourished under the Medicis in Florence, where *Christian Kabbalah* commenced its illustrious growth. Convinced that *Kabbalah* is the tradition encompassing the original revelation of the Divine to man, the Christian scholars went to great lengths to have access to primary sources and to understand *Kabbalah*. They studied Hebrew and had famous Kabbalistic treatises translated into Latin. Curiously enough, in the Renaissance the scholars of *Christian Kabbalah* had more primary Kabbalistic texts readily available to them, either in Hebrew or translated into Latin, than the average *Kabbalah* student had during the 20th century. Through the tireless efforts of Mirandola, some of the works of the greatest early Kabbalists, e.g. Nachmanides, Abraham ibn Ezra, Abraham Abulafia, Eleazer of Worms, Joseph Gikatilla, Azriel of Gerona, Todros Abulafia, David Kimchi, Levi ben Gershom, Menachem Recannati, etc., were translated into Latin in the early Renaissance.

The Christian Kabbalists had a great admiration for the concept of the "Divine Name." In this regard we might consider the teachings of Johannes Reuchlin, who was an extremely well read and informed student of this Tradition. He reformulated the Ineffable Name, *YHVH* (יהוה), "christianising" it *YHShVH* (יהשוה) which is often pronounced *Yehoshuah*. It should be noted that there is really no name, divine or otherwise, comprising that spelling in Hebrew. Reuchlin invented this construct in an attempt to show the importance and divinity of Jesus in kabbalistic thinking.

Reuchlin maintained that human history is divided into three ages. Deriving his ideas about these ages from the Jewish concept of three world ages, these being the "ages" of "Chaos," the "Torah" and the "Messiah," and combining these with the teachings of the millennianist Joachim de Fiore, who also spoke of three "Ages" on earth, the first under the rule of the "Father," the second under the rule of the "Son," and the third under the "Holy Spirit," Reuchlin linked his concept of "world ages" to "*JHS*," a common abbreviation used in medieval Christian manuscripts in reference to the Christian saviour. To understand his fabrication of the name *YHShVH*, you need to know what the three "Ages" meant to Reuchlin. He claimed that in the first age, which is that of the Hebrew patriarchs, God revealed himself through the name *Shadai*; in the second age, considered the Mosaic period, God made Himself known through the Ineffable Name, *YHVH*; and in the third age, the Christian period which Reuchlin maintained to be the one "redemption" and "grace," God is revealing Himself through a five letter name, which is the name *YHVH* with the interpolated letter, *Shin*, thus *Yehoshuah* which he claimed is the true name of Jesus. In fact, the letter *Shin*, according to Reuchlin, represents the *Logos*, the "Word" which became "Flesh" in the person of Jesus as God incarnate.

One wonders if there was any other reason for the choice of this letter, beyond the fact that this glyph is "three-pronged" in shape (ש), which gave them lots of ideas about the "trinity"; that it represents "Fire;" and that, interpolated in the Tetragrammaton, it can be pronounced "*Yehoshuah*." We might note that the Biblical *Yehoshuah* is spelled *YHVShA* (יהושע). A "five-letter-name" it is, but not comprising the letters claimed by messers Reuchlin and company. It is interesting how commonplace it is nowadays amongst Christians of the more fundamentalist mind set, to use this name so glibly and casually as a "genuine" reference to the Christian saviour.

Today Reuchlin is best known for his Kabbalistic treatise titled "*De Arte Cabalistica*," published in 1517 and the source of which was a Latin text called "*Codex Halberstam*." The latter comprised some writings by Todros Abulafia. Reuchlin dedicated his treatise to one of the Popes of his day. The English translation of this dedication reads "This book is dedicated to His Holiness Pope Leo X, by his humble friend Johann Reuchlin."[59]

Nearly one hundred and forty years after the publication of "*De Arte Cabalistica*," during the early years of the Reformation, the remarkable Jesuit Athanasius Kircher published his "*Oedipus Aegyptiacus*." Kircher derived much of his writings directly from Reuchlin. Called the "Egyptian Kabbalist," and hailed "the last man who knew everything,"[60] he was actually a plagiarist. He "lifted" material verbatim from other authors, and simply presented these as if he himself had been the author. Regarding "*Oedipus Aegyptiacus*" Gershom Scholem noted "vor allem aus Reuchlin und Galatin zusammengeschrieben" ("in the main a compilation of Reuchlin and Galatin").[61]

Now, as noted *Kabbalah* had a "high noon" during the Renaissance, and there were several prominent personalities associated with it, e.g. Giordano Bruno, the Dutch Franciscus Mercurius van Helmunt, Johann Trithemius, not forgetting the remarkable Heinrich Cornelius Agrippa. To this list one can add several more great luminaries of the time. Amongst these I have a great admiration for Guillaume Postel. This remarkable Frenchman had translated both the *Sefer Yetzirah* and the *Sefer ha-Zohar* into Latin, with lengthy personal expositions added, and he did this prior to the publication of even the original Hebrew texts. He had great Jewish contacts who readily shared information with him.

In this section I have thought to focus specifically on the birth of *Christian Kabbalah*, with brief references to its main protagonists. There were certainly many remarkable Jewish Kabbalists living in Italy and elsewhere during this period, who contributed enormously to Kabbalistic thought. Having been unable to devote any attention to these individuals, I thought I would next draw attention again to a remarkable period in the growth and development of *Traditional Kabbalah*, i.e. Isaac Luria and the incredible school he headed in Safed, Israel.

5. **Sixteenth and Seventeenth Centuries: Isaac Luria, the Safed School and the Rise of *Lurianic Kabbalah*.**
   Luminaries:
   a. Josef ben Efraim Karo
   b. Moses ben Jacob Cordovero (Ramak)
   c. Isaac Luria Ashkenazi
   d. Chaim ben Josef Vital Calabrese
   e. Joseph Ibn Tabul
   f. Eliahu ben Moshe de Vidas
   g. Isaiah ben Abraham ha-Levi Horowitz

   Texts:
   a. *Sefer Maggid Mesharim* (Book of the Minister of Uprightness) [Joseph Karo][62]
   b. *Pardes Rimmonim* (*A Garden of Pomegranates*) [Moses Cordovero][63]
   c. *Or Ne'erav* (*A Pleasant Light*) [Moses Cordovero][63]
   d. *Sha'ar Ru'ach ha-Kodesh* (*The Gate of the Holy Spirit*) [Chaim Vital][64]
   e. *Sha'arei Kedushah* (*The Gate of Holiness*) [Chaim Vital][64]
   f. *Sha'ar ha-Kavvanot* (*The Gate of Intentions*) [Chaim Vital][64]

g. *Reshit Chochmah* (*The Beginning of Wisdom*) [Elijah ben Moses de Vidas][65]
h. *Shnei Luchot ha-Brit* (*The Two Tablets of the Covenant*) [Isaiah ben Abraham Horowitz][66]

The rise of the "Safed School" would lead to "*Traditional Kabbalah*" being divided into two distinct periods—the "pre-Lurianic" and "*Lurianic Kabbalah*." The earlier *Kabbalah* could be termed "Zoharic," though not entirely correctly since there were several earlier Kabbalists, e.g. Abraham Abulafia, etc., who were unfamiliar with the Zohar and its teachings. This period culminated in the writings of Moses Cordovero. His pupil and son-in-law, Isaac Luria known as "the Holy Ari,"started a new trend which is now called "*Lurianic Kabbalah*."

This branch of *Kabbalah* comprises many novel doctrines regarding creation and our relationship with the whole of existence. These are addressed in the writings of the students of Isaac Luria, and have been greatly expanded upon by later Kabbalists.[67] Besides this primary literature, there are also several excellent studies by a variety of astute scholars dealing specifically with this topic.[68] Hence, we will rather focus now on certain unusual angles in the life of Isaac Luria.

The Ari is said to have had a number of remarkable "psychic" skills, e.g. he was able to diagnose demons, or rather whether someone had a *dibbuk* [e.g. an invading malevolent spirit intelligence], by feeling and listening to the individual's pulse. In Lurianic teaching this kind of pulse diagnosis is based on the ten types of pulse described in the *Sefer Tikkunei ha-Zohar*.[69] Each type is identified by its unique rhythm which is in turn associated with one of the Hebrew vowel forms, with which the specific pulse is believed to have an affinity. Besides this special ability which the Holy Ari shared with his disciples, it is said the master had other unique divinatory skills pertaining to the human anatomy. He was equally a master of "metoposcopy," i.e. he had the curious ability to analyse the character of an individual, by detecting and interpreting the Hebrew letters evident on the forehead of that person.

The art of recognising Hebrew letters on the forehead is based on the doctrine called "*Chochmat ha-Partzuf*,"[70] i.e. the study of the face on which arrangements of Hebrew glyphs might be traced, the latter being in turn based on the idea that the whole of creation was manifested through a divine language. The view that Hebrew was the primordial language of creation found expression in texts like the *Sefer Yetzirah*, the *Sefer ha-Bahir*, and the *Sefer ha-Zohar*, but was developed further in the commentaries and other writings of later Kabbalists. They were responsible for an extensive literature in which creation is not only considered to be the result of various combinations [permutations] of the glyphs of the Hebrew alphabet, but that all manifestation is actually clothed, as it were, with these letter combinations.

For Kabbalists the letters of the Hebrew alphabet corresponds to the ten *Sefirot*, the spheres on the Tree of Life, hence there is the further possibility of viewing those glyphs manifested on the forehead in terms of their sefirotic correspondences. In this way one can determine in those letters that are expressed particularly strongly and most frequently, the "soul root" of an individual understood as a "sefirotic root." Some actions strengthen as it were the revelation of the glyphs on the forehead. Reciting the "blessings" is said to be of special significance as one such empowering activity. In this regard Lawrence Fine wrote "The lights of the letters which appear on the skin as a result of reciting *berakhot* (blessings) are special insofar as there is light *surrounding* each letter; this surrounding light is more luminescent than that of the letter itself. If one sees that the opposite is the case, that the light of the letter is more intense than the surrounding light, it signals that the blessing was not performed properly."[71]

The multitude of speculations regarding this theme, was manifested in a most practical psychic ability in the case of Isaac Luria, who could "read" a person in accordance with the sacred glyphs "made flesh" in the being and body of that individual. In fact, these sacred forms are believed to be present in every aspect of one's being. In this regard, Chaim Vital, who was Isaac Luria's closest disciple, explained that the letters, also called "lights," are hidden beneath the skin of a wicked person, but in the case of a person who is purifying the different aspects of his or her being, the divine forces and their expression in the power forms of the Hebrew glyphs are openly revealed on the skin, where "the skilled eye" can observe them. He maintained that the letters of the soul are best displayed on the forehead, because the entire Hebrew alphabet corresponds to *Binah*, the sphere of "understanding" on the Tree of Life, of which the forehead is a symbol. However, the amount and clarity of the letters disclosed by each person is dependent on his or her level of purity and quality of service in this world.

While we have made special reference to the forehead as far as this divinatory art is concerned, it should be noted that the Hebrew letters as glyphs of power are said to manifest everywhere in one's anatomy, as Chaim Vital indicated saying "Know that in each and every organ of a person's body, there are letters engraved, informing us about that individual's actions. But the primary place is the forehead, as indicated earlier."[72]

Regarding the Ari's remarkable psychic skills, one of his followers, Eleazar Azikri reported in his *Sefer Haredim*, how Luria looked at the face of a sage and told him that "the transgression of cruelty toward animals is inscribed upon your countenance."[73] Apparently the sage rushed home in a state of great distress, where he found that his wife had forgotten to feed the turkeys. He promptly took appropriate care of these creatures, and returned to Luria. Not knowing what had transpired, Luria looked at his forehead and informed him that the misdeed is no longer evident, at which point the sage proceeded to tell the Ari what had actually transpired. Clearly the incredible Isaac Luria was a man of extraordinary talent and ability which goes way beyond the traditional study of Torah and Talmud.

On the demise of the Ari, his work and teachings are said to have passed to Chaim Vital, his recognised successor. Personally I find the generally held opinion that Chaim Vital is the most authentic representative of the teachings of Isaac Luria, to be seriously problematic. Vital was far too intent on blowing his own trumpet and discrediting the rest of the students of the Ari. In fact, his own messianic tendencies drove him to behave in a thoroughly unpleasant and egotistical manner towards those he regarded to be his "enemies," especially those fellow students whose reports and writings on Lurianic teachings did not quite align with his own. Close scrutiny of one of the reports on a "spirit possession" in Safed, in which Chaim Vital is certainly the major player, clearly reveals the "possession" to have been "rigged" in order to shame an individual who opposed Vital's messianic notions.

42 / *The Shadow Tree: The Book of Self Creation*

I am not suggesting that Chaim Vital's voluminous output should not be considered representative of *Lurianic Kabbalah*, but only that one should read the writings of other students of the great master, including authors of the day who resided elsewhere, in order to gain a more comprehensive insight into *Lurianic Kabbalah*.[74]

6. Seventeenth and Eighteenth Centuries: Messianic Frenzy and Lurianic Kabbalists.
Luminaries:
    a. Shabbetai Tzvi
    b. Nathan of Gaza
    c. Jacob Frank
    d. Moses ben Mordechai Zaccutto (Ramaz)
    e. Moses Chaim Luzzatto (Ramchal)

Texts:
    a. *Abraham Miguel Cardozo: Selected Writings*[75]
    b. *The Collection of the Words of the Lord [Jacob Frank] from the Polish Manuscripts*[76]
    c. *Shorshei ha-Shemot* (*The Roots of Names*) [Moses Zacutto][77]
    d. *Klach Pitchei ha-Chochmah* (*138 Openings of Wisdom*) [Moses Luzzatto][78]
    e. *Mesillat Yesharim* (*Path of the Just*) [Moses Luzzatto][78]

The 17th century marks one of the most momentous incidents in the history of world Jewry, the aftermath of which would impact in a most unpleasant measure on Kabbalists everywhere. I am referring to the occasion when Shabbetai Tzvi[79] made his "messianic overtures" to an overeager Jewish world. With the support of a huge publicity campaign launched by Nathan of Gaza, his closest disciple and promoter, he singled out the year 1666 to announce his messianic status.

Kabbalists at the time, basing their calculations on the Jewish calendar, believed the "age of the Messiah" would commence in 1646. Christians, on the other hand, *because* of their obsession with the number 666, believed the year 1666 marked the beginning of the "end times" and the return of their "Messiah." In this regard Shabbetai Tzvi, whose father was a representative in Smyrna of an English trading company, had been well informed on the sentiments of the Christian mystics regarding the triple six digit, especially those of the English "Fifth Monarchy Men" who believed the restoration of the Jewish homeland and the beginning of the messianic age, which they termed the "millennium," would commence in 1666. Hence, in order to impact on as wide an audience as possible, Tzvi selected that fateful year to proclaim his "messiahship." Talk about people being taken in on a massive scale! Literally thousands sold up everything and packed their bags to follow the "Messiah" to the Holy Land.

Eventually the clamour of denouncements from the rabbinical authorities, and his claim that he would some day appropriate the Turkish crown, led to his arrest by the Ottoman authorities and to him being condemned to death. However, Tzvi who had no penchant for death, averted execution by turning apostate when he converted to Islam. Many of his followers in Turkey followed suit, where they became known as "*Dönmeh*" ("converts").

So, depending on which side of the fence you are, Shabbetai Tzvi is regarded either as the "Messiah" or a "pseudo-Messiah." He certainly had many secret admirers amongst the mainstream rabbis of his day. Amongst those who flirted very briefly with Shabbatean ideas was Moses Zaccutto, an individual whom I greatly admire and respect. In fact, if I should ever entertain ideas about performing special invocations to cause an *ibbur*, a special "impregnation" of my being by the soul of a departed master of great renown, or perhaps tracing the "soulroot" of an outstanding Kabbalist so as to tie my soul to his by means of those very unique *Yichudim*, i.e. "unification" practices specially designed to expedite such intentions, I'd settle on Moses Zaccutto. I think there might have been just enough "waywardness" in the personality of this illustrious man, to guarantee me a modicum of success if I should ever attempt to enact what is now mere "speculation" on my part.

There is absolutely nothing ordinary about the charismatic "*Ramaz*." He led a most interesting life, however, tracing the history of this great man required a lot of "detective" work, since until very recently we knew hardly anything about him. He told us very little about himself, and it is now quite clear that much of what was written on his life by later biographers were actually faulty. Even the eulogy written by an admiring disciple, Benjamin Cohen from Reggio, turned out to be most unreliable.

We know for certain that Moses ben Mordechai Zaccutto was born into an affluent *"Marrano"* family. The word *"Marrano"* (plural *Marranos*) meaning "pigs," was coined by the Christian authorities in reference to those Jews and Muslims who did not leave Spain after the great expulsion of 1492, but who chose to "convert" to Christianity and afterwards continue to secretly practice their faith in hidden venues. The same term was used against Jews who lived in Portugal, and who chose to convert following the Inquisition enforced expulsion there.

The Zaccutto family hailed from Portugal, but during his youth our Rabbi travelled extensively and studied in so many different places. Under the careful tutelage of excellent mentors, amongst others Binyamin ha-Levi, a disciple of Isaac Luria whom the Ari sent to Italy to spread his teachings, Moses Zaccutto turned into a notable poet, dramatist, "Practical Kabbalist" and exorcist. He was apparently inclined towards mysticism since childhood, and *Kabbalah* remained for him the topic of special interest throughout his life. He organized his entire existence around the doctrines of this Tradition, and he literally excised from himself what did not appear to gel with Kabbalistic teachings. At one stage he considered the Latin he had previously learned to be irreconcilable with *Kabbalah*, and decided to employ a forty days fast to help him "forget" what he had learned of that language. We are not informed as to the success of this drastic activity.

Be that as it may, Moses Zaccutto initially planned to undertake a pilgrimage to the Holy Land, but yielded to the pressure of those who convinced him to remain in Italy as Rabbi of Venice, where he remained until 1673 when he was employed as Chief Rabbi of Mantua. He established a kabbalistic seminary, and amongst his students were the very young Moses Chaim Luzzatto, who was considered the child prodigy of *Kabbalah*, and who memorized all the writings on the teachings of the Ari by the time he was 14 years old; Abraham Rovigo, who was a follower of Shabbetai Tzvi, and Benjamin ben Eliezer ha-Kohen of Reggio, was also amongst the *ma'aminim* ("believers" in the messianic status of Shabbetai Tzvi).

Moses Zaccutto himself briefly flirted with the Messianic claims of the Sabbatianists, but later rejected these notions altogether. As said, he learned *Lurianic Kabbalah* directly from Luria's emissary from Safed, but he objected in the strongest terms to any intermingling of the teachings of Moses Cordovero, the representative of early *Kabbalah*, with those of the later *Kabbalah* of the Ari. Yet, whilst he familiarized himself with the full spectrum of Lurianic writings, he was particularly devoted to the traditions of the early *Kabbalah*.

He truly excelled in the field of *Practical Kabbalah*, and compiled much of the Jewish magical traditions into the text titled *Shorshei ha-Shemot*,[80] a mammoth compendium which, from its earliest inception, was widely circulated in manuscript amongst Kabbalists. The tome comprises 675 large pages, jam-packed with the most detailed descriptions of Divine Names, Angels, *Kameot* (amulets), "magic squares," and a host of assorted magical techniques. Today this text is readily available in a magnificent edition. This remarkable magical text could be considered a primary Hebrew "*grimoire*" of epic proportions, the scope of which simply dwarfs anything of a related nature, such as the "*Sacred Magic of Abra-melin the Mage*,"[81] a work which also includes the use of Divine Names, Spirit Intelligences, magical incantations and magic squares.

As we noted earlier, the young Moses Chaim Luzzatto was a pupil of Moses Zaccutto. The Ramchal would later rise in prominence as a philosopher and a poet, and was ranked the most important Kabbalist of the 18th century. It was a time when there were few who were willing to openly impart and expand the wisdom of *Lurianic Kabbalah*, especially during the immediate period following the Shabbetai Tzvi debacle. Then the slightest indication of interest in the teachings of Isaac Luria could get one into serious trouble with the Rabbinical authorities. In this regard Moses Luzzatto, who was a prolific author, soon caught the eye of the rabid rabbinate. He suffered the great tragedy of seeing his manuscripts burned and his Kabbalistic endeavours curtailed by a special ban. Luzzatto was forced to sign an agreement that he would not study the works of Luria, except in the company of an acknowledged authority after he had reached 40 years of age.

However, these draconian measures did not seem to have checked the activities of this humble Kabbalist. It would seem the Ramchal was destined to win, a point his more pragmatic detractors naturally failed to see. Regarding the mystical teachings, he was receiving very special instruction from a *Maggid*, a "Celestial Guide." It is said the guidance of "Spirit Messenger," as well as visitations by the Prophet Elijah and other "celestial visitors," inspired and raised the soul of the Rabbi to those incredible spiritual heights, where he perceived the great spiritual concepts which he wrote down at a prodigious rate.

Thus did the Ramchal not adhere to the terms of the agreement curtailing his actions, especially as it was signed under duress, and hence, despite these disasters that dogged his footsteps, he continued to teach *Kabbalah* and write remarkable ethical and Kabbalistic texts. He took the ideas of Isaac Luria and vastly expanded them as he explained the intricacies of the various concepts. Eventually he was accused of being a Shabbatean and of having personal messianic tendencies. Since he was surrounded by a sizeable number of admiring friends who were sharing his ideas, several Rabbis turned on him. His books were not only banned outright, but he was excommunicated. He attempted to find refuge in Amsterdam, where he wrote "*The Path of the Just*," and thence fled to the Holy Land where he died shortly after his arrival at the age of 40 years, the "appropriate age" at which he would have been "allowed" to venture into a study of *Lurianic Kabbalah*. Needless to say, his writings provide ample proof that he had been a master of this tradition for a couple of decades prior to his untimely death,.

Moses Chaim Luzzatto apparently wrote more than seventy-two works, many of them lost. However, several have survived the "fires of fanaticism." Some of these have been translated into many languages, and are still illuminating the minds of thousands seeking spiritual truth and enlightenment.[82] Having read these magnificent books, it is difficult to comprehend why this remarkable, outstandingly original thinker could have been considered "dangerous" by the Rabbinical authorities of his day. Interestingly those texts which have survived the ravages of time, space and events, are now enthusiastically recommended by both

Rabbis and scholars alike. In this regard it seems most odd that Gershom Scholem, being a scholar of such note, should have neglected this great mystic so badly. After all, Luzzatto's writings played an important role in the development of the Chassidic movement. Curiously enough, the famed Elijah bar Solomon Zalman, the Gaon of Vilna who was a formidable foe of the *Chassidim*, said that if Rabbi Luzzatto lived in his day, he would have travelled on foot from Vilna to Padua in order to be instructed by the great *Ramchal*.

7. **Seventeenth and Eighteenth Centuries: The Rise of the East European *Chassidim*.**
   Luminaries:
   a. Israel Baal Shem Tov.
   b. Dov Baer of Metzrich
   c. Shneur Zalman of Liadi (Alter Rebbe)
   d. Levi Yosef Yitzchak of Berdichov
   e. Nachman of Bratzlav

   Texts:
   a. *Likkutei Amarim – Tanya* (Anthology of Statements) [Shneur Zalman of Liadi][83]
   b. *Kedushat Levi* (*The Holiness of Levi*)[Levi Yitzchak of Berdichev][84]
   c. *Likkutei Moharan* (*Anthology of Our Master Rabbi Nachman*) [Nachman of Bratzlav][85]

Kabbalah started to decline in Western Europe following the messianic catastrophe of Shabbetai Tzvi. Notwithstanding this, the *Lurianic Kabbalah* made serious inroads in Eastern Europe, especially amongst the *Chassidim*. This movement of religious ecstatics had split into several groups after the demise of their founder, Israel ben Eliezer, the Baal Shem Tov.

Due to their intense missionary activities amongst world Jewry over the last century, the Lubavich faction (*Chabad*), had now achieved immense international prominence. This specific branch of *Chassidism* commenced with Shneur Zalman of Liadi,[86] whose legacy is heavily based on *Lurianic Kabbalah*. In fact, his *Kabbalah* is restricted virtually entirely to:

1. the writings of Chaim Vital, the earlier mentioned student of Isaac Luria;
2. the *Sefer ha-Zohar* and *Tikkunei Zohar*;
3. Nachmanides, about the only one amongst the early Kabbalists acknowledged by the Alter Rebbe; and to
4. some of the writings of Moses Cordovero, as well as the works of the Maharal, Rabbi Loew of Prague, who was one of his ancestors.

There might be a few I have missed, however I think the mentioned authors cover more or less the entire extent of Shneur Zalman's Kabbalistic interest. It should be noted that while he was influenced by these Kabbalistic writings, the Alter Rebbe remolded and reinterpreted the doctrines of this tradition in a most original and unique way. Here I would like to stress that the *Kabbalah* of these *Chassidim* is not the ultimate "one true and only" *Kabbalah*, as some of the more "militant" members of *Chabad* would have us believe. It certainly does not incorporate, nor does it acknowledge, the broad spectrum of Kabbalistic thinking.

Now, as we noted earlier, the *Chassidim* counted Elijah the Gaon of Vilna amongst their most vocal foes. The Gaon was a brilliant scholar who devoted his life to *Torah* study, but he was also an intolerant religious fanatic. One observer said that while he was a "profound investigator with a keen, analytic mind, he was at the same time a fanatical zealot who bowed down before every dead letter of the written law."[87] He detested philosophy, frowned upon Jewish mysticism, despite the fact that he edited the *Sefer Yetzirah*, and he persecuted mystics—especially the radical *Chassid* movement whom he branded "heretics."

One biographer apologetically maintained that the Gaon "acted out of purely ideological motives."[88] Of course he did! All violence spawned by a fanatical religious stance stems from the same motives, as we know from our experiences with modern day terrorists, whose dastardly deeds we would find extremely difficult to excuse on the basis of having been "acted out of purely ideological motives." The *Chassidim* eventually triumphed and managed to establish themselves as a force to be reckoned with in mainstream Judaism. So, while his vehement opposition did not exactly endear the Gaon of Vilna to the *Chassidim*, they are in turn the ones who dish out condemnation today on those who are not towing the line in terms of what they consider the correct manner of worship. Verily it has been truthfully said that there is nothing so conservative as an ageing radical.

While these ultra-fundamentalists are perfectly entitled to their own eccentricities on personal levels, their offensive invasive behaviour and condemnation of all and sundry around them, especially those who will not buy into their "group ego," should be denounced in the strongest terms. Some might still be able to tolerate this annoyance, but there is a much more sinister factor, which is the physical and spiritual militancy of Chassidic factions. There is a legacy of hate and violence to be found amongst many spiritual groups claiming to be profoundly involved in the task of expanding consciousness, and to be promoting real spiritual growth in our world.

Even in the ranks of such a venerable Tradition as our own, *Kabbalah* itself, we find a ferocity of a most virulent kind amongst "esoterically minded fundamentalists." This extends way beyond the physical assault of material bodies, or even the emotional onslaught on minds and psyches. It actually pertains to a spiritual targeting of perceived enemies through every means at ones disposal, whether such be physical, mental, emotional or spiritual—the latter referring to spiritual assault by psychic means, in order to expedite the destruction of our fellow humankind.

Here we might consider the so-called *"Pulsa Denura"* ritual (variously translated "arrow of fire," "lashes of fire," "ball of fire," "whip of fire" or "burst of fire"). Supposedly a "Kabbalistic death curse," it has actually nothing to do with *Kabbalah* at all, and high ranking Kabbalists in Israel deny it any historical validity. No evidence can be found that this practice derives from traditional Kabbalistic sources, whether of the pre- or post-Lurianic kind. There is further no trace of such a curse in the *Torah*, and neither can anything resembling it even remotely be found in primary Kabbalistic literature. Of course, lack of evidence does not mean anything, since this abhorrent custom could have been dreamed up by manic ultra-fundamentalists of the worst kind at a much later date, as recent as the 20th century perhaps? And thereby hangs a tale.....and a forked one at that!

50 / *The Shadow Tree: The Book of Self Creation*

Now, while there is no reference to the "Fire Whipping" death curse ritual in the Hebrew Scriptures or any other Jewish sacred writ, the expression "*Pulsa Denura*" is found in a number of Talmudic stories. One tractate, *Bava Metsi'a*,[89] describes how Rabbi Chiya, a veritable *Baal Shem* (Master of the Name), a comfortable term for someone who is really a sorcerer, was praying the *Amidah*, the central prayer of the Jewish Sabbath services known as the *Shemoneh Esrei* (Eighteen Benedictions),[90] on a day of fasting set aside for prayers to end a drought. We are told that a powerful wind promptly rose when the great Rabbi spoke "He maketh the winds blow," and when he got to the words "He maketh the dead rise," he caused a veritable panic in heaven as he was about to cause the premature resurrection of the dead, i.e. in advance of the arrival of the *Meshiach* (Messiah).

Apparently the Almighty enquired as to "Who has revealed such secrets to mankind," to which the Angels pointed an accusing finger in the direction of the culprit.....the prophet Elijah no less, who had to forthwith endure "sixty lashes of fire" (*pulsei denura*) from the "Divine Hand." It is said this caused him to look "like a fiery bear," as he hurriedly descended to earth to rectify the situation and to halt Rabbi Chiya's magical actions. Beyond this amusing tale of the furious Deity forcing a flustered and freaked out Elijah in a fiery fashion into hasty action, and a couple of other *Pulsa Denura* tales dotted here and there in the *Talmud*, there is no sign anywhere of a venerable ancient death curse of that name. I suppose for the fundamentalist ultra-right it is a small step from "celestial beings" to humans, especially as they view anything in the heavens and on the earth in opposition to their personal life stance, even if this be but a slight dissimilarity to their views, to be deserving of the wrath of God and eternal damnation at best. Just in case the Almighty should hesitate in this regard, they would work acts of doom on behalf of Deity, thus saving the Almighty the bother.....so to speak.

Now, serious research concluded that the *Pulsa Denura* is actually an updated, and a lot more sinister version of the old excommunication of heretics ritual which was used at one time in mainstream Judaism. It incorporated reciting a curse, blowing of the *shofar* (ram's horn), and extinguishing candles. It would seem the "*Pulsa Denura*" transformation of this rite was formally instituted in 1905. According to Meir Bar-Ilan, it was in that year that the foundation of secular Hebrew schools in Palestine by David Yellin elicited the *Pulsa Denura* death curse from the ultra-orthodox anti-Zionist factions in Jerusalem.[91] In this regard it should be noted that David Yellin, the first recipient of this curse, died in 1941 of nothing more than old age. In fact, it would seem that other than the belief that Yitzhak Rabin, erstwhile Prime Minister of Israel, was assassinated as a result of the "Fire Whipping" curse directed against him, the "*Pulsa Denura*" appears not to be working very well, considering those who have survived the ritual intact. Pope John Paul II, who had also been at the receiving end of such a "curse," eventually succumbed to old age.

It is said that initially the *Pulsa Denura* curse was adopted by the ultra-orthodox *after* the founding of the State of Israel, as a replacement for the rite of excommunication amongst those factions, both Zionist and anti-Zionist, who were struggling for religious supremacy in Jerusalem during the early years of the founding of the Jewish state. Likewise it is worked today exclusively by ultra-right political and religious activists. This "mystical hate politics" and racism of the ultra-right is absolutely sickening. As far as I can see, this deplorable situation amongst those of the ultra-right who call themselves "kabbalists," has absolutely nothing to do with true spiritual growth or with *Kabbalah*, the principles of which as set forth on the *Etz Chayim* (Tree of Life), reminds us:

1. *Keter* — That we should ever seek within ourselves the Single Spiritual Light which indicates our own Eternal Entity and will confer the **Cosmic Crown** of Everlasting Life upon us.
2. *Chochmah* — That we acknowledge **Wisdom** as an attribute of Deity mankind may share in some degree, and therefore dedicate ourselves to such attainment.
3. *Binah* — That we approach all aspects of our holy Mysteries with true humility and hopes of reaching revelation in the depths of a **Divinely Universal Understanding**.
4. *Chesed* — That we mediate the **Mercy** of our Maker to mankind, and care for our companion-creatures with compassion.

5. *Gevurah* — That we duly **Discipline** ourselves so that we will learn to live as a responsibly well-regulated member of these Mysteries.
6. *Tiferet* — That we attempt an actual arrangement of ourselves in **Holy Harmony** with all the Sacred Spheres throughout the Plan of our Perfection.
7. *Netzach* — That we so persevere with problems on our Paths that these will solve themselves and sublimate into a **Spiritual Success**.
8. *Hod* — That we should study matters of our Mysteries with **Respectful Rationality** and reason as a means of making up our minds.
9. That we firmly follow out the practice of our living Faith as we pursue the **Principles of its Foundation** and the secret of its spiritual strength.
10. That in this world we keep the laws of men intended for good government of all mundane affairs, yet live within the **Light of our Inner Kingdom** as active and initiated members of these Mysteries.

How tragic that one has to admit that even in the 21st century the scourge of religious fanaticism is still rearing its ugly head all over the world, as it did for over two millennia within the ranks of all faiths. Today this phenomenon has been appropriately called "Terror in the Mind by God."[92] Yet I believe it unfair to simply dismiss religion, the way through which many humans establish links with the "Infinite Source," as being a bad job altogether. The term "religion," a word simply meaning "to reconnect," originated from the Latin "*relegare*" meaning to bind. Religion is therefore a sacred binding, an obligation in the souls of true worshippers to reaffirm the original ties between themselves and the "Power" which they sense is controlling the universe and directing their destiny. Sadly it is humans who distort this basic meaning of religion with exclusivity claims, and who face those who march to the beat of a different drum with spiritual terrorism.

8. **Nineteenth Century: Mainstream Kabbalists and the Tradition in French Occultism.**
Luminaries:
1. Jewish
	a. Shlomo Rabinowitz of Radomsk
	b. Yitzchak Eizik Safrin of Komarno
	c. Tzadok Hakohen of Lublin
	d. Yosef Chaim ben Elijah ha-Chacham (Ben Ish Chai)
2. Christian
	a. Eliphas Levi
	b. Lenain
	c. Gerard Encausse (Papus)

Texts:
1. *Traditional Kabbalah*
	a. *Tiferet Shlomo* (*Beauty of Solomon*) [Shlomo HaKohen Rabinowitz of Radomsk][93]
	b. *Megillat Setarim* (*Book of Secrets*) [Yitzchak Eizik Safrin of Komarno][94]
	c. *Sichat Malachei ha-Sharet* (*A Study of Ministering Angels*) [Tzadok Hakohen of Lublin][95]
	d. *Ateret Tiferet* (*Crown of Beauty*) [Ben Ish Chai][96]
	e. *Da'at u-Tevunah* (*Knowledge and Discernment*) [Ben Ish Chai][96]
2. *Kabbalistic texts by French Occultists*
	a. *La Science Cabalistique* (The Kabbalistic Science) [Lenain][97]
	b. *The Book of Splendours* [Eliphas Levi][98]
	c. *The Mysteries of the Qabalah* [Eliphas Levi][99]
	d. *The Qabalah* [Papus (Gerard Encausse)][100]

I am sure many would expect me to focus now specifically on *Kabbalah* in "French Occultism." However, as this specific subject has been so well researched, documented and lavishly propagated, I would rather focus attention on those individuals of that time who were particularly devoted to the study of *Kabbalah*. In this regard there were still several astute Kabbalists in Eastern Europe in the 19th century, like Shlomo HaKohen Rabinowitz of Radomsk, author of the famous *"Tiferet Shlomo,"* who was a master of *Gematria* and Hebrew letter permutations. Besides having been a great Kabbalist, he was apparently also a wonderful singer who composed magnificent *Niggunim* (wordless sacred chants).

Assuredly one of the most illustrious Kabbalists of the time must be the ascetic Yitzchak Eizik Safrin of Komarno, who is said to have worked one hundred times through the entire set of works comprising Chaim Vital's *"Etz Chayim."* We are told that his uncle, who adopted him when he was ten years old, had introduced him to the mysteries of *Kabbalah* at an extremely young age. By the time he was sixteen, he had already mastered the teachings of Isaac Luria as well as the entire *Zohar*. This great visionary lived a most austere, reclusive life, surviving on bread and water alone, and confined himself to a small room in which he did not only receive literally thousands of visitors, but it is said he was also called upon by *Maggidim* (Spirit Messengers) in his dreams during the two hours he slept at night. These "spirit visitations" are described in his *Megillat Setarim*. He also wrote an excellent commentary on the *Zohar* titled *Zohar Chai*.

Another inspiring Kabbalist of the time was Tzadok Hakohen of Lublin, who again was a counsellor to thousands of *Chassidim* who sought his advice. Amongst the last great Chassidic Kabbalists of the 19th century, he appears to be one of the very few who seriously investigated the works of the early Kabbalists, combining their writings and the teachings of later Kabbalists like the Maharal and Nachman of Bratzlav, into a unique coherent system.

There were many great religious centres, frequented by thousands of students in both Western and Eastern Europe, where *Kabbalah* could be studied. There were equally important ones in the regions of the *Sefardim* (Spanish Jewry), e.g. in Salonika which, at the time, was a thriving centre for kabbalists and the study of *Kabbalah*; and in Baghdad which was still a very important centre for Kabbalists in the 19th century. In this city lived Yosef Chaim ben Elijah ha-Chacham of Baghdad, affectionately called the *"Ben Ish Chai,"* who was undoubtedly the greatest Kabbalist of the 19th century. There were certainly many outstanding Kabbalists amongst the *Sefardim* of Salonika; Turkey; the fertile crescent—current day Iraq and Iran; Yemen; North Africa; and elsewhere, but few were as prolific a writer as the Ben Ish Chai, whose fame spread throughout the Near and Far East, with his writings published and read by far off Sefardi communities, as far away from his native Iraq as Singapore on the one side and Tunisia on the other. Amongst his wonderful works is the earlier mentioned "*Da'at u-Tevunah*" mentioned earlier, a text offering a most lucid elucidation of the mysteries of *Kabbalah*, including a description of Kabbalistic meditation techniques.

One of the pupils of the Ben Ish Chai, Yitzchak Kaduri who also hailed from Iraq, became the most famous Jerusalem Kabbalist of the 20th century. He recently died at the great age of 106 years, and lived his whole life as a humble bookbinder and scribe. Rabbi Kaduri apparently also acquired the art of metoposcopy, the same ability Isaac Luria had pertaining to the art of reading the character and life of an individual in accordance with signs manifested on the forehead. A master of *Practical Kabbalah*, Yizchak Kaduri offered advice to literally thousands who flocked to his doorstep in search of "magical" solutions to their problems. We are told that he wrote numerous amulets for individuals ranging from the poorest to heads of state, these pertaining to protection, health, the alleviation of infertility, etc. We are told that in one instance he blessed a musician, then etched the names of angels into the skin of an apple, then instructed the performing artist to eat it with assurances that his health would be restored.

Of course, the 20th century also marks the rise and development of the "*Hermetic Kabbalah*," and here we find several luminaries, with special reference to my own mentor, William G. Gray. Unfortunately the size of this book precludes me from addressing *Kabbalah* in the 20th century in any greater detail. However, in the "*References and Bibliography*" I have included a list of texts on Kabbalistic themes, which were written from Hermetic perspectives over the last century.[101]

C. Ten and not Nine, Ten and not Eleven

So many people, having perused the voluminous output of Hermetic Kabbalists, and the constant rehashing of material by the same, inevitably suppose the Tree of Life to be the entire *Kabbalah*, and that there is nothing else to it. Hence the terms "*Kabbalah*" and "Tree of Life" have become virtually synonymous. In fact, most of the popular texts dealing with *Kabbalah*, especially those dealing with the subject matter from the perspectives of the Western Mystery Tradition, automatically address the topic in terms of the ten *Sefirot* with hardly any reference to anything else Kabbalism might entail. It is also worth noting that most of the modern studies readily available on bookshelves around the globe, pertain to attributions made to the ten *Sefirot* and twenty-two "Paths," always from the vista of "Hermetic Kabbalah."

On the other hand, when the same topic is raised in traditional Kabbalistic circles, it is equally automatically addressed virtually exclusively from the angle of "*Lurianic Kabbalah*," the general opinion being that the Lurianic treatment of the Sefirotic Tree is the only authentic one, and all others are invalid. Nothing could be further from the truth, and I believe it a serious error to simply dismiss earlier teachings, or consider them to be without any value. However, we should always remember that *Kabbalah* has its own "sacred language," and we need to keenly observe how its associated symbols, e.g. the *Etz Chayim* (Tree of Life), etc., were interpreted and reinterpreted, and how they are perverted into meanings they weren't designed for in first place.

Of course it is not only "sacred symbols" which have suffered abuse. The same can be said of our daily spoken languages in which ordinary words have been debased to such an extent, that their original plain meanings have been lost altogether. Many battles are being fought because we no longer have a uniform comprehension of the meanings of words, and they have come to mean different things to different people.

My contention here is that I have witnessed a hijacking and misapplication of Kabbalistic concepts for more years than I care to remember. This subject must be addressed, not from a specifically "finger pointing" angle, but from the clarity of consciousness which tells us that the words and symbols of all languages, whether the ordinary spoken ones or those of the sacred religious or "inner" traditions, need to be clearly understood in terms of their original intentions and meanings, before they are applied effectively and comparatively elsewhere.

Let me make it clear that I am not claiming that all modern interpretation of Kabbalistic concepts are "perversions." The history of this Tradition shows perfectly clearly that its concepts were of great interest to both Jews and Gentiles alike, and many amongst the latter were actually taught our hidden mysteries by astute Rabbis. History also shows that the concepts and teachings have undergone major transformations during the long period of their development. The doctrine of the ten *Sefirot* is a case in point, since it is vastly different in *Lurianic Kabbalah* from the way the early Kabbalists in the south of France, or in Spain, understood the topic.

The teachings of traditions get reinterpreted all the time, and while basic formulae remain the same, applications and exegesis have undergone many changes over the period of development. In fact, Judaism itself has undergone many changes since the destruction of the second Temple, and the modern religion can hardly be equated with the one practiced in the very precincts of that ancient "*House of God.*" Again this has been the case with all spiritual traditions. Change in all spheres of existence is the only constant we can be sure of, and the teachings of *Kabbalah* will probably undergo many changes in the future. Some of these *are* "perversions" and some are not. So what's the difference? Simply this, to speak and use any language, we must understand the "words" we are using. If you purport to speak English, you cannot tell me the word "hand" actually refers to a "nose." Those familiar with the vernacular know this statement to be false, however much you may argue philosophically or use the rules of formal logic to convince them otherwise.

The British have been "programmed" since early childhood to "speak" their language, as have the French, Germans, Dutch, Russians, etc. each nationality having a language understood by the native people using those tongues. The problem arises when someone unfamiliar, or perhaps having only the slightest acquaintance with the vernacular, attempts to argue about meanings and interpretations when they are very ill prepared to do so. Suddenly "red" is no longer "red," "green" no longer "green," and everything has to be reinterpreted. This can create enormous emotional, mental and physical stress. Those familiar with the language, and who "know" the meaning of each word, cannot simply be expected to override their conditioning. The same applies to Kabbalists and their teachings. They know the language. They have spoken it in many incarnations, and if you want to change meanings you better at least be on an equal footing.

This reminds me of a Talmudic story about a Persian gentleman who turned up at the home of Yehudah, a wise teacher, and after the exchanges of greeting and introduction, requested to be instructed in the Hebrew language. Yehudah agreed and proceeded to teach the visitor the letters of the Hebrew alphabet. He opened a book and indicated the first two letters of the Hebrew alphabet, saying:

"This is *Alef*.....this is *Bet*....."
"*Alef*.....*Bet*......" repeated the Persian.
"What is this?" asked Yehudah pointing to the letter *Alef*.
"*Bet*" replied the visitor.
"No.....that is *Alef*" repeated Yehudah.
"No.....*Bet*" insisted the Persian.
"What is this?" queried Yehudah, this time pointing to the letter *Bet*.
"*Alef*" exclaimed the visitor triumphantly.
"*Bet*" reiterated Yehudah.
"No.....*Alef*" persisted the Persian.
Our wise teacher paused momentarily as he briefly pondered how his presumed "pupil" is mocking him, and then boxed the ear of the visitor who exclaimed:
"Ouch!!.......My ear! My ear!"
"That is not an ear!" replied Yehudah, "It is a hand!"
"What are you saying?" cried the Persian, "Everybody knows this is an ear."
"Yes......," agreed Yehudah, and then, pointing at the letters in the book, continued: "and everybody knows that this is *Alef* and this *Bet*."

Now, the same argument applies to the "sacred languages" of "Inner Traditions" around the globe. Before you can talk about the symbols and teachings of a tradition, you need to be well acquainted with the original meanings and intentions behind those symbols. You must know your *Alef* from your *Bet*, you must know the difference between the "arses" and "elbows" of that tradition.

Again, let me make it clear that I am not saying that there cannot be any further innovations and developments today as far as this Tradition is concerned, but I believe it is important to understand the archetypal language behind the Kabbalistic concepts, so as to align oneself in a proper manner with the powers behind its symbols, all of which are, as it were, "programmed" in a "collective consciousness." Only those who know how to align themselves correctly with these "archetypal patterns" are able to effectively direct those "inner forces" for whom the mentioned symbols are special doorways.

Now, the concepts of *Ain Sof Aur* (*Or*), the "Tree of Life," and the so-called "Four Worlds" in *Kabbalah*, are only attempts to see creation from *Nil* to this world as a series of steps, so as to make that process more understandable. Each "world" is a single letter of the Ultimate Word, so to speak. The "World" concepts were so that humans might adjust their minds in easy stages, rather than try and grasp it all as a whole, which it really is. This is like reading a ruler inch by inch in order to realise the entire measurement.

The meaning of the *Sefirot*, Spheres on the Tree of Life, can be understood when one studies the term *Sefirah* (ספירה), which was derived from both Hebrew and Greek roots. The Hebrew part of the word means "numbers" and the Greek part "Sphere," as we would now say "field" or area. There is also a connection with the Latin "*Spiritus*," and so the whole word signifies "Numbered Sphere of Spirit" or "Spiritual Sphere, Number." *Sefirah* is singular, and *Sefirot* plural in a feminine sense.

The term *Sefirot* made its first appearance in the *Sefer Yetzirah*, the "Book of Creation," where they were enumerated as "ten and not nine, ten and not eleven."[102] This statement appears problematic for some contemporary investigators, who—being apparently unfamiliar with primary Kabbalistic doctrines—consider the Kabbalistic "Tenfold Tree of Faith" to be loosely based on this single phrase from the *Sefer Yetzirah*, which is considered far too rigidly applied "as an unquestionable law," and this is considered to be "silly."

Now, why "Ten and not Nine, Ten and not Eleven"? In one sentence, because the Sefirotic Tree is based on an ancient, fundamental mystical doctrine pertaining to a "sacred decad," similar to the concept of the *"Tetractys"* of Pythagoras. This doctrine was expanded and developed over a period of more than a millennium since its initial traces in the earliest teachings of Merkavistic mysticism and associated doctrines of early Gnosticism. In these we find frequent references to ten *"Ma'amarot"* (Sayings) which the Eternal Living Spirit is said to have used in the act of creation. These "Sayings" pertained to the *"Elohim* said....." verses found in the first chapter of *Genesis*, and while opinions varied as to exactly what constituted the "Ten Sayings," all were in agreement that there were exactly ten. This basic teaching was expressed in the sacred texts of the time, e.g. *Pirke Avot* (Sayings of the Fathers);[103] *Pirke d'Rabbi Eliezer*;[104] etc.

In conjunction with the "Ten Sayings" we find the Rabbis enumerated ten primal substances which they maintained were created on the "first day" of creation. The *Talmud* enumerated these as "heaven and earth, *tohu* and *bohu*, light and darkness, wind and water, the duration of day and duration of night." Additionally Rab, a third century Rabbi, stated "by ten things was the world created: by wisdom, by understanding, by reason, by strength, by rebuke, by might, by righteousness, by judgement, by loving-kindness, and by compassion."[105]

Whether referred to as "Ten Sayings," "Ten Substances" or "Ten Attributes," these were considered of fundamental importance in the creation of heaven and earth. In fact, what started initially as ten creative words, were later understood to be *"logoi,"* ten anthropomorphized creative agencies, each of which was explicitly instrumental in specific aspects of the original act of creation. Regarding our relationship with our fellow humankind, as seen in the light of the ten *"logoi,"* the author of *"Avot d'Rabbi Nathan"* tells us that "One who saves one person is worthy to be regarded as if he has saved the entire world, which was created by ten *logoi*.....And someone who causes one person to perish is to be regarded as if he caused the destruction of the entire world, which was created by these ten *logoi*."[106] Curiously enough, virtually identical doctrines regarding the ten "*logoi*" were promulgated by the early Gnostics. In this regard it is worth investigating the remarkable teachings of Monoimus, a second century Arab Gnostic.[107]

The notion of the ten *Ma'amarot* and ten creative potencies ultimately found their way into the primary texts of the early Kabbalists, in the form of the doctrine of the ten *Sefirot*, e.g. in the *Sefer Yetzirah*, the *Sefer Bahir*, the writings of Azriel of Gerona, those of the *Iyyun* mystics, the *Sefer ha-Zohar*, etc. However, before one can investigate these developments, it is important to note that the basic teaching did not only revolve around the mentioned ten creative qualities, but also incorporated ideas regarding the *unity* of the ten potentialities, i.e. the "decad" equals a "monad."

Again, ideas similar to these mystical musings of the Merkavah mystics can be found in the teachings of Monoimus, who is reported in the *"Refutation of All Heresies"* to have said "The monad, [that is] the one tittle, is, therefore, he says, also a decad. For by the actual power of this one tittle are produced duad, and triad, and tetrad, and pentad, and hexad, and heptad, and ogdoad, and ennead, up to ten. For these numbers, he says, are capable of many divisions, and they reside in that simple and uncompounded single tittle of the iota."[108] This aligns closely with the statement by Abraham Abulafia in *V'Zot li Yihudah* (*And this is Judah*) that those Kabbalists involved with "the way of the Sefirot" believe "divinity is ten Sefirot, and these ten are one."[109]

So we have "ten" being "one": the decad is a monad. However, there is a further aspect which we must consider, and that is the idea that there are three Divine attributes overseeing, as it were, the entire system. Hence we read in the *Midrash Tehillim* (*Shocher Tov*), "With three names did the Holy One, blessed be He, create His world, corresponding to three good attributes through which the world was created."[110] The same idea is found in the *Talmud* (*Berachot 55a*), but it is much more explicitly expressed in the merkavistic section of *Pirke d'Rabbi Eliezer*, specifically chapter 3, which reads ".....by ten Sayings is the world created and in three [Divine attributes] are these [Sayings] comprised, as it is said 'The Lord by wisdom founded the earth; by understanding he established the heavens, by his knowledge the depths were broken up' (*Proverbs 3:19, 20*). By these three (attributes) was the Tabernacle made, as it is said, 'And I have filled him with the spirit of God, with wisdom, with understanding, and with knowledge' (*Exodus 31:3*). Likewise with these three (attributes) was the Temple made, as it is said, 'He was the son of a widow woman of the tribe of Naphtali, and his father was a man of Tyre, a worker in brass; and he was filled with wisdom and understanding and knowledge' (*1 Kings 7:14*). By these three attributes it will be rebuilt in the future, as it is said, 'Through wisdom is an house builded; and by understanding it is established; and by knowledge are the chambers filled' (*Proverbs 24:3, 4*)."[111] Clearly these three "overseeing" qualities are "Wisdom," "Understanding" and "Knowledge."

Now in the period preceding the writing of the *Sefer ha-Bahir* the names and positions of the emanated powers, which ultimately developed into the scheme of the ten *Sefirot*, were not yet settled or fully agreed upon by the *Merkavah* mystics. As we noted, these mystics certainly referred to ten powers, or "sayings" (*ma'amarot*), through which the world came into being. In the *Pirke d'Rabbi Eliezer* these were divided into three higher and seven lower "attributes" (*middot*), but the three supreme attributes were then understood to be "Wisdom," "Understanding" and "Knowledge," which we saw were chosen because they appear together, in that exact order, in several Biblical verses.

It was only later that *Keter Elyon* (Supreme Crown) came to be seen as part of the powers in the scheme of Divine Emanation. Even in the writings of Eleazer of Worms (13th century), the term *Keter Elyon*, though appearing many times throughout his works, was never used in reference to the first *Sefirah*. It would seem that the first time "Supreme Crown" was used in reference to the first *Sefirah* on the Tree of Life, was in the *Sefer Bahir*, a work which is now well established to have been compiled by someone in the School of Isaac the Blind in Provence towards the end of the 12th century. This text was compiled from many, even Gnostic sources. It has been pointed out that Rabbi Isaac the Blind, who himself might have been the author of the *Sefer Bahir*, was the first mystic to devote his entire life-work to mysticism, and his many disciples disseminated his teachings in Southern France and in Spain. It was his initial input that stimulated the development of contemplative Kabbalism amongst the 13th century Spanish Kabbalists.

Isaac the Blind contributed a lot to the development of the concept of the *Sefirot*. However, for all its references to and discussions of the *Sefirot*, the teaching of these Divine Emanations were still not settled in the *Bahir*. For further developments, we need to look at the writings of the *Iyyun* circle in the 13th century. Well known amongst these is the *Sefer ha-Iyyun*,[112] but there are a number of short treatises circulated within this group, in which many novel deliberations were introduced regarding the *Sefirot* and the thirty-two "Paths of Wisdom."[113] The order of the emanation of the *Sefirot* varied a lot from one author to the next, and there were considerable differences of opinion amongst the members of this circle. It was really in the school of the Gerona Kabbalists, in the second half of the 13th century, that the doctrine of the Ten *Sefirot* began to assume a uniform pattern, and was finally presented in the manner we have become accustomed to, in the *Sefer ha-Zohar* of Rabbi Moses de Leon of Guadalajara.

So, ultimately this teaching of the "decad," which is a "monad" governed by three principles, developed into the doctrine of the ten *Sefirot* and the Kabbalistic Tree of Life—a unity of Ten Spheres divided into three groups, each overseen by a specific spiritual attribute, e.g. "Wisdom" to the right (Right Pillar), "Understanding" to the left (Left Pillar), and ultimately the centre pertains to "Knowledge" (*Da'at*).

Considering this brief delineation of the development of the doctrine of the "Ten *Sefirot*," we must assuredly consider that we are applying ideas initially gleaned from the *Sefer Yetzirah*, concepts which were finally settled in their current format more than a thousand years after the writing of that text. Hence, we are dealing with issues which the anonymous author of that text was not aware of, but this is not necessarily wrong on our part. There was much diversity in the development of the doctrine of the ten *Sefirot,* and even greater differences in the multitude of interpretations and applications of these by numerous individuals over the centuries—even to our times. In the case of claims being made that one approach is wrong and another right, I am reminded of Ludwig Wittgenstein who wrote: "Whether a thing is a blunder or not—it is a blunder in a particular system. Just as something is a blunder in one particular game and not in another."[114] Hence, what I do consider seriously wrong, are the exclusivity claims made for one or another particular system, which is equally as "questionable" as any other when viewed from broader perspectives.

However, having said that, it is equally clear that while one may understand and accept that much diversification has been going on regarding this Tradition, especially over the last century, and having closely investigated such "variances," we equally recognise that *Kabbalah* would become meaningless if its fundamental principles were compromised. In other words, principle Kabbalistic teachings and rudimentary reasoning cannot simply be altered in accordance with personal whims. Hence it is necessary to first understand the central, vital core teachings behind this Tradition, before adjusting parameters in alignment with personal perceptions. One simply can no longer speak of *Kabbalah* when the supposed stable primary doctrines of this tradition have been sacrificed in the fray. Sadly, such has been the case in a lot of works written in the name of *Kabbalah*, while they bear little or no relation to the Tradition. Often basic teachings of this tradition are sidelined and even dismissed out of hand.

When you come to think of it, *Kabbalah* is much more than the current assumption that the doctrine of the "Tree of Life" and the ten *Sefirot* comprise the entire teaching of *Kabbalah*. In fact, the "Tree-Concept" was originally only a small part of *Kabbalah*, and a relatively unimportant one at that. It is mainly Gentiles who expounded and increased it to its current central place in our system. It is certainly a lot clearer, more direct, and much easier to understand than the "letter-number" permutations of early *Kabbalah*. Yet, if the principles of *"Letter-Number Kabbalah"* are understood, some remarkable practices, meditations and "inner communications" can be found in this form of mysticism, which can produce some really far-reaching results for the individual who knows the system.

The entire arena of *"Ecstatic Kabbalah"* is based on this system. Few of these practices were, and still are, available to the modern public. A major part of the system often amounted to no more than mental exercises which enabled the brain to cope with the obscure problems of existence. To some extent it could then be likened to a cryptic crossword, in which the satisfaction came in the exercise of ones mental faculties. This was however never the only value of the *"Letter-Number Kabbalah."* There was certainly a lot more to it as the practices of *Shemot* (Divine Names), *Yichudim* (unification exercises) and *Tzerufim* (permutation practices) will show.[115]

Today the tendency is to think that there is really more than one *Kabbalah* so to speak, with three categories specifically identified: 1. *Traditional Kabbalah*— the one as understood to apply to Israel alone; 2. *Christian Kabbalah*; and 3. *Hermetic Kabbalah*. The latter two refer to the tradition as interpreted and worked on by Gentile scholars for the Western Inner Tradition at large, and we understand that though the basic formulae are the same, the application and exegesis are very different. End of story? Definitely not. This is a very simplistic and narrow viewpoint, in which the strictly Jewish origins of the *Kabbalah* are often ignored, not to mention that even in *Traditional Kabbalah* there are many divergent voices regarding practically every topic within that sector, that one would have to divide what is viewed collectively as "traditional" into many subcategories.

However, most modern researchers are still inclined to speak of *"pre-Lurianic"* and *"Lurianic Kabbalah"* in reference to the earlier mentioned two distinct periods in the development of *Kabbalah*. The first which could be termed "Zoharic," not entirely correctly as an early Kabbalist like Abraham Abulafia did not belong in this category, culminated in the writings of Moses Cordovero, while his pupil Isaac Luria started a new trend which is now called *"Lurianic Kabbalah."*

There are many who, in trying to indicate the distinction between *Traditional Kabbalah* and the one as applied in the Western Inner Tradition, use the spelling *"Qabalah."* It has been suggested by several authors, specifically from the "Hermetic Schools," that the spelling of the term *"Kabbalah"* should be varied in order to indicate variant applications, i.e. *"Kabbalah"* in reference to *"Traditional Kabbalah"*; *"Cabala"* to indicate the Christian variety, and *"Qabalah"* for the *"Hermetic Kabbalah."* I have found no use for this kind of variant spelling for a variety of reasons, amongst others:

1. The common use of the "K" spelling is a fairly recent one, apparently introduced to create a consensus. However, it should be noted that many Rabbis, historians and other scholars have been using the "C" spelling when discussing what we might loosely term *"Traditional Kabbalah."* In fact, to date there are still French, Spanish, Portuguese, Italian, and Swiss authors, amongst others, who are still using that spelling in their studies of mainstream *"Kabbalah."* The suggestion that the "C" spelling be used exclusively to designate a Christian variant of Kabbalistic thinking, would create confusion as far as a veritable host of works are concerned, which were written over a period of more than a hundred years. Likewise the "K" spelling was and still is being used by scholars around the globe in their discussions of *"Christian Kabbalah."*

2. The division of the Kabbalistic Tradition in this manner into the mentioned three categories is seriously problematic. It suggests a uniform pattern of thought to be prevailing within the "Jewish Mystical Tradition," which is patently an inaccurate portrayal of the tradition over the thousand and more years of its existence.

    Besides the obvious differences between, for example, the teachings of Isaac Luria and that of the author of the Zohar, marking distinct periods in the development of the Tradition, there are enormous differences and major disagreements between Kabbalists living in the same era, with regard to even the most basic tenets of *Kabbalah*, e.g. the ten *Sefirot*, etc. Pertaining to this specific concept, there were Kabbalists who did not like the sefirotic system at all, and rarely made use of it. Moreover, there were thinkers within this tradition who did not agree with Talmudic studies, yet these very individuals are considered part of that tradition. In fact, there are several absolutely distinct "Kabbalistic traditions" and diverse schools of thought which developed over the centuries, some of them considered to be heretical, yet many of the latter kind are now generically accepted as part of what mainstream religionists term *"Kosher Kabbalah."*

3. As far as I am concerned the word "*Kabbalah*" is a Hebrew term with only one spelling. The transliteration of this word has been somewhat problematic due to the fact that the sound of its initial letter is represented by two letters in the Hebrew alphabet, i.e. *Kaf* and *Kof*. The latter letter is the one used in the word itself, and has been designated "C," "K," or "Q" by different authors, thus the variants in the spelling of the word in languages using the Latin alphabet. Trying to use those variants to denote three different approaches within the Tradition does not work for anybody using the Hebrew, Greek or Cyrillic alphabet. Thus such usage cannot be universal.

Settling for one common spelling, i.e. "*Kabbalah*," and then clearly indicating a specific subsidiary of this tradition under discussion—*Ecstatic Kabbalah, Theurgic Kabbalah, Prophetic Kabbalah, Lurianic Kabbalah, Christian Kabbalah, Hermetic Kabbalah*, etc., is far more useful and accurate. Besides, there is in truth only one "*Kabbalah*," the teachings of which are wielded in as many ways as there are people to invent them from their personal perspectives. Provided the core principles and doctrines of the tradition are understood and upheld intact, there can be an infinite number of variant interpretations.

Now, since the subject of the Kabbalistic Tree of Life has been dealt with in detail by many authors, and in particular in a twentieth century fashion by my own mentor, William G. Gray,[116] I will only outline it here very briefly for a better understanding of this. However, considering the veritable mountain of trash written on the Sefirotic Tree in our times, it is certainly no wonder that the Tree of Life has turned into the most maligned aspect of *Kabbalah*. It is simply not good enough to claim that you can name the ten *Sefirot* and interpret these because you have acquired such knowledge via the teachings of late 19th century English authors who worked from badly translated Latin manuscripts.

Before one can even begin to address a single *Sefirah* like *Keter* (Crown), the highest *Sefirah* on the Sefirotic Tree, one should at least familiarize oneself with some of the fundamental doctrines regarding "the Crown of God," ranging from the teachings of the early *Yordei Merkavah* to those of the *Mekubalim*

68 / *The Shadow Tree: The Book of Self Creation*

of later *Kabbalah*, e.g. the Lurianic variety. This means one has to gather as much information as possible from as many of the primary Kabbalistic texts one can find, before jumping to conclusions.

As said, the Life Tree comprises ten "*Sefirot*" or Spheres and twenty-two "*Tzinorot*," "Paths" or "Channels of Power," named and numbered from the top downwards, as is shown in the following diagram:

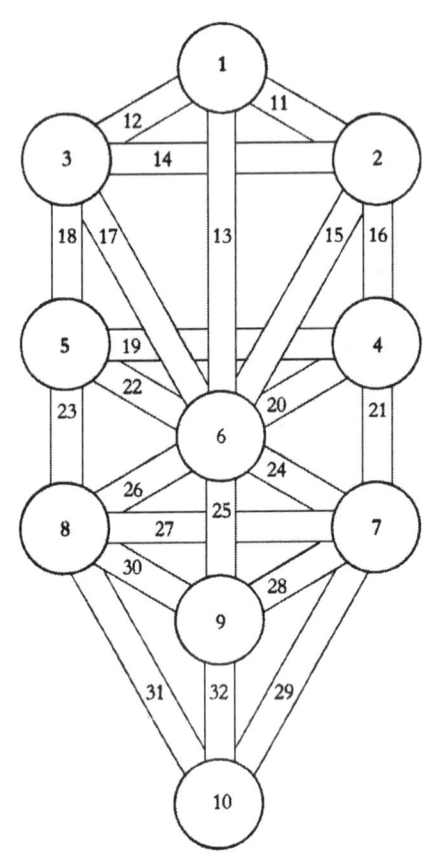

Here is a brief analysis of the different "*Sefirot*":

1. כתר—*Keter* (Crown), being the "Apex" or "Crown of Pure Consciousness." There might be an association here of the infinite extension of Consciousness as it encompass the Whole. In fact, the word "Crown" reveals a bit of this, since it derives from the Greek "*Koronis*" as a reference to anything curved or bent, to which is

linked the words "curve" and, believe it or not, "circus" meaning of course "a ring" or "circle." I think the ideas of encircling and surrounding should be obvious, and *Keter* as all embracing, all sustaining, all encompassing is well explained by the word "Crown."

2. חכמה—*Chochmah* (Wisdom), being Eternal or Supreme Wisdom, and

3. בינה—*Binah* (Understanding), being Omniscient Understanding.

    We will look at these concepts conjointly, as they represent the two great poles of perception. Regarding the expression "Supreme Wisdom" we might note that the term "Supreme" of course means the highest quality and intensity, while Wisdom refers to sagacity, acuteness of perception and sound judgment. On the other hand, "Understanding" literally means "to stand under," a quality which we should *be* ourselves. It is an openness which makes us capable of receiving or comprehending true meaning in life. "Understanding" means we are in a state of having apprehended something with clear awareness, and that this will bring discernment. *Chochmah* is said to refer to "undifferentiated Force" which is being differentiated, channelled as it were, into forms in *Binah*.

    In his remarkable book titled "*Meditation and Judaism*," DovBer Pinson summarized these concepts most eloquently saying "*Chochmah*, intelligence, is where kernels of thought begin to sprout. It is where new thoughts occur and begin to germinate. The word *chochmah* is comprised of two Hebrew words *choch* and *mah*, which means literally *the potential of what is*. *Chochmah* is the potential of all further thought that arises. Yet at this level the thoughts remain elusive; one can still ask 'What is it?' Thoughts the way they exist in *chochmah* consciousness are undefinable and incomprehensible. They cannot be explained in clear, logical terms, for they exist only in potentiality. It is the first flash of intuitive knowledge, the bare idea, that cannot yet be fully articulated in rational thoughts. Once the thought is brought into the domain of *binah*, the potential into the actual, one cogitates this seminal point into finer detail. *Binah* is the cognitive ability that absorbs the ambiguous seeds of *chochmah* and shapes it into transmissible form through the process of associative analysis. The kernel of *chochmah* is nurtured into maturity through the power of *binah*. *Binah* gives the thought form and configuration.

With the power of *binah* one constructs the details that constitute the totality of the thought, in its length and breadth. Examining and pondering a thought in its length involves taking the thought from a purely abstract state and making it into something more readily understandable. Broadening a thought means giving the thought greater implications, dressing and giving the thought comprehensible and rational connotations.

Chochmah is likened to the male, who supplies the semen, the germ of the concept, and *binah* is likened to the female, who receives the germ and develops it in the womb into a fully grown, particularized creation. In *binah* consciousness the kernel of *chochmah* incubates until it articulates into a comprehensible thought. *Chochmah* is the unchannelled creative force, which can only be brought into fruition when enclosed and channelled in the womb of *binah*.

In *Kabbalah*, *chochmah* is likened to a dot. It occurs as a flash of insight. It appears in the form of a concentrated intuitive lightning bolt. The thought flashes in front of one's eyes. It is as if one sees the thought and is certain of its existence but cannot yet explain it. *Chochmah* is the seminal idea before the details are formulated and externalized, while *binah* is where the abstract is made into rational sense. *Chochmah* is likened to seeing the thought, and *binah* is analogous to listening, that is, internalizing and making sense of it."[117]

דעת—*Da'at* (Knowledge), being the "Experience" to be gained in order to cross the Abyss, which separates the lower spheres of existence from the realm of "Pure Consciousness" represented by the first three *Sefirot*.

Some researchers claimed the term *Da'at* was initially used in reference to the uppermost *Sefirah* on the Tree of Life, which was then later renamed *Keter Elyon*. It was assumed that this must be the case, since the concepts of "Wisdom" and "Understanding" pertain respectively to topmost *Sefirot*, hence the term "Knowledge" must refer to *Keter*. However, we only need to peruse the writings of early Kabbalists, like those of Joseph

Gikatilla, to arrive at a clear understanding that the *sefirot* were sort of categorized within the three "Divine attributes," e.g. "Wisdom" comprises the collective *sefirot* on the right; "Understanding" those on the left; and "Knowledge" the set in the centre. In other words, the so-called "Three Pillars" on the Tree of Life, are respectively named the "Wisdom," "Understanding" and "Knowledge." Here there is no conception of any "hidden *sefirah*" named "*Da'at*" (Knowledge). In fact, not only the central "Pillar" but *Tiferet*, the central sphere of "Beauty" and "Harmony" in the process of reaching upwards along the central way to the "Crown of Cosmos," was also titled "*Da'at*." This topic is extensively addressed in "*Sha'arei Orah*" by Joseph Gikatilla,[118] and it is worth noting that the Latin translation of this text (*Portae Lucis*) had a major impact on the development of *Christian Kabbalah*, and ultimately on the later Hermetic varieties.

4. חסד—*Chesed* (Mercy), being "Perpetual Compassion," and

5. גבורה—*Gevurah* (Severity), being "Almighty Justice." I believe we should again consider these two *Sefirot* conjointly, since they are inseparable. Ultimately we need to realise the perfect harmony between mercy and severity, which is like the two sides of a door that opens and shuts. The term "mercy" derives from the Latin "*merces*" meaning to "reward" or "to pull together." So "mercy" unites and severity separates.

The sphere of *Chesed* is associated with what is termed "*Tzedakah*," acts of loving-kindness. This word, mistranslated "charity" in English, actually denotes "righteousness," and the meaning of "righteous" is simply to be "right" and "wise." Of course, everybody knows that the word "*Tzedakah*" indeed refers to giving charity or accomplishing "merciful" actions, but if we examine the motives of many gregarious philanthropists, there is very little in the giving pertaining to serving those who are in need, and a lot more to expanding personal egos through self aggrandisement. In this regard you might have noticed how the entrance halls of some places of worship are decorated with large wooden plaques, listing in gold lettering the names of philanthropical individuals—sometimes even the amount of money donated to some or other charitable institute. In fact, the most ideal form of *Tzedakah* is when the giver does not know who the receiver is, and the receiver does not know from whence the benefit derives.

Now, in mainstream Judaism as well as *Kabbalah* the subject of "bread of shame" is discussed in great detail. Basically what it means is that the person who is in the receiving position, should never be placed in a state of feeling inferior and humiliated by the giving. There is a lovely story about a Rabbi who wanted to invite a very poor member of his community to Sabbath dinner. This is more than a *mitzvah* (a good deed), it is in fact a religious obligation that one should have a guest at the Sabbath table.

Anyway, the story has it that the impoverished man responded to the Rabbis kindness with a polite: "Thank you very much Rabbi, but I am OK." The Rabbi again asked, and again the man who did not want to eat "bread of shame," replied: "Thank you very much Rabbi, but I am alright." The Rabbi suddenly found himself in a quandary, he wanted to do a kind deed, moreover he wanted to fulfil the religious obligation, and so, he again asked the poor man to share his Sabbath table, adding: "I need you at my table. I want to fulfil the law," and so forth. "Ah.....I understand Rabbi. You need me! Of course I will be there. Thank you very much." True service is when we ourselves have the need to give, in as great a measure as the other person has the need to receive.

Regarding all acts of "loving-kindness," it is important that we should afford all the opportunity to get somewhere by their own efforts. We should bear *with* them, submit *with* them, carry *with* them, endure *with* them, share *with* them, live *with* them but never *for* them. The smooth, soft, calm warmth of true clemency, compassion and mercy, does not allow slothfulness, indolence, idleness or laziness. In one sense mercy and compassion are passive, but only in the true meaning of the word, which comes from roots meaning "capable of suffering." Mercy and compassion are also active, nimble and alert. When you are aware, you are passive enough to receive what comes, and active enough to live out what you have received.

Now, obviously the word "severity" means to sever, separate, or cut apart, which is the antithesis and companion of "mercy." Most people only see graveness, austerity, harshness and sternness in severity. Look at "graveness" of which the source word is "grave." Grave in one meaning implies to carve and to dig, and in this sense we should carve, sculpt and engrave our lives, so that we may become fit for a god to live through. Only if you incise yourself to true action, can you impress and implant something indelibly in your life. On the other hand, "grave" also derives from linguistic roots meaning a cave or a trench, saying to the Companion: "Dig a grave for all that is dead within yourself." With the realisation of course that the "tomb" is also a "womb," and that burial is only insemination, gestation and all the preparations within the Earth Mother awaiting rebirth.

There is another meaning to "grave" which is generally not known and that is the meaning of renovating the wooden hull of a ship by burning off growths, and tarring or pitching while the boat is in the graving-dock. Each one of us is a boat afloat on the "Sea of Life," and we should occasionally enter the graving-dock, where the "Fires of Severity" and "Real Judgment" will burn away the unnecessary growths.

The final meaning of the word "grave," the one originally implied, is that of seriousness but not over-seriousness, so that consciousness becomes a pain in the arse. The Aryan base implies the word "important," and, by the way, the Sanskrit word "Guru" meaning important and honourable, comes from the same root. "Grave" in this sense implies seriousness and authority.

Now, we have to be most careful not to fall into the trap of associating this sphere with "divine retribution." I recall the conversation I had with my late mentor on this very topic. He did not believe in "judgment" or "divine retribution" after death, at least not in the generally promulgated sense, e.g. being "judged" and "punished" for our "sins" in the after-life. William Gray was an extremely direct man, and we had a particularly long interaction regarding "sin" and "divine retribution."

It all started when he mentioned how many years previously, when he had personal notions of entering the catholic priesthood, he had attended a sermon by the then great Father Martindale. This priest pointed out on that occasion that so-called Christians were making a mistake in claiming to be so good and holy because they did not, and had not, committed any serious sins. Merely because they had not murdered, robbed, swindled on a big scale, and so forth did not entitle them to any special sanctity, because the fact was that the ordinary person could not commit those sins on account of inability. Nothing else stopped them. What really mattered was the sins you could commit and prevented yourself from doing by your own will. First you had to have it in your power and ability to commit such sins, and then if you determined not to, you did deserve some merit.

I responded that whilst this was an excellent point, it was quite meaningless in the light of the different concept of "sin" which we were discussing. We agreed that the idea of a touchy, ill tempered God raging away at the antics of Man because those "offended" His ideas of propriety, did not "go over" any more. It was clear that "sin" is obviously wrongful behaviour which damages us by the doing in such a way, that we fail to achieve anything like the "Intention of God" in ourselves for our period of incarnation. Therefore, in "falling short" of the mark by so far, we hinder our progression towards "Perfection" by that much. In sinning against ourselves, we sin against the "God-in-us."

We felt that the old-time concept of "sin" as intentional offenses against a God, who laid down arbitrary dictates of behaviour, did not stand up very well in the light of experience. He referred to two old axioms which were felt to be very explanatory in this regard. One is "A thing is not just because God wills it, but God wills it because it is just." And the other is "We are not punished *for* our sins, but *by* them." For me it was a question of horses and carts, or plain cause and effect. Simply: "If I do this then that will happen," and taking things from there.

However, the one thing we both felt was vitally important, was to get away from the "Father Christmas" ideas humanity had of God in the past centuries—a totally benevolent and paternal Deity who could be stern, yet only demanded unthinking obedience to His presumed dictates, as translated by His faithful clergy on Earth. Two World Wars have stripped such an insipid creator of his trimmings in tinsel, and brought us up against the more terrible truth that everything was not created specially for our benefit alone, and we shall not be given everything free of charge if we flatter God enough. Oddly enough we are coming up against a God much more like our remote ancestors visualised. An enormous Power. Sheer *ENERGY* without emotions as we know them. Motivated, if one can call it that, by pure plus-minus-balance necessity with balance as the desideratum. The "swinging pendulum principle." It is we humans who translate this in terms of feeling such as Love—Hate; Like—Dislike; etc.

Anyway, William Gray maintained "Divine Judgment" to be a kind of inbuilt process of "compensation," a natural "rectification process," like the automatic pilot which gauges the motion of an aircraft and works automatic rectification (judgment) when it veers off its course in any direction. Compensation means that distress will lead to release, death to birth, the valley to the mountaintop, but also that the high peak is the limit and you need to come down into another valley—another death, in order to reach the next peak—the rebirth.

Before one can become slothful in ones freedom and release, the Eternal Living Spirit will allow one to be met with another pain, another distress, so that one may seek another release, bringing one every time closer to ones "True Home." Be thankful that Life chastises those who aspire, or as the old saying goes: "God chastiseth those whom he loveth," and "to chastise" simply means "to make chaste."

6. תפארה—*Tiferet* (Beauty), being Balanced Harmony. This is such a remarkable Sphere on the *Etz Chayim*, representing the "Solar Principle" on so many levels, that I want to be clear that we understand it properly. It has been said that it represents "sacrificed child gods," however, it represents all sacrificed "solar gods." For me *Tiferet* is the position of the Grail (*Sangreal*) on the Tree of Life. Some have associated a "triple image" with this *Sefirah*—a "Child," a "Priest-King" and a "Sacrificed God." These are all images of mediation between the lower half and the upper half of the *Etz Chayim*.

When we glance at the Tree of Life our eyes are immediately attracted to the central Sphere, and, as we know, *Tiferet* is the representation of the "Solar Principle" on the Tree, just as our hearts are in our bodies. *Tiferet* means "Beauty," and this is closely associated with concepts such as "Service," "Sacrifice" and "Restoration." In fact, there is a wonderful practice associated with what is called "*Tikkun*" (restoration) in *Kabbalah*, a practice pertaining to finding Beauty everywhere and, in so doing, raising the Divine Sparks which have fallen into this dimension of the *Klippot* ("shards" usually understood as demonic).

The central "solar sphere" of *Tiferet* is considered the specific focus of "Messianic consciousness." However, the way this is understood in *Kabbalah* does not quite align with the way it is often expressed in many contemporary books dealing with this topic. It would seem that due to the associated "sacrificial" ideas, many have assumed that this *Sefirah* pertains specifically and exclusively to the Christian saviour. In this regard it should be noted that while the Christian "messiah-deity" is acknowledged in "*Christian Kabbalah*" and some of its offshoots, this is not the case in "*Traditional Kabbalah.*"

Now, the term "*christ*" is the English translation of the word "*khristos*," which in turn is the Greek version of the Hebrew "*Mashiach*" (Messiah) meaning "an anointed one." The Kabbalistic view regarding this subject was well summarized by Robert Waxman, a lecturer and Kabbalist, in an essay titled "*The Messianic Idea in Jewish Kabbalah.*" He stated "Matter represents complete unconsciousness and spirit represents complete consciousness. As human beings we are evolving life forms or minds that have reached equilibrium between the lowest and the highest *Sephirot*.

What does it mean to reach equilibrium? It means that once we are aware of these two opposing conditions, we can choose for ourselves between these two states. The higher state of pure spirit represents our 'messianic consciousness' which is our spark of *Ayn-Soph*, or the *Neschamah* within. In the Hebrew Bible, Isaiah speaks of a coming messiah whose name will be *Immanuel*. The definition of this name from Hebrew into English is, 'The God with us.' Kabbalistically, the name *Immanuel* is defined with one slight modification to mean, 'The God with-IN us.' These two letters make all the difference in the interpretation of how to live one's life. There are those who are waiting for a liberating person of flesh and blood to do all the work by 'saving' them personally, along with the rest of humanity. Then, there are others who believe the 'messiah of *Neshamah*' has always been with them, and *it is they who must do the work* of *tikkun* to repair their Souls, and thus 'save' themselves.

But, what we must grasp is the idea that *we are now Life,* that *we were never anything but Life,* and that man in any sense means a life which has reached a given degree of spiritual, intellectual and physical evolution. This can be illustrated by the ascending nature of the *Sephirot*. Specifically, the *Sephira Tiferet* represents the 'messiah-within' (our own '*Immanuel*') who wants to spread the divine light of wisdom in each one of us, and thus 'save' a lifetime which otherwise may have gone to waste.....

It is not the kabbalist who is waiting for 'the coming' or 'the second-coming' of any messiah, rather it is the messiah-within (*Immanuel*) who is waiting for each one of us to wake-up, evolve spiritually, and thus experience the divine illumination from within....."[119]

Of course, there is and always was that sense that some great "Avatar" or "Messiah" is going to come and sort out all the troubles of this world, and yet he, or more probably it, will do nothing of the kind. Christians claim Jesus was the "Messiah," but the Jewish Messiah is much more of a nationalistic figure, a "Folk-Saviour" exclusively for Jews. And why not? Everybody should have a "Messiah figure" from time to time. The Christian concept simply built one around the personality of Jesus and made it multinational and multiracial, but unfortunately with the agenda of "Our God will swallow yours up, and we'll own the whole world in the end, because ours will then be biggest!"

Now, the view of William Gray in this regard—with which I personally concur, and which is fundamental to the teachings also of the Sangreal Sodality, the brotherhood we founded in 1980 in Johannesburg, South Africa, is that God incarnates through *all* life in existence, human or otherwise, but each to its own degree for that particular purpose. True, the "Salvation Principle" behind and underlying Christianity is the entire basis of our spiritual heritage under whatever name you care to give it. However, rather than pertaining to a specific historical or mythical personage, we would see what you might term the "Christ-spirit," to be the *liberative inherent instinct of humans seeking union with the Ultimate, regardless of any recognised religion.*

Robert Waxman's exposition is absolutely valid, since your "Salvation" is in your own hands, and the "Sacred Marriage" or "Divine Union" is meant to happen within your own inner being. Every individual should become a "Messiah" or an "Anointed One," specifically the "saviour" of his or her own "Self." In fact, the whole process of insemination, germination, etc., as a "Sacred

Sacrifice" causing a kind of breeding and birth, death and resurrection, was meant to occur inside oneself whilst alive in the physical body.

It is interesting to note that some of the early Christians, in particular the Gnostic sects, did not so much believe in a literal Jesus, but saw the "Real Self" under the title of "Jesus" or a "Christ," which one had to seek within ones own being. This view is expressed quite explicitly in some of the Gnostic texts discovered at Nag Hammadi in Upper Egypt in 1945. For example, one reads in the *Gospel of Thomas* that "If you bring forth what is within you, what you bring forth will save you. If you do not bring forth what is within you, what you do not bring forth will destroy you,"[120] or in the words of Monoimus, an early Gnostic teacher: "Abandon the search for God and the creation and other matters of a similar sort. Look for him by taking yourself as the starting point. Learn who it is within you who makes everything his own and says, 'My God, my mind, my thought, my soul, my body.' Learn the sources of sorrow, joy, love, hate.....If you carefully investigate these matters, you will find him in yourself."[121]

7. נצח—*Netzach* (Victory), being "Unceasing Achievement," and
8. הוד—*Hod* (Glory), being "Surpassing Splendour."

Since these two *Sefirot* are again so closely related, in fact so often confused with one another, I thought we should address them conjointly. *Hod* (Glory) and *Netzach* (Victory) represent respectively "thinking" and "feeling"; the "intellectual" and the "emotional." "Thinking" and "Feeling" are respectively linked to the left and right hemispheres of the brain, and are, curiously enough, placed that way on the Tree of Life as well.

Now, one can truly learn so much when one examines the basic meaning of the appellatives of these spheres. The plain direct translations of *Hod* and Netzach would be:

Hod—"Splendour"; "Glory"; "Majesty" and even "Beauty." Perhaps I can explain the meaning of the Hebrew term in the following way. You reside in Britain, a Kingdom, whose sovereign is addressed "royal majesty." Translated into Hebrew that would be "*Hod Malchut*,"speaking in the masculine sense of course. Associated with *Hod* we have the following terms: "Confess"—"*Hodah b'*—"; "Admission"—"*Hoda'ah*" (spelled with an *Alef*), "Announcement"—"*Hoda'ah*" (spelled with an *Ayin*}; "Acknowledge"—"*Hodei*," also associated with "thank" as in "thanks to"—"*Hodot li*–"; etc.

Hod is spelled *Heh–Vav–Dalet* (הוד). Here the letter *Vav* indicates the vowel associated with the term in question. However, the instant we drop the *Vav*, hence remaining with only the letters *Heh* and *Dalet*, we get "*Hed*" meaning "shout," "noise" or "echo." The latter term could be understood in reference to "reverberation." Naturally all these ideas are part of the overall meaning of the initial term pertaining to "splendour" and "majesty." Hence we have "*Hadar*"—to "adorn" or "honour" (also referring to an "ornament," "majesty," "glory," etc.); "*Heder*"—"splendour" (also "ornament"); as well as "*Hider*"—"to honour" also meaning "to be zealous."

It would seem the fundamental term has to do with the idea of a "persistent step by step ascendance," so to speak, hence when we say "by degrees" or "gradually," the equivalent in Hebrew is "*b'hadragah*." Notice the *Hod* inside this word. On the other hand, there are also associated ideas of "direction" and "guidance"—"*Hadrachah*," though the fundamental root in this case is not "*Hod*" but actually "*Derech*"—a "way"; "path" or "road." It has been said the "splendorous path" referred to here is the "Hermetic" one of the "intellect," the tool which aids towards the broadening of ones horizons via the thought processes of the reasoning mind.

On the opposite end of the same spectrum we have *Netzach*, a term linked with ideas of "shimmer" and "sparkle," e.g. *Natzach*—"to shine," "sparkle," but also meaning to be "victorious." Associated here is "*Nitzach*"—"to be enduring." In fact, the root meaning of the term *Netzach* pertains to "eternity" or "endurance" as in "*lanetzach*"—"forever"; and also to "eminence" and "glory," as well as "victory" as in "*Nitzachon*" meaning "triumph" and "victory." If we play around a bit with the word in question, we might find some interesting associated concepts. For example, *Netzach* is spelled *Nun–Tzadi–Chet* (נצח). What would happen if we dropped the letter *Chet*? We would still retain the fundamental meaning of "victory" and "endurance," but with quite lofty associations such as "unfolding" or "flying" in both the literal (nature) and metaphorical (spiritual) sense. Here we have *Netz*—a "blossom" or "flower" and also a "hawk." Many of us would like "to fly"—"*Natza*" (spelled with an *Alef* suffix) like a hawk, but many "flee"—"*Natza*" (spelled with an *Ayin* suffix) also meaning "to fall into ruin" as in "*Nitza*"—"to be laid waste," "to quarrel," or "made desolate."

Say we drop in turn the *Nun* prefix in *Netzach*, we will really emphasize the brilliant sparkle of the term in question with concepts like "*Tzach*"—"clear" and "bright," or to be "dazzling" as in "*Tzachach*," and in the extreme the discomfort of an extremely dry place, i.e. "parched"—"*Tzicheh*," etc. All the concepts associated with *Netzach* points to the "sparkle" of what has been termed the "Orphic" way, the one related to the emotional side of our natures. The eternal "yearn" inside ourselves, which can be a source of enormous pleasure or of pain beyond endurance.

On this "path" we sometimes experience the ecstatic heights of "Divine Realisation," at other times we sense a profound bleakness, virtually as if one has been deserted by God and man alike. I am referring to what has been called "aridity," that strange spiritual "dryness" which medieval "saints" wrote so much about and found so difficult to cope with. It is such a common occurrence really. Just the natural "infertility period" after spiritual "fecundity" or productiveness. One has to go with the other. Life being cyclic has its opposites, as we know from experience and commonsense, and such teachings as the Kabbalistic Tree of Life. All periods of spiritual activity and sense of "aliveness," must necessarily be followed, sooner or later, by a corresponding period of dullness and inactivity. Just as natural as Death following Birth forever.

All creative people are familiar with this pattern, and it is amazing how it can influence your life. Take book writing for example. Everything disappears when one is engaged in writing a book until it actually appears on the bookshelf, and then all the interest, concentration, and everything else in life sort of "goes flat" and one feels sort of "lost," wandering around and deserted. It is rather like being "between plays" if one is a professional actor or actress. For me as musician/composer "being between compositions" is just a blank bewildering experience. Then—*BANG!*—comes the necessary "Inner Seed," the necessary inspiration for a new work, and—*ZONK!*—life gets back in its groove and sails along again.

Afterwards it is back again to that "hiatus" position, where there does not seem to be a clear lead to follow in any direction. Then one marks time awaiting the next command which is so slow in arriving, which never seems to arrive, perhaps due to impatience. How many young mystics find this "dry" period or "hiatus" difficult to understand and deal with? No human being can stay in a state of being spiritually "high," any more than they can stay in a permanent state of sexual arousal. It means no more than that. What matters is knowing how to use a spiritual "down" sensibly and profitably. The answer of course is to switch attention intentionally and get on with something else. Maybe something quite mundane but necessary, like house-painting, or whatever needs doing on material lines. The worst thing to do is worry about it and suppose that God must have rejected you for some supposed "sin," or something stupid like that. Yet people do fall into those traps until they learn better. God knows, I have done this often enough in my life, but it does not worry me any longer, because I now know it to be a normal and natural part of the Life-process. "What goes up must come down," applies in more than material terms. Learning how to live through the long cycles of spiritual "ups and downs" is in a way like swimming through waves in the sea.

The point is, of course, one cannot have an up without a down following. Most people who live "flat" lives without much variation are not overly bothered, but for those with feelings it is a "Heaven and Hell" existence, until eventually you get to live above it, which few manage to achieve. It is worth noting that life is like a very choppy ocean with crests and troughs to its waves, the main idea being to propel oneself from one crest to another, but there are many troughs in between. Highs and lows, and many a time more lows than highs. So many esotericists, experiencing these "lows," wonder why—after having done all the concentrating and workings for some specific objective—nothing seems to happen, then, sometimes years later, the thing turns up apparently by itself long after they have ceased wanting it. I think we have all experienced this at some stage, and it is a pretty normal sort of happening. Anything involving time is a tricky business.

9. יסוד—*Yesod* (Foundation), being "Infallible Foundation." This *Sefirah* refers to the very basis of all existence, i.e. the "foundations" of our earthly "kingdom." Here we must address the topics of fertility and sexuality, since these pertain to the "seat of life," and hence are directly associated with *Yesod*. In this regard, we should again note the term "*tzedek*" (righteousness), the concept we encountered earlier in *Chesed*, but which is also associated with *Yesod*, if in a somewhat different sense. Very many pages have been written by Kabbalists on this Hebrew term and its associations, i.e. "*tzodek*"—rightful; "*tzedek*"—"righteousness"; "*tzadik*"—a righteous individual; "*tzedakah*"—to act righteously understood to be "charity" in English; and even "*tzedek*" the planet Jupiter. Much meaning has been derived from these ideas.

While there is no similarity between the "audible sound" of the English "righteousness" and the Hebrew "*tzedek*," I thought I would check the etymological origins of the English term, just in case there are similarities in the "hidden sound," i.e. the "esoteric meanings" of the English/Hebrew terms. The result was that I gained a greater insight into one of the most fascinating statements in the *Sefer ha-Bahir*,[122] one pertaining to *Psalm 18:12*. The original verse reads "He made darkness His hiding place round about, His *Succah* (tabernacle) the darkness of waters, thick clouds of the skies (*Shechakim*)." The indication is that the "place of hiding," "darkness" and "the sky," is the womb hiding the "essence" of the Almighty, the Divine Semen, described as "Brilliant Light" in the *Sefer ha-Bahir*. One could draw an analogy to the concept of the centre and circumference, e.g. "Darkness" is the circumference or womb—Light is the centre or seed. Connect to this the *Bahir*'s understanding of *Psalm 139:12*—"Even darkness is not dark to you, Night shines like Day—light and darkness are the same," as well as *Psalm 87:2*—"Cloud and gloom surround Him," and one gets an amazing understanding that God (the centre, the Seed of Light) perceives everything as Light, whilst creation (the receiver of the seed, the womb, in the position of the circumference) is seeing the surrounding darkness, cloud and gloom. Nevertheless the centre and the circumference are the same. God—the centre, inhabits His creation—the circumference, yet is at the same time His creation as well, since "there is nothing empty of Him."

You may well wonder what this line of thinking has to do with *tzedek*/righteousness associations. In the *Sefer ha-Bahir* the stanza "thick clouds of the skies (*shechakim*)" in *Psalm 18:12* is linked to *Isaiah 45:8* — "The skies pour down righteousness," a phrase which plainly alludes to rain falling to the Earth, that which allows man "to live and occupy the land." As you probably know, the ancients believed "Mother Earth" and "Father Sky" copulated and that the "fertilizing rain" was the "semen of deity." This ancient viewpoint is described by William Gray who explained that "Most people felt there was a Father-God somewhere in the Sky and a Mother-God in the Earth. This was because they sometimes heard Him growling away up there when He was getting a mood on Him. Then His shadow would lie heavily above the land as He enveloped Earth in His embrace and muttered. Suddenly His terrifying phallus of Fire would stab into Earth, and He would roar His triumph over Her with fierce passion. Sometimes Her rumbling responses could be heard quite clearly afterwards, dying into sighs of satisfaction. Again and again the action would repeat, and dense streams of Divine seed would descend all over Earth to fertilize Her willing and waiting womb. Eventually His passion would subside, and He would climb off Earth back into His clouds again, smiling from the Sun, while earth lay soaked and gently steaming. Her plentiful progeny would arrive later, and Man would eat some of them, as Earth would eat Man's body up when he had finished with it."[123]

Now, in the Kabbalistic text space, darkness and sky are seen on the one hand as feminine, but on the other hand again as being masculine. In relation to the Creator and Light, Space is considered a feminine concept and a symbol of "Darkness," but as the "bringer of rain to Mother Earth," the Sky is masculine. God is hidden in this sky since "cloud and gloom surrounds Him," and the "Presence of God" was observed in Lightning, and His "voice" heard in Thunder. Finally rain is poured into the "Womb of Mother Nature" and thus rain is called "Righteousness" (*tzedek*).

The Hebrew term *shechakim* (Skies) is said to refer to the spheres of *Netzach* and *Hod*, whilst the word *tzedek* (righteousness) pertains to *Yesod*, the latter considered in *Traditional Kabbalah* to refer to the phallus, which they associated with the scriptural statement "the righteous, the foundation of the world." The word for "world" in Hebrew is *Olam*, but it can also be read *Elam* meaning "Hidden," and this was thought to imply that *Yesod* (Foundation) is "righteous" when the male sex organ is hidden inside the "womb" (vagina) causing the rain of "righteousness" to fertilize "Nature" and to produce *Chai* ("Life"). No wonder the God-Name for *Yesod* is *Shadai El Chai*—"Powerful Lord of Life."

We might note that Kabbalists believed that when a couple mated, they were not only imitating God in the creative act, but that they were causing a "Supernal Coupling" in God. According to esoteric Tradition this dual coupling "above and below" is referred to in *Deuteronomy 16:20* as "Righteousness, Righteousness shall you pursue, that you may live and occupy the land." The double usage of the word "righteousness" was seen to imply the sexual union of the "Above" (the Divine One and the *Matronit*) and the sexual union of the "Below" (the human couple), which would lead to humankind to "live and occupy the land." Here the term "live" (*chai*) is again understood to allude to *Yesod* as the male, and "Land" to *Malchut* (the Kingdom), the Lower *Shechinah* or the Female Counterpart of God in Nature. On the other hand, the double usage of the word "righteousness" also meant *Malchut* (the female sex organ and womb) "opposite to Him" (*Yesod* — the phallus). It is for this reason that Kabbalists saw *Proverbs 10:25* — "The righteous is the foundation of the world" to mean the *Sefirah Yesod* (the "righteous") in sexual union, out of which "truth" is born from *Malchut*, the "Earth Mother" who received "righteousness," the divine semen flowing from the "Sky Father" as expressed in *Psalm 85:12* —"Truth sprouts up from the Earth, and Righteousness looks down from Heaven."

Now, if my late mentor, William Gray, was right in his suggestion that I would understand quite a lot more by examining the meaning of the English terms equivalent to the Hebrew concepts, we might scrutinise the term "righteousness" etymologically and see what we can get out of it. It appears the word "righteousness" is made up of three basic ideas: "*right*"–"*eous*"–"*ness*." "Righteous" without the "–*ness*" suffix is actually made up of the terms "*right*" and "*wise*" — the latter remodelled "*eous*." "Right" means to be straight and erect, here linked to the Greek "*orektós*" meaning "erect." The idea of "right" as a proper, suitable and correct design, likely to achieve a desired end, or appropriate to some particular end, might have originated from the idea of the erect, virile member of the male. Interesting that "right," besides its Greek root "*erektos*" — which also means stretched out and extended, is also linked to the Latin "*erectum*" meaning upright, lofty, to elevate and to be noble, from which derived the word "regal."

All things erect, lofty and upright, like trees, stones, etc., represented to the ancient mind the male sexual organ in its virile and fertile state, and the word "right" might have originated from the idea of the phallus in its "alive" or "erect" state, which is its proper and right function in life. However, while this is its "*right*," it may not be "*righteous*," which can only be achieved when its "right" is combined with being "wise," the root concept behind the term "*eous*" in "righteous" as said. "Wise" in this case is linked to roots meaning way, manner, to show, to guide, or literally to put wise, which of course pertains to having sound judgement, being sagacious and having true knowledge. I believe this has to do with a proper balance between "being" and "doing," again centre and circumference concepts.

Seen in the light of sexuality, this implies that for the sexual act to be more than a reproductive romp, sound judgement and understanding, the *Sefirot Chochmah* (Wisdom) and *Binah* (Understanding) should be present. That would be seen as being "righteous" in this sense, and coupled with the suffix "-*ness*," it becomes even more illuminating, since this suffix derives from Old English roots pertaining to a promontory, a headland or an extension of land, linked of course to the Old English "*nasu*" meaning a nose. Here one can compare Gothic words like "*thiudinassus*" and "*thiudans*," meaning respectively "Kingdom" and "King." To my mind the "*ness*" in "righteousness," besides being an usage to form an abstract noun expressing a condition or quality of being righteous, implies also royalty and regalness, the last mentioned already shown in my analysis of "right."

This exposition of "righteousness" may be a bit technical, but I believe it does help to accentuate the value which old-time Kabbalists placed on sexuality as a major factor in their philosophy, thus lifting it out of the "dry as dust" category which has surrounded it for so long. When you consider that the very same energy which motivates human sexual activity also motivates our attempts to "gain Godhood," you may realise that the Kabbalists were only trying to "intellectualize" this idealistically.

10. מלכות—*Malchut* (Kingdom), being Nature. In the Hebrew Bible the term "*Malchut*" is used in reference to 1. territory, e.g. "Kingdom"; 2. accession, e.g. "inheriting the throne"; 3. a period of rulership, e.g. "the seventh year of his reign"; and 4. anything considered "royal," e.g. a crown, a royal gown, a sceptre, etc. However, in the Hebrew Bible the term "*mam'lachah*" is also used to indicate sovereignty, kingdom or dominion, e.g. "And the beginning of his kingdom was Babel, and Erech, and Accad, and Calneh, in the land of Shinar" (*Genesis 10:10*). The word "*mam'lachah*" basically refers to both the "land" and the "people" constituting a "kingdom," and has been sort of used as a synonym for "*Am*" (People) and "*Goy*" (nation).

The kabbalistic concept of *Malchut* refers to the "Kingdom" of this world we are living in, the one in which we are supposed to be "Kings." Each one of us carries the weight of responsibility for the "Kingdom" comprising our bodies, homes and our world. Considering the track record of humans governing themselves and their planet, i.e. current conditions of life on earth, it is clear that humans have failed dismally in their collective responsibility as "Kings." As far as I can see there is only one word summing up this failure—GREED! We are eating up our planet! In this regard a dear Companion exclaimed in exasperation that the last bit of water will be running out of the golden faucet, and everybody will be running for the gold.

Our ancestors might have held ethical behaviour and other lofty principles in high regard, but what is being valued to the same extent today? Money! Everything is measured in terms of cold hard cash, even religion and spirituality, and many would gladly give their souls away for even the smell of money. In fact, the entire concept of money has become so tainted over the centuries, that a lot of "negative" energies, e.g. thoughts, feelings, etc., have become attached to it. These "negative aspects" impact on everyone, on both the giver and the receiver, crippling us in some or other manner, hence it is said there are "harsh judgements" associated with money.

In this regard Nachman of Bratzlav wrote "Money is related to strict judgments. Thus it is written, 'and all the living substance that was at their *feet*' (*Deuteronomy 11:6*), on which the Rabbis commented: 'This refers to a person's money, which is what enables him to stand on his feet' (*Pesachim* 119). From this we learn that money is the 'feet.' Now it is written, 'Justice attends his *footsteps*' (*Isaiah 41:2*), and 'Justice is the holy kingship (*Malchut*)' (*Tikkuney Zohar, Introduction*), and *Malchut* is judgment. This indicates that money is related to judgment.

It is necessary to sweeten the severe judgments at their root, which lies at the level of *Binah*, 'Understanding,' as it is written, 'I am understanding, power is mine' (*Proverbs 8:14*). This is why the Tzaddik places his hands upon the money in order to sweeten the judgments. For there are three 'hands' in *Binah*: the 'great hand' (*Exodus 14:31*) and the 'strong hand' (*Deuteronomy 7:19* etc.), which together make up the 'high hand' (*Exodus 14:8*). When the money—i.e. the severe judgments—comes to the hands, which allude to the three hands of *Binah*, the judgments are sweetened at their source.

The severe judgments have their hold in this world of *Asiyah*. They must be sweetened by means of the three hands in each of the three higher worlds, *Atzilut, Beriyah* and *Yetzirah*.....

It is most important not to be stingy in the amount of money one gives in order that no severe judgments should remain hovering over one. It takes exceptional wisdom to know exactly how much a particular person should give to make sure that no harsh judgments remain."[124]

Nachman of Bratslav talked extensively about the rectification of "harsh judgements" on many levels, and gave a lot of practical advice in this regard. For example, he said "Music has a tremendous power to draw you to God"[125] and that singing, dancing and clapping ones hands rhythmically would "sweeten harsh judgements." He believed acts of loving-kindness would do the same, and he maintained *Tzedakah* involving giving money to the poor to be especially meritorious. However, in the case of monetary donations, the crippling forces ("severe judgments") attached to the money should be lightened ("sweetened") by the understanding benefactor. One might consider money to be associated with *Gevurah* (*Din*—judgement) whilst the compassionate donor relates to *Binah* (Understanding), but in this instance we are informed that "money is the feet" and is associated with *Malchut* (Kingship).

It is clear the "harsh realities" or the "severe judgements" of cold harsh cash pertain to *Assiah*, this physical "World of Action" we all live in. Hence we are told to "sweeten the judgments" with the "three hands" in the "higher worlds" of *Yetzirah* (Formation), *Bri'ah* (Creation) and *Atzilut* (Emanation). My late mentor maintained the three "higher worlds" pertain respectively to "Mind" (Formation), "Soul" (Creation) and "Spirit" (Emanation). As noted in the quote, the "three hands" affiliated with *Binah* (Understanding) are the "Great Hand" and the "Strong Hand" conjointly forming a third titled the "High Hand." The two "hands" are actually ones own hands, while the third "hand" comprises the "Divine Power" which flows between your hands into the money intended as a donation. Likewise *you* are in fact *Binah*, and the quoted verse from *Proverbs*, "I am understanding, power is mine" (*8:14*), actually pertains directly to the donor who places his or her hands on, and directs the power of the "third hand" into, the money.

Money is really a form of energy exchange, but it is what has happened regarding human "addiction" to money which has impacted our world in such a horrible manner. This ugliness is not only to be found in the world of mundane living, but also in the spiritual domain. The internet is filled to the brim with "new theologians" trying to twist old-time religious theories around, so as to come up with anything a modern mass-media person is likely to believe in. Notice for example how Christianity is being sold as if it were a plastic-wrapped product with the hotel-sign "sanitized for your protection" plastered right across it. Selling church membership like one sells insurance, they are marketing faith and belief, both of which are an absolute necessity for mankind.

Money has become a most important "god" in our world, and I am greatly surprised that no one has as yet started a "Church of the Almighty Dollar" where a gigantic dollar bill forms the focus of worship on the wall. After all, many millions believe that if they spend enough money, they must get anything they want. God is thought to be buyable, and this derives from that fundamentalist idea of a "god" who sees everything in terms of wealth and well-being. The "Positive Thought" Archetype of a Supreme Racketeer, to whom one pays protection money for keeping the "Devil" away from one's business dealings. Give "*Gard*" enough dollars and he will save you from the "Devil." Many modern religions *do* think this way, and strangely seem to have the same fundamental beliefs as the ancient Egyptians. Heaven is for the rich, and simply a copy of luxurious Earth-Life. Gods could be purchased, and were bribable if enough priests were paid to "fix things." In the same way, many people appear to believe the dollar is an answer to everything in this world—and the next! Buy an expensive enough funeral, and a good place in Heaven is assured. As far as I can see, it all amounts to the old story of "What doth it profit a man." Many would gladly give their souls away for even the smell of money.

I certainly have no problem with earning well and making a decent living at all. In fact, there are works in which "money" is discussed from very lofty spiritual perspectives, including Kabbalistic ones like "*The Kabbalah of Money*" by Hilton Bonder.[126] It is absolutely clear that our continued physical existence requires cold hard cash. The same applies to *any* "organisation" with a physical presence in this world, and the more elaborate it gets the more money is needed. However, when spiritual principles are involved money should never be the first but the last consideration.

Kabbalah tells us that here the real problem is "*ha-Yetzer ha-Ra*," "the evil inclination," which is focussed in the "desire to receive." In fact, it says we have two inclinations: the "inclination to give" and the "inclination to receive." These must be balanced most carefully. If one should predominate or overpower the other, disastrous results will inevitably ensue. As an example we are told about a couple in love. Whilst they are enamoured with one another, the "desire to give" predominates and is very strong indeed. They want to share their lives, even their souls with one another. Yet, if they do not carefully guard and cultivate the balance between giving and receiving, the "desire to receive" will begin to rise and the individuals will start to separate from their "oneness."

Soon the erstwhile partners begin to "eat from the Tree of Knowledge Good and Evil," and they start to assert "rights" and claim what they consider personal entitlements. Nothing will satisfy the sense of personal betrayal and the need to receive—for which there is absolutely no compensation. Each feels that his/her "giving" is not properly reciprocated, and finally.....the "desire to give" disappears altogether. Should this trend not be brought under control quickly, the parting of the ways will be an ugly one! If this applies in family relationships, how much more so in communal and international relationships? It would seem that the entire problem of strife between nations, religions, etcetera, is the difficulty to find a happy medium between their "desire to receive" and their "desire to give." So, what are we supposed to "give" in order that we may compensate the *tsunami* of destruction currently besetting humankind and our world for that matter? The list is certainly extensive, but I believe it might be good to start with love and respect, and the mediation of the merciful Spirit of our Maker to all.

We might note that kabbalistic teaching distinctly informs us that much of our existence here, in fact, the very "path" we have to tread while manifested in the flesh, has everything to do with this world we live in. That is what the doctrine of *shevirat ha-kelim* (the shattering of the primordial vessels) and the work of *tikkun* (restoration), i.e. our divinely designated task of retrieving and redirecting the "Divine Sparks" which have fallen into this overmaterialised realm of manifestation, is all about. This is basic Kabbalistic teaching, and ultimately we need to understand that, while the ultimate aim is "Know Thyself," there is a much larger meaning to being.

It should be clear that divine destiny is not about each person being here for him or herself, i.e. those who will see the whole of manifestation lost provided their own little souls are saved. All aspects of manifestation are indeed "one," all intrinsically and primordially bound together.

D. Right, Left and Centre

A very interesting aspect of the Tree of Life is how it resolves opposites into a balance. This pertains to the concept of the *"Three Pillars."* In *Kabbalah* opposites are viewed as being basically on the same level. For example what is a virtue today may be a vice tomorrow, which could again reverse the day after, and so on. It is agreed that we live between opposites in this world, in fact we need both in order to find our way between them into the inner Adytum of Spirit. The Kabbalist believes that everything comes from God. Everything is the directing of Divine Energy. Man acts like a prism for this Energy for better or for worse. He has to direct the Divine Energy that comes down to him, and thus sin is only a misdirection or a misuse of Divine Energy, therefore "missing the point." It is still Divine Energy, and we humans have to realise that just as the good in us saves us from the worst in ourselves, so does the worst save us from the good in us paving a hell-bent path.

Now, in early *Kabbalah* the "Three Pillars" of the Kabbalistic Tree of Life were called "Three Lines." These lines were respectively named the "Line of *Chochmah*," the "Line of *Binah*" and the "Line of *Da'at*." However, while early Kabbalistic authors like Gikatilla did not specifically use the word "Pillar," there is no reason why we should not refer to the three "lines" as the "Pillar of Wisdom" on the right, the "Pillar of Understanding" on the left, and the "Pillar of Knowledge" in the centre. After all, today the "lines" between the *Sefirot* are generally referred to as "Paths," while in Hebrew they are termed "*Tzinorot*" which are best translated "pipes" or "conduits." Yet I see no reason why they should not be called "Paths" in English.

Regarding the three "Pillars/Lines," one of the differences between the early teachings and modern approaches pertains to their naming. Today they are respectively called the "Pillar of Severity" on the left, the "Pillar of Mercy" on the right, and some say the "Pillar of Mildness" in the centre. This is different in early *Kabbalah*. Does this matter? To some degree yes, since Kabbalists like Gikatilla, wanted us to understand that the *sefirot* comprising each of the "Pillars/Lines" are actually different stages of "unfoldment" of one central concept, e.g. those on the left were considered different levels of "*Binah*" (Understanding), those on the right different aspects of "*Chochmah*" (Wisdom), whilst those in the centre represented the different stages of "*Da'at*" (Knowledge). Hence they considered the stages from Malchut (*Kingdom*), through *Yesod* (Foundation) and *Tiferet* (Beauty) to *Keter* (Crown), to represent different levels of *Da'at* (Knowledge or perhaps better "Knowing").

Of course, this is an over-simplification in the extreme. While quite advanced for the average researcher, the teachings of Gikatilla in the *"Sha'arei Orah"*[127] represent only the very basics of a more elaborate topic, one greatly developed and expanded upon by later Kabbalists, until it eventually became a most complex "holographic" study, so to speak.

Anyway, as noted the "Three Pillars" are now referred to as the "Right Pillar of Mercy," the "Left Pillar of Severity," and the "Middle Pillar of Mildness" or "Balance." These stand for the opposites in life, plus their unique balance, which then forms that unique "Law of Threes" or Triads, the "Three-acting-together-as-One" principle which we will address in greater detail in the next chapter. It was in fact this principle which made *Kabbalah* popular amongst some Christians, who believed this teaching to substantiate the Christian doctrine of the Trinity. However, as we will see in the next chapter, Kabbalists were not thinking of Christianity when they formulated these mysteries, and neither does this law refer exclusively to the Christian concept and doctrine as a "one-true-and-only" teaching which is right, wrong or whatever. In fact, *Kabbalah* merely emphasised a principle which seemingly underlined manifestation on all levels, and most teachings as well.

I believe it is now the appropriate moment to address another contentious issue, an unnecessary one at that, which developed around the "Three Pillars" concept. This one revolves around the attributions of the *Sefirot* to the human anatomy. Some argue that the Tree of Life is, as it were, a "mirror," hence the "Left Pillar" applies to the right and the "Right Pillar" to the left side of our anatomies. In this regard I have heard an individual remark with absolute authority that "one always backs into the Tree." The only evidence I have been offered in support of this claim, is that it was derived from the "ultimate authority," the teachings of certain "Hermetic Schools."

As you may suspect, the matter is quite different in *Traditional Kabbalah*. In fact, consulting primary texts like the *Sefer Tikkunei ha-Zohar*,[128] and using some of the practical exercises of traditional *Kabbalah*, the consensus is the right and left "Pillars," as well as their respectively associated *Sefirot*, are aligned with the human anatomy in exactly the manner they are positioned on the Tree of Life—right to the right; left to the left.

However, I think there is a lot more to the positions of the "Pillars" than meets the eye. On closer examination of the concepts one would soon notice that the "Pillars" could be positioned on either side, depending on the way you are reasoning, i.e. the angle of approach. For example, in some modern Kabbalistic/Magical temples the respective positions of the two "opposing Pillars"— as represented by the door posts, temple pillars, standards and curtains behind the altar— are often switched or alternated. In one temple that I know of, the door posts at the entrance are painted white on the right side and black on the left. Inside the Temple the "Pillars at the Sanctuary" are white on the left and black on the right, and the curtains behind the pillars, against the wall of the "Sanctuary," are again black on the left and white on the right. Thus the Pillars switch and alternate all the time. In turn, the colours of the "Pillars" on the "Standard" in this temple are arranged in the same manner as the curtains within the Sanctuary.

The idea behind this is firstly that the "Pillars" on the Tree of Life are in actual fact the same, depending on how you look at things. Secondly, when you are practising, it depends on which way you turn. You are the "Central Pillar." If you are turning *into* the Tree, then you have the white on your right and the black on your left. If you are turning *out of* the Tree it is the other way around. You must pivot on an axis, always being the "Golden Middle Pillar." A further argument for the switching of the colours, is that often what we consider "severity" today, turns out to be "mercy" tomorrow, and thus the "Pillars" can switch around depending on circumstances, mind-sets and the manner of comprehension. All this is part of the symbolism of the opposing "Pillars" in a magical temple.

It has been stated in *Hermetic Kabbalah* that the "Right Pillar" represents the "Orphic Way," named so after Orpheus, the master of song, dance, creativity and artistic expression. On the other hand the "Left Pillar" is said to indicate the "Hermetic Way," called so after "Hermes," the fleet-footed messenger of the "gods," the master of calculation, the sciences, and intellectual pursuits. This would seem to correspond quite closely with our more recent notions about individuals being more "right brain" or "left brain," these referring respectively to their more emotional/creative/artistic and intellectual/rational/logical inclinations.

I do not believe one should focus on a hard and fast rule as far as the position of the "Pillars" are concerned. The "fixing" of concepts are, as said, based on the stances of individuals or groups, and definitely on the angles from which they argue, sometimes a little too heatedly because reasoning is applied far too rigidly, providing little or no flexibility as far as angles of approach are concerned. In other words, all argument is based on.....mind-set!

Each individual working with the concepts behind the symbols of the "Pillars" on the Tree of Life, should work out how they relate with these in accordance with personal approaches to the mysteries. Maybe the final criteria is the "Middle Pillar." In one "Initiation Ceremony" that I am familiar with, this is rather beautifully expressed. The Candidate is instructed:

> "Arise and take your rightful place between the Pillars of the North and South as an initiate of the Western Way. Stand straight and steadfast, holding Light with honour.
>
> Three are the Pillars of Life—Birth, Death and Resurrection.
> Three are the Pillars of Fate—Yes, No and Perhaps.
> Three are the Pillars of Power— Positive, Negative and Poise.
> Three are the Pillars of Principle—Might, Mercy and Mildness.
>
> Now learn to live that you may be
> The Central Pillar of all three.
> Between alternatives become
> Their perfect equilibrium."[129]

Now, one of the most helpful suggestions I received when I initially investigated the Tree of Life glyph some four decades ago, was to think of the "central pillar" as the "Pillar of Being" and the outer ones as the "Pillars of Doing." The *Sefirot* comprising the "Middle Pillar" pertain to specific aspects of the Self, whilst those on the outer "Pillars" respectively pertain to the way the central *Sefirot* are expressed. Hence, *Netzach* and *Hod* could be considered the "arms" of *Yesod* (*Nefesh* [Instinctual Self]); *Chesed* and *Gevurah* those of *Tiferet* (*Ru'ach* [Conscious Self]); and likewise *Chochmah* and *Binah* could be considered the "organs of action" of *Keter* (*Neshamah* [Divine Self]).

In the "*Gates of Light*" Joseph Gikatilla noted that the spheres of the "outer pillars" cannot "ascend any further than their place."[130] This is because they pertain to "deeds" which are expressions limited to time and space, e.g. past/future issues, whereas the "Pillar of Being," which Gikatilla termed the "Middle Line," pertains to that which always *IS*, the "Eternal Now" free from the constraints of space and time. Deeds could be likened to the circumference of a turning wheel, whilst the silent centre refers to the Being, the one who is eternally the "Now." Ones true "*IS-ness*" is ones Self, ones true Being, and this is what can "ascend all the way to *Ain Sof*."

Such an ascent necessitates a process of "awakening," the constant expansion of ones consciousness to embrace a bigger whole, until one achieves full "awakeness," the ultimate "I Am," which you termed "the knowledge that I am not separate from the Source." This "knowledge" must not be considered a cerebral activity in the cage of logic, but has to be a fully realised truth. In other words, rather than "knowledge learned" it pertains to "knowledge lived." Seen in this manner, the central "line of *Da'at* [Knowledge]" traces the journey commencing in the "instinctual knowing" required for our basic existence on this planet, e.g. self preservation and self perpetuation based on "knowing what," to the full "awakeness" of *Eh'yeh* ("I am" and "I will be"), where the initial "*what*" in the "knowing" process disappears and only "*who*" remains. "What" is *Malchut*, "Who" is *Keter*, and the journey in between *Da'at* (Knowledge).

Now, the last great principle on the Tree of Life I wish to look at briefly here is the "Worlds" concept. The Tree of Life with its Ten *Sefirot* exists on four levels or "Worlds." These Worlds are named and numbered in order of importance as *Atzilut*, the First World of Emanation or Origination; *Bri'ah*, the Second World of Creation; *Yetzirah*, the Third World of Formation; and *Assiah*, the Fourth World of Manifestation or Action. Each of these "worlds" comprises "subtle beings" or different types of consciousness, starting with the most subtle Energies in the World of Emanation, which is the world of "Divine Names," followed by the Archangelic Consciousness in the World of Creation, the Angelic Consciousness as "Hosts of Angels" in the World of Formation, and ending with the realm of "Planetary Spirits" and Elementals in the World of Action or Physical Manifestation, the world of our physical bodies. Each *Sefirah* therefore exists in every World, each having a different type of consciousness linked to it on every level.

For Kabbalists the path to real "occult power" is via the Tree of Life. They consider this glyph to be one of power. Sadly the mass of modern literature on this subject available on bookshelves everywhere, is either rehashed material better dealt with elsewhere, or simply pertains to the Tree of Life being used as a kind of filing cabinet comprising hundreds of items and ideas, e.g. this "Sphere" corresponds to that planet, animal, stone, ancient Greek or Egyptian deity. Actually, it would be interesting to see a set of related "emotions" included amongst those correspondences—a "Tree of Feelings." This would assuredly be a most beneficial application of the Tree of Life.

Here are two such uses of the ten *Sefirot* which William Gray discussed with me during his visits to South Africa.

1. ALPHABET OF CONSCIOUSNESS

0	Nil	The Unconsciousness	I AM NOT
1	Summit	Being	The I AM
2	Wisdom	Knowing	This from That
3	Understanding	Feeling	I and They
4	Compassion	Attraction	Loving, wanting
5	Severity	Repulsion	Hating, rejecting
6	Beauty	Stabilizing	Equanimity, normality.
7	Victory	Increasing	Gaining amount of awareness.
8	Glory	Improving	Quality gain of awareness.
9	Foundation	Constructing	Arrangement of Awareness.
10	Kingdom	Continuity	Memory.

2. INNER ARRANGEMENT OF THE TREE OF LIFE

0	*Ain*	Nil	Experience the All of Nothing. *OMNIL*.
00	*Ain Sof*	Limitlessness	Unbounded homogenous undifferentiated Being.
000	*Ain Sof Aur*	Limitless Light	Identify with boundless outpouring LIGHT. Nothing else. Just pure illumination by itself with no objective to illuminate.
1	*Keter*	Summit	Identify with fire awareness of individual existence. Feel I AM – THOU ART.
2	*Chochmah*	Wisdom	Realise faculty for gaining knowledge and experience through consciousness. See it as a *modus vivendi* and a major factor for continuing existence further than this point.
3	*Binah*	Understanding	Appreciate intuition and ability to extend consciousness through all else than "self." Try and do this.
4	*Chesed*	Compassion	Enter into understanding of necessity for everything. Empathise lovingly therewith. Be merciful and kindly. Anabolic.
5	*Gevurah*	Severity	Realise need for control and economy of energy. Nothing to be wasted. Law of retributive return. Discipline of self. Catabolic.

6	*Tiferet*	Beauty	Experience poise, balance, harmony, perfect equilibrium, radiance, and all sorts of solar wonders. Feel the centre of a universe.
7	*Netzach*	Victory	Feel triumphant and joyful. Be "in love" with everyone and everything. Experience security of affections. Feel loved and wanted.
8	*Hod*	Glory	Experience a state of intelligent interest in everything, good humoured, amused, alert for all information and very much "ready to go."
9	*Yesod*	Foundation	Have faith in the purpose of everything even if incomprehensible currently. Believe in life itself regardless of personal opinions. Feel strong and firm, vital and fecund.
10	*Malchut*	Kingdom	Experience individuality as human and the world around. Relate one with the other. Realise connections between Inner and Outer Life. Feel God behind Man as Ultimate Rule. Be, because of BEING.

Of course, the Tree of Life with its Spheres, Paths and associated concepts has been employed in numerous ways, as a means of achieving a state of Enlightenment or "Cosmic Consciousness." The methods are far too numerous to recount here. However, during the course of this work we will look at some relevant methods of God and Self realisation through the use of Kabbalistic methods.

These days so many people suppose the Tree of Life to be the entire *Kabbalah*, and that there is nothing else to it, whereas *Kabbalah* itself is a mixture of Past and Future considered from the *Now* standpoint—an extension of Consciousness into the Infinite each way, so to speak. It came down to us as a presentation of very ancient Lore, note the connection with Law, from our remotest past; the true "Old Religion," dated from our earliest times on earth, out of which emerged a curious synthesis from which we projected the conscious calculations which will produce the strange "Religion of the Future" which is carrying us toward Itself.

The "Law" which Orthodox Judaism and *Kabbalah* keep harping on about so much, *was* and *is* in fact God. All the scriptures, writings, concepts, and so forth called *Torah* are only symbols for God, and intellectual symbols at that. God is the *"Law of Life,"* and all the writings are only human opinions and beliefs about that Power, Energy, Control, or whatever you like to call *IT*.

In his book *"The Life of Moses,"* Edmond Fleg portrays the instance when God gives the *Torah* to the world, and grants Moses a vision of distant future teachers. Moses asks "Lord, how is this thing possible? I do not recognise the *Torah* thou gavest me. Is that new *Torah* thy *Torah*?" And God answers, "There are fifty gateways of Understanding: I have opened for thee forty-nine, but the last is closed, for no man, even though he be Moses, can know everything. The *Torah* thou understandest hath a thousand senses which thou understandest not, and which others in the course of the ages will come to know: for in each century it will speak the language of that century; but what each century will find is already there, and each new *Torah* will still be my *Torah*."[131] So while our Tradition may be based on earlier teachings and traditions, its origin is to be found in the Middle Ages when these "earlier traditions" were comprehended in new and meaningful ways, as we hope they will be today.

As I see it, "studying *Torah*" did not necessarily mean pouring over ancient scrolls at all, but *Living the Law of Life*. In other words just living according to ones beliefs that God was living through you, and respecting God in the way you lived; but with typical literalness, many spend wasted time with their eyes glued to papyrus and parchment scrolls in the honest belief they are "studying *Torah*" as an ideal way of spending a whole lifetime, and it is even their idea of "Heaven."

We need to be clear that *Kabbalah* has never been a fixed and rigid tradition. Its doctrines have undergone many alterations over the centuries, always relative to new discoveries and the broader perspectives of those who studied its teachings with the expanded mind-sets of later times. In fact, *Kabbalah* is really a constant change of consciousness relative to our causes and completions. It is not fixed and immutable, but fluid, free, and continually creative. Its fundamental basics are indeed stable in relation to ourselves, therefore we need to grasp them as firmly as we can while realising their essential "alterability."

Look at the way religion itself is changing in this world. In the last century alone we have seen it alter beyond belief. Two World Wars and our modern TV battles have caused this. I believe humanity as a whole has been forced into a very different position. Not so very long ago beliefs were fixed and very limited, mostly because to change them would have needed a lot of thought, and most humans just did not want to disturb themselves that much. The wars compelled even common ordinary folk to open themselves up to entirely changed conceptions of life. They would have changed anyway in the course of time, but the rate of acceleration increased incredibly. People no longer believe in olden forms, even though fundamentals remain relatively reliable. The possibility that our whole state of civilization can be wiped out in a matter of moments has altered our outlook on life forever. Our worst devils have materialised so to speak. They are no longer shadowy monsters lurking in some "underworld" to destroy us. They are right here beside us, within us in fact, and until we can make our "Gods" as real as our "devils," there will not be a lot of hope for us in this world.

I honestly do not know whether this will ever be achieved, but I believe it can be done, or should at least be possible. In other words in plainest language, can we beat the Bomb or not? Here I am not necessarily referring to the physical atom bomb, but a spiritual one. Are we building ourselves, the No-thing within us, into an "atomic Bomb," which would be likely to explode, and blow God back to the Chaos He is reputed to have emerged from in the first place? Can we, through our actions, form ourselves into a "black hole," so to speak, which could devour this dimension of the manifested universe? Is God's "primal scream" (the "Big Bang"), likely to result in man's "Last Blast"? Are they one and the same? The Alpha and Omega, beginning and end of everything which will blow us back to another kind of beginning altogether? What the Hindus call *"Pralaya"* or "rest state," during which the bits of the Universe which end in one unimaginable orgasmic explosion in the womb of space, drift around prior to re-grouping themselves into another beginning again. The fabled "Death of God" which awaits "Resurrection" or rebirth. That is the Ultimate Question, and only history has the answer somewhere in its future grasp.

. ...this one all blue, this all black, this all red, this all green, this all saffron and this combining two colours, where one is unlike the other... ... .

Chapter 2
FROM "NOTHING" TO "SOMETHING"

A. *Ain Sof:* "The Eternal No-Thing"

How can one speak of that which is unknown? After all, I am to speak of the *Nothing*, that which is not a thing, yet emanates all things and is at the same time all things. How shall I say it? Before the beginning there was *Nothing—No Thing—Nothing*, and yet this *No Thing* is *Absolute Essence, Absolute Potential*. It is difficult to steer the mind towards perceiving that which is beyond human conception, even though this Absolute Essence also comprises the ordinary mind. One cannot even comprehend *It* in ecstasy since *It* is stillness, and yet one can almost *feel* understanding, *sense It* somehow without mind or body in the silence of the spirit; *know It* within ones soul.

Prior to all things, to all creation, to everything that is manifested, including space and time, there was only *No-Thing*. It was coined *Ain Sof* (אין סוף – Infinite Nothing) in the Provence School of early *Kabbalah*. We are faced with seemingly two ideas—*Nothing* and *Infinity*, but, even though there is apparent duality, *It* is essentially One and not two. The *Absence of Things* and *Infinity* are essentially One. *Ain Sof* is the *Infinity of the Absence of Things*, and as the beginning of all things is the *No-Thing*, so is the end of all existence the *No-Thing*. This *Nothingness*, as *It* is sometimes called, is understood in *Kabbalah* to be the highest Level of Spirit.

So, we commence with the *Nothing* from which all "somethings" derive. Termed *Ain* in Hebrew, literally meaning "without" or "absence," *It* is *No-Thing* because it is the "Absence of Things." However, there is no finiteness here. *It* is infinite—*Sof* in Hebrew. *Ain Sof*, the closest description we have of Ultimate Reality, has been translated "the Endless One," "Infinite Being," "the Infinite," "The Ultimate Nothingness," and "The Nothingness without End." The *No-Thing* does not exist in Time, yet *It* emanates Time and *is* also Time. *It* is both *No-Thing* and *all things* simultaneously. *It* is an *Eternal Now*, which overtakes running Time while standing still. *It* is what *It* is within *Itself*.

This is a state of being most powerfully realised when ones "attentive awakeness" is focussing inwards on *Itself*, on the *Experiencer*; the One who mediates thinking and feeling; the One who is expressing these in actions; the One who is the *Essence* which binds all experiences together; the One who says "My thoughts.....my feelings." This is the *Self*, the "I" who, like the *Eternal No-Thing*, is beyond thinking and feeling, yet able to manifest all manner of thought and emotions. In fact, the *Self* is one with the *No-Thing*, yet, while *It* is God in its own right, *It* is only part of the Eternal Living Spirit. So, *Ain v'Ani*, Nothing and the *Self*, comprise the reason *for* and *behind* all existence, giving meaning to mind and soul. Again, this is the *Experiencer* who, being *No-Thing*, creates things out of *Itself*. Hence the Eternal Living Spirit is able to experience *Itself* through all manifestation, through everything *It* has projected into the realm of Time–Space–Events.

The full realisation of the *Self* is one of tremendous illumination and profundity. I recall my mentor William G. Gray, the late English Kabbalist and occultist, explaining how he experienced this incredible state of perfection, peace and profundity in World War II during the Battle of Dunkirk. It was one of those very rare moments when I witnessed my dear Father–Brother shedding tears at the recollection of that momentous incident. The manner in which he described the battle on the beaches of Dunkirk during the Great War was quite frightening. He depicted the slaughter of the English troops so vividly, that I was transfixed and literally experienced what he was relating through the subconscious channel which existed between our souls.

He said the noise of the battle was indescribable. There was the cacophony of droning aeroplanes, the noise of exploding bombs, all interspersed with the screams of soldiers being massacred on the beaches. They were literally "between the Devil and the deep blue sea." Bodies were being blown apart.....mangled hands, arms, legs, heads, and torsos.....blood and sand everywhere.

Boats, some of them quite small, were coming to the rescue. Many of them were bombed, sank under their load, or simply capsized due to the many men frantically attempting to clamber aboard. Wherever you looked, on land, in the sea or sky, there was horror, horror and more horror. For those soldiers it was as if the end of the world had come. It was their personal "Armageddon."

William Gray told me that he thought he was going to go mad, and he felt he was actually moving to the edge of insanity, which he reached and then crossed. Traversing that border between cosmos and chaos, he thought he would fall into an abyss of wanton extermination of his body, mind and soul. Instead, he found himself in the core of the most perfect stillness. He described this silence as so total, so perfect, that the motion of this solitary little planet in space could not interrupt the completeness and potency of that silence. He understood with absolute clarity that—as is the case with all of existence—noise begins and ends, but that the silence is eternal. In fact, he knew the silence supported the noise, the latter having no meaning without that support, just as the sky supports the clouds, yet remains empty like this page behind the written words.

During that fateful battle in the wars of a confused and enslaved humanity, my dear Father–Brother had reached what he later described in his works as a state of Perfection, Peace and Profundity. He continued to say that at that moment he turned to a friend who had been with him practically throughout the war, and who appeared to have reached the same state of consciousness, and asked him if he had his chess set with him. His companion replied in the affirmative, commenting that some of the pieces may have gone missing. William Gray responded something like "Oh! I thought we could have a game of chess."

I was awestruck! The two men had at that moment reached such a unique state of perfect peace in the midst of one of the worst battles of the time, that they were willing to play chess right there on the beaches of Dunkirk.....amidst all the fighting. He told me that from that moment on it was easy. He knew he would be fine.

The message is plainly "When you are *something*, you have *something* to lose. When you are *nothing*, you have *everything* to gain." In *No-Thing* all are the same and to understand this, you must not consider yourself to be *something*. You must be *absolutely nothing*, beyond Time–Space–Events, reigning with the *Absolute No-Thing* in complete *Unity*. In *No-Thing* all thoughts, senses and physicalities are nullified. In fact, as all things derive from *No-Thing*, so do they resort back to *It* every time they transform themselves in the *Eternal Life/Death Process*. Things cannot hinder the *Eternal Presence* of the *Nothing*, just as the movement of this solitary little planet in the vastness of space cannot disturb the *Eternal Stillness*.

So, in *No-Thing* is the state of *Perfection, Peace* and *Profundity*. At this level *Ain Sof*, the *Eternal No-Thing*, is beyond nature. *It* is the *Unthinkable, Life-Death, Creative Immanence*, elusive and timeless.[1] *It* has no past, thus no memory; no future, thus no purpose. *It-Is-what-It-Is-within-Itself. Ain Sof* is everywhere and nowhere, and the single glyph used to represent *It* is the Hebrew letter *Alef* (א), the image of that which belongs neither to time nor space. Phrased somewhat differently, we might say *It* is non-temporal, dimensionless *Life–Death* out of which comes all that is temporal. *It* is both imminent and transcendent. *It* is creation since "there is no place empty of Him," yet *It* is no thing. *Its* Essence is within *Itself*. *It* is a Unity to which it seems impossible to attach qualities. In fact, *every* term we use to define *It*, must also be created out of *It*, and since "thoughts are things," *It* is impossible to comprehend mentally. Yet we know, while the *Timeless, Immeasurable Immanence* cannot be understood intellectually, *It* is *inside* us, and thus somehow perceivable through the *Self* as the *Eternal Now*— Eternity within.

Now, to most people the term "Eternity" means "time eternal," which in itself is something impossible to grasp with thought alone. Time exists as past and future, and nobody is able to determine exactly when it is neither past nor future, until that juncture when the *Self* as *Experiencer* becomes the *Experience.* Then the instant between past and future is not a moment in time, but the Self as *Eternal No-Thing*. We have to turn inwards, in order to perceive the *Now*, and realise the "Great Time" is ones *Real Self*, ones "awakeness" as a child once expressed it. *It* is inside *all* life, and all life is likewise inside *It*. *It* is *everywhere* because *It* is *nowhere*. No wonder it has been said that "God is a Circle, the circumference of which is Everywhere, the centre of which is Nowhere."[2]

So, to bind all things together inside ones own being, one must reach the *Awareness* of the *Limitless Nothing*. "*Unborn, Unbeing, Unbounded, Unilluminate, Unmanifest,*"[3] in which the "me" is erased and only "I" remain. If the "me" can die and be born again *Now*, "I" will live eternally. In the *Now*, nothing is repeatable, everything *is* everlasting. Everything occurs eternally, for it is happening *now*. This is the *Ultimate Experience* which cannot be experienced, but which one must *be*.

In other words, if you are the *Experience*, you cannot really experience *It*. To be able to experience, you must be separate from that which is experienced and, in this case, *you are It*. That is why it is impossible to tell anybody what this *Experience* is like, because "me," the medium through which the *Experience* is to be transmitted, is no more, and only "I am." *It* cannot be explained or related in words or actions, but might be imparted in *Silence*. The *Experience*, the *True Knowledge* is there, but the *Experiencer*, the knower, is not.

It does not mean the *Knowledge* does not exist, because there is nobody to know *It*. Even ordinary, worldly knowledge or any so-called "new knowledge" we learn, was always there in the "Now," long before mankind *knew* it, prior to its physical manifestation; before it was separated from *Divine Wisdom* and emanated into the realm of physical existence.

Again, *Ain Sof* is the *Infinity* of the *Absence of Things*—both the *Centre* and the *Circumference*. Using allegory, one might say that wherever I stand is the centre perceiving the circumference about me. Likewise you may stand elsewhere within my circumference, seeing yourself as the centre and I would then be part of your circumference. The *Centre/Circumference* is part of the *selfsameness* of *That* which is *absent* yet always immanent. Centre and circumference imply space, but even this does not exist within *No-Thing*, since space is finite with respect to its absence. So is time finite with respect to its absence. Everything is finite, only *No-Thing*—the *Essence of Things*—is *Infinite*.

Ain Sof is *Absolute Ultimate Perfection*, or *Perfect Peace Profound* as *It* was called by the Rosicrucians. *It is Absolute Perfection*, since there are no distinctions within *It*. No differentiations whatsoever. *It is One*, eternally the same unborn non-being without bounds. Because *It is not*, it can be anything.

Absolute potential, without volition, except in *Its* relation to *Itself* within *Itself*. Now, vibrant with the potency of *Nothing*, *It* emanates *Infinite Power*—Now!

To better understand this, let us turn our attention to the idea that the Eternal No-Thing has a relationship with Itself within Itself—a relationship, as it were, between *Ain* and *Sof*. Let us imagine that when we contemplate *Nothing* (*Ain*) we are thinking "Infinitely Small," but the very term "*Infinite*" (*Sof*) implies "Infinitely Big."

The very idea of a relationship means a sharing of some sort of power. To relate is to use energy. In this case a force which would manifest itself, and be called "*Light*" (*Aur*). In *Ain Sof* this *Light* is understood to be *unmanifest potential* within the *Infinite Nothing*. When this *Light* or *Energy* is manifested, we talk of "God manifest," and *everything* becomes the manifestation of *Nothing*. As said, although one talks of *Nothing* and the *Infinity* of the *Nothing*, *It* is the same, and even though one talks of the *Aur* (*Light*) of the *Infinite Nothing*, *It* is still part of the *Selfsameness* of the One.

So, *Ain* (*No-Thing*) is *Ain Sof* (*Infinite No-Thing*) which a child might call the "small-big." The interplay inside the *Infinite No-Thing*, i.e. the relationship between the *Infinitely Small* and the *Infinitely Big*—in which there is no centre or circumference—results in, as it were, a *striving* to define a centre and circumference. There is an act of simultaneous contraction and expansion, which was termed *Tzimtzum* in *Lurianic Kabbalah*. This action results in the creation of primordial space, in which the attempt to define centre and circumference, respectively the "nowhere" and the "everywhere," causes a tension, the very beginnings of that energy which is termed *Ain Sof Aur* (*Limitless Light*). When *Ain Sof* is focussed into a dimensionless centre, this becomes *Keter* (the Crown), the first Sphere on the Kabbalistic Tree of Life, where the Creator is on the brink of manifesting *Itself*. Here the Creator is in the state of *Ehyeh*, normally translated "I am." However, while *It* is *pure consciousness*, *It* is still unaware of *Itself* as an *Identity*. It is *Yihyeh* (*I will be*). *It* is not yet. By projecting *Itself* as light into the realm of Time, Space and Events, *It* commences the path leading to awareness of Self.

Of course, regarding any primary "motives" behind the creation of the whole of existence, one must concede that any speculation about "primordial intentions" within *Ain Sof* is impossible. Whatever we may suggest in this regard is based entirely on human viewpoints. In other words, we cannot really "know" anything regarding the Creator, and in our attempts to understand the Divine One we are employing human logic to characterize what is beyond characterization, beyond definition, the unborn, unbeing and unbounded.

We know that when it comes to our human "creative" abilities, Kabbalists maintain that a. "From a man's actions we cannot determine his will"; and b. "From a man's actions we cannot determine the extent of his options."[4] If such is the case as far as human beings are concerned, how much more so when it comes to the "infinite unknowable," regarding "whom" Kabbalists wrote "from God's creations we can draw no conclusions about the extent of His ability." Nor can we draw any conclusions about primordial intentions, hence Aryeh Kaplan reminds us that "one of the basic axioms of the *Kabbalah* is that nothing can be said about God Himself."[5]

That being said, there have been serious thinkers within this Tradition who have "speculated" that in its state of "unmanifestedness" *Ain Sof* could not know Itself, and that by manifesting *Itself* into Time–Space–Events, *It* can know *Itself* through self experience. Thus the "*I will be*" becomes "*I am.*" Once again, the *Eternal No-Thing* is the *Eternal Now* out of which Creation is constantly being created, and in which Creation is eternally being reaffirmed. However, we cannot contemplate *No-Thing*, we must *be It*. We ultimately have to realise that *we are* in fact the *Eternal Now*. Each one of us must know this for ourselves, in our own individual ways, and then we must reach the first step of Creation —"Let there be Light!"

The cosmic *It* does not reveal *Itself* through "*knowledge learned,*" through man's understanding. We can only come to **be** *It* through knowledge *lived*, since there is no nature within *It* to really understand. All we can do is realise that the *Self* is part of *It*, and *It* is part of the *Self*. Only a tiny measure of the *Real Self* is incarnated in the body, the rest is *everywhere*. Try perceiving the *Omnipotence*, the "omni-potency" of the *Self* as the *God/man* or the *Man/god*, whichever way you wish to view it. *It* is the *Potency* within. *It* is the potency of everything! It is everything, yet no thing in its *Essence*. *It* is *Potential* manifesting *Itself* into existence!

As *Ultimate Principle*, *Ain Sof* is certainly the most important concept in *Kabbalah*; one which modern science might benefit from, if it cared to investigate it more closely. It is certainly interesting to see how modern physics with its quantum theory, is concentrating on some of the ideas of *Kabbalah* once considered most extreme and bizarre. Creation, it is speculated, encompasses a unity of complementary but opposing forces. For example, subatomic particles are believed to be both destructible and indestructible. Energy and matter are considered to be simply different aspects of the same phenomenon. Similarly, time and space have been combined in "relativistic physics." Yet over a period of centuries, Kabbalists have discussed these very ideas, and have at the same time insisted that our ordinary, rigid way of discernment, with its dualistic classification of this or that, does not encompass the real structure of manifestation. It is for this reason that Kabbalists continually stressed that we must enter an expanded and higher state of awareness, a state which would lift us beyond the limits of our restricted, everyday reasoning and judgment.

Clearly, most people are satisfied to maintain, throughout the whole of their lives, the mode of thinking they learned as children, without ever expanding their consciousness of themselves or their universe. *Kabbalah* recognises two different states of consciousness by referring to our normal everyday reasoning as "the mentality of childhood," while the developed, expanded and transcendent reasoning is called "the mentality of adulthood." In Hebrew, these mentalities are called *Mochin de Katnut* (the small, inferior, restricted and undeveloped mind), and *Mochin de Gadlut* (the great, superior, expanded and developed mind).[6] In the higher levels of consciousness, there is much greater perception and comprehension of the splendour and harmony of the whole of manifestation.

The idea that creation comprises complimentary forces in absolute harmony, is understood to be already present within the very "beingness" of *Ain Sof*. Thus, it is said that the being of the Eternal Living Spirit (*Ain Sof*) includes both the quality of Love

(Mercy) called *Chesed* or *Rachamim*, and that of Sternness and Judgment called *Gevurah* or *Din*. In *Kabbalah*, it is claimed the potentiality of all manifestation is in the "roots of *Din*," i.e. the forces of restriction. Naturally the study of how creation originated out of the Eternal No-thing is enormous, but from what has been said thus far, we can summarize it in the following manner.

We can postulate that "in the beginning" there was only *Ain Sof*, the Infinite No-thing as the Eternal Living Spirit. Being without past or future, without memory or expectations, *Ain Sof* could not "know," thus a process was initiated within *Its* "beingness" which would lead to an awakening of *Itself* to *Itself*. This activity is termed *Tzimtzum*, which is a process of Divine contraction and expansion within *Ain Sof*, termed *Histalkut* (contraction) and *Hitpashtut* (expansion) in Hebrew. This action led to the creation of a primordial space, as well as an eternal ebb and flow within this space. All creation would ultimately come into being because of the forces of contraction, understood in *Kabbalah* to be the forces of *Din* (*Judgment*), creating dimension and an apparent permanence.

Kabbalah teaches that everything we have been discussing thus far is only potential which must be made actual. Thus, a ray of the light of *Ain Sof* entered the primordial space, moving towards the mysterious infinite, non-existent centre, where a *Sefirah* (sphere) was created—a space within a space. The ray continued to move towards the centre of that space, creating another sphere—a space within a space within a space. It continued creating sphere within sphere.....within sphere.....within sphere, literally falling inwards due to the inherent forces of contraction or super-gravity. Each *Sefirah* formed in this way was filled with primordial divine energy. Chaim Vital referred to this, saying that "Through the contraction and diminution of the light, it was possible for a receptacle to come into being and become apparent."[7]

Lurianic Kabbalah teaches that a stage was finally reached where the primordial *Sefirot* (spheres within spheres) could no longer contain the divine light or force. An explosion, depicted as a shattering of the divine vessels or spheres, ensued outwards from that gravitational centre. This is called *Shevirat ha-Kelim* (the shattering of the vessels), described in Kabbalistic literature in the following manner: "When the light becomes too strong, the receptacle disintegrates due to its limited capacity to contain the powerful light."[8] This explosion or shattering resulted in a state of absolute chaos, which necessitated a second ray of light out of the being of *Ain Sof* to enter the now manifested universe of space–time–events, in order to regulate the chaos, establish the workings of cosmos, and focus the hidden elements into forms.

Yet it is understood that throughout the whole of creation the two inclinations of *Histalkut* (contraction) and *Hitpashtut* (expansion) continue to function within every aspect of creation, unto the ends of time. We might understand this more clearly, when we consider that even as I am writing these words and you are reading them, we continue to inhale and exhale. In fact, we might conceive the act of creation to be the enormous creative sigh of the Almighty.

This is beautifully expressed in an invocation, compiled from various sources by William G. Gray in his "*Seasonal Occult Ceremonies*," which reads: "Spirit of Light, Spirit of Wisdom, whose breath gives and takes away the form of all things. You before whom the life of every being is but a shadow which transforms, and a vapour which passes away. You who ascend upon the clouds and fly upon the wings of the wind. You exhale and the limitless immensities are peopled, You inhale and all which came from You return to You.

Be consecrated Endless Movement in the Eternal Stability. We praise You, we bless You in the fleeting empire of created light, shadows, reflections and images, and we aspire without ceasing towards Your immutable and Your imperishable Splendour. Let the ray of Your Intelligence, and the warmth of Your love descend upon us. That which is volatile shall become fixed, the shadow shall become substance, the Spirit of the Air shall receive a Soul and dream be thought.

We shall be swept away no more before the tempest, but shall bridle the steeds of the morning, and guide the course of the evening winds, that we may flee at last into Your presence.

We invoke You Eternal Spirit of Spirits, Soul of Souls, Imperishable Breath of Life, Creative Sigh, Mouth which issues and withdraws the life of all beings in the ebb and flow of Your Eternal Speech, which is the Divine Ocean of movement and of truth."[9]

Thinking of *Ain Sof*, the *Eternal No-Thing*, it occurred to me that when Voltaire said: "*Si Dieu n'existait pas, il faudrait l'inventer*" (If God did not exist, it would be necessary to invent him),[10] he hit on the secret of human existence in this world much deeper than one might suppose. What really matters is the *Principle Itself*. Everything else is subservient and secondary to that *Ultimate*. It is the "*Single Point*" at which we aim ourselves in Life that makes our lives worth anything at all. Without *That*, we have no point, purpose, meaning, value, or anything at all to justify our existence. Even whether *It* exists or not, is unimportant to us, since we cannot alter *Its* actuality in the slightest. What matters to us is our implicit belief in *It*. Our *Faith*. Our conviction that even if *It* does not exist, *it should*, and therefore *must be*. Perhaps in the end we shall find that "God" is an invention of Man, but if so, *It* is our finest and most valuable invention.

Interesting thought, is it not? The *Eternal Nothing* becoming *everything* in order to make our existence mean *something*. Back to the eternal *Ain* or *No-Thing* again. We can never escape *It* however hard we try. Everything comes from *It* and everything goes back to *It*. All the forms, fancies and factors of religion are only the categories and classes of human beings saying the same things in so many different ways. Jew, Christian, Muslim, Buddhist, or what have you, are all no more than variations on the same theme.

The common denominator behind all of them is *identification as a relationship with Divinity*. One might say: "This does not apply in the case of any officially atheistic State," like for example in the 20th century Soviet Union, North Korea or China today. Yet it does apply even there. They just call it *Humanism* or anything else they invent. It is still an *ideal*, however they may dress *It* up or disguise *It*. *It* is always something beyond and behind their material beings which motivates their behaviour. Whether they call *It* Communism or Marxism, *It* is inevitably an immaterial and metaphysical *ideal*, which accounts for their activity. Atheism is a devout belief in a *Nothing*–God. Whatever ones viewpoints in this regard, it is still a *belief*. You just cannot get away from the *No-Thing*.

We can speculate about the Eternal Nothing *ad infinitum*, and never really understand *It*, i.e. stand *It* under our minds. Yet,

114 / *The Shadow Tree: The Book of Self Creation*

when we close our eyes, sitting in a calm and relaxed manner, not doing anything, we might sense and perceive *It*, as we allow ourselves to invoke a state of consciousness which will help us to *be It*. This is eloquently expressed in the following words:

In the Timeless is the Formless
In the Formless is the Darkness
In the Darkness is the Stillness
In the Stillness is the Silence
In the Silence is the Seed

I.A.O.

Out of Nothing comes the Being
Out of Being Comes the Meaning
Out of Meaning comes the Motion
Out of Motion comes the Action
Out of Action comes the Deed

LIGHT!

And of Light — Law
And of Law — Love
And of Love — Life.[11]

B. "Three-Acting-Together-As-One"

Returning to the subject of manifestation as a whole, we understand there is really an entire hierarchy of forces holding the basic constituents of life together: molecule to molecule in liquids and solids, atom to atom in molecules, electrons to nuclei in atoms, protons to other protons and neutrons in nuclei. The first three types of force patterns are due to electrons and protons being oppositely charged, and hence attracting one another. However, the entire process is based on a "Law of Three-acting-together-as-One," which appears to govern all manifestation. All life-processes are based on a principle of three qualities acting together as one.[12]

The study of the Law of Threes, or what could be termed the "Ternary," is very interesting indeed, but of course we first have to understand the "Binary," the 1 + 1 or polarized qualities, which are only solved when they are balanced into a third quality between the two opposite poles of the binary. Here, instead of the logical 1 + 1 = 2, the binary 1 + 1 actually equals 3, and that 3 is a sacred number in many spiritual traditions. Its sign is the *Triangle*, the separate three corner points of which constitute a " Ternary," but when "acting-together-as-One," creates a fourth quality. Thus we arrive at the strange calculation: 1 + 1 = 3 = 4, or the "Tetrad."

For anything to manifest as an "Event" within "Time–Space," there must firstly be a positive, active and dynamic element or force to initiate the process of manifestation. Secondly there has to be a passive and receptive element receiving the flow from the positive element. A third principle then ensues as a result of the meeting between the active and the passive elements, combining them into the "neutral," and a new unit results from the "three-acting-together-as-One."

Take for example the *Atom*, comprising the positive proton, negative electron and neutral neutron. *Proton*, *Neutron* and *Electron* function together in a single unit called the *Atom*. Another example is the *Embryonic Disk* from which our physical bodies derive. It consists of three cells called an *Ectoderm*, *Mesoderm* and *Endoderm*, all acting together as the basic substance of our human flesh.

While not referring to it in such a direct manner, this process was delineated in our discussion of the Eternal No-Thing. In fact, *Ain Sof Aur* is this very process of "*Three-acting-together-as-One*," each of the "three" being part of the selfsameness of the *Great Unmanifest*. *Ain* is the *Infinitely Small* or the "*Positive Seed*," so to speak, whereas *Sof*, meaning "*Without End*," represents the *Infinitely Big*, or the "*Negative Womb*." These two factors are the "Divine opposites" or polarities, the balancing or relationship of which creates *Aur*, *Light* or Energy as a neutral force emanating everywhere at once. Finally *Ain Sof Aur* conjointly creates a fourth principle or quality, which is the three-dimensional reality of *Time–Space–Events*.

"As Above, so Below." We witness this process everywhere in manifestation, where all things express the principle of "*Three-acting-together-as-One*." This is why it was instinctively, or perhaps consciously, realised in so many

116 / *The Shadow Tree: The Book of Self Creation*

Traditions and religions. Here are some examples:

```
         SON                         TAO
          /\                          /\
         /  \                        /  \
        /    \                      /    \
       / CHRISTIANITY \            /  TAOISM  \
      /        \                  /        \
     /_____\                /_____\
  FATHER    HOLY GHOST        YANG          YIN
```

```
        SHIVA
         /\
        /  \
       /    \
      / HINDUISM \
     /        \
    /_____\
 BRAHMA      VISHNU
```

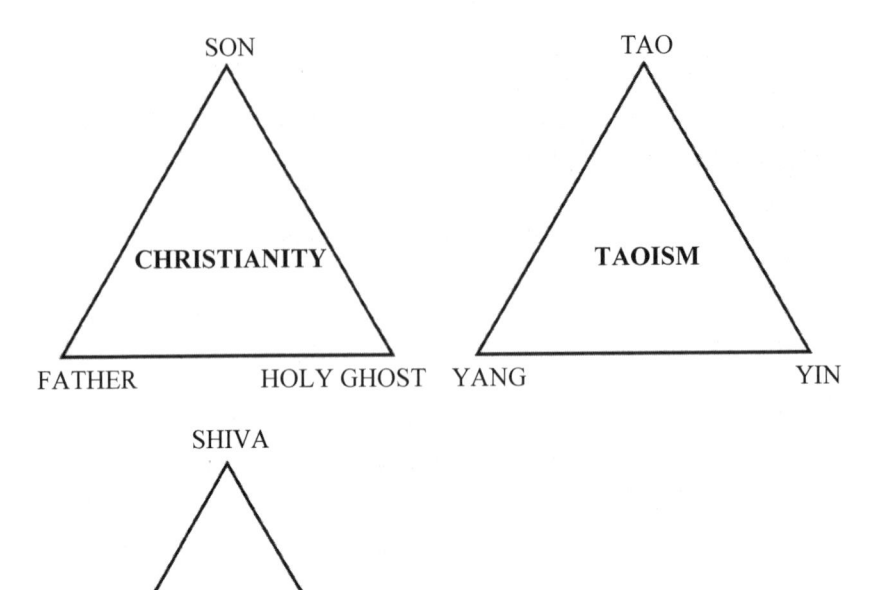

In Hinduism *Brahma*, *Vishnu* and *Shiva* refer respectively to the "Generator," "Operator" and "Destroyer" which a fellow Companion of the Sangreal Sodality indicated is quite a fair definition of the word "God," since the letters of this word spell the Ternary:

```
       DESTROYER
          /\
         /  \
        /    \
       /  GOD  \
      /        \
     /_____\
 GENERATOR    OPERATOR
```

Besides the mentioned religious examples, one can witness this "Law of Threes" in mechanics, polarity, logic, the family, etc.

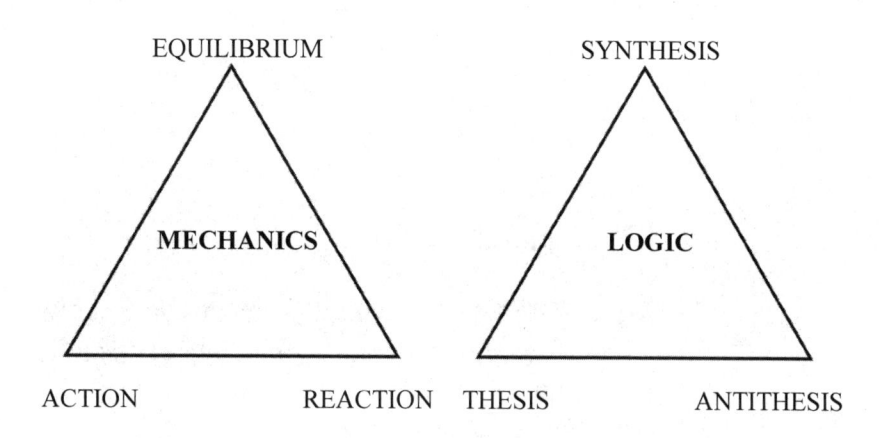

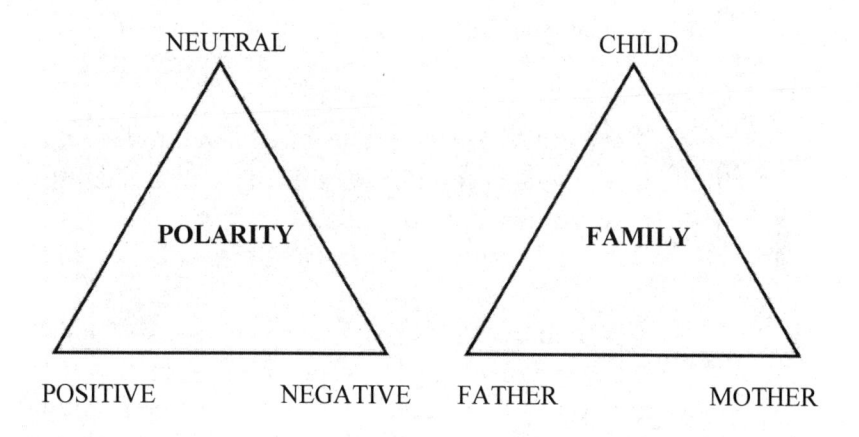

```
        EQUILIBRIUM              SYNTHESIS
           /\                       /\
          /  \                     /  \
         /MECHANICS\              / LOGIC \
        /          \             /         \
       /_____\           /_____\
   ACTION        REACTION    THESIS      ANTITHESIS


         NEUTRAL                   CHILD
           /\                       /\
          /  \                     /  \
         /POLARITY\               / FAMILY \
        /          \             /         \
       /_____\           /_____\
   POSITIVE       NEGATIVE    FATHER        MOTHER
```

In *Kabbalah* we might refer to this process as *Yod–Heh–Vav–Heh* (יהוה), which is the most Sacred Name of Divinity or the *Tetragrammaton*, "Four Letter Name," in which each glyph is part of the process of *"Three-acting-together-as-One."* This should not appear strange, especially in the light of several claims having been made that the four letters comprising the Ineffable Name refer to a process rather than an actual name.

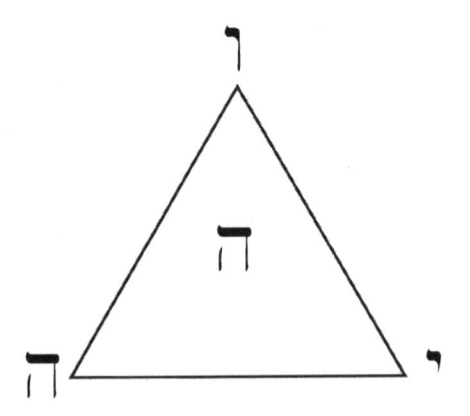

The *Yod* (Fire), the smallest letter in the Hebrew Alphabet, represents a flame, or the Male Principle, the Divine Essence as male, active, positive, dynamic and creative *Force*.

The *Heh* (Water) represents the Female Principle, seen as a negative, receptive and formative *Pattern*.

The *Vav* (Air) is the extension of *Yod* into *Heh*, and is a letter signifying fertility, thus literally representing the Principle of *Activity* as a neutral state, reflecting the qualities of both *Yod* and *Heh*.

The final *Heh* (Earth) in the Divine Name indicates the *Form* resulting from the previous three letters acting together as one, but is in itself representing Life as a Feminine Principle out of which more can evolve with the right insemination and gestation. Thus a new *Tetrad*, a fourfold process, can be born out of this last *Heh* due to the principle of "*Three-acting-together-as-One*."[13]

By the way, this teaching pertains to a principle, and does not specifically extol the doctrine of the "Christian Trinity," as some would have it. So, our reasoning thus far pertaining to two opposite qualities, the union of which is perceived as a third quality, out of which a fourth being realised, might be termed a

"Cosmic Sex Act," which brings to mind the statement that *"Nothing is created, but Everything is born."* This is understandable when *Yod* ('— the active) and *Heh* (ה— the passive) unite to give birth to *Vav* (ו— the neutral). The *Father* uniting with the *Mother* to give birth to the *Child*, which, together with *Father* and *Mother* forms the quality called the *Family*.

Examining the *Tetragrammaton* more closely, we notice that *Yod* might refer to "*Existence*" as *Time*, and *Heh* could mean "*Life*" within *Space*. Thus *Time* as "Male-Principle" and *Space* as "Female-principle" unite in "*Events*" as the "Neutral" or "Balancing Principle." In turn all three (Time–Space–Events) act together, in order to be the manifestation of the *Life/Death Principle of Consciousness*. *Time* and *Space* unite in *Events* in order to create *Awareness* which is as all-encompassing as *Space*, therefore the repeat of the letter *Heh* in the Ineffable Name indicating both *Inner Space* and the resultant *Consciousness*.

C. Space, Time and Events

I, like everyone else, have had my own personal *"sturm und drang"* about God and existence. However, in the back of my mind I always believed that, if I could get beyond this internal conflict, I might be able to realise *Ain Sof*. Eventually I reached a fundamental understanding that existence revolves around the still centre of the "Life/Death Principle." In my quest for what I perceived to be the hidden truth, I personified "Death" as a "Mother archetype," and through a most intimate communication with this anthropomorphized principle, I was led to comprehend a "Model of the Universe," that blueprint of existence which Kabbalists call the *Etz Chayim* or Tree of Life. With this tool I was able to face basic issues of existence, like the question of "Time."

It is certainly most important to grasp the "Ternary of Time" if one wants to understand what is happening within the womb of our Great Mother, which is the eternal process of genesis, the "*Ladder of Descending and Ascending Stages*" commencing in the "Hidden Origin," unfolding in the evolution of all existence throughout cosmos, and returning back into the "Infinite No-Thing." This is the fundamental meaning of the "Tree of Life," and once this is understood, one can reverse the machine of time for

120 / *The Shadow Tree: The Book of Self Creation*

oneself so to speak, and reach back to the original state of *Perfect Peace Profound* within the *Eternal Life/Death Process*.

In fact, the so-called "*Abyss*," shown on the Kabbalistic Tree of Life, is in one sense the vagina of the Great Mother, and the seven *Sefirot* below it the creation of all that *was*, *is* and ever *will be*, constantly emanating out of that "Dark Womb in the Now." Conjointly, the three "Supernal *Sefirot*," that is, the three Spheres above the *Abyss*, might then be considered the "Male Seed" of the *Great Emanator*, suggested by the Upper Triangle, or the Hebrew letter *Alef* (א), the *Life–Death* principle of all that is and all that is not. This would be altogether beyond time since even time must issue from the womb of the Great Mother. Comprehending this will facilitate the ability to reverse the machinations of time within ones own being, but *Time* itself is a Ternary.

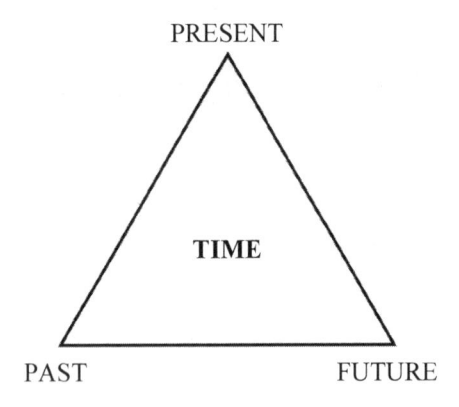

```
           PRESENT
              /\
             /  \
            /    \
           /      \
          /  TIME  \
         /          \
        /            \
       /_____\
     PAST            FUTURE
```

In accordance with our basic reasoning thus far, we might consider the *Past* and the *Future* to be united in the *Present*, but there is a hidden truth here which we need to understand, and that is that it is the *Present* which determines the *Past* and the *Future*. Literally the *Present* emanates both the *Past* and the *Future*. Yet we can view the *Past* as Passive, the *Future* as Active and the *Present* as Neutral, and by analogy comprehend the binary of *Man* and *Nature* the union of which results in the *Archetype*,[14] which neutralises the binary and creates the "*Ternary of Life*."

This subject requires more careful study, but for now we should understand that the "Highest Principle" also divides into *active* and *passive* elements, but as the "Highest" *diversifies* Itself, so does man and nature *unify* themselves in the Highest Principle. The *Archetype* is always between *Man* and *Nature*.

Now, it is the *Present* which is so interesting. In fact, the term "Present" does not only refer to an object at a certain moment in time, but refers also to the reality of something which is not an object at all. It is rather a *"State of Awareness"* in the process of emanation, or "birthing." That is why, when we use our "Will" to establish a certain mind-set for ourselves, or use suggestion to achieve certain aims, we should always use "Present" terms like "*I am* (whatever it is)" and never "I will be (this or that)."

However, the general way in which humanity experiences "Time" is through the "Past," i.e. the negative or the "Fate" way. They are literally looking backwards. This might be described as someone travelling in a vehicle moving from the *Past* into an invisible *Future*, and this individual is observing events through the rear window, thus travelling into the future by means of a "backwards" observation rather than a "forwards" one. Things appear out of the invisible *Future*, are framed momentarily in what is considered to be the *Present* moment, or the immediate sense experience—considered "True Knowledge," before it too recedes towards the Time horizon—into the *Past*.

All things appear to have beginnings and ends, and looking towards the *Past*, people can "clearly see" the lives of others they knew, all comprising beginnings and endings. All manifestation, both past and present, is understood to have derived from an infinitely remote beginning at the vanishing point in the centre of the "backwards view" in the past, and that "original beginning" was at one time the *Present* moment to be followed by later moments—all linked by chains of cause and effect, or *Karma* as some would have it.

However, let us be frank, no sense-experience at any moment is truly accurate, because there is always a fraction of a time-lapse between the actual encounter and the realisation of that experience in the brain. Thus, by the time anything is actually perceived, it has already moved towards the "Time horizon" into the *Past*. Hence there is never a true comprehension of what an event is really like, and all our experiences comprise personal creations in our minds. It seems to me that all our vaunted solidities are rather insubstantial, because they are constructed entirely from memories, and substantiated by what we believe to be real information about the *Past*. Furthermore, the *Future* is predicted on the basis of it being somehow related to the *Past* by means of a chain of causes and effects.

As far as I am concerned, this is pure illusion, and closer scrutiny will instantly diminish our sound solidities into insecure insubstantialities. Yet, everyone firmly believes that each individual, with his/her own "*Present*," is in some way moving through a universe of solid realities, even though these realities say nothing about the "Being" experiencing them.

It is so desperately tragic to see people preoccupied with the accumulation of physical objects, even though these "solid realities" tell us nothing about the person who is willing to beg, steal or borrow for a mere fantasy. *Being* is the important factor, the *Experiencer*, not the things encountered. Our true Self is the "*Eternal Present*," from which everything emanates. More and more people might realise this, when they discover that all they really "know" is the contents of their own memories, backed by what they agree is "fact."

So, we need to change this view. The *Past* filled with "objects" of *Fate* is no landscape determining the *Future*. Everything moving in Time is created, projected or emanated out of the *Eternal Now*, the *Present*. I cannot say I was born 40, 50, 60 or more years ago. I am born *Now*, and it is only my body that has existed for 50 or more years. My point of emanation is "*Now*." In fact, all so-called "reality" has to be constantly confirmed by me, the "observer" in the *Now*. This is most eloquently depicted by Lyall Watson in his book "*Gifts of Unknown Things*," when he summed up reality saying "When we open a book lying closed on the table in front of you, all those pages or states already exist, and any page is possible. The probability is not necessarily equal, there is usually a bias built into the binding which makes the book open more easily at a well-thumbed page. But with the covers closed, the system is open. It is a multiple state and enters a single state only when a reader comes along to take a measurement or make an observation.....There is only one nonphysical entity that is nevertheless real and sufficiently widespread to be held responsible."[15] Lyall Watson refers to this "entity" as "our consciousness," which I like to call the "Experiencer" or the

"Awakening One" who "self creates" throughout all manifestation, the One who hallucinates itself as an event in time and space.

Sure, the *Past* shows objects which look far away, almost beyond the reach of our imagination, and things still appear to "recede" towards an invisible point in the Time horizon, but with our perspectives widened to embrace much larger parameters, we come to know that things did not commence in the past at some imaginary point, but are eternally projected, or born, out of the *Now*, the *Present*. Thus "*In the beginning*" is *Eternally Now*.

All things are manifested through all of us, and the *Present* of every person is creating his or her world of knowledge and experience. The point of origin is not far away somewhere among the emanated objects, it is *inside* each one of us, within all of us. *This*, the real Self, is the *only reality*—not the things around us which seem so solid to our eyes. The crucial point comes when this is realised inside oneself. Then one can turn inwards, into the Self, and experience the beginnings and endings of all encountered reality, yet still continue to live as normal human beings with full awareness of what was, is and will be emanated into the realm of "Time–Space–Events."

It is true that when one watches the clock, seeing time never halting for even one instant to define a wink between past or future, it must seem crazy to say that the only reality is the *Now*. However, we will never find the beginnings of all things "somewhere out there," since their origin is in reality inside ourselves. The important point is that this cause, or origin, is our true identity which, while manifested inside our very genes, is yet beyond Time, Space and Events. While I look for my *Sangreal*, my Holy Grail, my "True Essence" inside my "Blood" as it were, I know perfectly well that it is not the physical blood which is my "True Identity" but the "Light behind the blood"—my "awakeness."

So, all I really have to do is turn away from this backward look, perceive *Ani*, my *internal No-Thing*, my *True Self*, from which all things originate. What is more, I must continue to live in my normal manner, emanating from this central point the continuing act of Self Creation. All ceremonies, rites and rituals have this "Inner Identity" in mind, and the act of *continuous creation* issues from the womb of the *Shechinah*, the Mother

Principle or Feminine Counterpart of God, due to a continuous infusion of Divine Semen or Essence from the Father Principle, in constant sexual delight.

I might add that discussing these "inner truths" is virtually impossible, and I am constantly thrown back to my initial query pertaining to how one can speak of that which is forever outside time, space and events. Our earthly communication skill is such a desperately inadequate tool in our attempt to describe "Instates." I am trying to speak of the *Unspeakable*, and the best way seems to recommend silence, and even this advice is violated by its very utterance.

"Experience of the *Eternal Living Spirit*" is a most inadequate description of the "Mystical Marriage," which is vastly different from conceptual grasping. It is so "direct" one could call it touching, and yet it does not need to be sensory at all. In my discussion of the "Eternal Present" I am crippled by the inability of language to rid itself of time, space and events. Words like "in," "out," "beyond," etc., are much too clumsy, and that is perhaps why Kabbalists invented the *Yichudim* (Unification exercises), through which one can touch the *Eternal Now*, whose "only begotten child" is the *Sangreal*, the *realisation of the Divine* within ones own being.

If you fully participate in your *Real Identity*, all distinctions of past and future pass away. In the "presence of the Present" there is no memory of the "has been" or awaiting the "might be." There are no regrets, there is no repentance, and no awareness of guilt pertaining to a *Past*. There are no fears of a deity punishing us, nor any fearful deliberations about the *Future*. Some may think that this would take away purpose and meaning in life, but surely it must be possible for *Life to be for Its own sake* and nothing else! In any case, the more we look at this "past–future" correlation of events, their manifestation out of nowhere and their decay into a finality of nowhere, the more we realise the insubstantiality of all manifestation.

The very best we can do is comprehend the *Eternal Present*, the *Eternal Now*, the *Experiencer*, who is eternally spewing events out of Itself. We might then understand that the "Ultimate Truth" is neither a thing nor an event, but the *Eternal Now*, you—the One who is both the *Experiencer* and the

Experience. Yet *experience* belongs to Time. Time is needed both to *do* and to *relate*, thus the ancients saw Time either as a deity, or as a river or stream emanating directly from Divinity itself. Time is really duration and change, a dynamic aspect of life in which nothing ever remains the same, and so only the *No-Thing IS*. Time might be *Eternity* as *Eternal Duration*, and the eternal recreation of what is created, but it *IS NOT*.

You probably recall how we earlier spoke of *Alef* (א) as the Hebrew letter for the *Eternal No-thing*, from whence *Light* or *Energy* flows into manifestation as *Life* and *Death*. Thus *Alef* is the unified *Life/Death Principle* of all, and, being exceedingly creative, *It* becomes diversified in existence as *Birth (Life)–continuum– Death*. The Hebrew letter for this *Continuum* (Time) is *Yod* (י), which is the projection of *Alef* into *temporal existence*. *Alef* is the *Stillness*, the *Formless* as said previously, in which the *inhalation/exhalation* of the *Eternal Living Spirit* is poised in that hovering pause, the rest of total surrender, the free fall between each cycle of breath, as it were, whereas the exhalation and inhalation respectively are the *Life* and *Death* of the *Time-continuum* of *Yod* (existence).[16]

Still too difficult to understand? Well let us look at it again. Whereas *Ain Sof* is *Life/Death* in total *Union*, *Time* is *existence* as *Life...Death...Life...Death*, not as a unity any more, but separated into a cycle of alternating opposites *Past.....Future.....Past.....Future.....* Time is a rhythm, a pulsation, an exhalation and an inhalation, or simply "existence." Time *is* rhythm, yet a relative one since the rhythm of Time is not the same for all events. It differs in terms of the fast moving cycles of manifested Life and the slow moving cycles of mega-molecules. In the realm of the subconscious as well, at very deep archetypal levels, what may seem a brief moment, could have taken long periods of earth time, and vice versa.

It has been suggested that Time is the continuity of existence without reference to any events occurring within it, and Time as *Eternal Existence* is in reality *opposite* to the *Infinite No-Thing*. In this instance Time as *Eternal Existence* is perceived to be "horizontal," while the *Infinite No-Thing* is posited "vertical," so to speak. It is as if Life/Death (א) and Eternal Existence (י) are playing a continuous game, in which Time/Existence is always the loser, since *Alef*, the non-moving centre, overtakes running Time while standing still.

So, *Alef* is the silent, imminent principle and *Yod* is the active, continuous sounding of *Alef* in existence. *Alef* is in fact non-existent, the Timeless, yet always *IS*, whereas *Yod* is the existence of *Alef* in Time, yet in truth *IS NOT*, since "*is*" is permanent and "*is not*" is temporal, and only there to allow the "*is*" to know Self. Remember that *Alef* has no past, no future, no memory, no purpose, but is what *It* is within *Itself*. Since all existence is within Time and Space, *Alef* does not exist but *is*, hence is the only reality. Knowledge of it is knowledge of *Self*.

Our problem is that while the **act of knowing** by necessity functions within Existence alone, the **state of knowing** is beyond deeds within "Being" itself. It is all a matter of "who" and "what." The only way we can *know* the *Self* is beyond thought, since *Alef*, the letter for the *No-Thing*, *is* beyond all mind. *Alef* is Eternal, again, not as eternity related to a remote past or a potential future, but as *Eternal Now*.

"*Yod*"-existence gives birth, yet in the end consumes its own offspring. By emanating continuity in Time, it annihilates that very continuity in order to create more continuity. The same is to be said of Life. As *Light* from *Immeasurable Alef* creates *Life*, so does *Life* sacrifice itself in order to maintain *Life*. The main purpose of this sacrificial maintenance of existence, is only to allow *Alef*—the *No-Thing* projected into manifestation—to become aware of *Itself*. Thus "the Word is made flesh" so that it may utter *Itself* to *Itself*. When *It* knows *Itself* ultimately, *Alef* and *Yod* can theoretically become one again, yet *It* can never know *Itself* completely since *It* has no centre, and therefore *Yod* can never be *Alef*.

Yod ("a hand" in Hebrew) is the "*Hand of Time*" continuously giving and taking in Existence. *Alef*, the *Eternal Life/Death*, perfectly balances the principles of give and take—neither giving nor receiving—yet knowing *Itself* more and more through the actions of *Yod*, which is basically *Alef* made manifest and separated into Life and Death. In the process of "Universal Evolution" *Alef* becomes *Yod*, the Centre becomes the Circumference, Life/Death becomes Existence in order to know Itself. Thus *No-Thing* becomes its own opposite by manifesting itself in a *Conditioned Existence*, which satisfies itself by *giving* Life and betrays itself by *taking* Life. However, whereas *Alef* (*Eternal No-Thing*) becomes *Yod* (Time/Existence), *Yod* can never become *Alef*.

Alef always remains the same and never changes in *Its Essential Self*, but through *Yod* (Existence) *Alef* gets to know *Itself*. *Alef* can never evolve, whereas *Yod*, as a continuous cycle of change and exchange, is evolving and revolving eternally in the *Now*, and so increasingly reveals the *perfection* of *Alef* (the *Life/Death Principle*), delivered into the "out-of-Self-created-realm-of-*Yod*" (the existence of Death in Birth and Birth in Death). Undiscovered and alone or "all-one" is *Alef*, the *Unknowable*. Even in its self-limitation within the realm of Existence, *Alef* remains unborn. Similarly, the Force inside and comprising every molecule throughout all existence, is unbounded, flowing freely throughout the entirety of existence.

Submerge a cup in the ocean, the content within the cup is also around the cup, and *is* the cup as well. Your body is the cup, but only a small part of the "real you" is incarnated in the flesh. The rest is everywhere. What is within is without, and what is without is likewise within. This was beautifully explained by William Gray saying "Nothing is the largest Cup existing since it holds all things within itself.....Hold Nothing yours, and you have more than you will ever need."[17]

Again the phrase "God is a circle, the circumference of which is everywhere, and the centre nowhere,"[18] has been used to describe this reality. Here the *Whole* is unified into the *expression* of the *No-Thing* as a *Self*, and therefore this *Unborn One* is like the wind which cannot be seen, but its effects can be felt. In the same manner we can witness the effects of *Alef* in *Yod* (Time/Existence). *Alef is the Question Mark, Yod the Questing for an Answer.*

D. Fate, Destiny and Free Will

Now, earlier we indicated that we could view the *Past* as "negative," the *Future* "positive" and the *Present* "neutral" in the *Time-ternary*. Compared to the *Man–Archetype–Nature Ternary*, it can be said that *Nature* and its manifestations are products of the *Past* comprising *Fate*, hence considered *Passive*, while *Man* with his *Free Will* pertains to the *Future*. However, it is the *Archetype* which is the *Eternal Now*—the *Present*—and which, because of *Its* wonderful inherent balance, can be called *Providence* or *Destiny*. Our *Destiny* lies in the *Present* and not in the Future, and this brings us to the following Ternary:

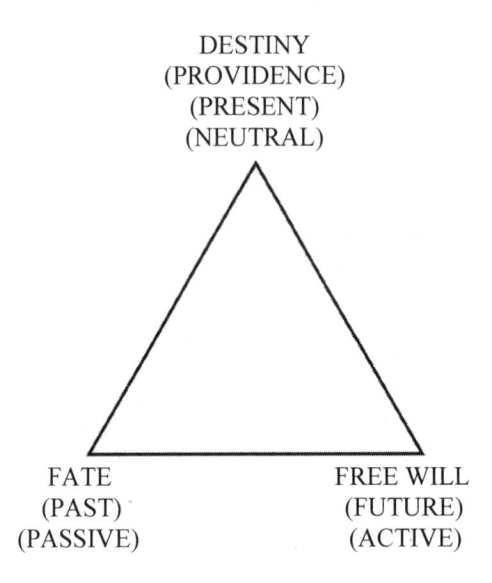

```
            DESTINY
          (PROVIDENCE)
            (PRESENT)
            (NEUTRAL)
               △
   FATE                FREE WILL
  (PAST)                (FUTURE)
 (PASSIVE)              (ACTIVE)
```

Free Will determines the *Future*, yet is controlled by *Fate* through the *Past*. *Free Will* becomes more powerful than *Fate* when it aligns itself with the illuminating influence of *Destiny*, *Divine Will*. History can thus be seen as a constantly unfolding evolution in the *Now*. History is not the "happened" but a "happening." If *Free Will* denies the influence of *Providence*, or *Destiny* (*Divine Will*), and then attempts to oppose *Fate*, the outcome is unpredictable and rests on a combination of the *Forces* of *Will* and *Fate*. In this instance *Fate* is inevitably the winner. If, on the other hand, *Free Will* decides to align itself with *Fate* (the Past) alone, forgetting *Divine Will* (*Providence*)—acknowledging material objects to be the only reality—results are rather destructive, because *Time* will always annihilate that which is created within it—or born out of it.

The terms "*Fate*" and "*Destiny*" are interesting in themselves. The word "fate" derives from the Latin *Fatum*, meaning "that which is spoken" and "that which is ordained." It is connected to the root *fari* which means "to speak," "foretell" and "to predict." Fate is also linked to the Latin *fabula*, also meaning "speech," which is the root for the words "fable," "fame," and so forth. Thus in "fate," "fable" and "fame," *Life has spoken*, the idea being that fate is an irresistible power controlling the course of all events.

In turn, the word "destiny" originated from the Latin *destinatum* which is "a mark," "aim," "design of purpose," and so forth. This certainly shows a vast difference between the concepts of "destiny" and "fate." Simply then, when God spoke the word of "*Light*" he created our "*Fate*." This means our course is set via the "*Way of Light*," and whereas "*Fate*" is the way we get to *Light*, "*Destiny*" is the *Light Itself* unto which we return, and in which we are fixed securely.

Fabre d'Olivet, a remarkable French Western Esotericist of the late nineteenth century, indicated the *Ternary* of *Fate–Providence–Free Will* in this manner:[19]

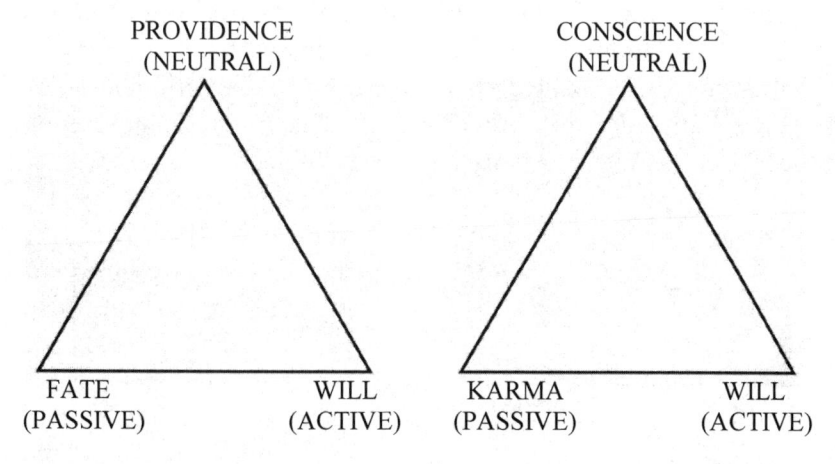

```
       PROVIDENCE                    CONSCIENCE
        (NEUTRAL)                    (NEUTRAL)
           /\                           /\
          /  \                         /  \
         /    \                       /    \
        /      \                     /      \
       /_____\                   /_____\
    FATE        WILL            KARMA         WILL
  (PASSIVE)   (ACTIVE)        (PASSIVE)    (ACTIVE)
```

In man *Providence* is *Conscience*, which, as the "neutral," does not attack or restrain, but rather *enlightens* by indicating how the binary is neutralized. *Free Will* determines future happenings, the choice being limited by *Karma* (Cause and Effect) which pertains to the *Past*. The best stance would always be to align *Free Will* with *Providence* (*Divine Will*), which, being stronger than *Fate*, can purify and rectify *Karma*. This is indicated in the Western Mystery Tradition by what is termed the "*Melchizedek process*," or the way of the "*Sacred Priest-King*," meaning the voluntary sacrifice or offering of *Free Will* to the *Creator* (*Providence* or the *Divine Will*), from whence all originate in the first place. William Gray said: "As the *One* willed Itself to become *Many*, so must the *Many* will themselves to become *One* in order that Consciousness should circulate around Cosmos, and Life continue Its own Creation.

Now, taking an ordinary soul of our species to be a mixture of human and Divine consciousness, the human part of this combination provides the Priest component which is willing to sacrifice its ordinary will to that of Divinity. The Divine Life-factor offers the Kingship element which wills that humans should be rightly ruled. Thus 'Kingship' (or the Blood Royal— *GREAL*) is of God, and the 'Priesthood' is of Man. When *that part of ourselves in God which is 'priestly'* encounters *that part of God which is 'Kingly' in us,* and the offering or sacrifice is exchanged between these extremities of Existence, then *the Grail is being gained.*

Put simply again, we as humans have to approach the 'Presence of God' as priests with something to offer (our human 'free will'), while the Divine Presence comes to us as a King or spiritual sense of Right Rulership in our lives. The action has to be reciprocal in order to work properly. This *is* the 'Melchizedek process' of the Western Holy Mysteries."[20]

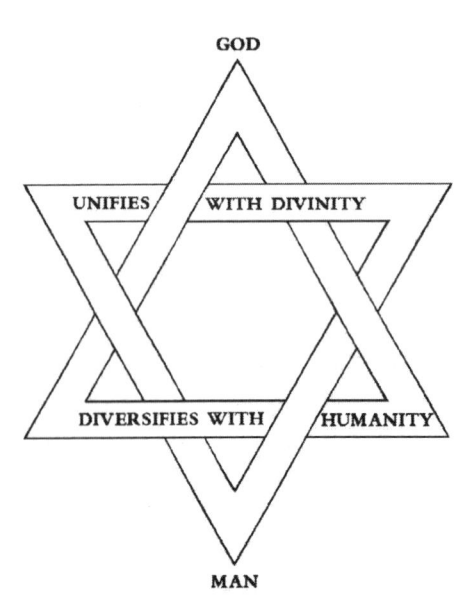

This is indicated symbolically by the interlocking triangles of the Star of David (also called the Shield of Solomon or the Hexagram), which William Gray called "the sign of the Macrocosm." Regarding this remarkable glyph he said "At the apex of the Symbol is God, seen as diversifying until the base of Its triangle represents all humanity. At the nadir is to be found Man as *one* of those souls (in this case, *you*). By extending yourself toward Divinity in a *truly* priestly fashion, you are uniting with the Divine Will ruling the lives of *all* for the sake of a Single Consciousness."[21] The triangles comprising the "Star of David,"

can be considered from a dual perspective. Depending on the nature of the Triangle or Ternary, the balance point between the extremities will be apex or nadir, up or down.

So, from *Light* we come and unto *Light* we go. In another way *Fate* could be seen as the *Irresistible Power* controlling the course of all events, while *Destiny* is the *Personification of that Power* which determines the *Way*, and here we again have the "word was made flesh"—"*et verbum caro factum est.*" This Latin phrase is actually correctly translated "the word is becoming fact." The "word" is "fate" and "destiny" the "fact." Maybe one should look more closely at the actual meaning of the word "Word." There is an interesting connection between it and *logos*—something tremendous; something that creates; the Creative Word with immense Light within it. In my mind's eye it is a vast ray of light. A "word" after all is only to create with consciousness. By using words, you are employing the same power as God in very reduced circumstances.

The root of "Word" means "name" and "order," i.e. creating order out of chaos. The Sanskrit *vratan* meaning "word" also means "order," and the Old Slavonic word *Rota*, meaning "an oath," is also connected here. The Gothic root for "word" means "accusation," while in Old Greek it means "orator."

This is telling all *orators* to be cautious when *naming* in their speech. We are reminded that we should create *order*, that we are *under oath* to do so, as it were, and that we may not misuse words and thereby gain an *accusation* of having misused our "Creative Powers" while we are on the "Wheel of Life." Curiously enough, the word *rota* is also Latin for "a wheel." With its added meaning of an "oath" in the Old Slavonic, it seems to say "The Wheel of Life is the Oath of Life." We have sealed ourselves to life with an "oath of service," and hence will remain tied to the "Wheel of Cause and Effect" until we have kept our end of the bargain.

Linked to the word *Rota* is the English "rotate," and the Sanskrit *Ratas*, meaning "a chariot," I am reminded of the early Jewish mystical tradition named the "Work of the Chariot" (*Ma'aseh Merkavah*) to which the roots of *Kabbalah* can be traced. Be that as it may, let it suffice that we are "carried" in the "Chariot of Life," our bodies being "pulled" along by the "power of the five senses" or emotional self which is "steered" by the "charioteer" of "mind–over–matter." While "*fate*" has decreed "the Way" of reaching our ultimate *destiny, free will* helps us apply "the Way" in whatever way we *WILL*, and "merrily we roll along" as the ancient Lithuanian word *Ritu* implies.

We might also note that the word *Rota* also means a list of members having certain duties, and every time the name of a person comes up in such a list, that individual is due to render some special service. If each one of us could but recognise our duties when it is our turn, but most seem to shy away from that responsibility of service we agreed to fulfil in the first place. Such inaction eventually leads to "accusation" and "judgement," as implied by the word *Karma* which has nothing to do with "revenge" but everything to do with exacting "compensation."

In fact, judgment is also implied in the word *Rota* itself. For example, in the Roman Catholic Church the word means a supreme ecclesiastical court of appeal, consisting of twelve prelates subjected only to the authority of the Pope. Here the "Twelve" suggest to me "the twelve dancing in the heavens"—the Zodiac, comprising "The Court of Twelve" who are rotating in the heavens and setting the circuit of our fates, while directing us back to our ultimate destiny.

A further meaning of the word *Rota* is the Old Netherlands meaning "to rot," and here the idea is disintegration. Of course, on the "Wheel of Life" we start to disintegrate the instant we are incarnated in the flesh. Our deaths are put into us by our births, and our births by our deaths. Every death is a new birth, and every birth a new death. It is like the two sides of a door which opens and shuts! One can only truly comprehend this, and untie oneself from the "Wheel of Death and Rebirth," when one no longer *knows* the *Eternal Now* from the "cage of logic perspective, but rather from the actuality of *being* it.

So we understand that *"Now"* is neither a moment in time, nor an event or any deed. It is the *Experiencer* as a *No-thing* and a *Self*. Kabbalists refer to this as *Ain v'Ani* (*Nothing and I*). Your *True Self* is both the *Creator* and the *Experiencer* of all creation, emanating the totality of existence in the *Now*, and herein lies great power. In the *Now* there are no regrets or expectations. It is only when we tie ourselves to experiences, that we suffer the effects of the past, of that which should have been buried long ago. In the *Now* exist all possibilities. This was made particularly clear to me in a remarkable way.

As Kabbalist/Magician I like working in what is termed an "open state." This refers to a condition in which your mind and perceptions are vastly expanded and strongly focussed into the present. In this state one recognises and understands *Being* in a state of *infinite knowing*, so to speak. In normal conditions this kind of expanded state of consciousness can last up to twelve hours after its induction, but I have had one which endured for a period of almost two weeks.

In one such condition, I was using my consciousness to "move" inter-dimensionally, as it were. On my return to normal focal levels in this world, I encountered two different "states of reality" pertaining to the same event. In one I saw an aircraft exploding in midair and falling on a village below, while in the other I saw the same aircraft complete its flight with the passengers disembarking safely in the usual manner.

Having experimented with different realities, I do realise that both the events described exist eternally as possibilities in the *Now*. In fact, all possible possibilities you can think of exist in the *Eternal Present*, almost like blueprints, so to speak. An example would be to lift your hand, hold it still, then to look at it and recognise that all the possible movements your hand can make are fully present at this very moment—all "predestined" in the now. When you recognise the number of motions you can execute with that hand, you can choose any one you please. So, which will you implement?

Again "As Above, so Below" and "As with the finite, so with the Infinite." All possible possibilities exist in totality in the *Now*, all *fated* by the *Divine Emanator* of all being. The more your consciousness grows and expands into full "awakeness" in the *Now*, the more you recognise the potential choices, all of which are fully present in the *Now*. All deeds and their possible expressions are fated in the *Present*. Thus, when you expand your consciousness enough to fully realise and embrace this, there are an infinite number of choices you can make in the expression of any deed. In this state all events are *Fated*, but *how* they will be expressed is a matter of *Free Will*, and this freedom of choice will depend on the abilities of the individual applying *Will*. Choices will be limited by how many of the potentials of expression can be perceived by anyone at any moment. In other words clarity of consciousness.

I am sure you are wondering which one of the two fated possibilities, recognised in my aircraft experience, was manifested or expressed in time–space. In this case it was the one pertaining to the exploding aircraft. I actually *saw* the event as it was happening. I did not know which reality was "realised" until I turned on the TV and saw the news report of the aircraft which exploded and fell on the village of Lockerbie. At the time I had the same strange feeling of emptiness William Gray said he had, when buildings were on fire next door to his own residence. He was watching the flames licking away very close to his property, which housed all his worldly possessions. He wondered how much longer he would own them, and told me that he felt *empty*, as if resigned to whatever fate might come, not exactly with total indifference, but with an abandonment of himself to *Life, God, Fate,* or whatever one calls it. *THAT* if you like, or the *inevitable.*

He told me it was much the same feeling he had at Dunkirk beach during World War II, which he described as "weird." While stranded there, he *knew* that *somehow* he would be saved from the ensuing disaster, because there was something for him to do in this world which he had not yet accomplished. In fact, this was confirmed in a rather fascinating visionary experience he had on the "dreary last night" at Dunkirk, while half-dreaming on the beach. It is worth quoting what he said in its entirety, for a clear indication of how each one of us has two "minds," so to speak. "*Mochin de-Katnut,*" the restricted consciousness functioning at normal, ordinary focal levels, and "*Mochin de-Gadlut,*" the expanded one, capable of recognising the universal meaning of being. He said: "What it amounted to was a weird double-consciousness where I knew quite well what was happening on the material level, yet at the same time was experiencing something totally different in another dimension of existence. I was being told somehow that my earthly adventures were only an interlude in something much greater than I was as a human person, and therefore I should not let them worry me unduly, but simply go on following the lines which would be shown me as I went along. I was not due to die here and now, but there would be a lot of work for me to do yet, before this incarnation came to an end and another set of adventures laid out for me to experience. What really mattered was that I should learn from what was happening on one level how I ought to behave on another.

I seemed to be living two lives at once and each was diametrically opposed to the other, yet both were *ME* at the same time. One was an ordinary frightened human, horrified at everything happening around him, and the other was a calm and almost disinterested observer, watching everything that went on with a mild interest, so as to assess it at its proper value in proportion to its importance as an item of experience. It was almost as if one 'I' were looking at another and wondering why it was making such a fuss about being alive, and having nasty things happen to it, which were so relatively unimportant when compared to this transcendent condition of consciousness.....

.....For me, those war experiences were my personal descent into Hell, which altered my soul to a degree which could only be described as dedicated to a completely changed course of consciousness. I was altered neither for the better nor for the worse, but for an entirely different direction. All that remained was to see where it would lead me."[22]

It is naturally difficult for human beings to realise that, despite our consciousness being very narrowly focussed in this particular three-dimensional level of existence, we are factually living in all dimensions of existence—on all Levels of Being. With expanded consciousness or "awakeness," and the recognition of ourselves as the *Eternal Now*, we could shift our consciousness to experience any, or "live" in any, dimension of existence we may choose. I am particularly fascinated by William Gray's description of his remarkable experiences at Dunkirk, and find the word "weird" peculiar in itself. It is an old Anglo-Saxon term for "a relationship between Gods and Men." Literally it means "to be" or "become." In other words the "whatever will happen, will happen" sort of thing. "Weird" somehow holds "destiny" within its inner meaning, the sense of "going with it because you have to." It is largely in Scottish usage, and you may recall Shakespeare referring to the Macbeth "witches" as the "Weird Sisters." "To dree his weird" is a Scottish term for coming to terms with ones own fate, and thus this is sometimes used for fortune telling.

Maybe the Spanish phrase "*que sera, sera*" fits here, meaning "What will be, will be." I suppose a practising Christian might call it "acceptance of the Will of God," or for a Hindu or Buddhist "cooperation with Karma." It all amounts to the same thing, an arrangement of attitude in conformity with circumstances.

It is very difficult to explain unless one has been in the same or similar circumstances oneself, where one watches something happening and knows there is nothing one can do about it, and one is more or less beyond feeling *anything*. I know that feeling so well, as such events have also happened several times in my personal life. There is a "certain uncertainty" or an "uncertain certainty"—I'm not sure which, combined with an almost detached interest just to see what will happen next, virtually as if it were happening to someone else instead of oneself. It is a sort of compulsory living for its own sake without any sense of being in control of anything, and yet, as my Teacher told me, "at the back of everything there was the strangest conviction that I'd be O.K."

Now, I am well aware that the concepts of *"Fate"* and *"Free Will"* have created quite a lot of controversy in this world, with beliefs varying from those in which all actions are considered predestined (here the concept of *Free Will* is thought to be purely an illusion), to those who claim total *Free Will* for man as a self-conscious living creature. It is also very clear that this controversy will rage unto eternity, and that my statements in this regard will certainly not be anywhere near conclusive for a great many people following the teachings of mainstream religions maintaining everything is known to God before it happens, and that Divine Knowledge knows no limit.

However, some of the more esoterically minded have argued that if man is truly free to do certain things, it is impossible that God should be aware of such actions in advance of their happening. They argue that while Divinity knows the order of an individual's life, i.e. the different possibilities open to that individual, the Divine One does not know how that individual will choose in particular circumstances, since everybody has the power to choose between the possibilities open to them. The famous/infamous Gersonides claimed this latter stance not only to be the most rational one, but to be in accord with the words of Sacred Writ which he then set out to prove.[23] You can imagine that this radical view caused many Rabbis to go rabid, and to forbid their students to read the works of the great Gersonides.

Yet, plain common sense informs us that concepts like "reward and punishment" and "Karma" will be nonsensical if all actions are predestined. Why should anybody be punished or rewarded for doing any action (even in the case of murder, rape, and every nasty action you can think of), when that individual is only doing what he/she was designed, destined, in fact even coerced to do anyway? Without the ability of free choice, punishment or reward would not only be unfair, but rather malicious on the part of a supposedly omniscient Creator. This Creator is claimed to have created beings who are able to recognise themselves, their environment, as well as that selfsame Creator in a fully conscious manner. They are then constrained into positions of acting out various scenarios which might hurt or benefit them, but that this is of no concern to a Supreme Creator whose only aim is that "the Divine Will be done." In this case, it is like the Divine One is saying: "My 'game' is to give you the freedom to think, to reason for yourself, but I will not allow you to act freely on your thoughts. All your actions will be as I determine. I will create a multitude of possibilities, but will allow you only to act on the choice that you are fated to make, and in all this you will be punished and rewarded on that act, which will appear to you to have been of your choice, but which was actually determined by me." As far as I am concerned, there would be no need to create "multitudes of possibilities" if you weree destined, even compelled, to act out only one of them.

It seems to me the concept of "predestination" requires a lot of explanation and argument, whereas *"Free Will"* appears to be purely a natural process of decision making as living creatures become aware of self, environment and the possible choices of interaction within that environment. The more aware the individual, the greater the recognition of possibilities within the myriad of choices of interaction. Here it is as if the Divine One is saying: "Since you are part of Me, I created you in the love and compassion I have for myself. My 'game' will be to give you the freedom to think and reason for yourself, and I will allow you to act freely on that awareness within the manifested realm of experience. I will not only allow you to comprehend your awareness, but to expand it, in order for you to recognise more and more choices within the myriads of possibilities. I will allow you to comprehend both the actions which would benefit you, as well as those that would be inimical. Understand this however, I created all possibilities, and in certain circumstances what appears to be benevolent may be malevolent; in others what appears malevolent may be benevolent.

You might not understand this at your current level of awareness, but, since I also granted you *Free Will* in the awakening of your consciousness, you will eventually be able to expand your awareness to comprehend all of this and more.....if you so desire. I create the possibilities, you make the choices, but know that you will be affected by your choices for good or ill.

I love you and will not punish or reward you, since your *free will* allows you to reward or punish yourself through your actions. I cannot stop you from being rewarded and punished by your exploits, without seriously obstructing the whole process of consciousness awakening to itself. So be warned! You will not be punished for your mistaken choices, but *by* them, and likewise you will reap reward from beneficial choices."

Now, which would you choose as the more comfortable, "Predestination" or "Free Will"? Either choice has its comfort zone and dangers. Maybe it is easier to allow a Divine Being to plan for you, and then to act according to His/Her/Its whims, whether these may benefit you in any way or not. On the other hand, it is difficult to decide for yourself as to where you want to steer your life, but somehow it gives you a casting vote over your destiny, and it is this possibility—though fraught with peril and uncertainty—that appears so attractive to some of those regulators of consciousness who call themselves "Kabbalists" and even "Magicians."

. ...Now when the light of the sun passes through them, the rays that strike the walls of the palace are variegated, with many colours, each different from the other, and none like the other... ... .

Chapter 3
THE TRIPLE SOUL & SHADOW BODIES

A. Introduction

The material presented here is purely introductory. The subject comprises many angles of approach, but I intend focussing for now on what I understand to be a model which you can apply practically with great success. Although it will be apparent that we could broaden this discussion, I am going to concentrate exclusively on what appears to me to be directly relevant to the basic aim of this discussion, which is to understand the "Soul in Man" in a functional manner from Kabbalistic perspectives. Again we need to remember that *Kabbalah* is a vast tradition, and that there is an incredible amount of material which can be called interesting. While we may want to study all of this intriguing knowledge, it would take more than this lifetime to do so. However, there are the pressing needs of living in this world which we must consider, not only as individuals in terms of our individual needs, but also in society where we are seeking to serve in order to make our world a better place.

It is for this reason that I have encouraged students to cut their spiritual activities to what can be termed "essentials." There is really no choice as far as this is concerned, because one cannot hope to achieve anything of relevance if attention is diverted into too many directions. Again, the problem with *Kabbalah*, as well as the whole of the Western Mystery Tradition for that matter, is that its doctrines cover a vast domain. These will keep your attention moving along all sorts of lines, but eventually you must move away from what is interesting to what is relevant in your life at any moment in time.

Looking in general at students interested in the domain of the "esoteric," one finds that they flounder an awful amount, not being actively concerned with the "Now," but more involved with what *was* and what *could be.* To sit for hours, days and years wondering "what should I do?" or "What should I be actively involved in?" is definitely the wrong approach. The fact of the matter is that we want to be better than we are at present. We are involved with *Kabbalah* and magic because we want to grow, have more power, more ability, and to function better as human beings on physical, mental, emotional and spiritual levels. We want to "realise" God, and affect the world around us for the better. All of us have very noble intentions, and we look at all the wonderful techniques, all being able to satisfy our requirements, provided they are suitable to the individual using them.

Eventually you bump against your own self and realise that the time has finally arrived when choices must be made, that you must get down to brass tacks or else flounder eternally as you try every single method in the book—of which there are in any case far too many. You have to find what is suitable and relevant to yourself and your needs. This is why many of the traditional rites and sacred ceremonies have to be rewritten, in order to make them more relevant and more effective in terms of getting people personally more actively involved in the procedures. That means everybody should apply their energies and actively participate, rather than listen to a barrage of words in which their minds wander aimlessly. Of course, words are fine to a certain degree only, if an inner response is invoked within your own being through the process of intense meditation on the meanings and intentions of the words. You have to literally "feel" meanings rather than think them.

Now I wish to raise the question of whether at this stage in your spiritual quest you should *apply* your knowledge, or whether you should *study* and investigate matters. "Studying" and "practice" are again the two opposing "Pillars" on the Tree of Life, being respectively the "receptive" and "applicative" sides of life experience. Both are required in the process of the real awakening of truth in our lives, but are you really ready enough to apply knowledge effectively at this juncture of your spiritual development? Even if practical activity is urgently required, will

The Triple Soul & Shadow Bodies / 141

your actions be really effective? I personally think that at this stage you should rather look at the "Shadow" side of your own nature, the "Laws" pertaining thereto, and then to attempt sorting and balancing your own nature.

Let us pursue this point a little in order to unravel the possibilities of you understanding and sorting your own "Shadow," hopefully aided by the information I am offering here. I do not only wish to discuss the three basic "Selves" comprising your being, but would also like to share some details pertaining to the "Shadow" side of your nature, body, and of life. This I believe will help you find the relevant activities in your quest for real power and true illumination.

Perusing the many diverse tomes dealing with the human soul from Kabbalistic viewpoints, one is struck by the fact that despite so much being written about the subject, very little is written about how the different "aspects" of the human soul actually interrelate. Investigating the various books, the profusion of diverse terms used can cause great confusion, which is why I have attempted to sift through the mass of material, in order to construct this chapter which will hopefully bring a clear understanding of both oneself and ones world, and also *facilitate* the practical application of this knowledge.

Viewed from Kabbalistic perspectives, the "Soul" is an extremely complex subject, comprising several levels and interrelationships, thus we would have to study the topic most carefully in order to understand the soul and its nature as seen through the eyes of Kabbalists.[1] Tradition has it that the human soul comprises three levels, i.e. the *Nefesh* (Instinctual Self), *Ru'ach* (Awake Self), and the *Neshamah* (Divine Self). The latter divides into two further aspects called the *Chiyah* (Living Essence) and *Yechidah* (Singularity or Uniqueness). There are further aspects within each "soul level," e.g. the *Nefesh* comprises a "lower bestial" (*Nefesh Behamit*) level and a "higher divine" (*Nefesh Elohit*) aspect.

For our purposes here, we will focus on the three basic levels of the "Soul." I will also address the power of the soul; the bodies of the soul (each aspect of the soul having, as it were, a separate *Tzelem* or shadow body); the different abilities of the soul; how they interrelate with each other, and what can be done with this information.

B. The Three Selves

1. THE *NEFESH*

Let us start with "Personal Consciousness," and look at its different degrees of expression in manifestation, i.e. the three aspects of the soul, or the three "Selves" of man. The grossest level of the three is the *Nefesh*, which we can rightly claim is the subconscious, or unconscious as modern psychology would have it. Through personal experience, many have come to know this aspect as an entirely separate consciousness, or "entity," from the conscious mind. I personally do not like the term "unconscious," since the *Nefesh* is certainly conscious, but it is not conscious that it is conscious. The animal "knows," but does not know that it knows. The same with the "Animal Self" (*Nefesh*) in us. It is an "Instinctual Self," but not the "Intuitive Self." Intuition is on a much more elevated level than instinct. The *Nefesh* is called the "animal–vegetable–mineral–soul." Everything, whatever and wherever in existence, whether it be a mineral, plant or animal, has a soul vital to its existence, and this is the "Instinctual Self."

The *Nefesh* is totally enmeshed with the physical body and is, in fact, responsible for keeping the engine of the body functioning in this world. If the "Instinctual Self" gets a phobia, which it can and frequently does, it can cause incredible harm to the physical body. It has a primitive, deductive form of reasoning, in fact, "logical" does not come into its frame of reference, since it behaves instinctively through the five senses. It creates a pattern inside itself, and then behaves in accordance with that pattern. In this regard the statement "caught in a destructive rut" can be quite apt. If your *Nefesh* is convinced that there is no longer a reason to live, it will attempt to destroy the body, even though you, the "Reasoning Self," might have no thoughts on suicide at all. The "Instinctual Self" will attempt to destroy you, and it will do so in a way peculiar to itself.

As said, the *Nefesh* acts through the five senses: hearing, smelling, seeing, tasting and feeling, and via these it gains impressions and "jumps to conclusions." It reacts, rather than responds, to outside stimuli, since it is in close harmony with the body and the physical world. Thus, if it has a phobia or something of that ilk, the *Nefesh* can give you things like psychosomatic illnesses as it commences its journey along the path of self destruction. I know of cases where the "Instinctual Self" caused serious illness requiring surgery, and when this was done it simply manifested another condition. Medical treatment did not solve the basic problem of the "Instinctual Self" having decided to destroy the entire organism. Only an attempt to actually confront the *Nefesh*, to befriend and support it, finally redeemed the situation. Thus the "Instinctual Self" has to be faced and convinced that life is worth living. It has immense power, and if you are not on friendly terms with it, you stand very little chance of success in your personal life and relationships. You might cope, but that is not entirely the same as being successful as a *complete* being.

The *Nefesh* is extremely important. It has been called the animal, vegetable and mineral soul, because all physical manifestation, be it mineral, vegetable or animal, has such an instinctual self, which is often called "bestial" (*Nefesh Behamit*). Kabbalists termed it the "vital principle" in man, and understood the *Nefesh* to be the first aspect given to a human, since it is the raw energy, which is not only vital in the maintenance of the body, but also in terms of survival and sexuality. We must not forget that life is a matter of balance. If balance is disturbed, something will happen to cause rectification or restitution.

The following saga will illustrate this point. In fact it does not only show the attempt of life to maintain balance, but it also indicates the action of the "Instinctual Soul" in plants. It started with Kudu, an antelope found in Southern Africa, dying of hunger in a local game park, and this despite their stomachs being filled with their natural fodder. This intriguing situation kindled the curiosity of a professor at a local university to determine the reasons for this strange occurrence. The outcome was so remarkable that it is worth relating here, in order to show how the "Instinctual Self" functions.

On analysing the bodies of the dead Kudu, it was found that the bacteria which normally digests the food for ruminants, were destroyed in the intestines of these buck. Thus they were unable to digest their food and hence died of hunger. It was found that extremely high levels of tannin in the food were responsible for the destruction of the vital bacteria. All plants have tannin, but this professor figured that perhaps the unnaturally high tannin level had something to do with these antelope overgrazing their natural habitat, and he set out to prove this idea.

It turned out that due to a serious local drought, there were too many Kudu and far too few trees to feed these animals. Normally these animals would feed on the leaves of local thorn trees. A tree would allow the animal to eat its leaves to a certain degree only. When the buck over-grazes, the plant will turn on its defences by increasing the tannin levels in its leaves. This would turn the leaves bitter, thus stopping the Kudu from eating more of that specific tree. In this situation the animal would normally move on to another tree, however, in the prevailing severe drought conditions, with too many buck and too few sustaining plants, the Kudu continued grazing the trees despite the high tannin levels, and so were killed by having their intestinal bacteria destroyed.

The remarkable part of this saga happened during the testing of trees. Measuring equipment was attached to a thorn tree, and the latter was "afflicted" by having leaves and branches pulled of it in order to test the tannin increase. As the tree was attacked, it started its usual defence, gradually increasing the tannin levels to a very high degree. On attaching the measuring equipment to adjacent trees of the same species, it was found that the tannin levels were at the same peak level as those of the "punished" plant. The trees had somehow communicated, maybe via scent. Thus there is a soul operating in plants as well, and this soul is again the *Nefesh*, a "Vital Self," which links all life. It is an "Instinctual Soul" whose existence is solely to keep the normal, instinctual survival functions going, i.e. procreation (the continuance of the species), as well as all the involuntary actions of the body like the heart beat and reflexes.

It is said that you, the "Awake Self" or *Ru'ach*, have no direct part in the *Nefesh*, no direct connection with it, yet you are able to control it if you manage to establish a good relationship with it. If not, its control over you could result in all sorts of psychological problems like schizophrenia, manic depressiveness, or what is now termed "bi-polar disorders." It has been indicated that the majority of humans over the age of three years, have a poor relationship with their "Instinctual Selves." This appears to be true when you study people, and discover that very few of them are friendly with, or even like, their own "Vital Selves."

The whole crisis of war for example, as well as the threats of hostilities globally, are signs of very bad relationships with the "Instinctual Self." The issue seems to revolve around egos, greed and emotions of "Instinctual Selves" out of control. In fact, observing the behaviour of certain world leaders clearly indicates what can transpire when the destructive power of a single *Nefesh* is afforded free reign, and it certainly shows how important the "Instinctual Self" is in the scheme of things.

The other Selves, i.e. the *Ru'ach* (Conscious Self) and the *Neshamah* (Divine Spirit), are only bestowed on the individual when the *Nefesh* is developed and purified. This needs reiteration. A person really becomes only in truth a "Self," when the "Instinctual Soul" has been developed and purified, because the *Ru'ach* is the "Self," and *Neshamah* is the Super-conscious, the "Higher Spirit." These loftier expressions of the "Self" are, as it were, higher "unfoldments" of consciousness, and therefore latently present in the *Nefesh*.

I know many will say that all people alive, who are conscious that they are conscious, are "Awake Selves," but this is not entirely the case. They are only partly manifested "Reasoning Selves." Their *Ru'ach* is not fully manifested, since most people live instinctual lives, with but a small smattering of the "Conscious Self" operating within their materially focussed existence. Most people are governed by their instincts, and thus it is not really true that they are at a level of being the *Ru'ach*, which is, as said, truly there when the "Instinctual Self" has evolved to such a degree that its higher aspect (*Nefesh Elohit*) is being expressed.

Of course the two, the *Nefesh* (instinctual self) and the *Ru'ach* (conscious self), are actually residing together inside the physical body. While some claim the *Neshamah* (Divine Self) is focussed in the head, it is generally believed to exist and function beyond the body. What is certain is that you and your *Nefesh* live in one body. Thus there are two of you in one body, and these are not seen as two definite, separate "selves."

When I was told this, it was at first extremely difficult for me to accept. Regarding the *Nefesh* I insisted that "It is my subconscious mind. It is nothing separate from me. I must take responsibility for my own subconscious, since it is me." I soon changed my tune when I discovered just how separate these different aspects really are in their behaviour. The *Nefesh* remembers but does not reason very well. The *Ru'ach* reasons but cannot remember. Why can it not remember? Because it is always in the "*Now.*" As an "Awake Self," you always live in the *Present*, while your subconscious, the "Instinctual Self," stores things. When you want to remember something, the instruction is given to your *Nefesh* who then retrieves it for you from the memory "where–house."

This process can be instantaneous, but sometimes the "Instinctual Self" refuses to present you forthwith with the required data. Left stranded, you think "Why can't I remember? It is on the tip of my tongue," and you grapple inside yourself in your attempt to remember, but *you* simply cannot retrieve the illusive memory. You need the *Nefesh*, the "guardian" of the "memory store–bank," to give it to you. So you surrender, and reluctantly concede "It will come to me later." You turn your attention elsewhere, and continue with your daily chores. Suddenly, while occupied with something completely different, the *Nefesh* throws the required memory at you, and you exclaim "I've just remembered!"

This happens to every person alive, leading often to very embarrassing situations. We need to realise that the "Instinctual Self" often needs time in searching the memory for the required information, and that it does not necessarily function in a logical manner. When it sifts through the "memory bank," it could latch on to anything which its deductive reasoning assumes is somehow related, thus it sometimes offers you wrong information. When I first attempted to befriend my *Nefesh*, it used to do this very often. This would annoy me, which would give stimulus to the "Instinctual Self" to get angry in return, resulting in it becoming uncooperative, until I was able to re-established peace between us.

Later I understood that the *Nefesh* must be given time, until a friendly behaviour pattern is established between us. The moment this happens, it will act in accordance with that new pattern. I have also learned that the more clues I give it, the quicker it finds what I am looking for. This has eventually turned into a fun game, and a joy to actually work with my "Instinctual Self." However, one has to be extremely patient because, as said, the *Nefesh* does not work logically. It is not illogical, it just does not work logically, and does not reason the way we "Reasoning Selves" do.

The *Nefesh* of both animals and humans can sometimes behave most strangely, and we should not always project our human or *Ru'ach* responses onto it. There are times when we see incidents in nature which appear totally incongruous with instinctual behaviour, and human onlookers are inclined to project their human responses onto the event, claiming personal reactions to be the same as the motives for that odd behaviour in the realm of the *Nefesh*. However, it is not always possible to use logic to explain what happens within the domain of the "Instinctual Self." There are within the *Nefesh* many activities which we do not understand, and anything can happen to trigger an alteration in its approach to events and life.

2. THE *RU'ACH* AND *NESHAMAH*

As said, the *Nefesh* and the *Ru'ach* reside conjointly in the physical body, each performing a unique and special task necessary for the proper functioning of life in terms of behaving and thinking as a human. However, the "mental" capabilities of the two selves are very different, since, as said, the "instinctual self" can remember, and has a deductive reasoning similar to all the animals on this planet, whereas the "conscious self" cannot remember a single thought after it has been released from the attention in the "*Now*, and thus has to rely on the *Nefesh* to retrieve required memories. If you have a very good relationship with your *Nefesh*, your memory ability becomes truly remarkable. One can literally turn into a "walking encyclopaedia," so to speak. Those who suffer from a very bad memory, also have a poor relationship with their own "Instinctual Selves." The *Nefesh* is not necessarily "out of control" in such instances. It simply means the relationship between their "Instinctual Soul" and "Awake Self" is not that good.

The two major abilities of the "Conscious Self" are *reasoning* —which is inductive, thus giving man an advantage over animals), and *will*—which it can use hypnotically, and is in fact stronger than the will of the *Nefesh*. In this case it is definitely a question of "brain over brawn." Certain animals, e.g. dolphins, might possibly be on a similar level of individuation as ourselves. In fact, these very special animals seem to have highly developed reasoning skills. Generally it would seem the reasoning of most of our fellow animal creatures on this planet is deductive rather than inductive.

So, the *Ru'ach* has reasoning and will, the *Nefesh* has the rest, i.e. all the emotions and all the power of survival—the brawn. I am reminded of a cartoon strip of a little dwarf bringing home his pet. The dwarf has this determined stance on his countenance, and he drags a pet along by a rope attached to a ring which passes through the nose of the animal. While truly huge in physical stature, the pet is a completely docile creature following his "master" in a totally subdued manner. It would take only one small sideways sweep of its head to send the dwarf flying, but it does not do so. Why not? After all, it has so much power and so much ability. The fact of the matter is the little dwarf has *will*, reasoning and determination, abilities the pet does not share. It has survival instinct and a lot of power, but "it does not know that it knows." The same applies to the *Nefesh*, the "Instinctual Self" inside all of us.

The *Nefesh* responds to hypnosis, whereas the "Conscious Self" does not. The "Instinctual Self" is not logical in its reasoning, the conscious naturally is. I am not saying that the logical mind is necessarily right, since this is certainly not always the case, and the "non-logical" Lower Self is often right in its instinctual behaviour. Two of my friends, a married couple, illustrated this very well when they arranged furniture in a room. The husband is sheer "mind," while his wife lives by her feelings. He calculated the light in the premises, combined this information with the shape of the room, and placed the furniture according to this data. However, though it seemed right "logically," the setup appeared all wrong. His wife, on entering the room, casts a single glance at the entire conglomeration, and commence pushing the furniture around in a helter skelter manner, creating a shambles. Eventually she steps back and the room is perfectly arranged. On querying how she managed it, she responded that she did what "felt right." In other words, she allowed the *Nefesh* to do the job.

In this regard, when one uses a method of divination, i.e. the *Tarot*, etc., it is not really the "Logical Self" but rather the "Instinctual Self" which is doing the "reading." However, one should not presume that the *Nefesh* does not make mistakes. It certainly does, and many to boot, but it is right most of the time, whereas when one attempts to read logically, one is more often than not proven wrong. At least with the cooperation of the "Instinctual Self," one is *sometimes* right.

In summary then, we have noted that the second aspect of the "Soul," the *Ru'ach*, is the conscious "Reasoning Self. One might call it the "Middle Self," if one sees the *Nefesh* as a "Lower Self." As said, the *Nefesh* remembers but does not have a very effective reasoning, yet it has all the emotions and controls all the involuntary functions of the physical body. On the other hand, the *Ru'ach* has no memory because it lives entirely in the present, in the *Now*. Besides reasoning ability, it has *will*, and with this it has more power than the brute force of the *Nefesh*.

The third aspect of the human soul, the *Neshamah* (the Divine Self), is the oldest and most developed part of the three Selves, and can in truth be called the "Parent Soul." This is what some call the "super-conscious." Its consciousness is truly cosmic, in the sense that it realises the past, present and the possible future in the same instant. It is said that this is due to what is being formed and planned in the present. This is understood in *Kabbalah* to be *Ehyeh Asher Ehyeh*, the "I am that I am," "the All in All" and "All with All."

Now, years ago, when I had just commenced my journey within this Tradition, my first *Kabbalah* teacher maintained that the "spiritual status" of each individual could be recognised by where his or her consciousness was focussed within the three levels of the soul, e.g. within the *Nefesh* (Instinctual Self), *Ru'ach* (Awake, Conscious Self) or *Neshamah* (Higher Spiritual Self). He maintained that the spiritual evolution of each individual pertains to the "awakening of Self to itself," in fact, this is the entire purpose of creation. For example, we might say that in the mineral "God sleeps," in the vegetable "God stirs," in the animal "God dreams," in man "God is waking" and in God the Eternal Spirit is fully awake. Hence the understanding that life is a process of "consciousness awakening to Itself" or "Knowing that I know." Here the "Knower," the "Knowledge" and the "Knowing" are One.

My teacher said that the different stages of "soul unfoldment" in an individual can be recognised in the following manner:

1. A person whose consciousness is still firmly focussed in the *Nefesh*, is mainly concerned with personal needs, and sees those of others only in terms of his or her own needs. The consciousness of such an individual is said to be focussed in *Yesod* (Foundation) on the Tree of Life, and his

or her life would revolve mainly around "self-preservation" and "self-perpetuation." On the lowest levels this means "eating" and "mating," and the greatest fear would be of dying and death.

2. A *Ru'ach* person, on the other hand, is the exact opposite of the previously mentioned individual. In this case the person is mainly concerned with the needs of others, and sees his or her personal requirements in terms of those of others. Such an individual is more altruistic, and seeks to make the world a better place for all. The motto here is "I seek to serve," and it is said the consciousness of this individual is focussed in *Tiferet* (Beauty) on the Tree of Life. Perhaps we might say that the greatest fear in this case would be "living death," which Henry Miller reminds us is an "unlived life."[2]

3. The level of *Neshamah* consciousness steers away from "needs" altogether. In this case, the awakening "Self" becomes aware of the "meaning of being." Here the consciousness of the individual is said to be focussed in *Keter* (Crown) on the Tree of Life.

In the lower, *Nefesh*, stages of development the river of life appears to be entirely chaotic and beyond ones personal control. On the other hand, in the *Ru'ach* degree an individual recognises patterns within the life stream, and attempts to understand these. In the higher, *Neshamah*, consciousness it is clear that all life and its patterns are expressions of the Self, and that these are emanated entirely in harmony with the "meaning of being." Again, in this case the "Experiencer" and the "Experience" are One, the centre and circumference perceived to be part of the self-sameness of one great "I am." Such an individual is truly "Present." Here there is no more fear, and no longer any need to hang on to the "scrapbook." One no longer lives by the rule "I have to be me"! Besides, in the "Eternal Now" the concept of "forever" no longer enslaves us.

It has been said that the three "Selves" are focussed, as it were, in specific organs of the human anatomy. The *Neshamah* is situated in the *Moach* (מח – Brain), the *Ru'ach* is focussed in the *Lev* (לב – Heart), and the seat of the *Nefesh* is said to be the *Kaved* (כבד – Liver).[3] The initials of these three words conjointly spell the word *Melech* (מלך – King). Those who master the Kingdom of their own beings through unification of body, mind, soul and spirit, can be truly called "Kings."

Today we understand that what the ancients referred to as "liver," is the area around the solar plexus which is in fact the "brain" of the *Nefesh*. In this zone one experiences all sorts of anxieties, fears, etc., the traditional "butterflies" or "Knot in the stomach" as some would say. The correct procedure would be for the Higher Spirit to govern the "heart"—the "mind" of the *Ru'ach* (the Awake Self), and especially the "liver" (solar plexus)—in turn the "brain" of the *Nefesh* (the Instinctual Self). The insightful *Neshamah* (Higher Self) should always be the "King" in the "Kingdom" of ones life.

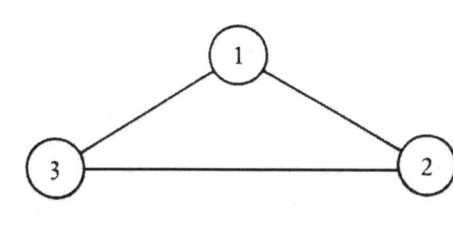

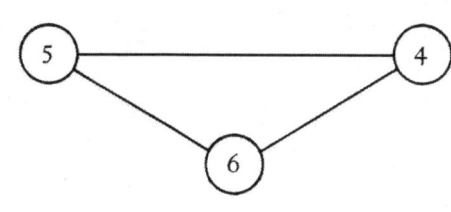

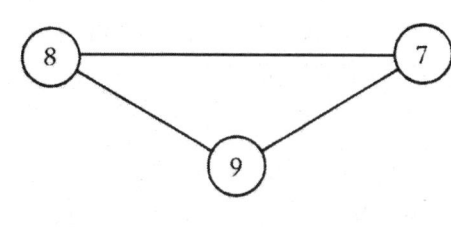

Perusing the *Etz Chayim*, we note each one of the three aspects of the Soul comprises three *Sefirot*. Basically there are three "triads" on the Tree of Life. The upper one comprises *Keter*, *Chochmah* and *Binah*; the middle *Gevurah*, *Chesed* and *Tiferet*; and the lower *Netzach*, *Hod* and *Yesod*. *Malchut*, the last *Sefirah* on the Tree is on its own, and balanced within itself, as it were, since it comprises the "Four Elements" of Air, Fire, Water and Earth in one.

Now, we noted the *Nefesh* comprises the lower triad of *Yesod* (Foundation) representing the sexual organ, or procreation, which is traditionally associated with the ego; *Hod* (Glory) representing the mind or thinking; and *Netzach* (Victory) representing emotions or feelings.

Reasoning is considered to be on a higher level than thinking. In this higher mode those amazing "*AHA*'s" happen, the moments of true realisation, which are somewhat like lights turning on in ones head, so to speak. Thinking does not necessarily "turn on the light," but in the higher reasoning mode "lights turn on" all the time.

The mentioned lower three *Sefirot* combined with that of *Malchut* (the Kingdom), the latter representing the *Guf* (the "phantom" or physical body), are in a very potent three dimensional relationship with each other. If one looks at the pattern they present on the *Etz Chayim*, it gives a much greater understanding of how they respectively impact on one another.

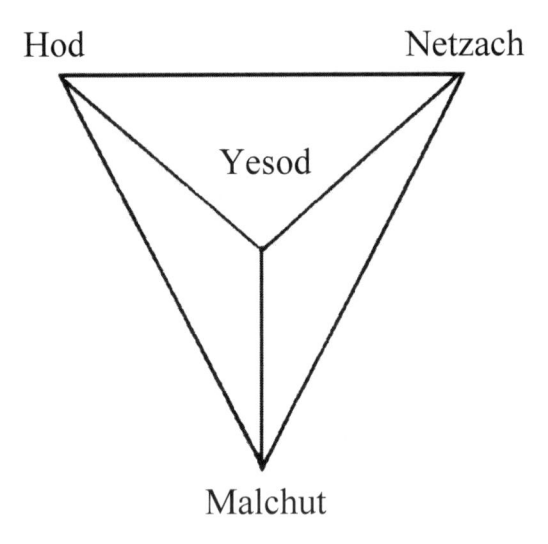

Hod Netzach
Yesod
Malchut

As you can see, the four *Sefirot* are interconnected, thus influencing each other continuously. *Malchut* is influencing *Hod* and *Netzach*. On the other hand *Hod* is equally influencing *Malchut* and *Netzach*, whilst *Netzach* in turn impacts on *Malchut* and *Hod*. This is literally true. What happens to you physically (*Malchut*) has an influence on both the way you think (*Hod*) and feel (*Netzach*), and the way you think can influence your body and your feelings. On the other hand your emotions also affect the way you think and the way your body reacts.

This situation does not only define conditions like psychosomatic illnesses, but determines our normal, daily behaviour in this world. *Malchut, Hod* and *Netzach* are in a reciprocal relationship with each other. What is more all three of these *Sefirot* contribute to *Yesod* (Foundation) in the centre, the ego or personality, which is as said the focus of the *Nefesh*. This means that your personality is made up of what *you* think and feel, what impacts on your body in your physical environment. The combination of all these aspects, as focussed in your inner being, comprises your reality and personality.

What has been said thus far only shows the connection of the *Nefesh* to the *Etz Chayim*. We might look a bit closer at how the *Ru'ach* is associated with the Tree of Life. The "Conscious Self" comprises *Tiferet* (Beauty or perfect balance); *Gevurah* (Severity or Strict Judgment), which one might call the "Principle of Taking"; and *Chesed* (Mercy or Loving-kindness), which might be termed the "Principle of Giving." This is also understandable when one realises that only when you are in truth a perfectly balanced Self, a *Ru'ach* firmly focussed in *Tiferet*, can you truly give and take, or act in harmony with the needs of life, without being affected by it. This makes perfect sense if we compare it to a scale, the "arms" of which might move up and down while the centre always remains still and unaffected.

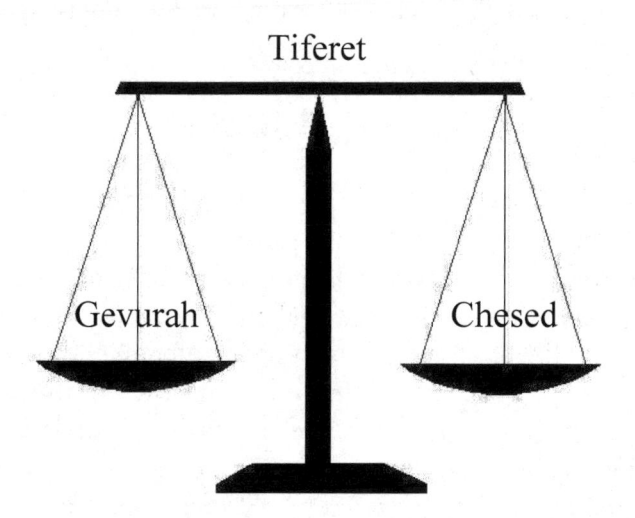

Tiferet

Gevurah　　　Chesed

If you are *Tiferet*, that is the *Ru'ach* or a balanced "Real Self," you are unaffected by the movements of the two arms of *Gevurah* and *Chesed*, and when you have achieved this level of awakening, you are said to be in a state of *Hishtavut* (equanimity), where you are no longer affected by insult or flattery. It is only when you are at this level of awareness, when you are in truth a *Ru'ach*, that you can truly give and take in life, without expecting recompense in your mercy or revenge in your severity. You behave according to the requirements of life, without expecting gratitude for your actions, since this expectation belongs to the ego or the Lower Self, and therefore has no value when it comes to conscious service in life.

Of course, it is important to know that all aspects of the Soul are *One* in truth, in the same manner as all of us are *One* in Spirit. Looking at Creation, we may see the two opposing poles of *Essence* and *Substance*, *Higher Self* and *Lower Self*, seemingly so far apart that they appear impossible to be united in a third principle. Again, it is easy to say that between *Essence* and *Substance* is *Nature*, and between *Higher Self* and *Lower Self* is the *Middle Self*, and then to see the separateness of each aspect of this ternary. However, real understanding comes when the three aspects of the ternary are part of a *Oneness*, a fourth quality, which offers us the realisation that there is no break between the aspects. *Essence/Nature/Entity* are *One. Higher Self/Middle Self/Lower Self* are *One*, a *Self-sameness*. This is the realisation of the *Tetrad* or *Ternary*, in which three can be seen but with an uninterrupted flow between them.

C. Shadow Bodies

From what has been said thus far, you understand that there are basically three aspects, or levels of Consciousness, to the Soul in Kabbalistic thinking, but there is more to this saga of the soul. It is claimed that each part has a body called a *Tzelem*, a word meaning "image" or "likeness" which is used in reference to a subtle or "shadow body." The use of the term "shadow" in this instance refers to something which is subtle and virtually imperceptible to all but the most sensitive individuals, whereas the same word is used in another instance in reference to something "dark," i.e. the "shadow" side of ones nature.

Each aspect of the human soul has a "shadow body." These get more subtle and refined as we move up the scale of the evolution of spirit. Thus the *Tzelem* of the *Ru'ach* is more refined than that of the *Nefesh* (the densest of the three), and the shadow body of the *Neshamah* is much more rarified than that of the *Ru'ach*. Since the *Nefesh* and the *Ru'ach* are closely connected with the physical body, their subtle bodies interpenetrate the physical body. In fact, the shadow body of the *Nefesh* is closely enmeshed with even the smallest cells of the body, whereas that of the *Ru'ach* is either centred in the brain, as some would have it, or according to others focussed in the heart. Since the *Nefesh* and *Ru'ach* are respectively connected to *Yesod* (Foundation) and *Tiferet* (Beauty) on the *Etz Chayim*, and these in turn are respectively associated with the Moon and the Sun, this relates with the early Greek teaching that humans have two subtle bodies called a lunar and a solar body.

Looking at the three subtle bodies, we notice that the *Tzelem* of the *Nefesh* tends to be adhesive, literally sticking to anything it encounters. In fact, it attaches itself to any object by linking with it through any or all of the five senses. It tends to create a kind of thread of its own substance, which remains attached to the object contacted. In other words, we become attached to millions of objects through a multitude of these sticky cords or bonds, which, though they are invisible, can be tangible. These strands can be charged with energy or vital force, to the point where they can be felt with the hands. In fact, via these invisible threads energy is transferred from one object to another. They also store vital force, and when they are strongly charged with this force, they can be used like a hand. This pertains to the phenomenon called "telekinesis," which is the moving of an object without the use of the physical hand.

These subtle bonds can be strengthened through constant attention, will deteriorate as the object fades from the mind, and can be severed through a conscious action on the part of the person practising such a severance. There is however a very important point to realise here, which is that everything, animate and inanimate, be they crystals, plants or animals, including thoughts as well as printed words, have such a *Tzelem*, which stays for a long time after the physical death of the object it was originally connected to. This also applies to thoughts and feelings. These are just as actual as any physical object. In fact, thoughts create forms, and related thoughts will form into clusters of subtle bodies.

Since these subtle threads are ideal energy conductors, and clustered thought forms can be carried on the current flowing through them, one of the most frequent uses of the *Tzelem* of the *Nefesh*, is to send a message along its bonds to somebody well connected. This is of course related to "telepathy." Yet the average person cannot really practice this at will. This is because "will" belongs to the Middle Self, the *Ru'ach*, as said, whereas it is the Lower Self, the *Nefesh* with its peculiar shadow body, who has to direct the thought forms created by and released from the Conscious Self, the *Ru'ach*. In fact, we need the help of the *Nefesh* in order to impart telepathic messages, and then simply wait and relax while it gets on with the job until it feeds the message into the Conscious Self, into the central conscious awareness, of the recipient. Experiencing this in the Now is actually the same as the process of remembering anything.

The other Selves of man also have a *Tzelem* each, but their subtle bodies are less solid than that of the *Nefesh*. Besides, the *Tzelem* of the *Ru'ach* is not adhesive, and there are no threads connecting it to objects. It is a conductor of a different force to that of the *Nefesh*. Its power is related to thinking and will, and brain waves are connected here. The *Tzelem* of the *Neshamah* (the Higher Self or Super-conscious Spirit), exists beyond the physical body as a "structure of light," which some psychics and other seers can actually see as strongly lit-up with "white light" when it is charged with a very high frequency of vital force.

In summary we realise that there are three aspects to the soul in man, each having a "shadow" or subtle body respectively having three different degrees of vital force. For every human being there are thus three units of ability. Firstly there is the consciousness working in a given situation; secondly, the power used; and thirdly, a subtle substance through which the power flows and acts. We noted each of the three selves in man has its own particular ability to express its power with a specific charge of vital force. Their related charges or frequencies can be used by the three selves for a number of purposes, and we should briefly look at these charges. For example, vital force of a low frequency can flow along the threads created by the *Tzelem* of the Instinctual Self. It is known that even chemical substances can move along these bonds from one person to another, and since it acts magnetically, the *Tzelem* of the *Nefesh* can accumulate and store such substances, vital force and thought forms. Practitioners applying such knowledge in a practical manner, can direct and store vital force in wood, permeable substances, and inside any object for that matter. It is further known that a powerful burst or emanation of this vital force from ones physical body, can cause sleep, trance states, temporary paralysis, or even catatonic states.

Of course, this force is not limited to physical objects and thought forms only, but is diffused as Universal Life Force, throughout the whole universe, and is called *Avir*. In *Kabbalah* there are two terms referring to "Divine Force." The first, *Avir*, as we noted, is used in reference to "Universal Life-Force," i.e. cosmic energy moving freely throughout existence. The second term, *Ruchaniyut*, pertains to the same power localized inside all material existence. All of us have this "Spiritual Power" within our beings, and so have trees, stones, the sun, moon and the stars. We should note that in *Kabbalah Avir* also refers to the atmosphere we breath, and there is a good reason for using the same term for both the Universal Life-Force and the atmosphere we breathe. Breath is one of the most important tools in the field of *Practical Kabbalah*, and therefore a lot of attention should be given to its usage, and the cultivation of strong, healthy breathing abilities. This subject has been addressed extensively by Franz Bardon, the Austrian Magus, in his *"Initiation into Hermetics,*[4] as well as in the "Huna" literature of Max Freedom Long.[5]

D. The Mantle of Righteousness

Regarding "Shadow Bodies" there is a unique literature in Kabbalah dealing with what is termed a *"Malbush,"* a special spiritual "garment." These writings are amongst the most interesting which have survived in the collection of Merkavistic documents. A fair amount of this literature weathered the travails of time, and some has been made available in English, e.g. in the translations of *Shi'ur Komah* material.[6]

The *Sod ha-Malbush* (*Secret of the Garment*) refers to a special vestment which spirit entities have to dress themselves in, acting almost like a skin as it were. It is said higher beings, i.e. angels, have to wear such a "garment" when they descend to a "lower world" like ours, in order to become visible in these lower domains. The following quote from an anonymous Kabbalistic text, the *Sefer ha-Meshiv* (*The Book of the Answering [Angel]*), apparently written in Spain in the first half of the 15th century, is most informative regarding angels descending and becoming visible through the power of a special spiritual garment:

"You should know that the secret causing the descent of the supernal book is the secret of the descent of the supernal chariot, and when you pronounce the secret of the great name, immediately the force of the 'garment' will descend downward, which is the secret of Elijah, who is mentioned in the work of the sages. And by this R. Simeon bar Yochai and Jonathan ben Uzziel learned their wisdom, and they were deserving of the secret of the 'garment,' to be dressed in it. And R. Chanina and R. Nechuniya ben ha-Kanah and R. Akiva and R. Ishmael ben Elisha and our holy rabbi and Rashi and many others learned likewise. And the secret of the 'garment' is the vision of the garment,' which the angel of God is dressed in, with a corporeal eye, and it is he who is speaking to you.....And the secret of the garment was given to those who fear God and meditate upon his name; they have seen it, those men who are the men of God were worthy of this state. And they were fasting for forty days continuously, and during their fast they pronounced the *Tetragrammaton* forty-five times, and on the fortieth day (the 'garment') descended to him and showed him whatever he wished [to know], and it stayed with him until the completion of the [study of the] subject he wanted [to know]....."[7]

By the end of the 16th century the doctrine of the *Malbush* was transformed in the writings of Israel Sarug, who saw it as the primordial *Torah*, a garment comprising the exact combinations of letters constituting the 231 gates referred to in the *Sefer Yetzirah*, which according to Sarug played an important role in the act of creation.[8]

Now, I chanced upon a statement comparing this donning of the *Malbush* to the saga of the "*Fall of Man*." In this case it is said that we ourselves were originally spiritual beings, but were obliged to dress ourselves in "coats of skin" in order to exist in this nether world. However, as in the case of Angelic beings having to wear a "garment" in their descent to this nether world, we too have to clothe ourselves in a garment of light in order to ascend into the loftier realms of existence.

Sometimes this "putting on the Name" was taken quite literally, as in the case of a work entitled *"The Book of the Putting on and Fashioning of the mantle of Righteousness"*[9] Here, a pure deer-hide parchment was chosen and a sleeveless garment, in the form of a high priest's *Efod*, was cut from this. It covered the shoulders and the chest, falling down the sides to the loins, and stretching down to the navel. A hood was connected to the garment, and on this "magic robe" the secret Divine Names were written. The practitioner was however not allowed to dress in this robe until the following conditions were fulfilled.

The wearer had to fast for a week, was not allowed to touch anything unclean, and had to follow a vegetarian diet. At the end of the week he was supposed to go to a body of water, such as a river or a lake, during the night, and call the Divine Name written on the parchment-robe over the water. If he saw a green shape above the water, something still unclean was within the individual concerned, and the preparations would have to be repeated for another seven days, accompanied by *Mitzvot* (good deeds) and *Tzedakah* (Acts of Righteousness mainly understood to be charitable deeds). If the shape over the water was red, "know that you are inwardly clean and fit to put on the Name. Then go into the water up to your loins and put on the venerable and terrible Name in the water." This "putting on the Mantle of Righteousness" was believed to give the wearer immeasurable power.

It is a mystery to me why seeing a green figure "above the water" should signify "uncleanness" or the vision of red figure should specifically be equated with "purity" or "cleanliness," but there are perhaps some clues in one of the first systems in *Kabbalah* of attributing colours to the various *Sefirot* on the Tree of Life, the colours then being mainly blue, red, green, white and black. Of course the last two are not really colours, but we should remember that the latter were definitely considered colours by these authors. Red, Green and White are by far the most important colours in this system, which Cordovero explained in some detail in his introduction to *Kabbalah*.[10] He said "colours are ascribed to the qualities [*Sefirot*] according to their actions," and originally these were:

Keter — White/Black
Chochmah — Blue
Binah — Green
Chesed — White
Gevurah — Red
Tiferet — White
Netzach — Red
Hod — Green
Yesod — White
Malchut — White

Rabbi Cordovero explained that as one cannot attribute any colour to Nothingness, no colour can be ascribed to *Keter*, a *sefirah* understood to be balanced between the states of pure being and becoming, but still hidden, as it were, within the Eternal No-Thing. He referred to *Keter* as being represented by the extremes of white and black. As white is understood to represent "Mercy," it shows the "Mercy of *Keter*." The attribution of black is said to indicate the true "essence" of Divinity, beyond time, space and events, hidden as said. Thus the great Rabbi wrote in *Pardes Rimmonim* "That essence does not change colour at all, neither judgment nor compassion, neither right nor left. Yet by emanating through the [*Sefirot*]—the variegated stained glass—judgment or compassion prevails."[11]

Cordovero referred to *Chochmah* as the "beginning of action" and referred to blue as the "beginning of the development of colour from blackness," or the first radiations of light from *Ain Sof*. He further stated that green is attributed to *Binah* since this colour "contains the colours of red and white, which are perceived together." He also claimed that it "contains the colour blue, which is from *Chochmah*." Cordovero is saying simply that *Binah* unites the principles of "Mercy" and "Severity," respectively "white" and "red," and is also channelling "Wisdom" (blue).

Now, while "white" is attributed to *Chesed*, its colour is considered to be quite different from that of *Keter*, almost as if the Light of Mercy, having been received via *Chochmah* and *Binah*, had become a bit contaminated and was thus somewhat grey, with a good dose of "blue" (Wisdom) in it. Now, while *Gevurah* is considered to be red (the colour of judgment), Cordovero attributed a number of colours to it. He said that blue can also be found here, since the "Light of *Gevurah*" also emanated via *Chochmah* and *Binah*, but he said this *sefirah* is also black because it contains that aspect of retribution that "blackens the faces of creatures." Cordovero considered the special link between *Gevurah* and *Binah* by referring to "the joysome wine which proceeds from *Gevurah* to *Binah*."

While *Tiferet* is traditionally understood to be white, Cordovero saw it as basically green, as well as comprising the principles represented by several colours at work within this special *sefirah*. Thus he wrote: "They ascribed to it sapphire in extension of *Da'at*. In its revealed aspect of determination, it includes white and red, that is, the green of an egg yolk, in truth. Now *Tiferet* includes the colour[s] of *Chesed* and Gevurah in one of two [manners]. It is either above them in the mystery of *Da'at*, which includes them in their roots or in its lower aspect, that is, the mixture of red and white. It also possess the colour of purple, which includes five colours. They are the mystery [of the angels] *Uriel*, *Refael*, *Gavriel*, *Michael*, and *Nuriel*."[12]

Netzach and *Hod* are respectively described as "red shading to white, for it is mostly mercy because of its orientation to the side of *Chesed*," and "white shading to red because it is mostly Judgment due to its orientation to the side of *Gevurah*."

Again, whereas *Yesod* was originally considered to be white, as were all the spheres of the "Middle Pillar"—being the "Pillar of Being" in contradistinction to the outer "Pillars of Doing," Cordovero maintained *Yesod* to be "a mixture of white shading to red and red shading to white," thus focussing the qualities of *Netzach* and *Hod* within itself. However, since the Light of *Yesod* is refracted via the preceding *Sefirot*, the colour of *Yesod* was also understood to be a kind of sapphire blue.

Finally *Malchut*, originally white, was seen by Cordovero to comprise all colours, i.e. all the Light derived from all the *Sefirot* was focussed in *Malchut*, which is like a rainbow.

Now, looking at this teaching in which the *sefirot* of the "Middle Pillar" are white, and the colours red and green are connected to certain *sefirot* on the "Outer Pillars" it is clear that "Understanding" and "Splendour" (or "Glory"), representing the top and bottom of the "Left Pillar" are "Green," while "Severity"

—which represents the forces of *Din* (Judgment) [also considered "Discipline" as well as *Pachad* ("Fear")], and *Netzach* ("Victory") [also considered "Endurance" and "Determination"] are "Red."

Using this information in order to comprehend the earlier references to the states of "purity" and "uncleanness" of an invocant attempting to put on the "Mantle of Righteousness," this being indicated above the water respectively by a "red figure" and a "green figure," and knowing very well that one is often confronted with that which one needs most in ones life, these messages might be interpreted this way:

Green figure: "While you perceive the splendour [*Hod*—green] of comprehension [*Binah*—green], you are in a state of imbalance [Left Pillar only]. You have not used self-discipline [*Gevurah*—red] in order to conquer [*Netzach*—red] lower desires [*Netzach*—red] and your fears [*Gevurah*—red]."

Red figure: "Your fears [*Gevurah*—red] have been conquered [*Netzach*—red]. Having proceeded with determination [*Netzach*—red], you were brought by your discipline [*Gevurah*—red] of self to a state of victory [*Netzach*—red] which will endure [*Netzach*—red]."

However.....there are many different ways in which these indicators can be read.....as many as there are people to interpret them. Everyone will understand in accordance with personal perceptions. Truly, each one of us perceives the world through "me"–coloured glasses!

. ...to the point that one who sees them will wonder and say that these differences are due to the light of the sun... ... .

Chapter 4
MAGICAL EMPOWERMENT

A. INTRODUCTION

What many people call "Magic" is in fact a hand-down of early "spiritual survival" systems, which enabled our forefathers to find souls of their own amongst all kinds of hostile conditions and circumstances. That is still its major function today. The English term derives from a root, "*maj,*" meaning "great," and the "Great Work" of our own spiritual survival and evolution is the only Magic worth bothering with. Any associated phenomena, or "marvels," are only side-effects and not necessarily good ones.

Part of the trouble with *Kabbalah* and the Western Mystery Tradition as a whole, is the absurd beliefs about it from fictional stories and misrepresentations. For so many people "Magic" means dressing up in important-looking costumes, participating in thrilling rites, where spirits appear, or fantastic phenomena happen, and all the rest of the theatrical performance takes place. That is why we need new approaches to the Tradition based on better grounds of belief, and 21st century outlooks. We need forward-looking people, who will not despise or deprecate the past, but use it to reach the best possible future. We really do need an appraisal and understanding of *Kabbalah* and the Western Inner Tradition, which modern minds and souls can accept with gladness and confidence.

We must also keep in mind a very important factor in spiritual practices. You have probably heard "Magic" defined as "the science and art of causing change to occur in conformity with will."[1] From what was said previously, we can assume that "will" refers to the *Ru'ach*, the Reasoning Self. Yet, from all the practical experiences I have had over the last four decades with this very subject, it is clear that while the *Ru'ach* might initiate a magical action, it is actually the *Nefesh*, the Instinctual Self, that has to work the "change," and it can only do so when there is no interference from the "cage of logic," the reasoning mind. One must reach that state of non-interference called *Hishtavut* (Equanimity or Unattachment), since the greatest pitfall in *Kabbalah* and Magic, leading to the worst frustrations and inability, is in fact the *desire to have results*. This lust for results annihilates all our efforts. *Desire destroys the deed*, because there is egotistical identification, fear of failure, and even a reciprocal desire not to achieve the original desire, and all this, arising as it does from our dualistic natures, will wreck any hoped for outcome.

Therefore I am asking you to do something extremely difficult, and that is to give up studying and working with a desire for results. You must literally work because you enjoy it, practising for the sake of the "art," i.e. "for the heck of it"! Perform a magical ritual because you want to do it, without caring whether it will work or not, or whether it will produce any effects or not. Do not seek any outcome, even if a working is done for a specific purpose, simply work "uninvolved," which does not mean "do not care" or not to put in effort. Just do not let spiritual, intellectual, egotistical, or emotional expectations cloud and destroy your efforts. Thus it is that at the end of the working, you should immediately wipe it from your mind.

As you proceed you will find that the process revolves, amongst others, around the following points:

1. Under all conditions, you must work on your *Nefesh*, your Instinctual Self. You must become your own best friend, and establish a total cooperation between you, the *Ru'ach*, and the *Nefesh*. This subject needs greater investigation, since spiritual growth and development are so vitally linked to the unfolding of the Instinctual Self. I concentrated over a long period on a lot of work in this arena of investigation, in which alterations within the psyche were directly affected through personal actions, and executed a great array of tasks through self impression while being in an expanded state of consciousness. After many years of research and practice, I have found that there still remain a lot of details left unclear and uninvestigated, which is the main reason for my inability to present the

subject here in absolute detail. However, I do know the process involves an expanded state of consciousness or trance states, as well as alterations within ones being, and cultivating the ability to map ones consciousness, as well as a variety of other functions.

2. It is important to become "empowered," as it were, through what can be termed "Universal Consciousness," in which all that exists and does not exist is within the sphere of your own being, literally *within* you. In other words, your consciousness has to expand to embrace a much larger whole, as it were. The true realisation of this is via a process of empowerment and divinisation. This is discussed in Chapter 8 under the title *"Ru'ach ha-Kodesh,"* the achievement of which is the aim of the practice titled *"Exercise in Absolute Reality."*

3. The next important aspect to consider here is what is called "The Power of Positive Feeling." In this part of spiritual training one starts to work with practices such as *"Picture Speech," "Acknowledging the God-Force,"* etc. This is discussed in Chapter 9 in which we address the topic of *Maggidim*.

4. Another important step is "Developing the Magical Will." Unless the "Will" of the practitioner is particularly dynamic, it will be difficult to control the chaotic movement of events occurring in a trance or altered state of consciousness. Hence a most commanding "Will" is required to be able to focus the energies flowing at tremendous rates while the Kabbalist/Magician is on an inter-dimensional journey.

B. Discovering the *Nefesh*

1. INTRODUCTION

We will now address the ability to "reconstruct" the physical self, and to achieve this, all aspects related to the procedure must be clearly understood. Through the use of these techniques you will literally renew your feet, hands, heart, mouth, eyes, brain, in fact, your entire physical body. In order to initiate this process, we will commence with exercises for purifying and illuminating the hands. As you know, you use your hands a lot, i.e. to greet people and to touch objects. You will learn to dedicate yourself and your hands in such a manner, that nothing is injured or annihilated by your touch.

Besides the reconstruction of the body, it is vital to transform the mind, i.e. to transmute it from a fairly ordinary state into magical consciousness. The purpose here is the creation of a "True Will" or the "Magical Will." Even the slightest ability to work a change in oneself is certainly more valuable than anything else the Universe has to offer us. What should concern us here as *Mekubalim* (Kabbalists), is the mind–body relationship, the nature of our consciousness and our capacity for transcendence. All of us are really *Yorde Merkavah*, "ones who descend into the Chariot" of the Self, despite the fact that some of us have not yet undertaken this "journey of transcendence" into the inmost areas of the unconscious, where true potential and the celestial vehicle, the *Merkavah*, is hidden and readied for the task of raising the consciousness of the Kabbalist through the *Hechalot* ("Heavenly Halls"), the inner dimensions, to the highest peak of Cosmic realisation.

This is not a journey to undertake unprepared, and thus it is important to be adequately trained, to know what to expect in terms of visions, feelings, etc., while traversing the difficult terrain of the "inner." For example, the Kabbalist should be carefully prepared in the usage of *Shemot* (Divine Names), which will banish the harmful images besetting the soul during this inward journey, and must be brought to a full realisation that all visionary experiences are entirely subordinate to the Kabbalist's own mind. Then, after careful preparation, a variety of practices such as fasting, breathing exercises, rhythmic chanting, etc., could be used to guide you into an altered state of awareness. In fact, it is the assurance of lofty bliss and ecstatic revelation in vastly expanded states of consciousness, which causes the demanding regimen of *Kabbalah* to have such a great appeal for the sincere practitioner.

The development of *Mochin de-Gadlut* (the "big" mind) is one of the major goals of Kabbalistic meditation. In such an expanded state of consciousness a variety of psycho-spiritual incidents could happen spontaneously or be consciously encouraged, such as the induction of specific, even prophetic dreams, transformed conditions of comprehension, automatic writing and speaking, etc. In this state a *Maggid*, a celestial being or inner guide, could temporarily occupy the body of the practitioner, and dynamically converse with the practitioner through the channel established through the surrender of the normal mental faculty. It is generally well known that continued repetition of Kabbalistic procedures induces the encounter of transcendent visionary experiences. However, the general stance in this work is that one should move cautiously and carefully in this inward quest, since intense concentration awakens a "fire" in the body, which could result in destructive mental, emotional and physical responses. Yet one must also understand that expanded consciousness is undoubtedly not enough to live effectively in this world. We live in the universe of *Assiah*, physical action, where tangible toil is demanded, and we realise that even the presumed most trivial deed has vast universal significance and effect.

Now let us investigate the process of altering ones normal daily life into a more efficient and spiritually active one. Try to understand that:

1. All things, whether near or far, are part of the irreducible, meaningful unity and order underlying all manifestation. All things in existence are in a continuous interrelationship with each other. There is nothing which exists which is not within you, and there is nothing you can do which does not also have an effect on the whole of manifestation. Nothing is chance, indiscriminate, aimless or chaotic, and the "reality" we encounter to be ours, is but one sphere of consciousness which we have become accustomed.

    Most importantly, this knowledge brings us to the full realisation of the unity of our physical, emotional, and spiritual selves. Thus it is known that "negative" feelings like melancholy, anger, hatred and depression, disseminate not only throughout the entire being of an individual beset by these emotions, e.g. creating disease in mind, body and soul, but also impact on the whole of manifestation. To confront these destructive tendencies you could use:

a. Breathing practices designed to bring a better state of balance, and above all facilitate greater concentration and control in your life;

b. Kabbalistic practices and meditation techniques like *Kavvanot, Yichudim* or "Taking on the Name," the primary aim being to bring the sacred into your everyday existence;

c. song and dance as powerful healing tools, and here we might recall those wonderful *Nigunim*, wordless chants, which have such a remarkable effect on the body, or you may use spontaneous chanting;

d. Cultivating joy, vivacity and happiness is the portal to the hallowed and sublime. In this kind of approach celibacy, austere abstemiousness, and asceticism are simply unacceptable. Castigating the body is hardly connected to a truly godly way of living. Laughter and joy are amongst the highest forms of worship, and you should make it a rule to be as cheerful as you can possibly be, even to the point of being comical and absurd. In this regard it is good to enjoy good jokes and hilarious stories. Your mind, emotions, and body keenly influence each other, and there is a fundamental bond between feelings like persistent anxiety, fury, melancholy, etc. and the commencement of bodily ailments. In this regard the great Nachman of Bratzlav maintained "When joy is blemished, the pulse is negatively affected. Illness can thus result from sadness and melancholy."[2]

e. Sexuality is also a powerful instrument in the fight against negative emotions, another topic needing greater investigation.

2. In order to aim for higher awareness, you should learn to direct the life force which is coursing your body. Again the methods used comprise:

a. Breathing practices in which Divine Energy and Life Force is drawn into the body;

b. sexuality which, when correctly used, is a most commanding spiritual exercise, able to demolish your temporal, ordinary mental approach, and transform it altogether. In fact, the most ecstatic states of sacred bliss are known to compare most strongly with the experience of orgasm.

3. The mentioned preparations of working against negative emotions, aiming for higher awareness, and knowledge through "inner states," i.e. dreams, will expedite the erasing of the barrier between the *Ru'ach* and the *Nefesh*, thus creating an integration of the two. The next step in the pathway to the divine would then be the awakening of your own inner potentials and abilities through methods such as solitary contemplation, breathing exercises, fasting, endurance praying, mystical weeping, and meditative practices. These do not only lead to the procurement of paranormal abilities, but also to "Divine Union" between God and the Kabbalist, resulting in those ecstatics states which some have aptly portrayed are like having "an orgasm with the Whole."

2. STARTING PREMISES

The methods discussed here involve what may be termed "Self Creation." If you are a true esotericist, you would prefer to go inside yourself and deal with your problems, rather than having anybody telling you what you should or should not do in this regard. With all due respect to psychologists, I want to say that you personally can affect the necessary transformations of your psyche.

Remember *Kabbalah* and the whole of the Western Mystery Tradition started with people who instinctively felt that they were "living patterns," living *by* patterns and creating new or adapting old ones all the time. The esotericist is one who always creates ever finer patterns in harmony with those of life, which he is consciously realising in his attempts to reach the Ultimate pattern locked up within himself, and which he may consciously live out as an entity restored to an original intention. The exotericist simply follows accepted patterns, which he/she may or may not be consciously aware of, with the promise that if he/she does "such and such," he/she will evolve unto a state of perfection.

The *EXO*tericist believes that God made laws, but never for one minute thinks that these laws might also have control over "God manifest," whereas the *ESO*tericist believes "As Above, So Below." Thus the esotericist, or "Inner Traditionalist," believes in a give-and-take between God and man, leading to an ideal

God–man relationship. The esotericist believes in an interpersonal relationship with Divinity. To this individual God is certainly not the all powerful super-being in the sky who waits to mete out justice at the end of time, who will even the score when everything is over. The "Manifested God" is the involved parent, whose "Breath of Life" can be blocked by the deeds of man, but who can really pour out the most intense love for His manifestation, his children, when they show genuine insight in their actions, whether these be physical, emotional, mental or spiritual.

One could say that exotericism is very group orientated, whereas the esotericist is very individualistic. Both these outlooks are legitimate of course, but only so in terms of the humans who work one way or the other. The exoteric viewpoint, as seen in orthodox religion, is well known and does not need explanation here, whereas the esoteric viewpoint needs probably more clarification. The esotericist is vitally concerned with rulership, or helping to rule the universe, as well as taking the responsibility for it. Having this idea of a man/God relationship, he has to work out symbols or systems by which he may connect man and Divinity. He wants to meet God on a common ground, somewhere halfway, like *Tiferet* (Beauty) on the Kabbalistic Tree of Life, which is connected to every other Sphere except *Malchut* (the Kingdom). Esotericists seek to meet Divinity face to face through an interpersonal relationship, where they may talk with God, and where God may talk with them; where they may fight with God, and God with them; where they may love with God, and God with them. Their relationship with Divinity is such, that they do not fear an argument with Divinity, in the same way as a child would have with a parent.

So, as said, you can alter your life and your being by yourself, and it helps a great deal if you start with the following premises:

1. There is a purpose to your existence. By viewing the broad spectrum of your life from your earliest beginnings to the present, you may be able to discern different periods all of which pertain to the expression of your purpose as an incarnate being. As a starting practice, attempt to write an essay on your life, its meaning, potential, purpose and how you wish to express it.

2. There is a need for inner growth and self-development in your life, and special conditions are required to facilitate this. Write an essay on these needed conditions according to your own estimation, referring to details such as challenge, stimulation, encouragement, support, etc.

3. The major factors in your life, such as your well-being, growth and purpose, are intensified through pleasurable experiences, thus these should be increased in your life. In other words, instead of suffering and wallowing in the misery of your existence, you should seek greater fulfilment in more agreeable expressions and aspects of being, i.e. those providing greater enjoyment and fulfilment. Write an essay regarding your own appreciation of this topic.

4. There is not a single especially effective method which will work for all people all the time. Each person is uniquely different from everybody else, has unique aspirations and must unfold his or her being in a personal manner. Therefore, for a Tradition to be really effective, it would need to provide a great variety of techniques from which you might select what is most suitable to you personally. Write an essay carefully commenting on this point.

5. You cannot really be compared with any other individual. Your development, quest and journey through life is unique to yourself. It would therefore be necessary to listen to, support and encourage all within your circle of friendship and companionship, to "walk" their respective personal ways of growth and spiritual unfoldment. Write an essay on this matter from your own perspective.

6. Your current problems and ailments are changeable, since most of them are persistent expressions of long-term anxiety and tension, often coupled with poor mental, emotional and physical nutrition. A confined, restricted life on all these levels will exacerbate stress and other afflictions. Methods are thus required to change these stressful situations and restore vitality. These should again incorporate, amongst others, breathing practices and relaxation. Write an essay, commenting on this vitally important point.

7. An important basic premise in *Kabbalah* is that your thoughts and feelings, your attitudes, shape not only your body, but your entire being and life. This means that you are entirely responsible for creating your existence, and shaping much of what you encounter in life. Yet most people are not aware of this source of control and creativity. To be able to have this consciously, you would have to fully understand your physical make up, being aware of the smallest detail of personal behaviour. This will cover everything from the way you sit to the manner in which you form preferences. Write an essay on this very important point in which your growth depends on surfacing these hidden aspects of your being, with specific reference to your own nature.

8. The current period of your existence must constitute a time of liberation from the repressions, the debilitating habits of childhood, and restrictive social customs and views. You have to inculcate a state of greater reality and truth in your life and existence. Commenting on this, write an essay discussing what you found was forbidden in your life, but which is actually part of the human condition. The more openly you are able to share this, the more you will accept the greater reality that is your life.

There are several psychological works dealing with programmes of this nature, some excellent, others extremely poor, some written without any acknowledgement of anything of a spiritual nature, while others incorporate the spiritual. In this regard I have found one of the best to be Mambert and Foster's "*A Trip into Your Unconscious.*"[3] Now, starting with the listed premises we can construct a programme that would counter the falsehoods and pretences one has learned to live with.

3. PRINCIPAL ACTIVITIES

To start with, we need to look at a schedule for practising the various exercises. If you intend working with a group, at least one group meeting of approximately two hours each week should be maintained. It would be better to have two in a week, the second one being of a much shorter duration of only one hour. However, life styles being what they are today, with time being limited, it might be better to have short regular practices rather than longer irregular ones, and then allow yourself the occasional intense session which could last up to four hours, or, time permitting, you might even devote an entire day to spiritual exercises. It has been found that a lot of momentum is gained from long sessions, which would include resting periods comprised of relaxation exercises.

In group work the first meeting of the week is reserved for the main spiritual practices, and the second, shorter one for relaxation exercises, breathing, related physical activities, interpersonal exercises, counselling, as well as listening to and discussing problems that members may encounter. In official magical lodges and temples members often arrange individual sessions to discuss personal requirements and find answers to personal queries. Yet, as is so often the case, individual sessions can be very difficult to maintain when there is only one person doing the counselling. There should be a delegation of duties to the main "officers" in Temples, such activities being allocated in accordance with individual ability.

Otherwise, when one is working on ones own, a set time of approximately one hour per day is normally kept for exercises and practices. Of course, this is virtually impossible for individuals who work all day, and who then after work have to attend to the home, kids, or whatever. In this regard it has been found that fifteen minutes devoted every day to spiritual practices, will furnish far better results than working an hour irregularly. However short the time you may have each day to devote to feeding your spirit, it should be strictly adhered to. Humans are controlled by habits, and the more we become accustomed to a rigorous regime, the stronger will be the urge to practice at regular times, which is a certain way to success. The following practices and exercises have been arranged with the busiest person in mind, and only one or two may be attempted at a time. If however more time is available, several could be practised.

These exercises and methods have been used to contact, communicate and befriend the Instinctual Self. I have placed them in the order I have been using them, but you may want to employ them in a sequence suitable to yourself, except for the first four which should be worked in the exact order in which they are presented here. They are extremely important and "transformative" practices, which you should experience at least once a week, or once a day in the case of chronic illness. However busy I am, I work them every day.

a. Surrendering

1. Sit comfortably, and consciously surrender to gravity, that is to become as heavy and as limp as possible. By surrendering in this manner, you allow the pull of the earth to draw all tension out of your body, as you simply sit quietly for a few minutes. *An important key is to feel yourself constantly smile warmly inside your solar plexus while doing these practices.*
2. Breathe deeply and remember to smile warmly inside yourself, and let the smile permeate throughout your body. Afterwards sit quietly doing absolutely nothing for a few minutes.

b. Body Awareness

The following practice, which I learned years ago from Franz Bardon's "*Initiation into Hermetics*,"[4] deals with control of the body. As Bardon noted, it needs great skill to sit quietly and comfortably, so one should not underestimate the value of this exercise. It is known to be an enormous stress reliever, and many of us living rushed lives can do with this kind of deep rest and peace for a half an hour every day. Do not say you do not have the time, simply claim a half an hour for yourself. Bardon delineated the practice very well, so I will merely paraphrase his words somewhat:

1. Sit in a chair in such a way that your spine remains erect. Sit relaxed, without straining the muscles, both hands resting lightly on your thighs. Set an alarm-clock for five minutes, then close your eyes and observe your entire anatomy. At first you will notice that the muscles are becoming restless in consequence of nervous stimulus.

Persevere in sitting quietly. As simple as this exercise may appear, it can be rather difficult for the beginner.
2. If you are able to sit without jerking, moving or exerting any special effort for five minutes, extend each new exercise by one minute. If you managed to sit for at least a half an hour quietly, comfortably, without any trouble, you have mastered the practice.

c. Toning and Tuning the Body[5]

This is a wonderful practice in which you are brought in direct contact with your body. It is known to have healing effects on the body, mind and soul. I have had incredible reports of the benefits derived by those who regularly work this exercise. A while back I was invited to present a one-day workshop in which I shared this exercise. Later I was asked to address another gathering and amongst those present I recognised a man who was at the previous workshop. He approached me and told me that this exercise had changed his life; that he had been suffering from chronic depression for as long as he could remember, and that nothing psychologically and medically had helped him in any way. He then started to work this exercise on a daily basis, and within a relatively short time he had rid himself totally of the debilitating mental condition. His words to me were: "You do not know the value of this practice!" I *do* know that it is a "healing" exercise, which is used to reverse very serious physical, mental and emotional conditions.

When you have prepared yourself with the previous two exercises, and you feel sufficiently calm and surrendered, take three deep breaths. Do not strain or over-breathe. Simply take three comfortable deep breaths, and sigh nicely on exhalation. Pause momentarily, and then take another deep breath but this time you hum during the exhalation and feel your body vibrating with sound. Feel your body surrender more and more while intoning. Do this three times, before continuing with the next stage.

This is an enormous meditation, in which you have to come in contact with the individual parts of your body. This could take a lot of time in the beginning. However, later you may replace group areas of your body, and "tune" these collectively. With practice you can reach a stage where, when time is extremely limited, you only need to take a few breaths and hum a few times in order to fully contact and vibrate your entire anatomy. Again a most important key in these procedures is to smile warmly and feel an intense friendship, as it were a union, with every part of the body you are approaching in this manner. The preliminary procedure is as follows:

1. Sit comfortably and close your eyes. Now look at your toes. This is easy. Do not think "How do I look at my toes with my eyes closed?" If you shut your eyes now, and somebody says "Look at your toes" what are you doing? Your attention is automatically in your toes. Do not make it an issue. Now, smile at your toes. Be very friendly with your toes. Feel the warmth of your smile reach inside and permeate your toes. Then imagine the very pores of the skin of your toes are like millions of little mouths, and you can breathe vital energy in through those pores. As you take a deep breath, imagine that you are sucking vital Life-Force directly into your toes. As you breathe feel your toes sucking in this vital energy through the skin. It is the same as drinking a cool drink while sucking at the end of a straw. Your toes are the straws or, perhaps better, sponges in this case. Keep smiling inside your toes, and on the exhalation hum and vibrate your toes, i.e. literally feeling your toes humming with you.
2. Next, shift your attention to your feet. Follow the exact procedure you used with your toes. Smile at your feet, and again feel the warmth of your smile permeate your feet. Again as you take a deep breath, also breath with your feet, imagining the life force flowing through the pores of the skin into your feet. Once more keep smiling inside your feet, and on exhalation hum and vibrate your feet.
3. Next turn your attention to your ankles, and repeat the entire procedure breathing with your ankles.
4. Repeat the procedure with each of the following parts of your body: lower legs, upper legs, genitals and anus. Each time look at the specific bodily part. Smile warmly inside it, take a deep breath while breathing *with* that respective

organ of your anatomy, that is imagining that you are absorbing the vital force directly into it while inhaling, and conclude by vibrating the part with sound on exhalation.

5. Next repeat the procedure with the area from the navel down to the genitals, and then with the middle portion of the torso below the chest, that is the area from the navel to the diaphragm. Remember to smile warmly each time, and to feel the warmth of your smile permeate the specific area you are focussing on. Always take a deep breath directly into that part through the pores of the skin, which means you have to allow your imagination to experience the skin as opening up into millions of little mouths as it were, and then to hum and vibrate the area you are focussed on.

6. Repeat the procedure with the chest, and here ladies should not forget to include their breasts. Then you should follow respectively with the shoulders, the upper arms, the lower arms and the hands. If you are doing it correctly, you will at this point feel so deeply surrendered and peaceful that you might lose any sense of the body having any dimensions whatsoever. It might be experienced as entirely made up of scintillating energy alone. You will experience each hand as a large locus of energy and warmth. Whatever you are sensing, keep smiling and let the specific bodily part you are focussed on experience the warmth of your smile.

7. Next repeat the procedure with your neck, and though you may focus on the neck in its entirety, give specific attention to the back of the neck. Afterwards continue respectively with the back of the skull, then the middle of the head, followed by the forehead and the ears. Continue with the eyes, followed by the nose and the cheek bones.

8. In conclusion, repeat the procedure with the mouth, teeth and jaws, and finally with the throat. Do not forget to smile warmly at each portion of your body, and whatever happens, stay with it. If your *Nefesh* suddenly becomes emotional, i.e. laughing or crying, let it do so freely while you, the *Ru'ach*, the Conscious Self, simply watch without trying to suppress the emotions in any way. Do not become uptight or frightened in the least. This working, as a

process of mental, emotional and physical healing, might surface hidden thoughts and feelings. Let them arise freely and clear out. After such a diversion, you simply continue with the exercise. Your Instinctual Self will soon realise that it can trust you completely.

9. Finally, pause for a few seconds, sensing and experiencing the vibrant energetic state of your body.

10. Keep smiling, but this time smile *with* your entire body. Literally experience every portion of your body opening up, like the bud of a flower unfolding and opening itself to the sun. Smiling with your body, breathe with your whole body, straight through the skin, and on exhalation hum and feel the entire body singing and vibrating with you. Do this breathing three times, and then move on to the next exercise.

d. Spontaneous Song

This practice follows on directly from the previous procedure. After having toned and tuned the body, keep on taking deep breaths, then, instead of humming, open your mouth and begin to sing. Simply sing and chant spontaneously. Do be concerned about any specific song you should sing. Simply let the voice move freely to produce a spontaneous tune using any sound. Croak or groan or or chant tones. Anything will do. There are simply no guidelines, when it comes to expressing yourself freely in this vocal manner. Continue with this for a few minutes, listening and allowing yourself to feel what is happening inside you. Should any emotional response rise in the body, do not try to suppress it, but simply let it express itself.

If the body should sway and move, let it express itself without any interference on your part. Simply watch what is happening, and do not analyse or attempt to interpret the process. Keep the analytical mind, the "cage of logic," altogether out of the process. Just enjoy and let be what will be. It is perfectly alright to go crazy, or to loose your reason while keeping your mind.

Constant practice of this exercise increases creativity and great freedom of expression. It breaks down inhibiting thoughts and feelings. Besides you would have used the creative side of your psyche, which is enormously satisfying.

4. THE MAGICAL WILL

Many of the exercises discussed in this and the following section, were again derived from practices suggested by Franz Bardon.[6] I worked these in the early 1970's, and later adapted and intensified them for easier personal use. Now, the following methods are practised to build a powerful "Magical Will":

a. **Motionlessness**, that is to make the body comfortable and try to maintain that position for at least 15 minutes, as discussed earlier. The important thing with this practice is not to move the eyes, tongue, fingers or any part of the body, and not to allow the mind to wander, but rather to observe yourself as uninvolved as possible, and to persist, even if it gets uncomfortable.

b. **Breathing**, that is to stay motionless and deliberately slow the breath to a long, deep cycle, using the entire capacity of the lungs without strain or effort. The mind should also be completely attentive on the breath cycle, and kept focussed on it for around 30 minutes. In other words watch yourself breathing.

c. **Withdrawal**. The previous exercises will improve health and well-being, but they will also prepare one for the practice of withdrawal, in which, while motionless and breathing deeply, you begin to withdraw the mind from any thoughts which may arise. It requires immense effort and willpower to achieve even seconds of mental silence. It helps to feel your consciousness contract, virtually into a dot somewhere inside your solar plexus, and then to continue shrinking into a state of nothingness. Do not worry. You certainly will not disappear, but this might help you achieve the required vigilance without thoughts. This might last only seconds, but with continued practice the periods of total inner silence will lengthen.

It should be mentioned that most of the practices described in this work develop the "Magical Will" and are most valuable.

5. CONCENTRATION

To get magic to work, ones ability to concentrate and focus attention must be raised to a very high degree. The following practices will again develop the "Magical Will," facilitate greater concentration, and can also be used to induce a trance state.

a. Object Concentration

The legend of the evil-eye comes from the ability to give a fixed dead stare. This can be practised against any object, a mark on the wall, something in the distance, a star at night, anything in fact. To hold the object with an absolutely fixed, unwavering gaze for a few moments will prove to be very difficult, yet you should practice until you can do it for at least 30 minutes. Every attempt by the mind to distort the object, or to find something else to think about, must be resisted, however I believe this "resistance" should rather be of the "soft" kind than "forceful." In fact, when I initially worked this technique, I quickly discovered that if I consciously allowed my mind to relax during the stare, I would avert all painful sensations in my eyes.

Object concentration helps to acquire hidden information about that object, but in the beginning it is important to work with objects which appear to you to be without any especial meaning, that is if you can find one.

b. Sound Concentration

The part of the mind in which verbal thoughts arise is brought under control by concentration on sounds imagined in your mind. Repeating a tune or a phrase from a song is relatively easy, hence it is better to select words of one or more syllables. Such words can be meaningless tonal constructs, or any simple term. In this regard I recall using *Omein (Amen)*, *Hu*, *Omnil*, and so forth. The chosen sound is repeated in the mind to block all other thoughts, and what is important here is to actually listen to yourself doing it, while being very careful not to attempt any explanation or analysis of the word or sound. You might even begin by uttering the sound aloud, and then saying it mentally, listening to yourself doing so. No matter how inappropriate the choice of sound may appear, persist with it. When the sound appears to repeat itself automatically, and even occur in sleep, you have mastered the skill.

This information applies to Kabbalistic meditation, and is a key to the use of "Words of Power."

c. Image Concentration

The portion of the mind in which pictorial images arise must be brought under control, and this is facilitated by choosing a simple shape, such as a triangle, circle, square, cross, crescent, etc. and holding it in the mind's eye without distortion for 15 minutes. Only the strongest efforts are likely to show results.

Commence visualising the image with closed eyes, and later, when some proficiency has been achieved, do the practice with open eyes, i.e. attempt to project the image onto a blank surface. This skill is fundamental to the internalizing and projection of "sigils" in talismanic work, and in the creation of thought-forms. Again I have personally found that the skill was mastered a lot easier when images were visualised in a specific area inside the head. For example, I was able to visualise circles, squares, and triangles a lot easier in my forehead than I could in the middle or back of my head.

Now, these methods of magical concentration are again useful in entering magical trance, and must be practised with determination. Remember these abilities are usually not accessible to the average human, hence they demand total concentration and commitment.

C. Self-Exorcism

William Gray taught that all the problems of life begin and end within oneself, and he maintained that before we attempt to rid the world of evil, we need to get rid of it inside ourselves. This is basically what his *"Exorcism by Effort"* and its accompanying *"Rite of Self-exorcism"* are all about.[7] I should mention that William Gray had lots of doubts and misgivings about exorcisms, and having been his student for fourteen years during which he raised this topic many times, discussed it in great detail, and having perused many case studies, I have to admit that I share the same sentiments. Often the claim that somebody is "possessed" is actually nothing of the kind. People are more often obsessed, and very rarely possessed. In fact, most of the time they are possessed by their obsessions. As it is, our obsessions are products of our own personalities, and while some of these are harmless enough, others might turn out to be extremely dangerous and injurious.

A while ago I was told of a regular doctor and psychiatrist, who was also a priest–missionary in China for some years, who claimed that he was getting remarkable results in healing mental troubles by exorcising patients from influences connected with departed ancestral spirits who themselves were troubled. He apparently specialised in *anorexia nervosa*, and was not only deadly serious, but absolutely devoted to his ideas of exorcism. Subsequent research raised the argument that the exorcism did not so much rid "victims" of "troubled ancestral spirits," but provided the patients with a symbolical means to deal with their own obsessions. In other words, what needed to be "exorcised" were their own thoughts and feelings, and the only way in which the exorcist ascertained whether the "exorcism" was effective, was when it was accompanied by some sort of cathartic action in which the "obsessed/possessed" individuals forcefully rid themselves of the obsession/possession with an evacuation of physical waste from their bodies—a nice way of saying that the catharsis involves patients crapping themselves, or vomiting all over the show.

In the past, very observant individuals noticing the effectiveness of this physical expulsion of "spirit forces," arrived at the conclusion that "demons" inside the body were situated in the colon. They decided that the easiest way to exorcise anybody was with a laxative or an enema. This is at least a practical start to the process. In this regard I have been sternly lectured by a concerned friend who informed me that a "dirty stomach" has been responsible for many of the mental and physical ills of mankind down the centuries. I smiled when he sang the praises of a "colonic lavage," and fell about with laughter when he informed me that Martin Luther suffered from obsessive hallucinations as a result of chronic constipation, and added "look what that did to our world." I thought this an absolute hoot, but my dear friend waved his forefinger unyieldingly in my direction, exclaiming "It is no laughing matter?" Later, after reading and hearing what William Gray had to say about our ability to rid ourselves of the worst within us, or as he put it, "If I could get rid of my spiritual detritus as easily as I am voiding this physical waste, I might be in a better state of spiritual health altogether,"[8] I understood that my concerned companion was actually trying to draw may attention to factors pertaining to our very survival on all levels of existence. Again, I think by and large we are losing a lot of information by being too "nice" about basic facts of bodily behaviour, covering everything up as "shameful" purely because it deals with excretion, etc.

"Self-Exorcism" pertains to ridding oneself of ones own "spiritual excrement." The basic premise is that we should not only rid our bodies of our physical detritus, this being vital for the survival of the physical side of our beings, but that we also need to expel the equivalent from our minds, souls and spirits. My late mentor, William Gray, insisted that there was no difference between matter and spirit beyond the physical being "materialised spirit" and the spiritual dimension of existence being "subtle matter." He insisted that one should look at the "whole." I remember saying to him how vastly different material existence must be from the "seventh heaven" one hears of in *Kabbalah*. A frown formed on his forehead as he listened. He paused momentarily and quietly got up, picked up an ordinary ruler, placed it on a little coffee table, and very politely requested "Now Jacobus, would you kindly raise the one end of the ruler without moving the other?" I retorted that this was impossible. "Exactly" he said, and proceeded to use the two ends of the ruler as analogies to matter and spirit, the two "ends" as it were of existence, each end intrinsically connected to the other.

In this regard, William Gray told me that the life process of eating and defecating applies on all levels of manifestation. He put it simply as "What goes in must come out somewhere." Of course, we physically enact this process every day when we evacuate our dross down the nearest "bog".....that is if one is not seriously constipated, a most uncomfortable condition which pertains not only to our physical bodies but also to the mind, soul and spirit. We can suffer just as much from constipation psychologically because we have become bogged down by what we are retaining from the encounters we have had to deal with in our lives, the residue of which we have not expelled from our psyches. In other words our so-called "hang-ups" might just as well be described as our "psychic excrement."

Some decades ago I discovered that it is no good blaming the worst in oneself on external events. You cannot blame your mother, father, whoever or whatsoever for your current psychological or spiritual condition. As difficult as this is to accept and understand, the fact of the matter is that most of our emotional difficulties are self-made, and there are quite a number of ways individuals respond to their emotional, mental and spiritual "dis–ease." While all reactions are meant to be "cathartic," results do not always proof satisfactory. Some might submerge themselves in the escapism of fundamentalist religions, shoving the lot on the "Lord" and trying to drown out the worst in themselves with the frenzied barrage of noisy prayer. Others try to drown themselves in a swamp of furious fornication, whilst still others try to sublimate pain with more "pain," enjoying the personal "suffering" as much as they can. Some respond with aggression and live with an anger which corrodes their souls. The latter category is only too familiar to me, representing aspects of my own life which I had to address.

It is really interesting to note how religion, sex, pain and violence often go hand in hand, like for example in the ancient rites of Cybele during which the priests castrated themselves in a state of religious trance. It occurred to me that a lot of those old practices, which Christians later found so obscene and disgusting, were in fact just sheer catharsis, or "letting go," so as to release all the strains of life and frustration. The modern equivalent is the disco session where the kids just scream, howl, contort and fling themselves around. We might note that revivalist religions do very much the same along different lines.

We might also recall "Primal Therapy,"[9] where the main idea is to push people past an ultimate in emotional stress until they "flatten out" on the other side, and supposedly come up again in perfect peace. It mostly pertains to a psycho-dramatic procedure involving the "Primal Scream," which is uttered until there is literally nothing left inside and therefore one becomes "perfectly purged." At least that is the theory. I suppose one could describe it accurately but crudely as giving someone a sufficiently hard kick in the guts to clear the psychic excrement out of them. This has been called an "abreaction," and I believe Israel Regardie, the well-known occultist and Reichian[10] therapist, was rather fond of this method. I was told he used to get his patients to vomit into buckets until they were exhausted.

The general idea is to literally drive the patients to the utter edge of endurance until they scream their heads off, vomit heartily, defecate themselves, or do something drastic physically in the way of expulsion, which is supposed to take the psychic cause of their troubles with it. In the past all these effects were noted by exorcists as signs of "demons" going out of a victim. The whole shooting match boils down to one thing. "Get it *out* of you, but *do not* keep it all bottled up." So we are dissatisfied with ourselves? That is as it should be, but these very severe ideas of clearing ourselves of psychological rubbish are often inadequate. So we have created these battlefields inside ourselves where we can combat everything we feel is spoiling our lives, and it is exactly *there* where we will have to fight it out. In old time language it would have been said that the "Dweller on the Threshold" has been evoked, and we are engaged in the necessary combat to control the beast.

Every human person has a peculiar life-problem which he or she has to deal or live with. In any case, if there were a single average sensitive person in this world without any hang-ups of some kind, I would personally not like to meet them. They would be too dull to bother with. So, we have unsublimated aspects in our lives. It is no good to "suppress" the worst in oneself with a ruthless imposition of will. A *secret* and *hidden* enemy is much worse than an open and honest one, which is far easier to deal with. The nature of that "inner enemy" needs to be transformed and changed rather than repressed and confined. In the latter case it becomes like an explosive—lethal, whereas dynamite can be burned as fuel. Put a light to it and it just burns. Compress and hit it, and it explodes.

William Gray claimed that the safest thing to do with one's "inner junk," is to evacuate it out of ones spiritual system down the "Abyss" on the Tree of Life. That is what it is there for. Alter the worst of your nature, just as your body does, to the spiritual equivalent of excrement, and shove it out to fertilize your Tree of Life.[11] In this regard I discovered a practical "formula for self-exorcism" when I realised that William Gray had addressed the same topic in his writings.[12] Afterwards I raised the subject in several private conversations I had with him. Here is the most simple formula for daily self-exorcism:

When you feel yourself to be in a state of great mental and emotional turmoil, you can rid yourself of this negativity by urinating and/or excreting whatever you are experiencing down the nearest toilet, literally forcing it out of your body with the urine or excrement. When you have bad thoughts, whisper or think while urinating "Toxic thinking—Go! like purest water flow!" Simultaneously imagine and feel all the "mental darkness" flowing out of you into the toilet. In turn, push bad feelings out of your system via the anus while whispering or thinking "Foul feelings—Forth! Return to cleanest earth!" Literally expel the disagreeable emotions from your body conjointly with the physical excrement.[13]

I have been, and still am, using this system with great results. I discovered that whatever my mood or mind-set may be, I have control over it. If I am thinking harmful thoughts, I rush into the nearest toilet and expel those thoughts, literally feeling them flow out of my system with the urine as I say "Toxic thinking go! Like clearest water flow," and if I get angry or have emotions which impact negatively on me or my world, I hurl myself into the nearest lavatory and evacuate these "negativities" from my being, literally expelling them with the physical excrement, with the firm instruction "Foul feelings forth! Return to cleanest earth!" I can assure you that this incredibly simple technique did not only save me from disastrous circumstances on many occasions, but it also brought balance into my life on more than just the material level of existence.

D. The Rite of *Noten Kavod* (Giving Respect): A Doorway to Higher Consciousness

It is not advantageous to work for peace in this world when some inanimate object is more respected and has more value than a human life, or, to put it differently, there will be no end to wars, abuse of the environment, etc., until respect for all manifestation returns to our world. Most people may consider this an impossibility, but that does not mean that those who have the intention of doing something to make this world a better place, should not at least make some attempt in the direction of bringing respect back into this sphere of existence by emanating and giving it from their own persons. The act of honouring all manifestation, from the mineral to the human, should be the first magical and ritual practice taught by any Temple of the Western Mystery Tradition.

This operation has the effect of influencing the environment in the same manner as that of the being of the practitioner. It slowly infiltrates and alters the thought and desire of all life to emanate and give respect to the whole of manifestation, and all its constituent parts. With this activity, peace and serenity are automatically encouraged in yourself, your reality and everything else you may encounter. Here is the practice in which the "Words of Power" are: *Noten Kavod*.

There are three stages in the "Rite of Giving Honour," each corresponding to one letter of the Divine Name יהו (*YHV*). Each stage is applied for one week, and during the third week the different stages are combined into a single procedure. When you are adept at doing this procedure as a matter of course throughout the day, it is a continual expression of יהוה (*YHVH*), the Ineffable Name of God.

Stage 1:

Whatever and whoever you meet through your five senses, whether it be an object, subject or person, e.g. a stone, a book, food, drink, animal or person, be gracious enough to bow in your mind to what you are encountering, and, while bowing, on an exhalation, mentally say the divine command: *Noten Kavod*. Smile warmly with your whole being. Feel your whole body, heart and soul smile and at the same time imagine that the warmth of your smile is flowing towards that to which you are giving respect, while you utter the "Words of Power." This stage causes a strong link to be established between your *Tzelem ha-Nefesh* (the body of your Instinctual Self), and that of what you are honouring. *Ruchaniyut* is then caused to flow from you towards the object, subject or person according to your intention.

Stage 2:

The next stage in this practice is to follow the same procedure as described in the first stage, but to imagine that you are receiving in return from that object, subject or person you are in contact with at that moment, the same respect, honour and warmth that you emanated. For example, if you are bowing and saying *Noten Kavod* to a tree, imagine that the tree is bowing and saying the "Words of Power" in return to you. By using imagination you are inducing a beneficial return flow of *Ruchaniyut* from the tree to yourself, provided you allow yourself to receive such an acknowledgement by being open to that return flow.

Stage 3:

In this stage you follow the procedure as described in the previous two stages, but you imagine that when you are saying the "Words of Power," the force flows out of your mouth or your entire being towards that which you are honouring in the form of a specific colour, element (fire, water, air or earth), with a specific associated quality such as love, health, etc., or even a combination of all of these. You should allow yourself to be guided by your own inner instincts as to what colour or elements you wish to emanate. This practice will become easier when combined with more advanced practices such as elemental breathing, etc., which will be taught later.

. ...And this indeed is not the case, for the change is due only to the receptors of the rays... ... .

Chapter 5
THE SCIENCE OF BREATH

A. *Avir:* Universal Life-Force

Very careful attention should be given to breathing, since there would be no life without it. To live in this physical realm, all that is animate (and maybe inanimate objects as well) must breathe, and all serious students should know that there is more to breath than the mere inhalation and exhalation of the physical elements comprising the atmosphere. Our bodies need both breath and food to exist, and the atmosphere is also food. Of course, as Franz Bardon indicated, the atmosphere is of a very much "finer degree of density" than physical food, yet, "according to the universal laws, both of them have the same nature."[1]

Since it is in breath where the power of the magician is situated, I have closely investigated and practised what Bardon had to say about breath. He indicated that when we look at the composition of the atmosphere we realise that oxygen belongs to the element of Fire and nitrogen to the element of Water. The element of Air balances Fire and Water, as the *Sefer Yetzirah*[2] explains, and the element of Earth is the gravity uniting the oxygen and hydrogen. *Avir* (the Spirit or Universal Element), is the mysterious fifth element, the Divine or Causal Principle, which underlines all the other elements, and is also experienced as a Universal Sea of Energy, or Life-Force if you like. As it is in the whole universe, the Four Elements of Fire, Air, Water and Earth, have polarities—the radiative and the attractive. Bardon called them the electric and the magnetic. During normal, unconscious breathing, only the elemental substances required for survival are absorbed by body. With conscious breathing however, different possibilities arise.

Amongst other techniques, one might decide to put a thought, idea or image, in the atmosphere to be inhaled. With conscious breath, it will be absorbed in *Avir*, the Universal Ether,

Universal Life-Force or Spirit Principle, from whence it is transmitted through the radiative (electric) and attractive (magnetic) currents, into the substance of the atmosphere. When this infused substance is inhaled, a double process takes place. Firstly the material components of the elements preserve the body, and secondly the electro-magnetic current, infused with a thought-form or an image, will carry the impregnated air from the bloodstream through the *Nefesh* to the *Tzelem ha-Nefesh*, the shadow body of the Lower Self, and from there it can be carried to the *Neshamah*, the Higher Self.

This is the secret of breathing from the magical point of view, but it is not the quantity of the air inhaled that matters, but the quality of the air impregnated with ideas. Therefore it is not necessary to pump the lungs full of air. Breath is probably the most important tool in the whole of the Tradition, and therefore a lot of attention should be given to its usage, and the cultivation of strong, healthy breathing abilities. *Kabbalah* teaches that when one breathes correctly one acquires certain life-giving elements from the spiritual universe, which increase and sharpen consciousness and awareness in the individual. Thus, proper physical health needs a good, breathing rhythm, and the relationship of the element of air to good health is expressed in the letters of the words *Avir* (אויר meaning "air") and *Bari* (ברia meaning "healthy"), which comprise practically the same letters in different permutations. Traditionally the letters *Vav* (ו) and *Bet* (ב) can be interchanged, since they belong to the group of letters (*Bet, Vav, Mem,* and *Peh*) called "labials," that is pronounced with the lips. Thus there is a connection between breath and health, and this tells us that we become healthy when we breathe properly. The letter *Bet* (ב) means "a house," representing archetypally a containing element, such as the body, the health of which depends on the function of the element of air within it.

Kabbalah tells how God created Light (*Aur* – אור), and then how He later added the letter *Yod* (י), thus converting the *Or* (אור) into *Avir* (אויר – Air). The *Yod* (י) is seen to be the element of oxygen, which is well explained in the word *Mayim* (מים) meaning Water, consisting of the letter *Mem* (מ) repeated twice, and since the letter *Mem* means water, it refers to the two hydrogen atoms, plus the *Yod* (י), the oxygen atom, which is exactly the atomic structure of water, H_2O. So in the beginning there was "Light" (*Or*), and much later was added the element of oxygen, which became the basis of all Life.

The word *Avir* (אויר) comprises the letters *Alef* (א) and *Yod* (י), connected by the letter *Vav* (ו). The final letter *Resh* (ר), expressing movement, as one can see in its pronunciation, represents the motion of Light and Air. Many words related to running in several languages contain the letter "R." The part of the body linked to *Avir* (אויר—"air"), is *Reyah* (ריאה), the "lung." The elements of air, א—י—ר (*Alef–Yod–Resh*), are also found in the lungs. These elements are said to maintain the body through ה (*Heh*) meaning "Life," whose numerical value is five which is said to refer to the five parts of the lungs.[3]

As we noted, *Avir* means more than just the physical air we breath. The term also refers to much more subtle essences. It is understood in *Kabbalah* to be the undifferentiated substance behind all substance, in total, inseparable unity with infinite creative potencies. It is said that *Avir*, the "very pure and imperceptible air,"[4] surrounds and is hidden in the first creative causes of the universe. *Avir* is thus what has been called, the "universal ether," the absolute essence of the four subtle, universal elements, as well as the four material elements in absolute unity. It is said that this ether is like a universal sea, and in its infinite receptivity, it is being played upon by the "Breath of God," thus it is connected to the *Sefirah Binah* (Understanding), seen as the "Mother Principle" of all Life, both subtle and manifested. The "Father Principle" is *Chochmah* (Wisdom), understood to be hidden in *Keter*, (the Crown of Consciousness), called the "Ancient of Days." *Avir*, as a "very pure air"[5] so to speak, is enfolded in *Keter*, but the moment *Chochmah* appears as an intelligible emanation, or spiritual flame, out of the "Ancient of Days," *Avir* as *Binah*, the ether sea, envelopes and unites with it, and then both the Spiritual Flame and the Ether together follow the process of manifestation, until they emerge as the mythological Adam and Eve in the "World of Manifestation" or "Action."

This creative process, in which undifferentiated substance is made manifest, is described by the Tree of Life with its Ten

Sefirot, as the "Ten Fundamental Revelations of God," manifested firstly on a universal level as ten heavens, in which *Keter–Chochmah–Binah*, the three *Supernal Sefirot*, are the three "Heavens of heavens," again a three-in-one principle, whose separate aspects are called *Shechinah–Metatron–Avir*[6] on another level. The Divine Presence as a Feminine Force in the Cosmos is the *Shechinah* in *Keter*, the active aspect of which is *Metatron* in *Chochmah*, the principle form emanating all manifestation. The passive aspect of the *Shechinah* is then *Avir* (the Ether as a manifestation of *Binah*), giving birth to all manifestation, emanated from *Chochmah*, whether subtle or material. The three-in-one principle of *Shechinah–Metatron–Avir* as an inseparable unity, is then said to comprise the Spiritual World of Creation: *Olam ha-Bri'ah*.

Now *Binah* is the place of atonement, *Teshuvah* in Hebrew, of which the Talmud says: "Great is *Teshuvah*, for it heals the world. Great is *Teshuvah*, for it reaches the throne of glory. Great is *Teshuvah*, for it brings about redemption."[7] Atonement must not be understood as a grovelling before a dictatorial deity, but rather as a unification process. Thus the word "Atonement" literally means At–ONE–ment. By being absorbed into God, man works the universal deliverance of not only himself, but also works towards cosmic redemption, which can only happen in its totality when the whole of manifestation, both physical and spiritual, has reached its rightful fulfilment in the worlds of manifestation, at which moment it is said that the "grand Jubilee" will take place as the complete and last liberation, an absolute reabsorption of the whole of existence into *Ain Sof*, the ultimate Eternal No-Thing. This again is said will be achieved at the end of "seven times seven millennia," meaning vast cycles of continuance, and this is believed to be the conclusive stage of *Tzimtzum*, or "inversion of inversions"[8] as it is called, which is the "contraction" of the manifested universe and the whole of the cosmos. This is understood to be the "withdrawal" of the whole of manifestation into its unmanifested centre. What finally remain are the inherent immaterial, divine sparks recapturing their original transcendent radiance, while all earthly and heavenly substances are reintegrated into the "higher ether."

Now let us turn our attention to several breathing practices, both ancient and modern, in use amongst Kabbalists today.

B. The Mother Breath

This exercise derives from the "Three Mother Letters" concept addressed in the *"Book of Creation" (Sefer Yetzirah)*.[9] Obviously the concepts that are of central importance in the *Sefer Yetzirah* are those of numbers and letters. The predominant theory of this text is that the letters of the alphabet, including those comprising the Ineffable Name of God, are symbols of divine power, the combination of which lead to the creation of the material world. In other words, the combination of the Powers as represented by the letters, brings forth physical matter, and the book explains how this is achieved. It is the second verse of the *Sefer Yetzirah* which refers to the twenty-two letters of the Hebrew Alphabet, dividing these into three sections. It reads "Twenty-two letters are the foundation: three Mothers, seven double, and twelve simple."[10]

Looking at the Mother Letters, these being the letters *Alef* (א), *Mem* (מ) and *Shin* (ש), it was suggested that they are "Mother" letters because they represent the three sounds used throughout the ages by all mothers in controlling their babies, but it is also known in some Kabbalistic circles that these three letters refer to a special breathing exercise called the "Mother Breath."[11]

In this practice the breath is inhaled with the mouth in the shape of *"Ah,"* and the exhalation being first through the nose as the mouth is closed for *"Mmmmm."* The exhalation is completed through the mouth as it is opened to the sound *"Shhhhh."* Thus during inhalation there is the silent sound of *"Ah,"* while on the exhalation the whispering sounds *"mmmm......shhhhh"* can be heard. These three sounds imitate the ebb and flow motion of waves of the ocean, sounding the *"Ah"* as the backwash contract, and the *"mmmm"* as the wave starts to swell, and finally the *"shhhh"* as the wave breaks on the shingle. The sea is our "Primordial Mother" from whom originates all life on earth, thus the Mother Letters, refer to both the action of the sea and our ability to align ourselves with it through this unique breathing exercise.

To start the procedure, imagine or feel yourself seated waist deep in the centre of a vast lake or sea of Universal Life-Force. It stretches around you way beyond the horizon. Sense the infinity of this force around you, and then, while taking an inbreath with the mouth shaped as mentioned, feel yourself inhaling this sea of energy via the anus into your body. Imagine that you are literally sucking it into your body during inhalation. On exhalation, while whispering the sounds as discussed, imagine and feel the force flowing out via your rectum, back towards the horizon and into infinity. Literally release it back to its original status. This is called: "breathing in the manner of power," and is a very intense practice which could be employed with all the breathing exercises. Yet, I should caution you to do this with extreme care, and to cease the practice if it feels in the least uncomfortable or overpowering. In such an instance it would be better to breathe in a normal fashion, while imagining that you are the sea moving backwards and forwards.

Another point worth noting is, that you should rest between each breath, and in that pause, immediately after exhalation you should become aware of a vast emptiness within yourself. Regarding this Avram Davis, one of the most inspirational authors, wrote "*Kabbalah* teaches that before and after any manifestation, there is emptiness, before and after any being, there is emptiness. Try this principal truth by listening to your own breathing: before inhalation, there is emptiness in your lungs, after exhalation, there is also emptiness in your lungs......This emptiness is eternal, outside boundaries of time, space, and events. Emptiness is what lies behind you, past events in your life that are but memories, but fragrances of flowers bloomed and faded. Emptiness is what lies before you, future events not yet known, lands yet to be explored. Emptiness is the present, it is you right now."[12]

So, during the pause between the outbreath and the next inbreath, say in your mind "After exhalation—emptiness. Before inhalation—emptiness," and feel the meaning of these words without attempting to explain them. Then repeat the procedure by becoming again aware of the vast ocean of *Avir*, the Universal Sea of Abundance and Life-Force around you, and inhale it again in the manner described. Since it is a wonderful meditation practice, which can be used in stress management, you may repeat the exercise as many times as you like. However, I would recommend that you work with around twelve breaths per exercise, and then to gradually increase the breathing cycles over time as is comfortable, and be careful to avoid discomfort. The "Mother Breath" is highly recommended for those who not only wish to still the mind, or as a preparation for other meditative practices, but also to bring about a state of balanced harmony within the psyche.

C. The Complete Breath[13]

One of the most fundamental Yogic practices, the Complete Breath can be considered a "Gestalt" exercise, since it brings the practitioner in contact with the different parts of his body. Again I regard one of the most important components of the practice, to be the ability to smile warmly inside yourself while doing the practice. It has been said many times that "energy flows where attention goes," and this is certainly the case here, even more so when you focus with great friendship on your body.

Now, here we learn the skill behind this exercise in stages, at the end of which you will have acquired the ability to take a "Complete Breath" in the best possible manner. What is more, the process delineated here is also a great meditation exercise.

1. Begin by surrendering yourself to gravity, i.e. becoming as heavy as possible.
2. Contrary to what is normally suggested, e.g. breathing through the nose, breathe in through the mouth and nose into the zone of your heart, letting your chest swell fully.
   While exhaling through your mouth, imagine breathing out through the top of the head. If you are worried about breathing in through your mouth, just remember that it is quite a natural manner of breathing, and that you are doing so every night when you fall asleep. Your jaw drops, and you begin to breathe very deeply, even snoring!
   Be that as it may, repeat this part of the procedure twice more.
3. While inhaling, imagine you are breathing in fully through the top of the head into the solar plexus.
   Again imagine on exhalation, that you are breathing out through the top of the head.
   Repeat this part of the procedure twice more.
4. Again combine your inhalation with imagining that you are breathing in deeply through the top of the head, but this time feel yourself breathing in fully downwards to just below the navel.

While exhaling, feel yourself breathe out through a hole situated directly below the navel.
Repeat this part of the procedure twice more.
5. Breathe in deeply through the mouth and nose, allowing the breath to flow deep down into your genital/rectal area. You can facilitate this a lot by pushing down slightly on the anal sphincter while inhaling.
Breathe out whilst imagining that you are exhaling through the top of the head.
Repeat this part of the procedure twice more.
6. The following stage is what we were aiming at in the first place, and is "The Complete Breath" proper.
Breathe in through the mouth and nose filling your entire torso, that is all the mentioned areas of the genitals/anus, navel, solar plexus, and heart/chest, all simultaneously.
Breathe out normally with a sigh.
Repeat this part of the procedure twice more.

D. Advanced Breathing Programme

Your entire existence on this planet is based on breath. That is certainly obvious, but not always clearly recognised since you breathe unconsciously, and are not normally aware how your breathing skills impact on your health, wealth and happiness. All your communication skills are dependent on your breathing ability. Your moods can be controlled by breath, i.e. fast, shallow, intercostal breathing creates anxiety and can lead to tears, while deep abdominal breathing brings relaxation, surrender, openness, etc. Good conscious breathing skills are vital in all meditation and magical work. In this regard, the following breathing techniques should be carefully practised, because they are used to:

1. improve vitality and health and increase the flow of *Ruchaniyut* (Spiritual Power) throughout your being.
2. strengthen concentration, expand sensory perception and increase creativity.
3. build rapport with all life, aid in the building and transmission of thought-forms, and assist one in becoming a transmitter of Life-Force and vitality in this world. In this regard breath plays a vital role.

4. consciously control the quantity and quality of the flow of *Ruchaniyut* between yourself and all life around you.

The following programme of breathing exercises can be worked in a course lasting three weeks, during which an hour a day, that is a half an hour in the morning and a half an hour at night is devoted to breathing. However, following such a regimen of intense breathing exercises can have detrimental effects in the hands of unskilled practitioners, hence in this case it is advisable you devote a maximum of half an hour daily to these exercises, that is either a half hour once a day, or two quarter hours twice daily. In this manner you can develop your breathing skills slowly over a number of months.

PROGRAMME 1

Exercise 1

1. (5 to 10 minutes) Place both hands on the abdomen. Inhale as deeply as possible against the hands, expanding the abdomen as much as possible without allowing the chest or ribs to expand in the least.
    a. Inhalation counting five.
    b. Pause counting six.
    c. Exhalation counting four.
    d. Rest counting six.
2. (5 to 10 minutes) Place both hands on either side of your ribs. Breathe in deeply, pressing out the ribs, but without allowing either the abdomen or the upper chest to expand.
    Breathing cycle is the same as described above.
3. (5 to 10 minutes) Place both hands on the upper chest, just below the throat, and breathe with this portion of the lungs without allowing either the ribs or the abdomen to expand.
    Breathing cycle is the same as described above.

Exercise 2

For 15 to 30 minutes, breathe Complete Breaths only, that is breathe simultaneously into all three areas discussed previously.

    e.   Inhalation counting five.
    b.   Pause counting six.
    c.   Exhalation counting four.
    d.   Rest counting six.

Exercise 3: "The Rising Breath"[14]

This exercise, as well as several of the following ones, are part of a set of breathing practices recommended in acquiring the skill of consciously leaving the body, generally called "astral projection."

Part One (for 5 to 10 minutes)

    a.   Stand straight with heels fairly close together, and the feet turned outwards, i.e. "V" shaped. This is important, since it is impossible to maintain balance, and is most uncomfortable, when you attempt rising up on your toes when you feet are facing directly forwards.
    b.   Inhale steadily counting six, at the same time rising up on your toes as the air fills your torso.
    c.   Hold your breath and your stance counting six. Be careful not to tense up at this point. Holding the breath simply means to pause, to hover as it were, between an inhalation and an exhalation.
    d.   Exhale slowly through the nostrils counting six and lower yourself accordingly.

Part Two (for 5 to 10 minutes)

Repeat the practice exactly as described in the first part of this exercise, but raise your arms at the same time as you inhale and rise up on your toes, and lower your arms as you exhale and lower your heels. The general feeling should be something like a preparing your spirit to "take off" into flight when you rise, and settling back into yourself when you exhale and lower your arms and heels. Here you should aim for a smooth movement of arms, breath and body.

Exercise 4: "The Prolonged Breath"[15]
(For 15 to 30 minutes)

a. Stand or sit erect.
b. Breathe in slowly to a count of eight.
c. Pause and count to ten, or as long as you can without strain. Again it is vitally important to pause rather than hold, the difference between the two being that "holding" can be a sort of up-tight, locked-in state as opposed to the relaxed hovering required during the pause.
d. Exhale by forcing the air out of your body through the mouth in three short gusts.

Exercise 5: "The Cleansing Breath"
(For 15 to 30 minutes)

1. Sit or lie in a relaxed position.
2.
   a. Inhalation counting four.
   b. Pause counting one.
   c. Exhalation counting four.
   d. Pause counting one.
3.
   a. Inhalation counting five.
   b. pause counting one.
   c. Exhalation counting five.
   d. Pause counting one.
4. Increase the counts with each cycle, until a cycle of seven counts on inhalation and exhalation is reached.
5. Decrease the counts with each cycle until the return to a cycle of four counts on inhalation and exhalation.

Exercise 6: "The Advanced Cleansing Breath"
(For 15 to 30 minutes)

1. Sit or lie in a relaxed position.
2.   a. Inhalation counting seven.
      b. Pause counting one.
      c. Exhalation counting seven.
      d. Pause counting one.
3. Repeat twelve times.
4.   a. Inhalation counting four.
      b. Pause counting one.
      c. Exhalation counting twelve.
      d. Pause counting one.
5.   a. Inhalation counting five.
      b. Pause counting one.
      c. Exhalation counting thirteen.
      d. Pause counting one.
6. Increase counts by one each cycle on the inhalation and exhalation until a count of twelve on inhalation and twenty on exhalation.
7. Decrease the counts on each cycle until the original inhalation four counts/exhalation twelve counts cycle is again established.

Exercise 7

When all the previous exercises are mastered individually, you should practice them collectively for 30 minutes every day.

PROGRAMME 2

Exercise 1
(For 15 to 30 minutes per day)

1. Do the cleansing breath as described previously of the previous week, until the cycle of inhalation counting twelve (pause) and exhalation counting twenty (pause).
2.   a. Take a Complete Breath (no pause).
      b. Exhale in four short breaths through the nostrils, blowing out the last part of air.

	c.	Pause counting ten.
3.	a.	Repeat steps a and b in section 2.
	b.	Pause counting fifteen.
4.	a.	Repeat steps a and b in section 2.
	b.	Pause counting twenty.
5.		Repeat the entire practice for as long as time allows.

Exercise 2
(For 15 to 30 minutes per day)

1.		Do the cleansing breath as described previously, until the cycle of inhalation counting twelve (pause) and exhalation counting twenty (pause).
2.	a.	Inhale counting fifteen.
	b.	Hold counting twenty.
	c.	Pause one second.
	d.	Out fully with a sigh.
	e.	Pause one second.
3.	a.	Inhale counting fifteen.
	b.	Hold counting twenty-five.
	c.	Pause one second.
	d.	Out fully with a sigh.
	e.	Pause one second.
4.	a.	Inhale counting fifteen.
	b.	Hold counting thirty.
	c.	Pause one second.
	d.	Out fully with a sigh.
	e.	Pause one second.
5.		Repeat reducing the counts during the pause until the original count of twenty during the pause.
6.		Repeat the entire practice time permitting.

Exercise 3
(For 15 to 30 minutes per day)

1. Take a Complete Breath.
2. Pause counting four.
3. Pucker up the lips, as though you are about to whistle.

4. Without puffing up your cheeks, exhale a little of the air through the opening with great vigour. Pause briefly, and exhale a little more air. In other words, blow the air forcefully out in short gusts through the opening. Repeat until all the air has been exhaled. Use vigour in expelling the air through the lips.
5. Repeat the entire procedure for as long as time allows.

Exercise 4
(For 15 to 30 minutes per day)

1. Inhale a Complete Breath.
2. Hold counting four.
3. Pucker up the lips as described in the previous exercise.
4. Exhale very slowly through the opening. Attempt slowing the outbreath more and more during each repeat practice, in order to get the exhalation to last for longer periods.
5. Time permitting, repeat the entire procedure several times.

Exercise 5
(For 15 to 30 minutes per day)

1. Light a candle.
2. Sit facing the candle with the flame at the level of your mouth.
3. Inhale a Complete Breath.
4. Hold counting four.
5. Open the mouth, and exhale slowly without moving the candle flame with the breath.
6. Repeat the entire procedure for as long as time allows.

Exercise 6[16]
(For 15 to 30 minutes per day)

1. Sit or lie down comfortably.
2. Clasp the hands and raise them to your mouth, letting the thumbs rest on either side of the nose. Rest the elbows comfortably on the sides of the body.

3. Close the left nostril with your left thumb and inhale through your right nostril, filling the lungs to capacity, but not to where you feel uncomfortable.
4. Close the right nostril with your right thumb, thus closing both nostrils, and begin counting from one to hundred until you can no longer hold your breath comfortably.
5. Open the left nostril and exhale slowly through your left nostril, without straining or forcing the breath.
6. This time inhale through the left nostril, keeping the right nostril closed.
7. Close both nostrils and hold the breath again while counting.
8. When the same number of counts is reached as before, open the right nostril and exhale slowly and comfortably.
9. Repeat the whole procedure if time allows.

The object of this exercise is to hold the breath for longer and longer periods, but this must be done gradually. A harmonic ratio should be introduced between the inhalation, hold and exhalation. The ration begins with 12 seconds for inhalation, 48 seconds for holding, and 24 seconds for exhalation. Slowly over the next weeks, the ratio should be increased to 16:64:32, and then ultimately to 20:80:40. There is no need to go beyond this, and what is also important to realise is that it is not important to achieve these high ratios at all. A ratio of 5:20:10 or 6:24:12 is also perfectly acceptable for our work. Thus do not get yourself into a state of anxiety, but realise that it is the ratio which is important in this case, and simply work at it as far as is possible, and never force the breath.

Exercise 7

When all the exercises of the second programme are mastered, they should be worked collectively, for a period of about 30 minutes at a time.

PROGRAMME 3

(This practice could be done for 15 to 30 minutes per day, and developed over a period of several months)

1. For 5 to 10 minutes, repeat the "Rising Breath" exercise as described in Programme 1.
2. For 5 to 10 minutes, repeat the sixth exercise as described in the Programme 2, starting with the ratio 12:48:24, and gradually increasing it to 16:64:32.
3. For 5 to 10 minutes:
   a. Imagine your head extends 12 inches longer from the top of your head, and as you breathe in and out physically, inhale and exhale mentally into and out of that extended part of the head.
   b. Imagine your fingers extend 12 inches longer from the tips, and as you breathe in and out physically, inhale and exhale mentally in and out of the extended fingers.

These breathing exercises should be practised for at least six months, and attempt to increase the ratio gradually to 20:80:40. However, considering the spiritual activities we are addressing throughout this book, it is certainly not necessary to acquire these higher breathing ratios. It is best to work on a comfortable ratio and stick to that.

Having acquired these breathing skills, it will be quite easy to work meditation and ritual practices requiring the focussing of "Divine Energy" within your own being. Here is one such special technique of this genre:

E. Taking on the Name

In this technique the Ineffable Name is visualised as if the constituent letters were being written on different parts of the human anatomy. The practice is addressed by Chaim Vital in his remarkable *"Sha'ar Ru'ach ha-Kodesh."*[17]

Now, the use of a custom like "Taking on the Name" facilitates the "drawing down" (*hamshachah*) of a powerful current of "Divine Force" (*Avir/Ruchaniyut*) from the Source, the Eternal Living Spirit, from your "Infinite Point of 'Is'–ness." Each time you repeat the practice, a quantity of this Spiritual Force is drawn into your own being until the self begins to transform, and is liberated from anxieties, repressions, constraints, and ailments. When this transformation is achieved, one is able to communicate this Divine Power to anyone and anything you may encounter in your daily life.

The potency of this technique derives from the repeated inhalation of the *Avir/Ruchaniyut*, drawn from the Eternal Living Spirit. The power must be absorbed from the Divine, and thus the principal perception must be of a great wellspring of Divine Life-Force which you are willing to draw from and having its effects integrated into your own being. So it is extremely important that you start with an exercise in which you unite your consciousness with that "Infinite Point of 'Is'–ness" or "Infinite Point of Radiance," the "Eternal No-Thing," *Ain Sof* or God, which we will now address in greater detail. To work this special alignment, you need to use a little imagination in the same manner as those who have come before us have done.

In many of the Alchemical, Hermetic and Kabbalistic works written during the Renaissance, the power of the Almighty is often illustrated as an eye in the sky from which a ray of light extends downwards. Sometimes this ray is seen as striking the kneeling Kabbalist or worshipper in the forehead. While one would not necessarily visualise the power of God as deriving from an "eye in the sky," the idea is a good one, and one might envisage a line of force extending from an invisible and infinite "Point of Radiance" — sort of diagonally above ones head — from which a ray of Divine Life-Force is streaming into the forehead or the top of the head. This is in fact a technique which has been used over many centuries, in which the imagination (image making part of your being) is employed to facilitate a direct link between the human worshipper and his or her "Divine Source."

The technique is rather simple. You start by directing your attention upwards, almost as if you are reaching with your consciousness, your thoughts and feelings, into the endless infinity above you, until you sense — more or less diagonally above you — an "Infinite Point of Radiance." You can draw inspiration, health, strength, etc. from this infinite source of well-being. The instant you feel this connectedness with this Infinite, Invisible Source, breathe in and focus on your forehead or the top of your head. Then, on exhalation, breathe a ray or beam of your consciousness — like a beam of light or energy — in the direction of this Infinite Point of Radiance. Feel this ray being beamed like the light of a laser from your forehead, and attach it to your Infinite Source. You may want to repeat this action several times, until you are comfortable within yourself that such a bond has been established. As said, you may repeat the exercise until *you* are happy with the results. The feeling of connectedness via a radiant beam of light with your Point of Radiance is a little like being a puppet on a string.

After having established contact with your Infinite Point of Radiance, take a deep breath, and as you inhale, imagine that you are absorbing Divine Power from that Infinite Point, drawing it along the line of light which you have established, literally sucking this force into your forehead or into the top of your head. Then, on the exhalation, simply release this power by allowing it to flow downwards and suffusing your entire body. You can repeat this practice as many times as you wish, but the important thing is not how long you do each exercise, but how regularly you do it. Rather practice every day for three minutes, than for an hour once a week. You are establishing a conscious connection between yourself and your Infinite Source, and only regular practice will make this real for you.

When you feel this bond with the Divine is becoming potent and strong, and that it is relatively easy and comfortable drawing down Divine Force into your body, you can continue with the actual "Taking on the Name," in which we again use the four letters of the Ineffable Name combined with five vowels. In this *Yichud* one is required to memorize the four letters of the Ineffable Name:

יהוה

As you probably know, Hebrew is written from right to left thus your first letter (*Yod*) is the small one on the right, followed by *Heh–Vav–Heh*. When you are able to easily recall the four letters, you need to practice visualising them in the form of golden flames.

Keep in mind that with the practice of "Taking on the Name" you align yourself with the Eternal Living Spirit behind all existence and literally "robe yourself in light."

Do not be too concerned if you find it somewhat difficult to visualise the four letters of the *Tetragrammaton* exactly. In fact, you can work the *Yichud* equally successfully by "feeling the power flow." Of course, it would be even better if you could combine "thinking" and "feeling," i.e. visualisation and sensory experience. Let us commence with a preliminary and preparatory exercise, which helps you expand your being beyond the limits of the body.

1. Stand, close your eyes and let your arms hang comfortably. You need to smile a very warm inner smile while doing this practice.
2. Focus on your skull, now draw Divine Energy from your Infinite Source into the centre of the forehead while inhaling. On exhalation imagine that your are breathing out into the skull, and in so doing you are expanding it with Divine Energy. It should be a kind of swelling sensation, almost as if the skull is a balloon blowing up with Divine Energy. You should feel as if you are pushing your real Self out of the body, or expanding it beyond the limits of the body.
3. Repeat this practice with the rest of your body, that is to start by breathing the Divine Energy in through the centre of your forehead, or the top of your head, and then to exhale it into the respective parts of your anatomy, each time attempting to blow up, expand, or swell beyond the bodily limits. The different parts are processed with this expanding procedure in the following order:

   a. **Skull** (Top of the Skull [*Keter*—Crown];
   b. **Right Brain** [*Chochmah*—Wisdom];
   c. **Left Brain** [*Binah*—Understanding])
   d. **Right Arm/Hand** (*Chesed*—Mercy)
   e. **Left Arm/Hand** (*Gevurah*—Severity)
   f. **Torso** (*Tiferet*—Beauty)
   g. **Right Leg/Foot** (*Netzach*—Victory)
   h. **Left Leg/Foot** (*Hod*—Glory)

i. **Sexual Organ** (*Yesod*—Foundation)
j. **Entire Body** (Malchut—Kingdom)

You need to master this portion of the work very well in order to continue with the "Taking on the Name" practice, thus you need to practice regularly until you become used to the sensation of being larger than your physical body. The exact sensation is that your body is inside you rather than you being inside it. Constant practice actually leads to you becoming expanded beyond bodily limits, this being actually the case with your normal existence in this realm of manifestation where a very small part of you is really incarnated inside the body — the rest of you is everywhere. This is very well expressed by William Gray in the "*Sangreal Sacrament*" reading:

> **O Perfect Peace Profound, of Utmost Inexistence, Infinite Eternal Nil, Unborn, Unbeing, Unbounded, Unilluminate, Unmanifest. THOU ART THAT. Originate Ourself. Utter forth the Willword**
>
> **LIGHT**
>
> **Make manifest thy majesty. Begin thy LIFE by LOVE, according to the LAW of Cosmos and Creation.**
>
> **BE WHAT THOU WILT WITHIN THEE**
>
> **In the Name of the Wisdom**
> **And of the Love**
> **And of the Justice**
> **And the Infinite Mercy**
> **Of the One Eternal Spirit**
> ***Amen.***[18]

In the "Taking on the Name" practice, the Ineffable Name (*YHVH*) is thought, whispered, or intoned with different vowels, each associated with an associated part of the human anatomy, which is in turn associated with an affiliated sphere on the *Etz Chayim*, the Kabbalistic Tree of Life, as shown in the following table:

Divine Name	Sefirah	Associated Bodily Part
YahHahVahHah	*Keter* (Crown)	Skull—from the forehead over the skull to the back of the head
YahHahVahHah	*Chochmah* (Wisdom)	Right Brain—from the back of the head around the right side of the skull to the forehead
YayHayVayHay	*Binah* (Understanding)	Left Brain—from the forehead around the left side of the skull to the back of the head
YehHehVehHeh	*Chesed* (Kindness)	Right Arm—from the shoulder down to the palm of the right hand
YuhHuhVuhHuh	*Gevurah* (Strength)	Left Arm—from the palm of the left hand up to the right shoulder
YohHohVohHoh	*Tiferet* (Beauty)	Torso—from the left shoulder diagonally across the chest to the right hip
YeeHeeVeeHee	*Netzach* (Victory)	Right Leg—from the right hip down to the right foot
YooHooVooHoo	*Hod* (Splendour)	Left Leg—from the left foot up to the left hip
YooHooVooHoo	*Yesod* (Foundation)	Sexual Organ—along or around the sexual organ
Yod Heh Vav Heh (*EE-AH-OH-EH*)	*Malchut* (Kingdom)	Entire Body—head [*Yod*] – shoulders/arms [*Heh*] – torso [*Vav*] – pelvis/legs [*Heh*] – this is sometimes pronounced: "*EE–AH–OH–EH*," these being the four vowels respectively associated with the head, heart, solar plexus and throat

Here the following vowels are respectively associated with the *Sefirot*:

Keter and *Chochmah* — **AH**
Binah — **AY**
Chesed — **EH**
Gevurah — **UH**
Tiferet — **OH**
Netzach — **EE**
Hod and *Yesod* — **OO**

Armed with this information, and prepared through the regular use of the preparatory exercise, you are almost ready to undertake the "Taking on the Name" practice. To complete your preparation, you need to study the "path" the Divine Light will follow as you direct it through your body. You also need to know the manner in which the Ineffable Name is "written" in "fiery letters" on or inside the respective parts of your body. Hopefully you have memorized the four letters of the Divine Name well enough to be able to clearly recall each glyph in your mind.

In "Taking on the Name" you will "draw down" Divine Energy in the form of golden light, in appearance not unlike the brilliance of the Sun. You will absorb this Divine Force into your body, simultaneously visualising the four letters of the Ineffable Name being written over the bodily zone you are working with at that moment. This is done while you think, whisper or intone the Divine Name with the appropriate vowel associated with that bodily part. For example, you focus on your "Infinite Point of 'Is'–ness," your link with Divinity, diagonally above and in front of you. Sense a line of force stretching from your forehead and linking you with this "Infinite Source." You must literally feel this *Tzinor* (channel) stretching between you and your "Infinite Point of Radiance." Then, while inhaling (we usually inhale through the mouth using "*ah*"), imagine that you are "drawing down" the Divine Power in the form of golden light into your forehead. On the exhalation you simply allow this golden light to flow over your head as you think, whisper or intone the Divine Name, simultaneously "writing with fire" its component letters evenly spaced over your head as you express the associated syllables silently or verbally. On completion you should have, as it were, a ribbon of Divine Energy stretching over the top of your skull from your forehead to the back of the head, and the four letters of the Ineffable Name "flaming" on top of or inside your head.

This procedure is repeated with the other parts of the body associated with the *Sefirot*, until you have a whole circuit of golden Divine Energy spiralling through your body, and nine sets of Divine Names flaming along this "ribbon of light" entwined around your anatomy from your forehead to your sexual organ. Finally you complete with the utterance of the *Tetragrammaton* when your entire body is "lit up" with the Divine Force, i.e. each of the associated bodily zones (head, shoulders/arms, torso, pelvis/legs) filled with the golden light of the Divine Energy. Your image of yourself should then be something like this:

An important point to remember here is that, each time you take a new breath to deal with another bodily part in the procedure, the entire "path of Light" is traced from its origins in the "Infinite Source" to its last conclusion. The Divine Light is always drawn into the forehead and along the spiralling pattern to the new zone you will be dealing with next, and then on the exhalation you continue by allowing the Light to flow further along the pattern it is tracing in your body.

Of course, it would be a lot easier to illustrate this procedure in person, but while it is somewhat difficult to describe it on the written page, I think you would be able to make quite good sense of the way it functions with a more detailed description of the procedure. So here it is:

1. Stand, and let the arms hang comfortably by your side. Close your eyes, and remember to smile warmly while doing this practice.
2. Focus on your forehead and sense the line of force which ties you with your "Infinite Source" diagonally above you. If you find it difficult to sense this connection, you need to establish or re-establish this link by taking a deep breath and on exhalation (mouth shaped "*OO*") imagine that you are beaming a line of force from your forehead to your "Infinite Point of Power." It is not important how strong you feel this link. It is more important that you do this, and feel that you have established such a channel.
3. Now, breathe in and imagine that you are drawing Divine Energy in the form of golden light along this line into the centre of your forehead, and then, as you exhale, imagine that the Divine Force is flowing from your forehead over the crown of your head to the back of your skull. Simultaneously write the constituent letters of the Ineffable Name (יהוה) in fiery letters over your head as you express the Name, **Yah–Hah–Vah–Hah**. Each letter is "written" as you express its associated syllable in the Divine Name.
4. This practice is repeated next with the Right Brain associated with *Chochmah* (Wisdom). Again you need to draw the Divine Energy in through the centre of the forehead, but with this inhalation you need to draw the energy along the "path" it has traced thus far to the back of your head. As you do this, you should also be aware of the letters of the Divine Name flaming over the crown of your head. Then, as you breathe out, you allow the golden Divine Light to flow along the next portion of its path in your body, that is to flow from the back around the right side of your head to the front, returning to the spot where it entered your head. As you do this you simultaneously express the Divine Name, **Yah–Hah–Vah–Hah**, and again write its associated letters in fire on or in your right brain.
5. Next this entire procedure is repeated with your Left Brain associated with *Binah* (Understanding), remembering to trace the entire completed path as you draw the Divine Power into, over and around the right side of your head

during inhalation. As you do this, you must again be aware of the two sets of fiery letters flaming over and around the right side of your head. On exhalation you allow the Divine Power to continue its flow along its designated path in your body, this time from the forehead around the left side of your head to the back of the head, while uttering the associated Divine Name, **Yay–Hay–Vay–Hay**, and writing its constituent letters in fire as you utter each syllable. At the completion of this portion of the procedure, you should feel as if you have a "Crown of Divine Light" on your head.

6. Next you repeat this procedure with each of the bodily parts associated with the lower *Sefirot*, every time remembering to trace the completed path and to sense the flaming letters as you inhale the Divine Power into your body, before continuing on exhalation with the next portion of the circuit. The remaining pattern is as follows:

   a. **Right Arm:** Divine Power directed down your right arm into your right hand, as you write the letters and express the Divine Name, **Yeh–Heh–Veh–Heh**.

   b. **Left Arm:** During inhalation you draw the golden Divine Light via the forehead into your body, tracing the entire path it follows to the right hand from whence it jumps, as it were, into your left hand. Then, on exhalation, you allow it to flow from your right hand up your left arm to your left shoulder, simultaneously writing the associated letters as you express the Divine Name, **Yuh–Huh–Vuh–Huh**.

   c. **Torso:** Again you breathe in the Divine Light from its "Infinite Source of Radiance," tracing it along the path it has completed previously, and on exhalation you let it flow from your left shoulder downwards diagonally across the torso to your right hip, while writing and expressing the Divine Name, **Yoh–Hoh–Voh–Hoh**.

   d. **Right Leg:** The Divine Light is inhaled and drawn along its completed path, as you simultaneously experience the different sets of flaming letters. Then, on exhalation, it is directed from the right hip down the right leg into the right foot, as you write the flaming letters and utter the Ineffable Name, **Yee–Hee–Vee–Hee.**

e. **Left Leg:** As you inhale, the golden Divine Light is drawn in through the forehead and, as before, allowed to flow along the path it has traced before, but this time it jumps from the right foot to the left foot, from whence, on the exhalation, it is directed up the left leg to the left hip. Again you simultaneously write the letters in fire and express the Divine Name, **Yoo–Hoo–Voo–Hoo.**

f. **Sexual Organ:** You breathe the Divine Light in the manner you have done thus far, tracing the entire path and sensing the sets of flaming letters along the way, until you reach the left hip. Then, on the exhalation, you allow the Divine Light to flow in, around or along the sexual organ, while you write and express the associated Divine Name, **Yoo–Hoo–Voo–Hoo,** and so conclude the spiralling circuit of Divine Power in your body.

g. The final step is to draw down a final stream of Divine Force into your forehead during inhalation. On the out breath you expand your head while thinking, whispering or uttering *"Yod"* or *"EE"*; your shoulders and arms while expressing *"Hay"* or *"AH"*; your torso as you utter *"Vav"* or *"OH"*; and your pelvis and legs as you express *"Hay"* or *"EH."* While it is good enough to execute this concluding stage of the procedure only once, I have come across individuals who do it three times.

This completes the practice titled "Taking on the Name."

. ...to the many coloured glasses that are set in the windows... ... .

Chapter 6
INVOKING DIVINE POWER

A. Introduction

Now I would like to introduce you to the art of invoking and controlling "Divine Power," or as some would say "working with Psychic Energy." To be able to do this in a conscious and controlled manner, you must understand that the "Abundant Power" (*Shefa*— Divine Influx) of the "Eternal No-Thing" is continuously generating and regenerating every single particle in manifestation. This is an endless process in which the entirety of existence is constantly reaffirmed in the *Now*, and in which *Ain Sof* is the *Eternal Presence*. *Avir* (Universal Life Force) emanating from beyond time, space and events out of this "Fountain of Eternal Youth," so to speak, is forming into all aspects of life. In fact, it is powerfully present in everything on all levels of existence.

This "Divine Power" is termed *Ruchaniyut*, and very interesting discoveries have been made about this force, firstly that it does not only form itself into matter (from the most subtle to the gross), but that it flows quite freely through and around matter, and secondly, that the more evolved and aware the materialised aspects (e.g. humanity) becomes, that is its level of Self Awareness, the more it is able to control and direct the abundant flow of the Universal Life Force in accordance with *Will*. In fact, the skill of controlling the flow of creation, or creating a personal reality, is entirely based on the ability to direct this power flow.

This is where we need to examine most carefully what *Kabbalah* has to say about Divine Power. The word *Ruchaniyut*, a term which today means "spirituality," originally referred to "Spiritual Force" as an active link between man and Divinity. This is no mere fantasy, since those who have devoted their lives to finding the true meaning of Being, are quite adept at perceiving the inmost Being, the Divine Presence, the *Ruchaniyut* which is not only sustaining all existence, but as we noted is also *within* all. Wherever one may look, the Divine Being is visible. It is therefore not so strange that the Hebrew word *Havayah*, translated "Being," is closely associated with the Divine Name *YHVH*. Having discovered *Ruchaniyut* inside matter, Kabbalists can for example attract the Spiritual Forces (*Ruchaniyut*) of the celestial bodies, etc. It is understood that the very existence of our world hinges on this hidden force, which can be consciously drawn down through certain actions into the body of the Kabbalist, who is thereby able to achieve modifications in the terrestrial realm and even exert some control in *Tzeva Marom* (the celestial domain).

Naturally you may wonder how this "drawing down" (*Hamshachah*) is achieved. One should start by recognising that an alignment is required with those forces which are loftiest within ourselves, as well as with the "Highest Power" of all, the very "Is"–ness of the Infinite which Kabbalists termed *Ain Sof*. Our first task would then be to seek out this alignment. The word *Hamshachah*, deriving from the root *Mashach* meaning to "pull" or "draw," describes a threefold action: 1. The gravitational centering of force at a definite focus; 2. the focussing of the mind; and 3. the "drawing down" of *Shefa* (the sacred influx of Divine Power).

Adjusting the focus of ones mind is the most arduous part of the training, since the analytical mind often finds it difficult to be aware of, or even to accept, divine revelation. The major problem here is that mankind lost its sense of oneness with the whole, and has "fallen" into the illusion of "separateness." Out of this is born the illusion of "evil," an imaginary phantom resulting from humans being deluded into believing that they are separate entities. By buying into that delusion we "cut the limbs"—we sever ourselves from the "Infinite Oneness" of the "Divine Presence." Why should humanity do that? Because of the "veiling of Divinity." Kabbalists maintain the very process of scaling down of Divine Power, so necessary for our continued physical existence, actually traps us into believing that we are separate from God. We begin to believe that God is "out there somewhere" and we are here, and "never the twain shall meet." It is an illusion, since we are One.

Kabbalah says "evil" results from the "veils of manifestation," the "garments." Tricked by their many skins, their many protective layers, humans forget the infinity of their real "Selves," their union with the Infinite One. They forget they are not "things," and start to seek for truth and meaningfulness externally in creeds and conducts which overwhelm them with a compulsion to conquer creation in hopes of finding fulfilment in the materiality of time, space and events—whether perceived from physical or spiritual perspectives. The more they act on their sense of "separateness," the more intense the feeling of lack becomes, and the more they need to satisfy it at any cost, but all actions of this nature will only increase loneliness and emptiness, self-indulgence and self-pity, all disintegrating conditions which inevitably insulate perceptiveness.

In the task we have set ourselves to be the "Restorers of Peace and Well-being," and to achieve this aim we have to start with the cultivation of certain conditions in our own beings if we hope to succeed in our endeavours. First and foremost should be the task of bringing about a condition in which our service is not experienced as a struggle. We have to cultivate working with love and joy. You will certainly find that you would have to discern between necessity and demand. This might appear difficult but is not necessarily so in practice, since when there is need, your heart will want to satisfy it, whereas where there is demand, your heart will refuse participation and your mind will find a reason to refuse its fulfilment. So it becomes a question of listening to both the heart and the mind, to both the Instinctual Self (*Nefesh*) and the Reasoning Self (*Ru'ach*).

It should go without saying that the techniques addressed here must be experienced and lived every day in order for them to become part of your everyday living experiences. We work with techniques involving Divine Energy, Life-Force, Psychic Power, or whatever you care to call it. If you name it "*Light*" you might have a working analogy to aid you towards your own "en–*LIGHT*–en–ment." Whether you will literally perceive this "Light" you breathe daily into your body is irrelevant, since all that really matters is that you *feel* it in the very depths of your being. In fact, this power is immediately invoked when you bring it to mind, and is influencing you whether you are conscious of it or not.

Remember, you always become what you attach your mind to. Seeing and feeling is analogous, since sensation can be so intense that it parallels vision.

The second condition to bring about, is never to match your experiences with those of others, since we all respond individually, with some procedures appearing less difficult than others. There is often a tendency to ignore the difficult exercises and work only those liked personally. This is a serious error, since several factors are needed in the process of freeing every part of the mind and body from conscious and unconscious fears and debilitating habits, and often it is exactly the practices personally disliked which work on these very factors. Another major point is to *do* the exercises and not merely peruse them on the written page. Book-work never advanced anyone, unless it encourages and entices you to act out what is written, realising that you can become a very powerful channel for "Divine Energy," literally making it a *living* experience.

The common aim of the procedures we are discussing here, pertains to the perpetual task of reconstructing and unfolding the Self, which includes the material body. The transmuted Self becomes a channel for directing fresh Life-Force into all nature, in fact, straight into this planet itself. The method for doing this is to draw Divine Force directly from its source, the Eternal Living Spirit, the Infinite Point of "Is"–ness, God, or whatever you care to call It. Each time you practice, a quantity of this Sacred Power is conveyed to the Self, which will eventually be transformed and liberated from all its anxieties, repressions, constraints, and ailments, and you will also be able to transmit Divine Force to all you meet on the way.

The power of these techniques does not originate entirely inside the Self, but, like the material body, the success of these practices is reliant on factors in its surroundings. So the power of these techniques originates in the repeated inhalation of the Life-Force of the Eternal Living Spirit. The power must be drawn from the Divine, and thus the principal perception must be that there is an Infinite Source of Divine Power which you are willing to integrate into your being. In the related spiritual practices we refer to the "Source" as the "Infinite Point of 'Is'-ness." However, you may consider It the "Infinite Point of Radiance," the "Eternal No-

Invoking Divine Power / 219

Thing," *Ain Sof Aur*, or simply "God" if you so prefer. All the practices are based on the action of the Higher Self, *Neshamah*, as the converter of Light (Divine Energy) into energies and powers which humans can absorb.

You are the medium through which the splendid Divine Force is to be established and relayed in the world. You are the receptive conclusion of the operation, and your work is to acquire and relay the bright Being of the Divine every moment of your life. In this manner you may construct within yourself a fresh and hallowed essence, and in conveying this to your world, you contribute towards the *Tikkun*, the raising and restoration of both the human race and this planet. However, it should be noted that very few people, if any, can survive a direct exposition to any cosmic light or energy, whether it be spiritual or physical, if they are unprepared and unconditioned for such exposure, hence it is important to devote oneself to the preparatory work discussed in this book.

Now, most people think that the way to direct Divine Power is simply to beam what they call "Love," "Beauty" and "Kindness" indiscriminately in all directions. This sort of "Compassion Radiation" motion, where you just let "Divine Love" flow through you towards your fellow man regardless, is not only impractical, but as dangerous as over breeding without some sort of balancing factor controlling the process. "Compassion" without a balancing "Severity" would be worse than useless, and would literally just "glue up" everything. What we really need is *Tiferet* (Beauty), which is a beautiful balance of *Chesed* (Mercy) and *Gevurah* (Severity), because this is how the "Universal Collective Consciousness," or "Eternal Living Spirit," functions. An overbalance in either direction of the two "Opposing Principles" could not only slow down the "Awakening Consciousness," but actually stop the whole process of "Awakening" and "Illumination." Therefore in our attempts to direct Divine Power, we should always attempt to combine the practical application of the "Universal Laws of Life" with the merciful warmth of true clemency.

Here it is important to realise just how much power and responsibility you have as a Self-aware manifestation of Divine Energy. In fact, you should:

1. Know that you are one of the most powerful Creative Potencies on earth, and also remarkably powerful in the whole "Hierarchy" of manifestation. As a materialised entity you comprise all four "Elements" in one, and as a human you also comprise the subtle aspects of these same "Elements," thus having immense ability in terms of the Creative Forces of Life.
2. Realise and accept that you are immensely powerful *Now*, and can really alter life circumstances in conformity with your Will.

    Do not be too concerned as to the reasons why these applications of Divine Energy actually work. Rather get down to basics and start practising these techniques, and then, when you have achieved some results, you can get down to understanding things more intellectually.
3. Accept that Universal Life-Force as energy, both physical and spiritual, is flowing endlessly through you in the Eternal Present, and that you can use it *Now*.

    As an extremely potent Creative Force, Divine Power is not dormant in the vastness of space, and you do not have to hunt for it. It is extremely dynamic, surrounding and flowing through you constantly. It is *in you* and *around you*, and in effect it *is you*. Therefore you can never *be* or *exist* without it, but realising this does not necessarily give you any control over it. To achieve this, you have to accept it fully and desire to use it consciously, and not only unconsciously as you do automatically.

Knowing and understanding what is said thus far, is not going to cause a fanfare to sound, and "Cosmic Consciousness" to descend upon you. What is intended, is to awaken the "aware" part of the manifested Life-Force (which is you), to use the subtle, dynamic, controllable and creative part of the Life-Force (which is also part of you), and then to manipulate it *as you Will*.

Again your question is of course "How do I do it?" The first answer is that you should learn to communicate your desires, especially to your own *Nefesh*. The second response is that you should attempt to work on your own needs first and then on those of others. The third is *never* to accept any adverse conditions in your own life. Learning to express your needs clearly is of primary importance. By this I do not mean that you should simply say "I want to be happy," etc. In fact, whilst succinct you must be simultaneously as explicit as you possibly can be. Really *know* what you want and then *express* it. Ask yourself what it is you want, why you want it, how much of it you really want, what it will do for you, etc. Having gained some clarity in this regard, you can next focus on the "Invocation of Subtle Energy."

B. Invocation of Subtle Energy

It was Franz Bardon who, in referring to the skin, said: "Our skin has a double function i.e. the breathing and the secretion. Therefore we may consider the skin as a second piece of lungs and a second kidney of the body."[1] The following practice which he titled "Conscious pore breathing" is very effective in the invocation of Life-Force. The manner in which this exercise is presented here is somewhat different from Bardon's, but is one I have found to be most easily and successfully executed.

1. PRELIMINARY PRACTICE

This exercise has a remarkable cleansing and restorative effect on the psyche and the body alike, bringing you in contact with subtle forces.

1. Stand with arms and hands resting comfortably by your side. Imagine your arms down to the wrists are strings, and that your hands are heavy weights dangling on the bottom of those strings, almost as if they were pendulums. Of course, the strings are attached at the shoulders. The keywords here for the arms and hands would be "loose" and "heavy."
2. Surrender your entire body to gravity, be limp and heavy, and feel all tension flowing down into the earth while your body becomes heavier and heavier.
3. Now close your eyes, and put your attention on your hands, sensing them as if they were the weights of the pendulums hanging next to your body.

4. Begin to swing your hands and the arms, rotating them in small, inward circles, i.e. circles in which the hands are moving inwards, towards your body. Gradually increase the size of the circles, until the orbits are big enough to swing the arms outwards and upwards. Then bring the hands towards each other in front of the body, so that the palms face, almost as if you were holding a large beach ball.

5. Now let the elbows settle nicely into the sides of the body, while letting the palms of the hands face each other as if, as said, you are holding a large ball or balloon between them. Keep your eyes closed during the entire procedure, and keep your attention focussed on your hands. Practically *look* at the hands, even though your eyes are closed. Sense especially the palms of your hands, and feel as if you are smiling warmly *with* your hands. You should already begin to experience the palms of your hands glowing somewhat, or something of a similar nature.

6. Now, think of your hands as two strong magnets capable of reversing poles alternately on your inhalations and the exhalations. Thus when you breathe in they will pull together closely, though not touching, and on the outbreath they will push quite far apart. Do this over and over during several breaths. Inhale and the hands pull together closely, but do not let the palms touch. Exhale and they push apart. Try to experience the reversal of the poles quite strongly. Next imagine you are breathing with the hands themselves, literally sucking in the Life-Force through the pores of the skin on the palms, absorbing the energised air filled with *Ruchaniyut* through the palms into your hands, and exhaling negativity out of the palms. On the inhalation your palms will once again pull closely together, and on exhalation they push apart. Practice this again using a number of breaths. Always ensure the movements of your hands are strong and intense. Repeat this practice over and over until there is a feeling that Subtle Energy is powerfully present in the palms of your hands.

7. Return to normal breathing, and begin to play with this power in the palms of your hands. Push it together like

putty, pull it apart like gum, roll it like a ball of clay in the palms of your hands, and, in order to relax as deeply as you can while standing, surrender completely to gravity. Move the hands quite a lot and experience the force between them. For some people it is a bouncy sensation, somewhat like pushing against a soft balloon or something of that ilk. Keep your eyes closed and attention focussed on the palms of your hands, again as if you were looking at them, while smiling warmly inside and with your hands.

8. Next, allow the movements of your hands to become spontaneous. In other words, stop doing the actions, and let them move by themselves without trying to control or steer the movements. Let the Divine Energy move your hands. Surrender completely to the *Avir/Ruchaniyut*, respectively the Divine Presence around and within you. Be like a plant at the bottom of the sea, which, while anchored in the earth, is moving freely as the currents of the ocean wash over it. Feel yourself in a sea of Divine Energy, and while your feet are strongly "planted" in the earth, you can move without any restraint as the currents in this sea of *Avir*, of Universal Life-Force move your hands and arms. All you have to do is relax and surrender, and let happen what will happen. Above all, *do not be afraid*. You certainly will not go insane or die, and nothing horrible will ensue.

9. Continue to surrender your whole body and feel yourself bathed in this sea of Divine Energy, again as if you are a plant rooted at the bottom of a sea of energy, and allow the currents that are within this sea to move your whole body. Feel yourself sway and move, but do not *do* anything yourself. Let it move you while you surrender deeply to gravity and the Life Force around you.

2. WHOLE BODY PORE BREATHING

Now you can return to breathing with the entire body. This practice as well as the succeeding ones, were derived from Franz Bardon's groundbreaking work in this regard. I certainly have no intention of reproducing the entire text of Bardon's seminal work here. It is addressed well enough in a most accessible translation. While I had devoted myself some decades ago to working his entire "*Initiation into Hermetics*,"[2] my intention here is to share only those practices which play a role of immediate importance in the workings we are addressing. I have again paraphrased Bardon's words, and am sharing the techniques as worked in an easy, personal manner.

In the following practice you need to be really relaxed and surrendered. With each inhalation, imagine that not only your lungs and hands are breathing, but that you are breathing with the entire body from stem to stern, literally sucking in Life-Force through your skin. You might have a sensation of your skin contracting as you draw Divine Energy into your body, and perhaps one of expansion when you breath out through the skin. Feel your body absorbing *Avir* through every pore into your body. By sucking the Life-Force into your body in this manner, this vital force will pass from the atmosphere into the very depths of your being. Of course, personalities being so different, each individual experiences this process quite differently and uniquely. When, after repeated practice, this exercise is well mastered, you may use it in the procedure called "*Desire Inhalation*" which refers to inhaling from the vast resources of the Universal Life-Force, whatever you are aiming for or require most urgently. I will address this technique shortly, but for now let us focus on developing related skills.

3. BREATHING WITH INDIVIDUAL ORGANS[3]

Return to the practice of breathing with the individual parts of the body, which is only slightly more advanced than the exercise of "*Toning and Tuning the Body*." The position of the body must remain unchanged while doing this exercise for about thirty minutes. In this case pore-breathing with the whole body is limited to breathing with single organs, i.e. consciously allowing any part of the body to breathe through the pores of the surrounding skin. Start again with the feet and finish with the head, as you did with "*Toning and Tuning the Body*." The procedure is as follows:

1. Sit in your usual, comfortable position and close your eyes.
2. In the same manner as you did while "tuning the body," observe one of your legs with closed eyes. You may

commence with either one. Smile warmly during this practice.
3. Imagine your leg and foot to be like a sponge, and in the same manner as you did with the palms of your hands, inhale and exhale *Avir* into the leg, imagining you are absorbing it through the skin from the infinite resource of Divine Power and breathing it out again.
4. Continue with this for seven or more breaths, until you feel you have acquired some success, then repeat the procedure with the other leg.
5. Next proceed to repeat the exercise with both legs simultaneously.
6. Repeat the entire procedure with the hands and arms, and afterwards with other parts and organs of the body. You can breath with the heart, head, chest, anus, genitals, whatever. You might follow the same pattern delineated earlier in the "*Toning and Tuning the Body.*"

You should be able to breathe with every part of the body you choose to focus on. Not a single portion of your anatomy should be left out, since this is again an important "Gestalt" practice, which will give you complete control over your body, filling it with *Avir*, and is again most beneficial in the process of healing and rejuvenation.

If you managed to work this exercise with a definite sense of intensity and success, it becomes quite easy to transfer *Ruchaniyut*, the Divine Power within you, to others.

4. ACCUMULATION OF VITAL POWER[4]

We have already learned how to inhale and exhale vital power from the universe around us through "Whole Body Pore Breathing." Now let us look at the accumulation of the Divine Power.

Sit in your usual position, and in the same manner as you have done earlier, inhale the *Avir*, Divine Life-Force, from the atmosphere around you. Breathe it into your body through the lungs and the pores of your skin. However, this time do not exhale the Divine Energy out through your skin back into the universe, but retain it in your body. Breathe out in a regular manner, at the same time feeling the Divine Force gradually compacting and condensing inside your body. Accumulate more and more Divine Power, building it steadily in your body, until you start to feel that the stored force is beginning to radiate out of you. With each breath the pressure and radiation should increase, becoming stronger and radiating further and further away.

When you sense that you have accumulated enough Life-Force, you can commence reversing the procedure, i.e. breathe in normally and on exhalation release the accrued power through the skin, especially the skin of the hands, back into the air around you. You may have to use a number of breaths to release the accumulated energy and to return to normal focal levels. If you do not manage to rid yourself of the accumulated force, you can clear yourself by kneeling, placing your hands and forehead on the ground, and then breathing the "psychic tension" into the earth, at the same time feeling it being absorbed into the ground. In this manner you inhale pure air only, and breathe out the tension of the vital force until a sensation of balance is achieved. Later you will be able to release the lot in one go.

You should regularly work this accumulation of *Avir*, and radiate it as far as you like, since there is in reality no limit or distance at all. It is only the mind which sets limits. With repeated practice you will be able to emit the Divine Energy without feeling limited by any inhibiting factors. Begin by inhaling seven times and increasing by one inhalation as you practice every day, and work each exercise for a maximum of 20 minutes a day.

Regarding this practice Franz Bardon warns "These exercises have to be practised mainly in such tasks and experiments as require a great and intense expenditure of vital force, say, the treatment of sick people, telepathy, magnetizing of objects and so on. If the vital power is no longer wanted, in this accumulated form, the body must be brought back to its original tension, because it is not advisable to walk about in every-day-life, in an over-dimensioned tension. It would over-strain the nerves, and cause irritation, exhaustion and other bad side effects."[5]

Having acquired a certain skill, you may go on to slowly work the same technique with single parts of your anatomy, that is to compress Divine Power into single organs of the body. Franz

Bardon recommended that one should work this procedure especially on the eyes and hands. Having very poor eyesight, I paid particular attention to the eyes during this practice. Not only did it develop "Will," but as I expected, it definitely improved my sight. On the other hand, working it with special focus on the hands, develops what is termed "healing hands."

C. Practising the Presence: Spontaneous Dance

This technique is a continuation of the earlier preliminary "Invocation of Subtle Energy" practice, in which you build the power in the palms of your hands, then play with it, and finally allow it to move your arms. In this case you simply allow your body to express itself in spontaneous dance in the same way as you let your mouth open and chant spontaneously earlier.

1. Start by repeating the earlier preliminary practice of "Invocation of Divine Power."
2. Next, play with the Energy between your hands, taking deep breaths. As you did when you "tuned" the body, start to hum and vibrate the body on exhalation. Move the body experiencing the infinite sea of Divine Force, and feel the sound play in the body, as if dancing spontaneously.
3. Again allow the movements of your hands to become spontaneous, and once again stop doing anything, and let the Divine Energy move your hands. Surrender completely to the Force, the Divine Presence you should be sensing all around you, and feel how it moves your hands and arms. All you have to do is relax, and let happen what will happen. Above all do not be afraid.
4. Surrender your whole body and feel yourself bathed in a sea of Divine Energy, again as if you were a plant rooted at the bottom of this ocean, and allow the currents to move your whole body. Feel yourself sway and move, but do not personally *do* anything. Let yourself be moved without resistance while you surrender deeply to gravity and the Divine Life-Force around you.

    Let your arms and body sway and move spontaneously as if you are dancing involuntarily, as you move deeply into the state called *"Practising the Presence."* Continue to let the body dance and express itself freely, until there is a feeling that the movements are beginning to subside.

5. Slowly drop your arms so that they return to rest, hanging heavily and relaxed alongside your body. Feel the pull of gravity on your fingertips, or generally experience whatever sensation is now prevailing in your hands.

At a more advanced stage, or after some practice of the preceding exercises, you may begin to chant freely while your body is dancing spontaneously. Do not force anything during this procedure, and stop when you reach the stage when all starts to subside. Then slowly lower your arms, bringing them to rest next to your body. Make fists, open your fists, take a deep breath and stretch.

D. Exercising the Spirit Body

The execution of several techniques discussed in this work, requires the use of both ones physical and "spirit" hands. To accomplish this, you need to regularly exercise your "spirit body," i.e. *Tzelem ha-Nefesh*, in the following manner:

1. Stand with your arms and hands hanging in a relaxed manner by your sides.
2. Put your attention in your right hand. Slowly raise the right hand sideways, feel the movement, then lower it slowly again feeling the movement. Be intensely aware of the motion of your hands. Do this six times.
3. Now, in your imagination, raise your right hand as you did before, but without doing so physically. Then lower it back to its original position. Again be intensely aware of lifting and lowering your hand, but do not do so physically. Do this six times.
4. Repeat the entire procedure with your left hand.
5. Next, physically raise your right forearm slowly in front of your body until your palm is positioned over your chest, and trace the movement with your feeling appreciation

ability. Afterwards, lower it slowly to its original position, again tracing the movement as before. Do this six times. Again be intensely aware of the motion of your arm.
6. Repeat the practice in your imagination alone, feeling your arm rising and lowering, without lifting your physical arm. All the time you need to be intensely aware of the movement. Do this six times.
7. Repeat the entire procedure with your left arm.
8. Starting the process all over again, lifting and lowering both hands and forearms. Sense your "spirit" (imaginary) arms moving first, to be followed by their physical equivalents, almost as if your "spirit" body pulls the physical along with it in the action.

If you have accomplished this, you will be able to work the ritual techniques addressed later in this book with great ease.

E. Creating Your Own Reality

1. INTRODUCTION

What I am going to share with you now is certainly very controversial indeed, and quite the opposite to the opinions of those who believe that you have to literally investigate your entire past to understand your current behaviour patterns. Of course, I acknowledge that approach to work well enough, but so does this one which Dr. George Weinberg called *"Self Creation,"*[6] and which is more designed for the individual who is seeking to find the answers inside his or her own being. This approach claims that you do not have to be concerned with the reason why you currently behave in a certain manner. To use Dr. Weinberg's metaphor, one which was reiterated by my own mentor, William Gray, who told me quite coolly "Well Jacobus, it is entirely your business if you wish to ascertain which pebble caused the avalanche," you do not have to know which pebble caused the avalanche in order to deal with the catastrophe. You do not have to find the reasons and answers externally in past events. In fact, from the perspective I wish to share here, you need to know that you cannot blame whatever you are, whatever you do, or whatever happens to you on anybody or anything. You have to accept that you and you alone are responsible for the entirety of your life experiences; that you and only you have created and are creating your own circumstances; that you and you alone can alter them in any way your intentions direct, i.e. "as you Will."

Not a single word I am writing here will work the change in you, unless you actually *act* on it. I am therefore adamant that you should understand that you will not get very far if you try to gain inner knowledge of a Tradition or spiritual awareness by correspondence courses or any amount of book reading. Words on paper are valid symbols, but they are not *live* symbols, which makes all the difference. People, plants, creatures, and even places via minerals comprise "Life," and it is the way we react *with* Life which builds or alters our actual "Inner Nature." The most that paperwork will do is to stimulate our intellectual faculties to act as drives, which might impel us to try and live out in actuality what the words represent as symbols.

Insofar as reading might encourage us to live out the teaching, writings can be useful, but no more than that. No amount of merely intellectual achievements should ever be mistaken for genuine spiritual actualities. You have to align yourself to the meanings, intentions and principles behind the words, which must then be lived out in actuality, and ultimately it is only that which flowers inside you which is real. I can go on explaining the principles involved here *ad infinitum*, and you can go on comprehending these in as many ways as you like, which in itself is only understanding your own interpretation of what is being imparted, but all of this will be to no avail if you cannot "live out" in actuality what the written or spoken words represent. You have to "make the words flesh."

In the process of "Self Creation" you know that you need to realise that you are constantly creating *everything* out of yourself. Literally everything about you, your entire personality, all your attitudes comprising your body, mind and soul, are mostly unconsciously, and rarely consciously, created by you. You cannot lay the blame for anything you are and encounter, on external impulses. Your life is based on your responses and reactions, and you *do* have control over these. The mere decision that you have control, affords you control. It is as simple as that. Make a *decision*, and then *act* on that resolve. Know that you can deconstruct anything you have constructed, and *vice versa*. You simply have to shift your focus on that which you seek to develop, and not on that of which you seek to rid yourself. You should strengthen the "positive," as it were.

All of this is based on the "Four Worlds" idea of *Kabbalah*. As we have seen earlier, *Kabbalah* teaches that there are four levels of existence. Again these are called: *Atzilut* (Emanation or Origination); *Bri'ah* (Creation); *Yetzirah* (Formation); and *Assiah* (Action, Making or Expression). You could name these four "Worlds" or dimensions: Spirit (Origination); Soul (Creation); Mind (Formation); and Body (Action). Take any idea or concept. It *originates* in the Spirit, is then *created* in the Soul, *formed* in the Mind, and *expressed* in the Body. Maybe this process is better understood in reverse, so to speak. Take any word you like. Its *written* and *uttered form* is its "body," i.e. its existence in the realm of *Assiah*, the "World of Action." Its *meaning* is another dimension of existence, the more formative one behind the physical expression, which is *Yetzirah*, the "World of Formation." Next, behind the *meaning* of every word, is an *intention*, which belongs to the more creative realm, thus *Bri'ah*, the "World of Creation," and behind all of them is a *principle*, the realm of spirit, the "Emanator" from whence the initial impulse originated. Thus we could say that if we really "know" a word, it would comprise:

Body	**Mind**	**Soul**	**Spirit**
Word	**Meaning**	**Intention**	**Principle**

Every idea starts as an impulse in our "Spirits," which is created in our "Souls," formed in our "Minds" and expressed in the "Flesh," and so again the "word becomes flesh"! To make this easier to apply practically, we can say that "body" refers to the physical manifestation; "mind" is the reasoning, thinking or "left brain" side of our beings; "soul" refers to the feeling, emotional or "right brain" side of ourselves; and finally "spirit" is the true "Divine Self" beyond feelings, thoughts and actions, in fact the "Supreme Originator" in this case.

I understand that this needs a lot more explanation. However, it is enough to know that every time we express an idea in the "World of Action," we are empowering it, and the more we act on it, the stronger it becomes. This is a universal principle, pertaining to any action conjoining your feelings, thoughts and personality. It is simply this: We can look at the "Four World" process as following the order of Spirit, Soul, Mind and Body, or we may start, by following the opposite sequence of Body, Mind, Soul and Spirit. The latter order as a process is extremely important, since it applies directly to our ordinary existence as humans on this earth. It is saying: "*Do* this — *that* happens." It is not saying, "*that* happens — *do* this." You must be absolutely clear about this, because this rule stays the same throughout creation. The effect *follows* the impulse, and not the impulse the effect.

Every time you *act*, the action is followed by a whole range of feelings, thoughts, beliefs, etc. Here the position is not: "As a result of me *feeling* and *thinking* this way, I am *acting* in this manner," it is rather "As a result of me *acting* in this manner, I am *feeling* and *thinking* this way." Note that the behaviour pattern is a result of the action. *First the action then the thoughts and feelings*, and these effects are basic to the constant creation and recreation of your personality. Each time you *act* for any reason, you are going to have a resultant feeling, and you are entirely responsible for both the action and the outcome. You create your life and your world. You reward yourself for your "good" actions, and you punish yourself for your "bad" ones. So again, we should remember we are not punished for our sins, but *by* them.

Now, how can we explain this principle in the simplest terms possible? Dr. George Weinberg in his book "*Self Creation*" puts it this way: "Every time you act, you add strength to the motivating idea behind what you've done.....Every time you do something, the motivating idea or feeling that prompted you to do it is intensified. It can be an idea about yourself, about others, about the world. Whatever it is, it's reinforced when you act on it. It's as though the act retypes the motivating message in your mind. When it's not acted on, the messages becomes weaker, as if fading from an electronic screen. When it *is* acted on, it becomes brighter, louder, recharged, prompting still more of the same acts. The sheer fact of acting on any belief or feeling makes you believe or feel it more.....Perhaps the most important is that often we do not recognize the motivating idea behind our acts, so we do not make the connection between the motive, the act, and the intensification of the motive..... How many times have we seen people 'carrying on' and known instinctively that if only we could get them to slow down — to curtail what they were doing — they'd stop building their anxiety, or hatred, or even their misplaced high hopes? Why? Not just because they were 'keeping the adrenaline flowing.' Because in some way we knew they were *convincing themselves*. By their very actions..... Through the ages writers remarked on this one way or another: Do a man a bad turn, and you will find it hard to forgive him. Attack a man and he comes to seem worthy of attack."[7]

This principle is well-known in the world of pot-boiling littercrap journalists and purveyors of porn for money alone, and it is greatly exploited by the international media. One of the main principles of unarmed combat is to keep your opponents off balance as much as possible. In the same way a political or economic struggle depends on exactly the same principle. "Disinformation" in politics and its equivalent economically is the same "unbalance." Keep shoving *Yesod*, the Foundation or "ego principle" on the Tree of Life, out of line as much as you can, fill it with fantasy, and upset it as much as possible for everyone else, while keeping your own connection straight, because you know where you are pushing it and others do not. That is the shocking situation today. The media is of course responsible for its behaviour, but the people who act on this, who make it real, are equally responsible for their own realities.

So, it is a question of, if you can get people to act on what you say, they will soon make your words fact, whether it be the truth or not. Hence I personally do not immediately accept and act on *anything* the media proclaims from the roof tops, without careful consideration of *all* factors involved. They have successfully duped nations and the whole world for centuries, and why should they not do so now? *Pravda*, "truth" in Russian, a word espoused and bent to suit the personal pursuits of many a control freak, not only in the old Soviet Union but as much in Russia today as in every other country, has certainly turned out to be far removed from "truth," and this applies equally to the same term in other languages. I will not buy into the reality of others, especially not if it is based on factors presented in an orchestrated manner by those who are creating reality in conformity with *their* wills, and this may incorporate, politicians, the media, and even the conspiracy mongers.

The reality I choose to act on in this case is plainly and simply, that *all* information presented in the media is biassed, and thus one has to allow for the fact that you will have to filter the lot through a screen of caution and commonsense, and then one might get some ideas to act on. Yet, as the world stands today, one must not only look at the political and economic situations. On the public side the fact is that very many people do not *want* to think, that is to say really use their minds to arrive at original thoughts. They are terrified of doing so because of what they might discover. As long as their conscious minds are just occupied with anything invading them in a non hostile manner, they are happy. So they welcome almost anything at all which will do no more than fill the foreground of their focal consciousness, and obscure or anaesthetize the deep awareness which is trying to find out what Life is all about. The Zulu medicine man, Credo Mutwa, was perfectly right when he told my old Teacher: "Man will never amount to anything until he finds out *who he is*."[8]

To continue, there is a wonderful song in the musical "*Pippin*" a verse of which reads:

> "What good is a field on a fine summer night
> When you sit all alone with the weeds?
> Or a succulent pear if with each juicy bite
> You spit out your teeth with the seeds?
> Before it's too late stop trying to wait
> For fortune and fame you're secure of
> For there's one thing to be sure of, mate:
> There's nothing to be sure of!"[9]

So what are you to do? Die or wallow in your misery like a blabbering blob of protoplasm? No! Be sure who you are, and create your own reality! You are doing just that anyway each time you decide to act on any impulse. With every action you align yourself to all kinds of powers and responses, and as Dr. Weinberg said: "The greatest propagandists in history knew this essential truth which springs directly from the Principle: If you want to build dedication to the 'movement' in your followers, do not just preach your text, however true. Get them to *do* something. Something based on a belief in the movement. That is how you inculcate belief....."[10]

To illustrate his reasoning, Dr. Weinberg quotes the saga of a nineteenth-century French play *Le Voyage de Monsieur Perrichon*,[11] which is very apt: "Perrichon is rich, and he has a daughter. Daniel and Armand seek her hand in marriage. They know the choice will be made by Perrichon, so they court his approval. Armand's strategy is to do what he can for Perrichon. Daniel's is to get Perrichon *to do things for him*. He arranges a series of plights for himself from which, by certain actions, Perrichon can save him. His final coup is to pretend to be stuck in a crevice on Mont Blanc freezing to death. Perrichon struggles to rescue him, and with each new effort his determination to save that worthy boy increases. He succeeds in the apparent rescue and, hugging the estimable lad to his bosom, he chooses him for his daughter. Just in time Perrichon overhears Daniel gloating about his strategy, and the old man gives his daughter to the right man after all. Manipulation? Yes. But where Daniel merely entices Perrichon to act in a certain way, it is Perrichon who manipulates Perrichon's feelings. Daniel understood the Principle. If Perrichon had too, he never would have come so close to making a tragic mistake. And that's true of all of us....."[12]

Now, we said that every time you act on an impulse, you reinforce that impulse. A good example is drug addiction. The drug addict takes the substance to alleviate the desire, but that does not happen. There is first stage relief yes, followed by reinforcement of the desire for it, which is in turn followed by taking the substance again to take away the desire, and.....I am sure you know the rest. The same is true in the case of paranoia. You are worried. Extremely worried. Did you, in fact, lock the front door before you went to bed. You cannot sleep. You get up to check. Ah! You did lock the door! Oh my God! That lock is not good enough! You have to buy a new one in the morning. You buy and install another lock. Locks are no good anymore! Anybody can get in! You buy a security gate and a good security system — oh no! — the people who install the system know how to turn the damn thing off! And as you act to *alleviate* your fears, you are in fact acting *on* your fear, and so *reinforce* it more and more. Finally you surround yourself with a huge wall and an electric fence, and live inside a jail of your own making.

Do you recognise this scenario? There are many such examples, but some are so subtle you do not know that you are acting on hidden impulses which are being reinforced, and which are slowly becoming stronger, until you find yourself in very unhealthy conditions physically, emotionally, mentally and spiritually. I am talking from personal experience, and the support of my late mentor, William Gray, who would not let me get away with anything. Today I still have to observe most carefully what emotional stimuli I am reinforcing through my actions. Sometimes what you think you are trying not to empower, is having exactly the opposite effect because you are *trying*. I like the example given by Dr. Weinberg. He wrote "......it is the premise behind the act that is reinstated, reinforced and strengthened when we act. All of us 'tried to like' someone at some time. We are congenial, but we still do not like him. We end up feeling disturbed and frustrated, filled with an increased desire that we perceive will be thwarted. At last we throw up our hand. 'To hell with him. I just cannot like him. God knows I tried.' So we cease trying, and promptly even the desire to like him wanes. Because we are no longer continually reinstating the desire by action stemming from the desire. Of course, sometimes when we make an effort to like someone, we do end up liking him. How's that? Many possible reasons. Very likely our friendly attitude gets perceived by John and he begins to open himself up in a way he never has before. He reveals some unexpected aspect that we do like. The aspect pleases us enough so that we make a sincerely genial gesture, we say or do something motivated by our liking and, bang! our liking starts to build. The Principle at work....."[13]

There is what Dr. Weinberg calls "the two-stage effect of any act," which is what I was talking about when I referred to drug addiction. It is worthwhile quoting a good portion of what the doctor has to say about this, since he explains it very well indeed. He said "The *immediate* effect of any act is to satisfy, ease and reduce the motivating impulse behind it. But the ultimate effect is to strengthen it. This is most keenly observable with a habit. You feel the impulse to indulge it. If you do, the impulse is reduced, even eliminated — temporarily. But the very fact of acting on it ultimately reinforced it. Picture a habit as our whole life-style in microcosm. Whatever impulses we act on are entrenched by the act. Ultimately. The first stage may appear to be a reduction, but this only serves to obscure the lasting effect. The paranoid who checks and rechecks his locks feels first-stage relief, and ultimate reinforcement of his paranoia....."[14]

I will leave you with Dr. Weinberg's words and hopefully your own self examination. *Kabbalah* has a lot to say about this very subject, but for now I would like to encourage you to do a lot of personal evaluation, or finding out how your actions derive from impulses reinforced by those very actions, and how these are impacting on you physically, emotionally, mentally and spiritually. Now let us turn to the practice of "Desire Inhalation."

2. DESIRE INHALATION

As is the case with several procedures discussed in this book, I am again greatly indebted to Franz Bardon for the following and other techniques addressed throughout this text. While these have been reworked and explained in specifically Kabbalistic terminology, this exercise derives directly from this astute ceremonial magician's great teachings.[15] Since the following technique is closely associated with practices we have addressed earlier, you would by now have acquired enough background in order to work it successfully. The exercise is based on the idea that everything you are looking for in life is already in the atmosphere around you, and that this is continuously strengthened by everyone who has been, is and will be successful, healthy, loved, or whatever it is you are looking for. All you need to do is to align yourself with what you are seeking, and then to absorb it into your body. To do this, accept that whatever you are looking for is everywhere around you in the *Avir*, in the "Ether" as some would say.

So, sit comfortably and relax your body in your accustomed manner. Then inhale, using the "Whole Body Pore Breathing" we have discussed earlier. While doing this, imagine that everything you are aiming at in life, whether it be health, wealth, success, love or peace, will pass with the inhaled air into your body via your lungs and the bloodstream. Sitting or even standing quietly, close your eyes and sense that which you desire to be all around you, literally saturating the vital atmosphere you breathe every day. In your mind repeat a simple statement about yourself being linked to this quality you are seeking, such as: "I am healthy" or "I am successful" or whatever it is, but note that this declaration is always expressed with an assertive stance in the present tense. Think the affirmation and inhale the quality you seek.

Surrender and smile with your whole body while doing the exercise, i.e. your feet and hands, legs and arms, torso, genitals, anus, shoulders, back, etc. In fact, every part of your anatomy must open like a flower as you surrender to the "Divine Presence" you are invoking through this intense attachment of your mind and heart, your thoughts and feelings. What you are calling on, and aligning yourself to, must also be experienced in the present, in the "*Now*." It is never "I will be." It is always "I am."

While breathing whatever it is you are looking for, the "feeling" or "emotional stance" of having it, and better still — *being it*, must be gradually built to an enormous intensity. This can be considered to be the "*Power of Positive Feeling*" rather than the "*Power of Positive Thinking*." However, I do believe that both *Hod* and *Netzach*, respectively "thinking" and "feeling" should be employed in these activities. You must focus only on that quality you wish to inhale from the Universal Life-Force around you. Again, like a chalice submerged in the ocean, you should experience yourself in "it" and "it" inside you. That which is within this cup is also outside it, and *is* in fact it. All you have to do is consciously focus your mind on it, and then, very importantly, you must *act* on it. That is vital. You have to manifest what it is "in the flesh," and that happens when you act on it. This is most important. Remember that every time you act on an impulse or an idea, you empower that impulse and idea; you allow it to become the motivating factor in your life.

So, when you have concluded this "magical breathing practice," you should go out into your normal day with the "stance" you have acquired because of your alignment with it. Do not bring yourself to constantly think about your "desire," since, as explained before, desire kills results. Once again, you should do this working with as little desire in it as possible, which means you should do it in a surrendered manner as an act of exuberance and enjoyment. However, if at any moment you find you are losing your stance, becoming unaligned as it were, immediately close your eyes, and, using a few breaths, re-establish your contact by allowing that which you were aligned to initially, to flow again into your body and re-establish your stance.

Here are a couple of important points to keep in mind. Do not use this technique in an attempt to rid yourself of what you might consider "negative aspects." Rather use it to increase "positive aspects." Everything is a question of balance as said earlier. We should understand clearly, that we are here to experience life, and you are today the full expression of *all* your past experiences, the *totality* and not merely of one or two which we wrongly term *positive* or *negative*. Keep that in mind always. It is also not what you experience that is eventually important, but *how you react or respond personally*. You should always remember that you, the *Experiencer*, stand between thinking and feeling inside yourself, and that you are the *Essence* which joins all experiences into life stances or attitudes.

3. IDENTIFICATION

The practice of "Identification" is an important one for those who would like to get a closer understanding of the world around them. This refers to the ability to experience anyone and anything as if you are him, her or it. A lot of moralistic arguments can be hurled at this practice, but eventually we have to admit that the exercise in itself is only as bad or as good as the intention of the user, in the same manner as is electricity or any other use of energy for constructive or destructive purposes. Enough said! I do not have to defend the pros and cons of this working here, since you will surely be able to do that for yourself, and arrive at your own conclusions.

To understand the practice of "Identification," I need to draw your attention to the way people usually function in this world. We are all looking at the world through "me-coloured" glasses, so to speak. I mean, when you say to someone "I understand," you are in fact not understanding anything that individual is saying or encountering. You are understanding your own interpretations and the emotions triggered by that individual. When you say "I love you," you are in fact loving your own feelings about the individual in question. Yet, having said that, and perhaps leaving you in a state of bewilderment as far as your relationship with the world is concerned, one might ask whether it is at all possible to experience anything and anyone as if you are that thing or person? Yes it is possible, but you have to get yourself out of the way. You have to step aside as it were.

I remember William Gray telling me that if I truly want to experience anything in this or any other realm of manifestation; if I truly want to get to the point where I can say "I know," I have to be nothing. Absolutely nothing. I remember asking him if I could be just a little something, and he stamped his walking stick on the ground saying: "No...no...no... you must be nothing!" When you are nothing, you are unaffected by insult or flattery. For heaven's sake, you always know where you stand with somebody who insults you. Yet, you never know where you are with somebody who flatters you. It is an important point to keep in mind.

However, I personally found it difficult to be nothing. It had something to do with my personality. Eventually, however, I discovered that it was because I was holding on to *things*. Maybe it was "insecurity," but eventually I learned that being nothing did not mean I had to disappear at all. It meant I had to *surrender*. Surrender to the Divine Presence which is around me and in me. Surrender to life. When I surrender, I move with ease. When I don't.....I struggle, and I used to struggle so very much! I still do on occasion. I remember my grandmother telling me: "Don't wrestle....nestle!" She really snuggled up to life!

I can assure you that I am no master of the art of instant surrendering. I have to work at it. I deliberately surrender, and part of that is to smile with every portion of my body, since this causes the pores of your body to open up to the Universal Life-Force, in order to allow it to flow easily in and out of your body. Smiling at your world with your whole being and body, is like a flower unfolding its petals and basking in the sun in a surrendered fashion. Have you ever tried smiling with your stomach....or perhaps with your ear....or maybe with your left breast? I mean you should deliberately and consciously smile at your world, using all the different parts of your body. In one instance, my Teacher had me going through an entire day imagining that I had no face, and that I could do with my right thumb everything others do with their

Invoking Divine Power / 241

faces. I thought it quite kinky to go the whole day smiling with my thumb, literally experiencing my thumb smiling at the world around me. I tried using other organs, and soon discovered that it was difficult in certain instances to work this exercise, but it is good to persevere with it. You might want to try it for yourself some day.

Now, the practice called "Identification" here is very similar to what is termed "shape shifting," and is, as already indicated, the ability to identify very closely with an object or whatever, so that you can experience that object as if you are it. You must take great care with this kind of exercise, because, with continued practice, you will soon realise that you are in fact inside the object you have chosen to identify with, and that whatever instruction you are mentally giving that object, plant, animal or person, will be strongly implanted in his, her or its being, especially in cases where this "instruction" is backed with intense emotions.

You should always be most careful as to what you talk about in your mind, while in this deep state of meditation and identification. It is a good idea to decide beforehand what it is you wish to implant in yourself, your world, and its inhabitants — whether these be minerals, vegetables, or animals. You should also consider the old rule *"and Thou harm none"* always applies in this work. It has been truthfully said that "what goes around comes around," and you will find that what you emanate comes straight back at you. Always keep in mind that as you are doing the practice of "Identification," you are in a deeply receptive state. While you are identifying, you are also implanting the ideas inside yourself. If you say: "Be at peace," you are also instructing yourself to be at peace, etc. This working is therefore as much *integration* as it is *identification*. Here is the procedure:

1. Sit or lie down comfortably, and consciously surrender to gravity. Again this is to become as heavy and as limp as possible. By surrendering you allow the pull of the earth to draw all tension out of your body, as you simply sit or lie quietly for a few minutes. Once more an important key is to smile constantly with your entire being while doing these practices.

2. Take a number of deep breaths using "Whole Body Pore Breathing," and always remember to smile warmly inside yourself, all the time feeling the warmth of the smile permeating your body.
3. Next, sit quietly, doing absolutely nothing for a few seconds, besides smiling your inner smile, which you can trigger by smiling physically as well.
4. Now, take three deep and complete breaths in a relaxed manner. Do it calmly, gently and smile warmly while you are breathing. The important thing to do here is to let the breath rise and fall by itself, and to allow a pause between the exhalation and the next inhalation. In fact, simply wait calmly between breaths, until the next inhalation occurs by itself. Do this in a surrendered manner.
5. Take another breath, and hum on the exhalation while letting the sound vibrate in your body in the manner you previously learned. Do not worry about the pitch, simply accept the first sound that appears when you start to hum, and remember to keep your warm inner smile.
6. Practice *"Toning and Tuning the Body,"* the exercise we discussed previously, which is to look at different parts of your anatomy with your closed eyes. You will recall that in this practice you focus on a part of your body, and smile warmly while observing it. Then, while your attention and senses are still focussed and smiling, breathe deeply with that part and hum on the exhalation, thus feeling the sound vibrate inside the chosen part of the body. At the end of the humming, keep looking and smiling for a few seconds at the part on which you are focussed, and while you surrender, opening your gates as it were, allowing yourself to experience, i.e. to feel the after effects. When you feel the next breath starting to rise, repeat the entire practice with a different part of the body. Keep on repeating with separate parts of the body, and remember to keep on smiling warmly.

   In this instance we add an additional directive to this procedure. While you are humming, mentally instruct the different parts on which you are focussed to *"understand,"* that is to simply talk to each part. Pause for a few seconds. Then repeat the entire procedure of looking, smiling and humming in different parts of the body, but change the instruction to *"surrender,"* again simply talk to each part individually. Rather than "thinking" them, try to "feel" these instructions.

7. Next simply smile with your body, feeling the warmth of the smile permeating your entire physical structure. Breathe in using all of your body, and vibrate your entire anatomy while humming

8. Remain quiet for a few seconds, doing absolutely nothing. Do not think specific thoughts, or feel special feelings. Simply do nothing, but feel yourself fully identified with your body, since you have just completed the first part of the identification practice, which is to relate to your own physical being.

9. Next, get Divine Power moving in the body by doing Pore Breathing with your hands. This is done as described before, but this time you need to be seated.

10. Again you need to continue by letting go of the movement of your hands, and for a couple of minutes simply watch the hands either being held still, or being moved without you doing anything. Again do not forget your warm inner smile.

11. Now, bring to mind a chosen object, plant, animal or person with which/whom you wish to identify. Mentally see, feel or think of your chosen object, etc., and smile warmly at it. It is not ultimately important that you visualise the object in absolute clarity, in fact, it is best to work with its "shadow" which can be visualised as entirely black. What is very important is that you smile warmly at it. Feel the warmth of your smile, or the energy moving towards it with your smile. Surrender totally while smiling. Open up like a flower, without any fear. Let there be no hindrance between yourself and the object or whatever. Surrender and smile. This should be experienced very intensely, since with the smiling and surrendering you will begin to experience that curious phenomenon of feeling yourself being drawn towards and into the object.

12. Keep looking at your chosen object or whatever, until you feel you are becoming it. What you should allow to happen, is to feel as if the object, plant, animal, or human is acting like a magnet, drawing you towards itself, until you feel you are being absorbed into it, the sensation of which can be described as being surrounded by the object of your choice, with you being right inside its structure or body.
13. Continue to smile warmly, and feeling the warmth of your smile radiate as energy out of you into the structure, or body, of what you identified with. Do nothing more, except sit calmly and quietly, sensing the structure or body you have become.
14. Then commence breathing deeply and hum on the exhalations, and while you are humming you can mentally give an instruction or "implant," as if you are talking to the object or whatever, all the time smiling warmly. An alternative would be to give these instructions without humming, but it is always done on exhalation. The key here is once again the warm inner smile which radiates the instruction into the body and mind of that with which you have identified. When I was taught this practice, I was told that it was a good idea to align oneself with Divinity by imagining above you an Infinite Point of Radiance; your "Point of 'Is'-ness"; your "Source" which some term the "Higher Self" or the *Neshamah*, and then to feel yourself linked to that Radiance by a "line of light" along which you can breathe and draw Divine Energy into your body through the top of your head. This is usually practiced and mastered prior to doing "Identification." This specific practice is then used during the current procedure to direct the Divine Energy into the being with which you are identifying.
15. You usually keep breathing in this manner during the practice of "Identification," and on exhalation repeat the instruction while humming, or simply exhaling, until you feel or sense inside yourself that the practice has been

completed. Slowly return to normal focal levels, as if you are surfacing from a great depth. Open your eyes, make fists, open fists, take a deep breath and stretch. End of practice.

F. Directing *Ruchaniyut*: Spiritual Force

1. PREPARATION FOR THE CREATION OF CONSCIOUS PSYCHIC BONDS

Let us return to the topic of the "shadow body" of the *Nefesh*, and the possibilities of communication and sharing Divine Power with anything anywhere, because of the peculiar qualities of the *Tzelem Ha-Nefesh*, the subtle body of the Instinctual Self. To understand and practise the procedures we will be discussing here, you might want to review the section titled *"Shadow Bodies"* in Chapter 3, with special reference to the *Tzelem Ha-Nefesh*. The "Shadow Body" of your "animal, vegetable, mineral soul" is "sticky," so to speak, and it automatically creates energy bonds between yourself and any object you come in contact with via the five senses, as well as through thought. Knowing this, you can prepare yourself to consciously create powerful bonds between yourself and any chosen object.

Here you will learn how to create strong conscious psychic bonds between yourself and a chosen object, in preparation for which you should work the following technique for a couple of days:

1. It is important to sit in a calm and relaxed manner, or to lie down comfortably. Close your eyes, and surrender to gravity. Always remember to smile your warm inner smile, which opens you to the very best these exercises can offer. Take several "Complete Breaths," and then settle into a comfortable breathing rhythm.
2. Now, focus your attention on the top of your skull. Take a deep breath, and on exhalation imagine you are extending yourself about 30 centimetres out of the top of your head. It is almost as if your "spirit head" is sticking out of the top

of your material head. Then, as you continue to breathe in and out physically, imagine that you are inhaling and exhaling Divine Power into and out of that extended portion of your "spirit head.".
3. Next, turn your attention to the soles of your feet. Take another deep breath, and this time imagine on exhalation that you are growing 30 centimetres out of the bottom of your feet. Again, feel yourself inhaling and exhaling *Avir* in and out of those extensions.
4. Lastly, turn your attention to your hands and fingers. Take a deep breath, and on exhalation feel your fingers growing 30 centimetres longer. It is as if your fingers have suddenly elongated. Become intensely aware of your long, spindly fingers. Then, while continuing to breath normally, imagine that you inhale and exhale vital Life-Force in and out of your extended fingers. The sensation of inhaling into your fingers is almost like feeling your fingers sucking in the Divine Vital Force, while the exhalation is like a kind of outpouring, a kind of radiation from the extended finger tips.
5. When you are ready, focus your attention back into your body, i.e. in your face. Feel yourself return to normal focal levels. Make fists, open fists, take a deep breath, and stretch.

When these exercises are experienced intensely and powerfully, you can commence drawing and giving vitality.

2. DRAWING AND GIVING VITALITY

Again it is important to understand that there is *Ruchaniyut*, Spiritual Force and vitality powerfully focussed in the air, light, colour, in fact in everything, and all of us have the innate ability to work with this Divine Power. Most people do so instinctively in any case, but we will now learn how to work with *Ruchaniyut* in a conscious manner. Remember again that *Avir* is the abundant "Universal Life-Force" emanating freely out of the "Eternal Living Spirit," while *Ruchaniyut* is the transmuted "Spiritual Force" inside everything.

Invoking Divine Power / 247

As said earlier, everything exists within your own being. Kahlil Gibran expressed this rather well when he wrote: "All things in this creation exist within you, and all things in you exist in creation; there is no border between you and the closest things, and there is no distance between you and the farthest things, and all things, from the lowest to the loftiest, from the smallest to the greatest, are within you as equal things. In one atom are found all the elements of the earth; in one motion of the mind are found the motions of all the laws of existence; in one drop of water are found the secrets of all the endless oceans; in one aspect of you are found all the aspects of existence."[16]

Every state of separateness you experience in your life, is caused by you. You are responsible for your own separation, and yet, though you make mental statements that nothing can penetrate your being, everything is still moving through every aspect of your body, mind and soul. It is purely a question of altering your awareness to that state of reality which never ceases to be. As indicated earlier, just like the rest of existence, separateness is self-created, but isolation does not necessarily mean insulation. The fact that we *think* we are isolated from Cosmic Energies by having a roof over our heads, does not preclude those energies from penetrating the roof and passing straight through the earth. With this information and clarity of understanding the reality of our existence, let us look at the workings entitled "Drawing and Giving Vitality."

Exercise 1

1. Always adopt the mental, emotional and physical stance we have discussed in all the exercises and workings in this book. These will always provide the proper mind-set, making for both a good working and a good result.

    Focus your attention on, i.e. look at, an object such as a candle flame, or a strongly coloured object (no pastel colours at this stage), etc., ***but do not practice this exercise on humans or animals, as it could harm them.*** Drawing vital force from humans, animals and plants without knowing exactly what you are doing, can be very destructive indeed, and might in some instances even lead to the death of that individual or animal. Thus you must avoid practising on humans, animals, and even plants for that matter. Certain plants, like trees, have the ability to restore themselves rapidly, but some plants are more sensitive than others. Thus it is good to wait till you have gained more experience and understanding, before you use these techniques on plants.

2. Focus on your body, and select one of the following areas:
    a. Forehead
    b. Throat
    c. Heart
    d. Navel
    e. Sex organ

3. Inhale Spiritual Power from your "Infinite Point of Radiance" via the top of your head. As you inhale, feel this Divine Force flow into the chosen area inside your body.

4. Focus your attention on the flame, colour, crystal or whatever you have chosen to link with, and while puckering your mouth and whispering "*OO*" as you exhale, feel the force flow directly out of the chosen area in which it was focussed inside your body, simultaneously imagining or rather feeling how you are projecting a line of force, like a laser beam, from that part of the body from which you are exhaling, and how this line attaches itself to the object of your choice. There is no need to visualise this thread, since it happens automatically anyway when you look at something. You are only doing it consciously and strengthening the bond. Choose only one object at a time to work with, and project the thread from only one of the listed areas of your anatomy.

5. Next, during inhalation, draw *Ruchaniyut*, the Spiritual Force inside the light, colour or object, along the line or thread linking you to that object. As you inhale, literally suck the force into your own body, and feel yourself retain it inside yourself on the exhalation.

6. Repeat the exercise with each of the respective areas of your body mentioned above.

Exercise 2

In this working you will follow the same procedure discussed in the previous exercise, but try to establish several conscious lines or threads during the initial exhalations, projecting these from the same area in your body to different objects. On each inhalation draw *Ruchaniyut* via the top of your head from your "Infinite Source," directing it into the selected part of your anatomy. Radiate your "bonds of Power" during the exhalations, attaching them respectively to separate objects. For example, project three lines from your throat, one to an object, another to a colour and the third to a candle flame. Then, during inhalation, draw *Ruchaniyut* from all of them simultaneously along the threads. Inhale the Spiritual Force into your body during the inbreath, again feeling yourself retaining it inside yourself during exhalation. It is important to practice this with all the different parts of the body referred to in the first exercise.

Exercise 3

Now you can take the practice to a much more advanced stage, during which you follow the same procedure as described in exercise two. However, instead of projecting many threads from one area in your body, you should project single threads from all the mentioned areas in your body and attaching all the lines to a single object. In other words, during an exhalation project a line from the forehead and attach it to say an amethyst crystal. Inhale, and this time project a line from your throat during the exhalation, attaching it to the same spot on the chosen object. Repeat this action individually with the heart, solar plexus and the sexual organ. Thus you will have five force lines linking five important centres of your being to one object. Afterwards, you again draw *Ruchaniyut* from the object into your body along those threads on inhalation, and retain this vital Spirit Force inside your own being on exhalation. Keep in mind that while you are establishing the links between yourself and an object during exhalations, that the "Universal Life-Force" should always be drawn from your "Infinite Point of Radiance" via the top of the head into the bodily area from which you will be projecting, and then establish the link on the exhalation.

Exercise 4

It is important to do this work as intensely as you possibly can. In simple words, work with maximum intensity. You will notice that each new exercise advances out of the previous practice. Again you need to follow the same procedure as described in exercise three, but this time you must project several threads from all the mentioned major bodily areas. Thus you will project several lines of force from your forehead, throat, heart, solar plexus and sexual organ linking you to different objects, flames and colours. Of course, you should handle each bodily area separately, using separate breaths. You can project several lines from a single area during one exhalation, but it is far better to use a different breath for each strand of vital Spirit Force you project. Afterwards you will again draw *Ruchaniyut* back into your body along these threads during inhalation and retain it during exhalation.

Exercise 5

Continue by repeating the practice as described in exercise four, but this time also project lines of force or "psychic threads" from the fingers of both hands, and attach the threads to objects, colours, the earth, air, flames, etc. Then draw *Ruchaniyut* from all these objects, colours, lights, etcetera, along these threads on inhalation and retain it on exhalation, as previously described. If you feel comfortable doing this, you can now begin to work with plants, but never with humans or animals.

Exercise 6

1. Choose one plant, object, colour, but do not choose any living object other than a plant for the following practice, since you might draw the life-force out of it. Raising your hands, point your fingers at the object. In this case you will be directing *Ruchaniyut* into the chosen objects, rather than drawing the "Spiritual Force." Do not tense the hands or fingers, but point in a relaxed manner. Using the technique you have learned thus far, project lines of power, or force threads, from the areas of your body referred to previously, as well as from your fingers, and attach them to your chosen objects. Here it is possible to use one breath to

achieve this, but until you are able to do this with total ability, comfort and force, it is good to use several breaths in executing this task.
2. Now, focus your attention again on the top of the head. Draw *Ruchaniyut* into your body from your "Infinite Point of Radiance" via the top of the head.
3. Pause for several seconds whilst holding the breath comfortably, and deliberately surrendering to gravity.
4. Then reverse the process, giving *Ruchaniyut* to your chosen objects, plants, or whatever along the threads on exhalation while puckering the mouth and exhaling slowly whispering the sound "*OO*."
5. Repeat by drawing more *Ruchaniyut* into the body through the top of the head, and then pause again for several seconds, holding the breath, before exhaling *Ruchaniyut* along the threads to the receiving object.
6. It is good to work in accordance with a comfortable breathing ratio, and you should never feel strained, uncomfortable or exhausted after these workings. You might feel surrendered and even sleepy, but not exhausted. If you have reached this point without too much physical, emotional and mental stress and discomfort, and have mastered all the previous stages, you can start to work with humans and animals.

Exercise 7

In this final working, you need to re-practice exercise six, but this time choose a living being and focus *solely on the projection of vital force*, which is the only portion of these workings applied to creatures of flesh and bone. The practice is done in the exact manner as you did before, and you impart *Ruchaniyut* by drawing it again from your "Infinite Point of Radiance," and then exhaling it in the direction of the chosen human or animal creature.

However, you could also give a mental instruction such as "I love you" or "You are getting well," etc., while projecting the "Psychic Force" during the exhalation. This means that you are infusing the Divine Power with a quality required by that creature. This is usually repeated several times. Finally, stop when you sense inside yourself that you have done enough.

. ...So too we may understand the rays of
the effluence of the Unique Master... ... .

Chapter 7
FOUR IN THE HEAVENS, FOUR ON THE EARTH

A. Introduction

In many primary Kabbalistic texts the "Heavens" and the "Earth," in fact the whole of creation, are described in terms of the "Four Elements." For in depth comprehension, ordinary Hebrew words have been analysed in accordance with the "Elements," e.g. the Hebrew term for "Heavens" is *Shamayim*, a word which is said to comprise *Esh* (Fire) and *Mayim* (Water).[1] From this it is deduced that the "heavens" comprise the Elements of Fire and Water, and this is sometimes portrayed symbolically as a hexagram inside a circle:

The circle represents *Ain Sof*, the triangle pointing upwards portrays the Element of Fire, and the one pointing downwards the Element of Water. Curiously enough, this symbol has been referred to as the "Philosopher's Stone" in Hebrew alchemical writings.[2]

As I am sure you may realise, the "Four Elements" are extensively addressed in the primary texts of *Kabbalah*, ranging from the *Sefer Yetzirah* the very source of much subsequent speculation and practice), through the Hebrew magical texts, the writings of the *Chassidei Ashkenaz* (e.g. Eleazer of Worms), Hebrew Astrological and Alchemical texts, to even medical textbooks, e.g. the beautifully illustrated "*Ma'aseh Tuviah*" by Tobias Cohn.[3] Here is an interesting illustration of the Four Elements from this work:

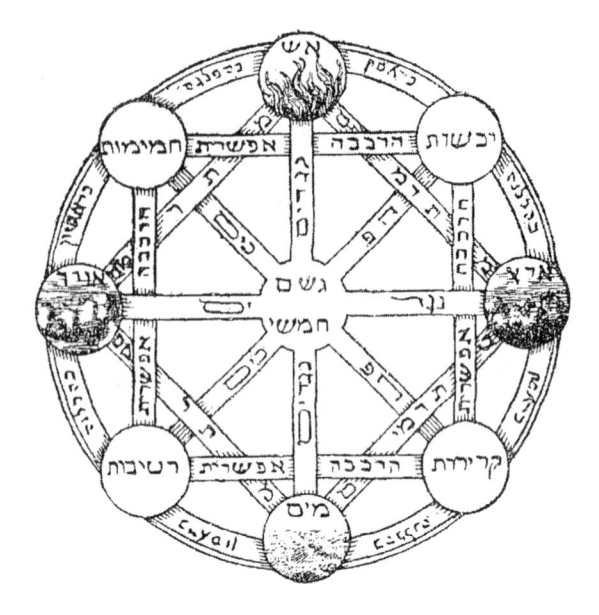

In Hebrew the "Four Elements" are called "*Arba Yesodot*" (*Yesodim* in the Zohar), which could equally well be translated "Four Foundations." They are respectively called:

Fire — *Esh*
Water — *Mayim*
Wind — *Ru'ach*
Earth — *Afar*

Two further appellatives have been suggested for the "Element of Earth,"i.e. "*Aretz*" and "*Adamah*." While the first of these two has been employed as a reference to the Element of Earth, I have as yet not found an instance in the primary works of our tradition, which I have had the opportunity to study, in which "*Adamah*" was used in reference to the Element of Earth. In most primary Hebrew and Yiddish literature dealing with this subject, which includes works on *Kabbalah*, astrology, alchemy, medieval medicine, etc., "*Afar*" (dust) is the most prominent term for the Element of Earth. The same word appears in the literature of "*Hermetic Kabbalah*," usually written "*Ophir*." Obviously the "*ph*" in this case is meant to sound "*f*," but the mispronunciation of the initial vowel is basically because the authors of that specific literature, not familiar with spoken Hebrew, thought the letter "*Ayin*" should be pronounced "O."

Regarding the three words listed as "earth," *Afar*, *Aretz* and *Adamah*, it is worth considering how they are generally employed in standard Hebrew. Firstly, the term "*Aretz*," while meaning "earth," refers more to "the land," a country, in the Bible the planet on which we live, or "*the* earth." On the other hand, *Adamah*, which could be accurately translated "red earth," actually refers to the material substance we till for planting, the actual ground or solid soil. While both these terms mean "earth," their fundamental meaning makes them unsuitable in reference to the concept of "Earth" as an "Element." On the other hand, the word *Afar*, the meaning of which is essentially "dust," related as it is to *Efer* (ash), was mainly used by Hebrew alchemists, astrologers, and so forth, as an accurate reference to the "Element of Earth."

I should also mention that both *Ru'ach* (Wind) and *Avir* (Air) have been used interchangeably in reference to the Element of Air, again with the first term being the more predominant one and the second more rarely employed in this manner. However, as shown in earlier chapters, *Avir* is used as a title for the Universal Life-Force, the very important "Universal Element." Again, *Avir* is the fundamental quintessence of all existence. It is understood that *Aur (Or) Ain Sof*, the Primordial Light of the Eternal No-Thing, transforms into *Avir*, the undifferentiated "Universal Air." The "Universal Element" is extensively addressed by Leo Schaya. He wrote "'And there was light.' When God uttered his formatory and redemptive word, it was revealed as the 'light (*avr*) which spreads out and issues from the mystery of the ether (*avir*),' causing all the 'details' of the material universe to unfold in perfect order and setting all the terrestrial and astral bodies in harmonious movement.....

The four material elements, penetrated by all the corporeal forms imprinted on them by the radiation of the *Fiat Lux* ['Let there be light'], unite in their sacred movement towards the four cardinal points to which they respectively correspond. '.....these four winds were then joined to the four elements of the lower world: fire, air, earth and water. And when these winds and these elements were thus mingled, the Holy One, blessed be he, formed one body of wondrous perfection (in the image of the heavenly and spiritual worlds). Therefore it is plain that the substances composing man's body belong to two worlds, namely, the corporeal elements to the world below and the subtle elements.....to the world above.....'"[4]

Now, with most of the primary Kabbalistic literature on the topic of the Four Elements being still available in Hebrew only, readers unfamiliar with this language are gleaning whatever they can regarding this topic from the writings of those contemporary authors who have derived their knowledge from the teachings of the 20th century "Hermetic Schools." While it is certainly true that much of the Western Magical Tradition is based on Kabbalistic concepts, the teachings of the "Hermetic Magical Orders" are perhaps not the most ideal way to garner information on primary Kabbalistic doctrines. However, from "magical perspectives" one has to acknowledge that there certainly is much well researched material on this topic to be found in "Hermetic" sources, like for example the writings of my mentor, William G. Gray, who wrote extensively with great clarity on the "Four Elements," and in this regard offered many practical applications.[5] Furthermore there is a set of outstanding practical techniques related to "Four Elements," including their "balancing" within ones own body, to be found in Franz Bardon's superb *Initiation into Hermetics*," from which all the following practices were derived.[6] These are of primary importance to all would-be ceremonial magicians.

B. Identification with the Elements

To be able to identify and literally become the "Magical Elements" is vitally important. This is usually done by responding in a "sensing" way to what these Elements represent, that is to have a "feeling appreciation" rather than a "thinking appreciation."

Writing about the Four Elements, William Gray said: "Air is atmosphere, lightness, life, freshness, uplift, exhilaration, freedom, and the like. Nothing but the finest and purest qualities that can be imagined into an 'Air-Concept' are fit to incorporate into our Inner Cosmoi.

These must be dwelt on to a degree where we actually feel and experience an Inner experience caused by concentration of our consciousness for that particular purpose. The degree of intensity will depend largely on the individual Initiate, but it should always be kept at controllable levels.

Fire is thought of as Light, Illumination, clarity of consciousness, equable temperature, Inner vision, the Divine Spark shining, heavenly Radiance, and so forth. Let the pure Inner Element be as perfect as possible, free from all the fears it suggests to us as mortals. Again we must work until an experience of radiance, clarity, or suchlike is actually undergone inside ourselves.

'Inner Water' is not wet, cold, or anything that might be unwelcome. It is flowing, friendly, protective, sustaining, amenable, powerful, rhythmic, and anything else of a beneficent associative nature. We have to sufficiently 'waterize ourselves' to obtain a definite experience.

Earth represents objectivity, solidity, gravity, weight, fertility, mass, incarnation, definition and so forth. When we feel properly 'Earthed,' we should come back to the Centre again, and from there contemplate the Cosmos around us as a dynamic construction driven by its own Elements. As a crudely effective analogy, we may think of a mythical perpetual motion machine wherein Air blows Fire, which boils Water, which dissolves Earth which becomes Air and so on and so on. The end-product at this stage ought to be an Inner experience of being a balanced entity around a central Point of Poise, with an Elementary Cosmos in working order humming happily on its Divine-Human axis to the Keysound of its own Name. We should hear this in ourselves, and even hum it under our physical breath as perhaps '*OMMMMMMMM—AYNNNNNN*' or the rightly resonated '*Amen.*'

No attempt should be made to go beyond this framework until it can be built up rapidly and satisfactorily as an easy exercise. Even to achieve this may take more material time than might be supposed. The exercise has to be persisted with until we become aware that such a state of cosmos has actually been built up around us and we are indeed living in it as a natural everyday condition."[7]

Here is a very easy practice, which allows very rapid identification with the Element or anything else for that matter:

1. Select one of the four Elements, i.e. Air, Fire, Water or Earth. Bring to mind an image associated with that element, e.g. a whirlwind for Air; flames or glowing coals for Fire; a waterfall, flowing river or a deep cool pond or lake for Water; and dry soil, a big boulder or a large crystal for Earth. Smile warmly at your chosen Element. Feel the warmth of your smile, your *Ruchaniyut*, linking with the Element. This should be experienced as intensely as you possibly can.
2. Keep looking at the image of your chosen Element, and sense the specific quality associated with the chosen Element, these being "lightness" for Air, "warmth" for Fire, "coolness" for Water, and "heaviness" for Earth. In this regard you should again develop a "feeling appreciation" rather than a "thinking" one about each quality. Try to keep your mind, the "cage of logic" out of these practices. While continuing to smile warmly inside yourself, keep sensing the quality of the Element in question until you feel you are becoming it. What you should allow to happen, is to feel as if you are being absorbed into or turning into the image of that Element.
3. Keep on smiling warmly, and let the quality of the chosen Element radiate out of you as *Ruchaniyut*, Spiritual Force, and simultaneously let the body freely express the element either in stillness or in spontaneously expressed motions.

C. Breathing the Elements

The task here is still to acquire, accumulate and control the qualities of the Four Elements, producing and dissolving them in the body at will. We are already familiar with this practice through the foregoing identification practice, but we will need to look more carefully at mastering the skill.

1. THE ELEMENT OF FIRE: ACCUMULATION & DISSIPATION

1. Sit in your usual comfortable, surrendered manner. Close your eyes, and smile warmly inside yourself. As in the

previous exercise, feel yourself in the centre of an immense sphere enveloping the entire universe which is filled with the Element of Fire, e.g. red fiery energies, flames, etc.

2. Now inhale the Fire Element through your nose and mouth, simultaneously imagining it being absorbed into the body using deep "Whole Body Pore Breathing" without straining in any way. Keep breathing and with each breath increase the quality of the Element (warmth) in your body, condensing it inside yourself more and more with each inhalation. Bardon recommends that one commences with seven inhalations only, which is increased by one breath with each successive exercise, settling eventually for an average of about 20 to 30 breath cycles. He also suggested that one uses a string of beads or knots to count the breaths, so as to avoid being distracted by having to count mentally.[8]

3. Finally, using again "Whole Body Pore Breathing," dissipate the Element of Fire from your anatomy with a number of exhalations equivalent to the number of inhalations you employed to accumulate Fire. You should count these exhalations with the string of beads or knots.

2. THE ELEMENT OF AIR: ACCUMULATION & DISSIPATION

1. Prepare yourself once again as you did in the previous practice, i.e. sitting comfortably and surrendered, closing your eyes and smiling warmly inside yourself. This time sense yourself in the centre of a vast sphere comprising the Element of Air. This could be visualised as billowing orange clouds, this colour having been associated with air and the lungs.

2. Inhale the Air Element through your nose and mouth, and directly through your skin into your body using again "Whole Body Pore Breathing." Using a number of breaths, increase the quality of this Element (lightness) inside you, i.e. feel your body becoming lighter with each inhalation. Start again with seven inhalations, and increase with one breath during subsequent exercises, again finally settling

for around 20 to 30 breath cycles. Once again use the string of beads or knots to count the breaths.
3. Conclude again by dispersing the Air Element in the same manner as you did with Fire, that is using a corresponding number of exhalations to breathe the Element of Air out of your body.

3. THE ELEMENTS OF WATER & EARTH: ACCUMULATION AND DISSIPATION

Repeat the procedure of accumulating and dissipating Elements in the manner described above, employing respectively the Element of Water and Earth. In the case of Water, you could sense yourself in the centre of an enormous sphere comprising blue water, and focus on the quality of "coolness" as you inhale the element using "Whole Body Pore Breathing."

With the Element of Earth you might feel yourself in the centre of a sphere comprising a green crystalline substance, and the associated quality would be heaviness. Be sure to gather and diffuse each Element initially with seven inhalations and seven exhalations, and increasing these with repeated practice.

Now, the system of colours suggested here: Red for Fire, Blue for Water, Orange for Air, and Green for Earth, do not quite align with those suggested by Franz Bardon. However these colours do work, and align with further practices addressed in this and other titles in this "Shadow Tree" series. Regarding such colour attributions to the four Elements in these exercises, Bardon noted "Colour vision or sensation is quite individual, but not absolutely necessary," and he added that "what chiefly matters in our exercises is the sensory imagination."[9] I might add that with these procedures it is once again important to "feel things out," rather than to reason about them.

D. Amplification of the Elements

Having acquired the skill of absorbing the qualities of the respective Elements into your body via your lungs and the pores of your skin, you will now concentrate on drawing these same Elements into individual bodily organs. Franz Bardon recommended two methods to achieving this:[10]

Method 1

1. Excluding the brain and the heart, select any part of your anatomy.
2. Repeat the practice of accumulating the respective Elements in your body using Whole Body Pore Breathing. During exhalation focus your attention on the chosen segment of your body, and feel the "elemental force" flow into this bodily part.
3. Accumulate and compress the quality of each Element into that sector with each consecutive outbreath.
4. When you sense maximum intensity has been reached, the Element is dissipated back into the Universe via successive exhalations comprising same number as those ones used to compress the Element into the chosen part of your anatomy. You may also disperse the elemental force directly from the chosen bodily part during one forceful exhalation.
5. Repeat the exercise with various parts of your anatomy, and using each of the four Elements. In this regard, special attention should be given to the hands and fingers, since these organs are extensively used in the magical practices addressed in this work.

Method 2

1. Repeat the practice of accumulating the respective Elements in single parts of your anatomy. However, instead of employing Whole Body Pore Breathing and directing the elemental force to flow into chosen organs, simply breathe directly into the specifically chosen bodily part.
2. Use again successive inhalations to draw the quality of an Element directly into the chosen organ, retaining and accumulating the inhaled force inside the selected location.
3. Again, when you feel that you have accrued enough elemental force inside that bodily part, relieve that portion of your anatomy from psychic tension by releasing the garnered power directly back into the universe with the same number of successive exhalations, or with one powerful exhalation.

E. Balancing with the Elements

The human body is divided into four principal regions, corresponding to the elements. The feet up to the buttocks, correspond to the Earth Element. The genitals, the abdominal region with all the internal organs such as the bladder, bowels, gall, liver, stomach, etc. up to the diaphragm relate to the Water Element. The chest, lungs, heart, arms and the neck correspond to the Air Element, and finally the head and its organs pertain to the Fire Element.

The following task would be to "load" the four regions in the physical body, with the respective qualities associated with the four Elements.

1. The different elements are invoked by feeling yourself positioned in the centre of an enormous sphere filled with a specific Element. For example The "Earth Sphere" could be made up of a subtle "crystalline substance," the "Fire Sphere" with fiery energies; etc.
2. It is customary to commence by loading the Element of Earth in the lower regions of the body, followed by Water in the lower torso, Air in the upper torso, and finally Fire in the head. When you sense yourself fully centred in an enormous sphere comprising a chosen Element, take a deep breath and absorb the Element and its quality via the pores of your skin into the sector of your body associated with that specific Element. Do this seven times.
3. Repeat the procedure with all four Elements and their respective regions in the human anatomy.
4. Continue by separately focussing on each of the four "elemental sectors" of your body. Smile warmly, take a Complete Breath, and on the exhalation vibrate the part you are focussing on with sound, while mentally giving it the instruction to "*Understand.*" Again you should "feel" rather than "think" the meaning of this word. Repeat this portion of the procedure, but change the instruction to "*Surrender.*"
5. In conclusion, simply smile with your body, feeling the warmth of the smile, the *Ruchaniyut*, permeating your

whole physical structure. Then take a Complete Breath and vibrate the whole body while humming, followed by sitting quietly for a few minutes doing absolutely nothing. Finally get "Spirit Energy" moving in the body by doing "Whole Body Pore Breathing," and then allow yourself to enter the state of feeling the Divine Presence moving you (*Practising the Presence*).

6. A more advanced procedure is to accumulate as much of the qualities of each element as possible, i.e. load each bodily sector with its respective Element until the force commences to radiate out of your anatomy, then release it back into the universe in the usual manner.

This practice definitely affords one greater balance, and a sense of profound peace and serenity. There are many benefits to be derived from these procedures in which one learns to control and align oneself with the Four Elements, for example:[11]

1. The practitioner will become protected against the harmful affects of the adverse aspects of the elements.
2. The exercises facilitates practitioners the opportunity to be balanced and centred in their personal environment. This allows one to sense the fundamental laws and processes governing existence in a powerfully spiritual manner.
3. The practitioner becomes immune to many diseases, and gains a certain amount of control over issues affecting his or her personal fate.
4. A greater resistance is gained against malevolent influences, such as psychic attack.
5. These procedures have a cleaning effect on the different levels comprising the being of the practitioner, and in this manner restores and strengthens the psycho-spiritual aspects, which Bardon[12] terms "magical faculties," of the practitioner.

F. Projecting the Elements

The Practitioner will now learn how to project the elements. I am once again greatly indebted to Franz Bardon for these exceptional exercises. I have selected only three, as well as one procedure pertaining to mastering the "Universal Element," amongst the many included in his highly acclaimed training course, these being the ones relating to the material addressed in this book.[13]

Exercise 1

1. Sit in your usual comfortable position, smiling warmly inside yourself. Close your eyes.
2. Using Whole Body Pore Breathing, inhale and accumulate the quality of the Element of Fire in your body via your lungs and pores. On each inhalation breathe in more of the Element, and retain the elemental force inside yourself during exhalation.
3. When you feel the Element adequately compressed inside your anatomy, focus on your solar plexus and during successive exhalations, permeate the room you are working in with the power of the Element in question, clearing it out of your body.
4. Repeat the procedure of inhaling and accumulating the Element and then impregnating the room with it, a number of times.
5. You will have achieved your aim when you can distinctly feel the increase of heat in the room, at which point you should diffuse this power into the universe, back into Infinity. This is done by taking a deep breath, and then, on exhalation, to feel yourself push the elemental force out of the room.
6. Repeat the entire procedure with each of the four Elements.

If this practice is worked outdoors, it would be necessary to first create and define a working space. This procedure is addressed below in the sections titled *"Clearing the Sacred Space"* and *"Defining the Working Space."* When this is achieved, you simply work the exercise of projecting the elements in the manner described. Bardon[14] recommended working either with one Element each day, or working with all four Elements, employing each at a different time of the day, e.g. Air at dawn, Fire at noon, Water at dusk, and Earth at midnight.

Exercise 2

In this exercise the practitioner will learn how, through breathing with lungs and pores, to emit an accumulated element, not only via the solar-plexus, but through "Whole Body Pore Breathing," and in this manner amassing Elements in the surrounding atmosphere.

1. Sit in your usual comfortable and relaxed position. Focus on inhaling the Element of Fire into your entire body using Whole Body Pore Breathing. Accumulate the element with successive inhalations, until you strongly sense the heat quality of the fire Element.
2. Again, when you sense the Element strongly compressed inside your body, permeate the room you are working in with the power of the Element in question, by exhaling the accumulated elemental force out of your entire body, releasing it via the skin into the surrounding atmosphere, again dispersing it afterwards into Infinity. Repeat the procedure with all the Elements.

Exercise 3

1. Commence again by sitting in your comfortable, surrendered position. This time, breathe elemental force directly into separate parts of your anatomy, in the same manner learned previously, and gradually increase the specific force inside the selected part until the quality of the Element is felt with great intensity. Conclude by releasing the element directly out of the chosen organ, and in this manner once again impregnating the surrounding atmosphere, from whence it is redirected into the universe. As usual, repeat the practice with all the Elements.
2. Pay special attention to working this exercise with your hands and fingers, since you will mostly employ these in your magical practices. The element must be accumulated by pore-breathing in one hand or both of them in such a manner that through a movement of the hand, like a flash, the element is emitted from the hand into the selected space, impregnating it instantly. Repeated practice makes

perfect, and all the elements should be applied and mastered. Then continue with the following practice.

G. Mastering the Universal Element

A fair amount has been written regarding a primordial "universal element" in Kabbalistic texts—much of which can be found in the works of those who were also practising alchemists, or at leased versed in alchemy. However, our problem here is that while this "universal element" is understood and discussed by modern authors in a fairly simplistic manner, e.g. "ether" as the primordial power behind the "four," and, for that matter, behind all manifestation, the topic is a lot more complex in the primary literature of Jewish mysticism. For example, in the *"Prayer of Unity Rabban Gamliel,"* a text which deals extensively with the "Primal Ether," we read "He is emanator of the entire unity from a single power that He created prior to everything. This is the Primal Ether which is called supreme exaltedness (*rom ma'aleh*), because it is first and the intelligence of everything that is emanated, above and below. Moreover, it is the source of all supernal blessings."[15]

While this statement is plain and clear in my estimation, the instant one begins to investigate the topic in the broader spectrum of primary Kabbalistic literature, one is faced with terms like *"Avir"* ("Ether"), *"Avir Kadmon"* ("Primordial Ether"); *"Avir Sovev"* ("Encompassing Ether" or "Surrounding Ether"); *"Avir ha-Ne'elam"* ("Hidden Ether"); etc.[16] Again one might think that all of these are references to the same basic concept, yet one soon discovers that these terms pertain to different qualities of the "universal ether," so to speak. There are higher levels as well as lower ones.

What I find particularly interesting, and personally most meaningful in terms of a practical understanding of what the "universal element" is all about, is the idea that a *Tzadik* (a righteous [enlightened] individual) is in fact the "simple element" (*"yesod hapashut"*)—Nathan Nosson Sternhartz (Nosson of Bratzlav), wrote "The four elements stem from a single source element. This is alluded to in the verse, 'and a river flows from Eden to water the Garden; from there it divides and becomes four major rivers.' That is, there is a single source which divides into four—the four elements. The single source element is the *Tzadik*, the righteous person in whose merit the world is sustained, as in 'And the *Tzadik* is the foundation of the world' (*Proverbs 10:25*). He is likened to the 'apex of the *Yod*,' the source of the four letters of the *Tetragrammaton*. This source element is called the *yesod hapashut*, 'the simple element,' in that, at the source, everything is united as one, without differentiation.

Everything in the world is composed of four basic elements. Each element contains traces of all the others, even if only in microscopic proportion. Thus, *domem* (mineral) has 'earth' as its main component, but one can find traces of 'water.' 'air' and 'fire' within. The continued existence of the world is based upon the proper combination and interaction of these elements.

Each element is radically different in makeup from the others, yet God in His infinite wisdom created them in such a way that they could coexist and sustain life in an almost endless array of combinations—as long as that which they are sustaining is alive. When its 'life' ends, the elements disperse—creating a situation, conceptually, of the 'World of Separation.' Thus it is the life force that binds the disparate elements together so that man can exist. This life force is the single source element, the *Tzadik*, who has ascended above the materialism of this world. He acts as a bridge between the spiritual and the physical, and can therefore transmit spiritual life force to the physical world.

In their source (the single source element, the *Tzadik*), the four elements are actually one—conceptually, the World of Unity —sharing a peaceful coexistence and interaction. Even when they leave their source, the four elements can exist in perfect harmony as long as they continue to receive their life force from the *Tzadik*. Only when the elements are cut off from this life force for any reason is their harmony upset. At this point, degeneration and dysfunction set in, leading to illness and suffering.

Although every person is made up of all four elements, there are four main roots, corresponding to the four letters of the *Tetragrammaton*. Each individual is rooted in his particular letter more than all the others. Correspondingly, he is also rooted in the specific element and character trait that derives from that letter. This is what accounts for the tremendous differences we find in people's temperaments. Some temperaments are rooted in fire, some in air, some in earth, some in water. The main thing is to harmonize their differences, for when difference, rather than harmony, is stressed, strife becomes the norm and people resist and oppose each other. This strife reverberates into their root elements, causing disharmony Above. As a result, the world is visited with destruction and sickness.

The main controlling force which can harmonize these differences is found in the single source element, the *Tzadik*, The *Tzadik* knows how to establish a proper balance between the various elements in his domain. This brings harmony and peace to each individual and to humanity as a whole."[17]

Now, the general tendency is to think that the term *Tzadik* refers to specially chosen, "hero worshipped," better still, "guru worshipped" individuals who are untouchable spiritual leaders in their communities. Such is certainly the case in numerous instances, especially amongst ultra-fundamentalist religionists. However, the term *"Tzadik"* refers to any individual who has reached a most lofty state of spiritual growth, an individual who has turned into the "perfect channel" through which "divine force" may be directed into the world. Hence, Reb Nosson and his master, Nachman of Bratzlav, maintained that everyone can grow spiritually to the extent that all four elements are harmonized within their being. This would lead to enormous control over the physical body and personal nature, and ultimately to gaining the state of great perfection, peace and spiritual profundity, which would afford personally suitable levels of *"tzadik-*hood."[18]

Again, such individuals are understood to be both "channels" and "buckets," able to convey and pour out *Shefa* (Divine Abundance) into the manifested world for the benefit of all. Hence it was said that when such individuals raise their arms in blessing and spread in the "priestly position," that the four spiritual elements are conducted via the spaces between the fingers (two spaces per hand—one space between the two sets of conjoined fingers and one space between the thumb and fingers), with the "primal element" transmitted from the large space found between the hands, i.e. from the very being of the one who combined the "Four Elements" in perfect harmony. It is certainly clear that the simple lives of many of the individuals who have reached such levels of "cosmic alignment," clearly indicate that "messianic madness" and "hero worship" do not feature at such exalted levels of spiritual excellence.

We will now learn how to master the Spirit-Principle or Universal Element. All the elements originate in the Universal Element, which corresponds to the Cord in the "Magical Instruments," and they are dominated and kept in the correct balance by this element. If the practitioner achieves good results with the elements, the practice of controlling the finest principle, *Avir* (Ether) can be worked with:

1. Sit in your usual comfortable and relaxed position, and close your eyes. Sense yourself floating in the vastness of space. Attempt to lose all sense of dimensions and directions. Imagine the vastness around you to be filled with *Avir* comprising a most radiant colourless substance.
2. Commence inhaling this primordial ether by breathing normally. When you are well settled, employ Whole Body Pore Breathing to absorb *Avir* via your skin into the whole of your anatomy. Continue breathing in this manner until you feel yourself, as it were, merging with the "Whole." You need to reach the stage where you begin to sense yourself at one with this scintillating force, virtually as if it is breathing you.

H. *Arba Ruchot:* The Four Winds (Directions)

1. INTRODUCTION

In *Kabbalah* the "Four Elements" have been attributed to the four letters of the Ineffable Name, four Archangels, four *Sefirot*, four directions, the four seasons, the four phases of the Moon, etc., etc. However, attempting to find a uniform set of attributions from primary Kabbalistic literature is extremely difficult, since there have been major differences of opinion in this regard. In fact, nowhere does the statement "there is only one thing Kabbalists agreed upon and that is that they don't agree," apply more accurately than in this instance.

270 / *The Shadow Tree: The Book of Self Creation*

In many instances authors were dealing with the topic from a single perspective alone, without consideration of any "broader implications," so to speak. As a case in point, consider the traditional bedtime prayer (*Kriat Sh'ma al ha-Mitah*) from the *Siddur* (Hebrew prayer book).[19] Here we find the invocation "To my right *Michael* and to my left *Gavriel*, in front of me *Uriel* and behind me *Rafael*, and above my head *Shechinat El*." This portion of the evening prayer is claimed to be based on *Midrash Bamidbar Rabbah 2:10*[20] and the *Pirke d'Rabbi Eliezer 4:1*.[21]

Now, in this night-time prayer the four archangels are aligned with the "position of service" each archangel held around the "Throne of Glory" in early Jewish mysticism, e.g. as depicted in the large merkavistic portion of the *Pirke d'Rabbi Eliezer*, where we read (4:1) "Four classes of ministering angels minister and utter praise before the Holy One, blessed be He: the first camp (led by) *Michael* on His right, the second camp (led by) *Gavriel* on His left, the third camp (led by) *Uriel* before Him, and the fourth camp (led by) *Rafael* behind Him; and the *Shechinah* of the Holy One, blessed be He, is in the centre."[22]

Here it is clear that *Michael* is in attendance to the right of the "Throne of Glory," hence is guarding our right; *Gabriel* to the left, thus guarding our left; *Uriel* [*Auriel*] to the front, and guarding our front; and lastly *Rafael*, positioned behind the "Throne of Glory," is protecting our rear. Keep in mind these attributions were made in very early *Midrashim* some centuries prior to the appearance of the *Sefer ha-Zohar*, and long before the Tree of Life was fully formulated in its current order.

If one is facing East while uttering this bedtime invocation, the positions of the four Archangels would naturally be *Michael* in the South, *Gabriel* in the North, *Uriel* in the East and *Rafael* in the West, and this set of attributions is in fact maintained in some Kabbalistic writings. However, inspecting the positions of the archangels in *Midrash Bamidbar Rabba* (2:10), considered one of the sources of the bedtime protection invocation, the entire issue gets quite confusing. Scrutinising the "four directions," which the four archangels are respectively said to be associated with in this verse, suggests that those who originally listed the positions of these "spirit entities" around the "Throne of Glory," did not have specific directions in mind, i.e. East, West, etc., when they listed the positions of the archangels around the "Throne of Glory." Such directional attributions appear to have been added somewhat later, and are simply not reconcilable with the associated celestial positions of the four archangels.

Of course, problems inevitably arise when one attempts to broaden the application of a set of attributions initially employed in a singular manner, unrelated to any broader perspectives. Regarding this issue we read in *Midrash Bamidbar Rabbah 2:10* "As the Holy One blessed be He created four winds (directions) and four banners (for Israel's army), so also did He make four angels to surround His Throne — *Michael, Gabriel, Uriel* and *Rafael. Michael* is on its right, corresponding to the tribe of Reuben; *Uriel* on its left, corresponding to the tribe of Dan, which was located in the north; *Gabriel* in front, corresponding to the tribe of Judah as well as Moses and Aaron who were in the east; and *Rafael* in the rear, corresponding to the tribe of Ephraim which was in the west."[23]

Here the archangels are attributed to the directions in the following order, and despite alternatives listed elsewhere, this order became generally accepted:

> *Rafael* to the West.
> *Michael* to the South.
> *Gavriel* to the East.
> *Uriel* [*Auriel*] to the North.

Consider that according to the bedtime prayer, *Michael* is to my right, and we are told in the *Midrash* that he is associated with the "South".....so I must be facing East, which I am! However, *Gavriel*, located to my left according to the same sources, is associated with the East....which is in front of me? Worse still, *Uriel* is supposedly in front of me but, hold on to your seat, if I am facing East—because *Michael* is on my right, and *Gavriel* is associated with the East, which is somehow supposed to be to my left—how in blazes can *Uriel* be in front of me when he is associated with the North? Even *Rafael* appears to be oddly placed. Also, if I keep *Michael*, the archangel associated with the South, to my right, i.e. as if I were facing the "Throne of Glory" myself, I would be looking in the direction of *Rafael* who is positioned "behind the Throne".....that would be East.....but this archangel is associated with the West? If the traditional bedtime invocation was aligned with this arrangement of their respective positions, it should read "To my right *Michael* and to my left *Uriel*, in front of me *Gavriel* and behind me *Rafael*." Keep in mind that there are other variations to this Angels/Directions theme, e.g. South – *Uriel*; North – *Gavriel*; East – *Michael*; West – *Rafael*; or again South – *Michael*; North – *Uriel*; East – *Gavriel*; West – *Rafael*. There is simply no general agreement on this topic to be found throughout the primary texts of *Traditional Kabbalah*.

It is worth noting that much of the early "angel teachings" in both Judaism and Christianity, were derived from Zoroastrianism. In this regard, it is recognised that the archangelic protection portion of the bedtime prayer was derived from the ancient Babylonian incantation which reads "*Shamash* before me, behind me *Sin*, *Nergal* at my right, *Ninib* at my left."[24]

Now, considering this subject and related issues, we should also peruse the attributions made of the mentioned four archangels to the "Four Elements." In the *Sh'lah al Sefer Vayik'ra* by Yeshayahu ben Avraham we are told that "*Micha'el* is the base source of Spirit Water, *Gavri'el* of Spirit Fire, *Auri'el* of Spirit Air, *Rafa'el* of Spirit Earth."[25] These attributions are based on teachings found in Kabbalistic literature in which the archangel *Michael* is attributed to the *Sefirah Chesed* (Mercy), *Gavriel* to *Gevurah* (Severity), *Uriel* to *Tiferet* (Beauty), and *Rafael* to *Yesod* (Foundation). In this case, *Chesed*, attributed to "Spirit Water," is the domain of *Michael*, while *Gevurah*, the domain of "Spirit Fire," belongs to *Gavriel*. In turn, the sphere of *Tiferet*, being the balancing central *Sefirah* between *Chesed* and *Gevurah*, is attributed the "Spirit Air" and *Uriel*, this being aligned with the statement in the *Sefer Yetzirah* about "Air tipping the scale" between "Fire" and "Water." Finally, in this instance, *Yesod* is attributed to *Rafael* and "Spirit Earth."

As we know well enough by now, these attributions are by no means universally accepted amongst Kabbalists, and there are again numerous variant attributions of these four, as well as other archangels, to the ten *Sefirot*. Some of these attributions are decidedly odd, but they are always in accordance with specific mind-sets. Here are a few examples of attributions of the four archangels to the *sefirot* to be found in traditional Kabbalistic literature:

1. *Michael – Binah; Chesed; Tiferet; Hod; Yesod;*
2. *Gavriel – Binah; Gevurah; Netzach; Yesod;*
3. *Rafael – Tiferet; Hod; Yesod;* and
4. *Uriel (Auriel) – Tiferet; Netzach; Yesod.*

It gets even more befuddled when we investigate the related planetary and zodiacal attributions. We can be certain that it took a lot of careful investigation and consideration of all the details involved, including a study of related material, i.e. the writings of Averoes and the literature of ancient astrology, in order to arrive at the neat, coherent and efficient systems used in the Hermetic Orders.

As said, the four letters of the *Tetragrammaton* (*YHVH*) have been linked to the "Four Elements." In fact, the four letters comprising the Ineffable Name have been attributed to a great variety of "tetrads," e.g. four "Divine Elements" respectively focussed in *Chochmah* (Wisdom), *Binah* (Understanding), *Tiferet* (Beauty) and *Malchut* (Kingdom); the four "Divine Countenances" (*Partzufim*) — Father, Mother, Son and Daughter; the four "Winds" of Isaiah; Ezekiel's four "beasts" of the *Merkavah* (Divine Chariot-throne) — Lion, Eagle, Man and Bull; the four "Fixed Signs" of the *Mazalot* (Zodiac) — Leo, Scorpio, Aquarius and Taurus; etc. In this regard there are a number of primary kabbalistic sources on this topic, e.g. the *Sefer ha-Zohar*, etc. There are also some very informative essays regarding this topic available in English.[26]

I spent many hours investigating this subject, eventually ending up with a hefty document comprising a chaotic cacophony of opinions and dissenting voices. Yet, while curiosity had me delving into this confusing mass to broaden personal perspectives, I did not find any need to adjust the tidy, straight-forward system I learned from my astute mentor. This one, as shown in the following table, I applied as successfully in the realm of "*Practical Kabbalah*" as I have in scrutinising the theoretical variety. The set of attributions is both logical and practical.

EAST	SOUTH (NORTH)	WEST	NORTH (SOUTH)
LIFE	LIGHT	LOVE	LAW
RAPHAEL	MICHAEL	GAVRIEL	AURIEL
Divine Healer	Divine Resembler	Divine Strength	Divine Light
AIR	FIRE	WATER	EARTH
Mercury	Sun	Moon	Venus
Sword	Rod	Cup	Shield
MAN	LION	EAGLE	BULL
Spring	Summer	Autumn	Winter
First Quarter	Full Moon	Last Quarter	Dark Moon
Dawn	Noon	Dusk	Midnight
Light Arising	Light Increasing	Light Descending	Light Returning
Commence	Continue	Complete	Cease
In	On	Out	Off
Birth	Adulthood	Maturity	Age (Death)
Tongue (Voice)	Spine (Nerves)	Heart (Veins)	Flesh (Skin)
Thinking	Being	Feeling	Doing
Listen	Consider	Reply	Reflect
Hearing	Seeing	Tasting	Touching
EE (*Yod*)	AH (*Heh*)	OH (*Vav*)	EH (*Heh*)

I believe I should explain the four "vowel associations" listed at the conclusion of this table of attributions, especially as they are important in the use made of the Ineffable Name (*YHVH*) in several practical workings discussed in this book. These vowels present a pronunciation of the Ineffable Name.

Tradition has it that the pronunciation of the Divine Name *YHVH* is lost, and currently the name *Adonai* is generally used in its place in mainstream Judaism. However, I have perused several theories regarding the pronunciation of the Ineffable Name, ranging from its component letters being used as consonants uttered with vowels in various ways, to the name being entirely comprised of vowels, the latter said to be "*IAOE*" pronounced "*EE–AH–OH–EH.*" However, why should this Name, whose pronunciation is claimed to be lost in the mists of time, be pronounced in this manner? I will try and explain the background to this curious custom.

The "Ineffable Name" is the most sacred Divine Name in our tradition. We know that the "Essence" of Divinity is truly beyond time, space and events, and therefore cannot be referred to by *any* name. "Divine Names" therefore relate to the various attributes of God in manifestation, and *YHVH* refers to the most sublime attribute of Divinity. It is said this Name derives from the terms *Hayah* (היה — was"), *Hoveh* (הוה — "is") and *Yiyeh* (יהיה — "will be"). In this sense *YHVH* expresses the totality of "Being," the totality of time, space and events, that is the totality of existence.

Many authors have contemplated the meaning of the *Tetragrammaton*, some more successfully than others. My late mentor, William Gray, also shared with me what the *Tetragrammaton* meant to him as an Englishman. Viewing the component letters of the Ineffable Name as an acronym, *YHVH* or *IHWH* can in English be thought of as an anagram for "It-Him-We-Her." As a God-title this would be "***ITHIMWEHER.***" This interpretation of the *Tetragrammaton* certainly describes Deity in Its highest sense:

   IT — an ultimate of anything;
   HIM — the male polarity of Existent Energy;
   WE — the unity of Entity; and
   HER — the female polarity of Life.

This is the Life-Spirit as a complete "Whole"— unique and entire. I do not think for one minute that any "orthodox Kabbalist" would approve, yet see what it opens up! Look how it forms a cycle: Neutral–Positive–Total–Negative. In fact, it aligns nicely with the fourfold patterns shared in the table of correspondences. In this sense the *Tetragrammaton* represents "The Wheel of Life" in ever turning circles.

Be that as it may, the Ineffable Name is said to be the "Integral Animating Force" behind all manifestation. Kabbalists use this Name to link their own mortal power with this Ineffable Force which radiates throughout all manifestation. To achieve this end, the Name is invoked and meditated upon, but first we have to consider its pronunciation. This is somewhat problematic since, as said, it has been claimed to be lost somewhere in the mists of time. Yet, it is not lost and is easily recognisable if one studies the Name closely.

Firstly, Hebrew is written without vowels. All the letters of the *Otiot*, the Hebrew Alphabet, are consonants. Of these the letters י (*Yod*), ה (*Heh*) and ו (*Vav*) are the only ones employed in the indication of vowels. As a vowel, the letter י is vocalized "*EE*"; ה is expressed "*AH*" or "*EH*"; and ו is sounded "*OH*" or "*OO*."

Secondly, it is interesting that these three consonants used in that order in combination with the letter ב (*Bet*) or ל (*Lamed*), are pointing respectively to three identities: me, her and him. Thus the words בי (*Bi*), בה (*Bah*), בו (*Bo*) respectively read "in me," "in her" and "in him." The words לי (*Li*), לה (*Lah*), לו (*Lo*) in turn respectively read "to me," "to her" and "to him." Here the sound "*EE*" refers to oneself, "*AH*" to the feminine "other," and "*OH*" to the male "other."

Thirdly, in the *Sefer Yetzirah* we note that only three letters of the *Tetragrammaton* are said to have been used to establish or "seal" the six directions with its various permutations, and these are *Yod, Heh* and *Vav* (יהו).[27] In the likelihood that these letters refer to the vowels "*EE*," "*AH*" and "*OH*," this exact order of vowels aligns with *IAO* (*Ee–Ah–Oh*), a popular Divine Name used by the Gnostics.[28] They derived it from a Hebrew original, as they did "*Sabaoth*" (Hebrew: *Tzva'ot*), etc. As indicated, the *Sefer Yetzirah* refers to the six permutations of *YHV*, and curiously enough the exact permutations of the name *IAO* or *YAO* can be found in the Greek magical papyri.[29] We also know that the Ineffable Name, or at least portions thereof, are incorporated in Hebrew personal names, and there are angelic names as well which include the letters of *Tetragrammaton*, e.g. the very important angel *Iaoel*,[30] etc.

Taking all of this into consideration, we realise that the first three letters of the Ineffable Name (יהו) should similarly be pronounced "*EE–AH–OH*" with the last ה (*Heh*) taking on the second pronunciation of the letter as a vowel, which is "*EH*." The full pronunciation of the *Tetragrammaton* would then be "*EE–AH–OH–EH*." In her remarkable book "*The Secret Doctrine of the Kabbalah: Recovering the Key to Hebraic Sacred Science*" Leonora Leet[31] wrote similarly regarding the pronunciation of the Ineffable Name.

As indicated, the sounds for the four "Magical Elements," i.e. Air, Fire, Water and Earth, are respectively "*EE*," "*AH*," "*OH*," and "*EH*." Thus the Ineffable Name invokes the Past, Present and Future; the Personal, the Male and Female; the four "Magical Elements"; in fact the very "Essence of Life" itself! Armed with this information, we can now continue with related practical activities.

2. THE SIGN OF A CROSS

a. The Kabbalistic Cross [32]

"The Kabbalistic Cross" is a formalized ritual procedure in common use amongst Hermetic Kabbalists. I believe it was designed to impact most beneficially on the Self, to focus and centralize personal consciousness, and to act as a "seal of protection" for the practitioner. In this regard, because of its remarkable efficacy, the "Kabbalistic Cross" has been adopted and adapted by some practising Kabbalists, as well as many outside the tradition.

This procedure is not directly associated with "*Traditional Kabbalah*" *per se*, but was developed and practiced by the Hermetic Order of the Golden Dawn. It is based on the last stanza of the Christian "Lord's Prayer," i.e. "Thine is the kingdom, and the power, and the glory, for ever. Amen."[33] This phrase was loosely transposed into Hebrew, and sort of aligned with four spheres on the Tree of Life, specifically "Thine is" (*Atah*) – *Keter*; "the Kingdom" – "*Malchut*"; "and the power" (*v'Gevurah*); "and the greatness" (*v'Gedulah*), "forever" (*l'Olam*), the latter being perhaps a reference to *Tiferet*. The Hebrew words are not direct translations of the English expressions concluding the Christian prayer.

Terms like "kingdom," "power" and "glory" are frequently used conjointly in the Hebrew Bible, but it would seem that the origin of that statement at the end of the Christian prayer is *1 Chronicles 29:11* which reads "Thine, O Lord, is the greatness, and the power, and the glory, and the victory, and the majesty: for all that is in the heaven and in the earth is thine; thine is the kingdom, O Lord, and thou art exalted as head above all."[34] This specific verse inspired both Jewish and Christian authors alike, including Kabbalists like the poet Ibn Gabirol who included it in his great mystical poem "*The Royal Crown*" which reads "Wonderful are Thy works, as my soul overwhelmingly knoweth. Thine, O Lord, are the greatness and the might, the beauty, the triumph and the splendour. Thine, O Lord, is the Kingdom, and You are exalted as head over all."[35]

As I am sure you have noticed, the words comprising that phrase from *First Book of Chronicles* are actually tracing the six *Sefirot* from *Chesed* to *Yesod* in their exact order on the *Etz Chayim* (Tree of Life), i.e.

> "Thine, O Lord
> is the **Greatness** — ***Gedulah***
> and the **Power** — ***Gevurah***
> and the **Glory** — ***Tiferet***
> and the **Victory** — ***Netzach***
> and the **Majesty** — ***Hod***
> for all that is in the heaven and in the earth is thine
> (**Foundation**) — ***Yesod***"

It would be interesting to know whether the individuals who came up with the "Kabbalistic Cross," based their construct exclusively on the Christian Lord's Prayer, or whether they were influenced in any way by the mentioned verse in the Hebrew Bible.

Now, the formula of the "Kabbalistic Cross" reads as follows:

>   *Atah* You are
>   *Malchut* The Kingdom
>   *v'Gevurah* And the Power
>   *v'Gedulah* And the Glory
>   *l'Olam* Throughout Eternity
>   *OmEin* Amen

Tracing the "Kabbalistic Cross" on your body requires the use of both your "spirit" and physical hands. The action and movement of your hands should be felt as intensely as possible, and you should literally experience the "Divine Force" flowing in and from your hands.

> Touch forehead say: ***Atah***
> Touch solar plexus, say: ***Malchut***
> Touch right shoulder, say: ***v'Gevurah***
> Touch left shoulder, say: ***v'Gedulah***
> Moving hand over the head, encircle all points, say: ***l'Olam***
> Raise both hands in prayer position over the heart, say: ***Amen*** (*OmEin*).

The best way to work the "Kabbalistic Cross" is to keep your eyes closed, and employ both your physical and energy hands. Slowly move your hand into position on inhalation, pause and sound the appropriate word on exhalation. It should feel somewhat like you are dragging your arms into position with your breath. Thus, you inhale and drag your right arm to your forehead, and while pointing your middle and forefinger at your forehead, sense an energy bond between your forehead and your fingers, then chant "***Atah***" extending the sound over the entire out breath. With the next inhalation, drag your arm downwards in a circular motion to your solar plexus or navel, again pointing the two fingers at this location, sensing the energy bond between it and your fingers, and on the exhalation chanting "***Malchut***," ensuring that you are sounding the word over the entire extent of the outbreath.

Continue by dragging the hand on the next inhalation diagonally upwards to your right shoulder, point the two fingers, sense the bond between the fingers and the shoulder, and chant "*v'Gevurah*" over the length of your exhalation. Then, on the following inbreath, drag your hand in a circular motion from your right shoulder to the left shoulder, point the two fingers, feel the bond between shoulder and fingers, and chant "*v'Gedulah*" in the same manner.

Now, on the next inhalation drag your hand in a circular motion over your head to your right shoulder, then on exhalation chant "*l'Olam*" while continuing the circular motion downwards from your right back to your left shoulder, thus encircling all four points: Forehead—Right Shoulder—Solar Plexus (or Navel)—Left Shoulder.

Finally, with the next inhalation slowly drag both hands upwards towards your face, then with hands positioned in front of your mouth and sensing a ball of energy between the palms, exhale and chant directly into this sphere of force, saying: "*Amen*" (*OmEin*). Conclude by inhaling, and on the exhalation slowly lowering your hands back to the side of your body.

Remember to intone the words as intensely as you can. Each vocalization is extended over a single breath in a single tone. Another point worth noting, is to move the hands (spirit and physical) while inhaling, almost as if the inhalation is pulling the hand in the direction it needs to go, and then to chant the associated word while the hand is pausing, and directing *Ruchaniyut* into the part of the body corresponding to the sentence or word.

b. The Cosmic Cross

William Gray's understanding of the Western Mysteries is heavily based on what is termed the "Cosmic Cross" or "Circle Cross of Cosmos."[36]

The humble symbol of the "Circle Cross" represents the oldest pattern of universal order.[37] Like all cross symbols, it incorporates the idea of humanity (the horizontal line) and Divinity (the vertical line) meeting (the lines crossing) in the centre. William Gray celebrated this great symbol by establishing its pattern as the primary "ritual signature" of the Sangreal Sodality. This entails the tracing of the "Cosmic Cross" pattern on ones torso, incorporating the same format used in forming the "Kabbalistic Cross." The "Cosmic Cross" should equally be traced with both the physical and "spirit" fingers. While chanting the words in a very resonant manner, the subtle energy and movements of the hands should again be experienced as intensely as possible.

The "Cosmic Cross" is formed in the following manner:

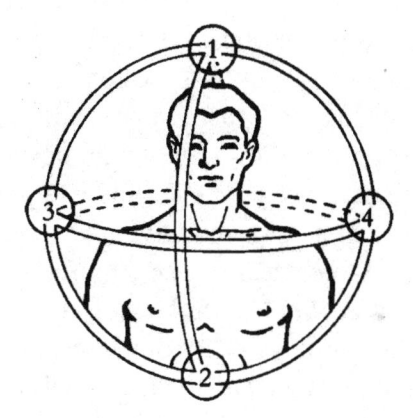

1. Pointing the forefingers of your right hand at your forehead, say: **In the Name of the Wisdom**
2. Move the hand downwards, and point to the solar plexus, say: **And of the Love**
3. Slide the hand upwards and sideways, and point to the right shoulder, say: **And of the Justice**
4. Slide the hand across the torso to the left shoulder and point the forefingers at this locale, say: **And the Infinite Mercy**
5. Moving the hand over the head, encircle all points while saying: **Of the One Eternal Spirit.**
6. Bring both hands into prayer position in front of the mouth, palms slightly apart, and say in the space: *Amen (OmEin)*
7. Breathe in and on exhalation lower the hands to the side of the body.

You should trace the sign of the "Cosmic Cross" with "Spiritual Power" flowing from your hands.

3. CLEARING THE SACRED SPACE

The intention here is to abolish from your temple, meditation room or sacred working space, all forces which might impede the task you have set out to achieve, and equally to attract and allow certain powers which would impact beneficially on your work. Now, the procedure is here delineated for individuals living in the Northern Hemisphere where the movement of the Sun is East-South-West-North. The positions of North and South are switched in the Southern Hemisphere, since there the daily cycle of light is East-North-West-South. The Sun moves anti-clockwise in the Southern Hemisphere, and anyone living in that part of the world should align their ritual activities with this motion of the Sun.

Keeping this in mind, position yourself in the centre of the space in which you intend to meditate or work your ritual activities. Facing east, close your eyes and imagine yourself in the centre of a sphere, one large enough to encompass the entire working space. Imagine the floor or ground on which you are standing to be exactly in the middle of the sphere, with you standing in the upper half. Be aware of the large dome of the upper half of the sphere above you, and the lower half beneath you, with the floor suspended centrally.

Next, sense directly below your feet an invisible axis extending upwards from the bottom centre of the sphere through your body, and out through the crown of your head into the top centre of the sphere. In fact, just as you *are* the axis of this sacred working space, so are you the axis of your personal universe.

When you feel yourself ready to continue, focus your attention on your hands and invoke spirit force in the palms in the usual manner, and trace the "Kabbalistic Cross." On conclusion of this activity, while still facing East, sense directly ahead a powerful sphere of light, positioned like a "gate" in the Eastern quarter of the dome surrounding your sacred space. This is the light of Archangel *Raphael*, the Element of Air and LIFE. Now, trace with your mind along the central axis through the top of your head,

Four in the Heavens, Four on the Earth / 283

reaching into infinity and feeling yourself linked to your "Infinite Source" via a line of force. Then, while inhaling deeply through your mouth shaped *"OO,"* draw *Avir* (Universal Spiritual Power) in the form of golden light down along this line through the top of your head into your heart or solar plexus, and on the outbreath, while mouthing *"EE,"* think *"Raphael*—Air—LIFE" as you direct a beam of golden light from your heart (or solar plexus) with your imagination towards the sphere of light in the East, thus linking your heart with the "Spirit of Life."

Next, we come to a slightly tricky portion of the task at hand, but one offering a skill easily learned. You will light the entire sphere surrounding your Sacred Space, and to do so, you will start by dragging the light from the Eastern position to the South (North in the Southern Hemisphere). First you have to trace with your mind an exceedingly thin light stretching from the "Eastern Gate of Light" upwards along the dome to the axis above your head, and downwards to the centre below your feet. This line of light you are going to drag from East to the South while simultaneously imagining that portion of the dome lighting up as the golden illumination creeps along from the Eastern quarter to the Southern one. The pattern is like this.

You have just breathed out and established a line of light between yourself and the East. During the pause between the exhalation and your next inhalation, quickly sense the mentioned thin line of light along the dome in the East, then on the next inhalation, while mouthing *"EE—AH,"* drag the light to the "Southern Gate of Light", in this manner illuminating the South-Eastern quarter of the sphere surrounding your Sacred Space. During the pause between inhalation and exhalation sense on your right a powerful sphere of light positioned in the South—the light of Archangel *Michael*, the Element of Fire, and LIGHT. On the exhalation breath, while mouthing *"AH,"* think *"Michael*—Fire—LIGHT" simultaneously directing a beam of golden light from your heart towards the sphere of light in the South, thus linking your heart with the "Spirit of Light" on your right. On the next inhalation, while mouthing *"AH—OH,"* drag the light to the "Western Gate of Love," thus illuminating the South-Western quarter of the sphere surrounding your Sacred Space.

Again, during the pause between the inhalation and exhalation, sense a powerful sphere of light positioned in the West behind you—the light of Archangel *Gavriel*, the Element of Water, and LOVE. Then, as you mouth "*OH*" and thinking "*Gavriel*—Water—LOVE," direct a beam of golden light from your heart towards the sphere of light in the West, and so link your heart with the "Spirit of Love" behind you.

On the next inhalation, while mouthing "*OH–EH*," drag the light to the "Northern Gate of Law," thus illuminating the North-Western quarter of the sphere surrounding your Sacred Space, and sense on your left a powerful sphere of light located in the North—the light of Archangel *Auriel*, the Element of Earth, and LAW. During the next exhalation, while mouthing "*EH*" and thinking "*Auriel*—Earth—LAW," direct a beam of golden light from your heart towards the sphere of light in the North, thus linking your heart with the "Spirit of Law" on your left. During the next inhalation, while mouthing "*EH–EE*," drag the golden light back to the "Eastern Gate of Life," thus completing the illumination and linking with the Archetypes of the quarters.

During the pause between the in breath and the next inhalation, sense the lit sphere surrounding your Sacred Space as well as the four lines of light connecting you with the quarters, then on a forceful exhalation, mentally sweep the inside of your sphere with light from East around the South, West and North respectively mouthing "*EE–AH–OH–EH*" (*YHVH*), simultaneously expelling all adverse forces via the four "gates."

Return your attention to the "Eastern Gate of Life" in front of you, where you sense *Raphael*—"Spirit of Life." On inhalation, while mouthing "*EE*," think "*Raphael*—Air—LIFE" as you draw the Element of Air and the "Power of Life" from the East, along the beam of golden light towards your heart (or solar plexus). On the outbreath, while mouthing "*EE—AH*," move your attention along the circumference to the "Southern Gate of Light." Then, during the next inhalation while mouthing "*AH*" and thinking "*Michael*—Fire—LIGHT," attract the Element of Fire and the "Power of Light" from the South towards your heart along the beam of light.

Continuing in the same manner, on exhalation while mouthing "*AH—OH*," move your attention along the perimeter to the "Western Gate of Love." Then, as you mouth "*OH*" and thinking "*Gavriel*—Water—Love" during inhalation, attract the Element of Water and the "Power of Love" along the beam of light from the West towards your heart. Afterwards, during exhalation, while mouthing "*OH—EH*," move your attention along the circuit to the "Northern Gate of Law." During the next inbreath, while mouthing "*EH*" and thinking "*Auriel*— Earth—LAW," draw the Element of Earth and the Power of Law from the North towards your heart along the beam of light. Conclude by moving your attention back to the East and mouthing "*EH—EE*" during the inhalation. During the pause between the exhalation and the next inhalation, sense the four "Gates" as well as the lines of light connecting you with the quarters, then while breathing in powerfully, draw from all four quarters the powers of Life, Light, Love and Law, along the beams of light towards your heart, respectively mouthing "*EE—AH—OH—EH*" (*YHVH*) as you move your attention along the circumference, from East, to South, to West and to North. On the exhalation direct the inhaled force via the top of your head, back into your "Infinite Source" breathing "*OO*" along the line of light.

Focus your attention on your heart during the pause, then chant:

b'shem YHVH	In the Name of Infinite One,
Elohei Yisra'el	Power of the Godwrestler,
mil'fanai Rafael	Before me *Rafael*,
u'mei'achorei Gavriel	and behind me *Gavriel*,
u'mi'yemini Michael	and to my right *Michael*,
u'mis'moli Auriel	and to my left *Auriel*,
v'al ro'shi	and above my head is,
Sh'chinat el	the Feminine Presence of the Power.

Conclude the entire procedure by repeating the "Kabbalistic Cross" in the manner described earlier. Then prepare to circumambulate the circumference of your "Sacred Space" and so define your working space, while invoking the aid and support of the Eternal Living Spirit.

4. DEFINING THE WORKING SPACE

Repeat the following chant rhythmically while circumbulating the Sacred Space seven times, following the "Way of Light" set by the movement of Sun in your part of the World, e.g. clockwise in the Northern Hemisphere, anti-clockwise in the Southern Hemisphere. Simultaneously draw the "Sacred Circle" with your forefingers or with a Rod, chanting:

> *hineini* Here I am,
> *hineini* Here I am,
> *hinei ani YaH* Here I am *YaH*,
> *ana hoshi'a* I invoke your support

> (*Breathe, then continue*)
> *ani v'ho* I and It (Unknowable One)
> *ani v'ho* I and It

> (*Breathe, then louder*)
> *ani v'ho* I and It,
> *ani v'ho* I and It,
> *hoshi ana* I invoke your support.[38]

The rhythmic step used in this circumambulation is as follows. Using a stomping dance, step on the highlighted portions of the words, indicating the rhythmical accents, and fit the words into the exact rhythm of the sacred dance.

    The first phrase is meant to be uttered in one breath. If this should cause discomfort or a feeling of stress, it is better to take small, convenient breaths at points indicated by the commas.

Hee–nei–**Nee**   **Hee**–nei–**Nee**   hee–**Nei** ah–**Nee** YAH (*pause*)
Step   Step   Step   Step   Step   Step   Step

ah–**Nah** ho–**Shee**–ah (*pause*),
    Step   Step   Step

Take a quick breath and continue with the next phrase within the beat, keeping in mind that the dance continues rhythmically from the last step in the previous phrase to the first step in the next phrase.

*ah–**Nee** ve–**Hoh** ah–**Nee** ve–**Hoh** (pause.....)*
   Step   Step   Step   Step Step Step

Continue with the following phrase in one breath.

*ah–**Nee** ve–**Hoh** ah–**Nee** ve–**Hoh** hoh–**Shee**–ah–**Nah** (pause.....)*
   Step   Step   Step   Step   Step   Step Step Step

Repeat the entire chant until the circle has been circumambulated seven times.

Having completed the creation of a "Sacred Space," you can now proceed with working meditations or ritual practices within this protective sphere.

. ...One and unchanging, without addition or diminution... ... .

Chapter 8
"THE FIVE-FOLD PATH"

A. *Kavvanah*:[1] Attitude
or
Focussed Awareness

1. INTRODUCTION

Free will and the capacity for inner growth are vitally important in our quests to control our lives, especially when we appear to be so often beset with depression and despair. Yet, since we live in *ha-Olam ha-Assiah* (the Universe of Action), action is the necessary antidote for depression. Our darkest emotions must be confronted through sincere self-analysis, since the quest for cosmic consciousness is a personal one, which must be realised through personal endeavours. It is however also important to recognise the power of our lower feelings, like fear, anger, and sadness, and their effective use in our lives.

In this section we will encounter *Yichudim* and *Kavvanot*, procedures particularly devised to direct the mind during meditation, prayer, ritual activity, and other exercises. Diligent training is necessary if one is to become truly conscious of the "Divine Design" behind creation. Regular and precise practice is required, with total mental and physical focus, composure, patience and persistence. This is vitally important since there are many dangers in venturing, without proper preparation, into the domain of "Ecstatic Meditation" with its incredible visionary experiences.

One of the main dangers of Kabbalistic meditation is the fact that it can cause a state of awareness in which the physical body cannot cope with the intensity of the influx of the *Kavod*, Divine Glory or Energy, which can then lead to death. Another danger is the possible inability of the consciousness of the meditator to return to normal focal levels after the Ecstatic experience, thus leading to catatonic states in the body. It is also possible that mental and emotional instability not only interfere with the process, but that these instabilities can be enhanced and amplified. Because of these dangers, it is vitally important to pay a lot of careful attention to each of the "Stages of Awareness" addressed here, before venturing into the next stage, and so on.

Kabbalistic thinking describes five "Stages of Awareness" in ones Spiritual Awakening. These are:

1. *Kavvanah* (Intention, Motivation and Dedication).
2. *Devekut* (Divine Union or Adhesion).
3. *Hishtavut* (Equanimity).
4. *Hitbodedut* (Meditation or Aloneness).
5. *Ru'ach ha-Kodesh* (Spirit which is Holy or Enlightenment).

These stages correspond to the "Middle Pillar" on the Tree of Life, i.e. *Kavvanah* at *Malchut*, *Devekut* at *Yesod*, *Hishtavut* at *Tiferet*, *Hitbodedut* at *Da'at*, and *Ru'ach ha-Kodesh* at *Keter*.

Now, *Kabbalah* considers the mind to be an extremely powerful instrument, and it is clearly understood that what you think of, to that you attach yourself. Think physical things and you bind yourself to the physical. Think higher matters and you bind yourself to the higher. In this regard it has been suggested that one should start with a definite decision to realise Divinity inside oneself, and then to alter ones actions, whether they be spiritual, mental or physical, accordingly. This practice of altering ones behaviour or approach in life to be in harmony with a definite attitude, opinion, viewpoint, outlook or perspective, is called *Kavvanah* in *Kabbalah*. The whole realisation of your "True Identity" is based on intention and focussed attention (*Kavvanah*), since what you intend is what you will attach yourself to. When you think or contemplate something, you are mentally and emotionally filled with that "something."

This world of multiple objects is therefore acting as a barrier between you and the realisation of the "Inner Truth of Pure Divine Consciousness" behind matter. Yet remember, the door that shuts you out, can also open so as to make you aware that "Cosmic Consciousness" is realisable inside matter. After all, nothing is separate from its source, and since the real identity of everything is in God, so is God inside everything, inside oneself. Realising this is already a state of *Devekut* (Divine Union).

Inner devotion, intention and contemplation are all terms for *Kavvanah*. These expressions are strongly stressed in *Kabbalah*, since the right attitude is needed in order to aid one towards a proper inner centring, resulting in a linking of the ordinary mind to the Divine Mind, thus leading to *Devekut* (Adhesion or Divine Communion). Intention means that you will only have your ultimate goal of "Identity Perfecting" in mind. This aim is *all*, and no amount of mental, emotional and physical pain should be able to wreck it. In fact, if one creates a mould for oneself, and then becomes the clay within it, life can go on knocking one left, right and centre, adding pain upon pain without doing any real harm in the end. If the mould is strong enough, these very pains will shape you in the form of that fundamental construct. Your mould will only be as strong as your faith and trust in it, and a lack of these qualities of *Kavvanah* can mean that a relatively weak push from life can smash you, breaking it and leaving you one big, pulsating pain, desiring only death.

A point worth considering is that *Kavvanah* also means solitary contemplation, that is to allow the world to continue around you as normal, to live in it as far as necessary, yet to reduce all relations to a minimum but with maximum intensity, rather than maximum relations with minimum intensity. Hence all communications and service with, and in, the world are connected to your single "Intention," realising that being *in* this world is not necessarily being *of* this world. This also means that one should learn to *Keep Silent*. Practice your real spiritual communication only when in company of those linked to you on a profound spiritual level, and then again address the "God-aspect" inside these fellow-companions. In this manner you ensure that your communication will be a constant practice of *Devekut*, and your relation with the physical world will be through the God embodied in matter.

Before you can begin to "know" anything, it is vitally important to get your "Intentions" right. This is supremely needed before embarking on that "Inner Journey" leading to *Devekut* (Divine Union). Kabbalists believe *Kavvanah* leads to the

"Mystery of *Devekut*," a term also meaning "Attachment" or "Devoutness," and signifying a close and intimate communion with Divinity.

Now, in order to help you in the cultivation of a contemplative mind in your life, i.e. making it a normal condition of your existence here, it is customary to employ mottoes, set viewpoints, set approaches, or attitudes. This also aids greater *Kavvanah*, and is rather like feeding codes into computers, thus coding your instinctual self. A motto means of course a "word" coming from the French *Mot* meaning "word." It refers to a "guide word" used by an individual, family, tribe, nation, or whatever, to incarnate by their own being or becoming. Hence the importance of a "Magical Motto" for everyone, or a self-selected guide-word for "living up to" or "making flesh." When you come to think of it, what else are "Key codes" that you feed into computers in order to link with whatever area you want? Computers are operated according to the old laws of *Kabbalah*, which used to be so secret centuries back. All the "Words of Power" and all the mysterious "God-Names," what else are they except "Cosmic output" on the VDU or Screen of your own "Inner Awareness"? We are only watching all our old "Magic" being mechanised, and this is just the start we are seeing. Maybe there will come a time when computers will put out more than any human programmer puts in. Where will that "extra" information come from? I am certain there will be no guarantee it would necessarily come from a good source.

Be that as it may, the meaning of a word is a point one has to be very careful of in the "Occult." William Gray taught me to run down the root-meanings of all words, and only apply them in their correct context. That was really good advice, and I owe a lot to him for it. Have no hesitation in passing it on. One should preferably obtain dictionaries in several languages, all with root-meanings. That is the important point. Get back to origins, and it is amazing what one learns. A word is "alive" in that it has a "body" — its alphabetical spelling, and a "soul" — its meaning on several levels. The same is true of symbols, all having a body, which is the outer visual form, whereas the meaning behind it is its "soul." A symbol may be overloaded with meaning, and ultimately die thus by its own soul, which is a form of suicide or murder by humans placing too much or too little value onto a symbol.

Taking ritual magic as a case in point, the compression of consciousness into specific words is part of the process, and that can only be done if the "soul" of a word matches its body well enough to produce a concept which "lives" on "Inner Levels of Life." I deplore the modern murder of languages, resulting in many thousands of words being written which have scarcely meaning in any of them. Luckily a number of writers are hitting back and are resisting this rubbish. Believe it or not, there are actually words that have in our days acquired totally negative connotations, when they were originally filled with hope and aspiration. In this regard I find the expression "weasel words" to be very apt, since a weasel is a nasty little animal of the rodent type being both intrusive and vicious, which is exactly what such warped words are. Typical examples are "parameter," "fascist," "witch," and "situation," perfectly clear words in themselves, yet twisted through slanted misuse until they are made to mean something quite different to the original intention behind their construction.

Words are of course symbols of consciousness which they are supposed to express in sonic or visual form, and it is the actual consciousness which is all-important. No wonder in old times when "primal sounds" were uttered, which reached right into the very depths of awareness and released a powerful response of feeling, those "words" were considered "Magic" ones — hence the advice not to change what were then the "barbarous words of invokation." They believed such sound could call up gods and demons, and so in truth they did, but these "entities" were actually responses surfaced from the deepest levels of either their individual instinctive awareness, which were in touch with much higher (or lower) forms of intelligence than human ones, or they were responses in the "Collective Consciousness" called "God," where these higher (or lower) "Forms of Intelligence" actually reside.

Those reputed "Magic Words" were most likely very primitive sounds of an animal nature, calculated to arouse fear, anger, sex, etc. You can hear them in "mating-calls" or "challenge-calls." The roar of a lion or hiss of a snake — our earliest "God-Names." Both inspire apprehension in humans to this day because of their implied threats to safety. That is to say, it is not the actual noise itself which frightens, but the thought of what that noise may mean in terms of damage to a human body, resulting in almost certain death.

As human language improved and evolved, terms for much more abstract concepts became possible, and humans reacted accordingly. Eventually it was realised that this over usage was beginning to devalue the "words," and so they brought out prohibitions against "taking the Lord's Name in vain." They were thereby protecting their heritage. That worked for quite a while, but nowadays virtually all our "Magic Words" are gone. We have simply used them to death until their impact is altogether lost. Long ago, words like that were used as battle-cries. That is to say, noises calculated to evoke the utmost fighting spirit in the user. Very often these were the clan mottoes or family names; something the fighters held in special honour or valued greatly. That was always the important point: a value, or worth of the utterance to the utterer.

That was supposed to be the idea of taking a "Magical Name" at an initiation, which was an identity no other human was ever to know, so that it became a code between the individual and Deity Itself, which could effect a direct connection between the two when used. Much like the emergency telephone number for calling Fire, Ambulance, or Police at moments of desperate need. The factor that really works everything is the depth of response as an intensity. It has to react at primal level, and these days that is becoming increasingly difficult, since we have eroded our values so greatly.

In a chapter on "Words of Power" William Gray explains that "As a rule, a Word is a vehicle formed on any Life-level for the containing and expression of energies from other levels. If we accept the conventional classification of Life into the four categories of Spirit, Soul, Mind and Body, we can see that a 'soul-Word' would bring forth the energies of Spirit towards Mind, and those of Mind towards Spirit. Direction of force-flow depends on the pressure-point from which Will is applied. If again, we follow the 'Word becoming Flesh' through these levels, we shall find it is Originated in Spirit, Created in the Soul, Formated in Mind, and Expressed in Body. Such are the 'Four Worlds' of the Qabalist, which, of course, return cyclically back to the point of Origin to complete the Circle of Cosmos."[2]

We need to recover some of that old ability to react with special sounds so as to release related currents of consciousness at significant spiritual levels of living. That will take a lot of training and experimenting, but I believe it would be a worthwhile project.

2 *KAVVANOT:* TRAINING THE LOWER SELF WITH "ATTITUDES"

Now, what mottoes do we use to programme the computer of the "unconscious" or subconscious mind? They should be at least of the kind which can be used in your ordinary daily life while working, and which will make you more aware of your intention of "realising God within." Obviously the best way is to invent your own in conformity with your own requirements. All you have to do is adopt one motto each day as an actual attitude, and then approach everything around you from this specific standpoint. For those who might find it useful, here are some "Attitudes" as compiled by the William G. Gray. I can recommend these for those who intend using the Kabbalistic system of "Self" and "God Realisation" through experience and meditation, rather than just through book work. I would suggest the following pattern:

1. Alter your approach to life so that your day starts at night. When you retire to sleep would thus be the commencement of the current procedure.
2. Now, select a motto or an attitude before you go to sleep, and write it down on a piece of paper.
3. Read the motto/attitude aloud three times. Say the sentence slow enough for you to sense the meaning of each word, but fast enough not to loose the overall meaning of the sentence. This is also an important point in meditation and other related practices.
4. Fold the piece of paper and place it under your pillow. Now retire to bed and while your head is resting on the pillow, repeat the attitude again slowly in your mind. Do this over and over until you fall asleep.
5. On waking, immediately retrieve the piece of paper under your pillow, and again read your motto or attitude aloud three times. Then attempt to do your daily duties,

approaching all activities from the standpoint of that attitude.

6. Carry a small notebook in your pocket and make a mark in it every time you become aware that you did not keep to your adopted stance, but were drawn out of yourself, so to speak, into a reaction to what happened, or were affected by outside activities. Do not get angry or depressed about it, but simply note it down and be aware that you did this, even if it happens hundreds of times.

7. At the end of the day, before you retire to sleep when your new day will start, retrieve the little notebook and review the results. Do not judge yourself, simply note your achievement or non-achievement. Then select a new attitude, as you should do every day, without being overtly concerned if you were not successful in keeping to the previous attitude the entire day. If you could do so, you would not need to do this practice anyway. Thus start every day with a new attitude.

8. Below you will find a list of suggested "attitudes." To work through these will take many weeks, after which you could attempt keeping two a day. Afterwards you should attempt to increase the number of attitudes per day, until you are able to have all the attitudes as one, complete, conscious, personal life stance, approaching all situations and experiences from that angle.

Here are some Kabbalistic attitudes compiled by William Gray.[3] As said, it is best to write your own, and if you are well acquainted with the Tree of Life, you could even connect these mottos to the ten *sefirot*:

1. I am here to experience Life.
2. Everything matters.
3. I can get all I ought.
4. It is impossible to exist without Spirit.
5. I cannot live on Earth without a body.
6. What matters in Life is that all should have a chance.
7. Be responsible in living.
8. Place faith in "no thing."

"The Fivefold Path" / 297

9. Growth under control.
10. Life is certainly All.
11. You cannot cheat Life without paying.
12. Know the import of being a Self.
13. Take every advantage to benefit others for your own good.
14. Be not deceived.
15. Don't steal it—earn it.
16. It is foolish to enjoy flattery.
17. Grasp what being means.
18. Be clever, make others think.
19. Admire the possibilities of learning.
20. Laugh with others at what happens.
21. Overcome Evil with Good.
22. Achieve what is right.
23. Be master of your Self.
24. Desire to be satisfied.
25. Make your forces obey your will.
26. Be it against your will to use compulsion over others.
27. Let no cost be unaccounted for.
28. Break nothing you cannot make.
29. Conquer hate.
30. Oppose all intending to destroy you.
31. Control chaos, then create what you will.
32. In a universe of Eternal Beauty, all ugliness must fade away.
33. Whoso rules out Beauty blasts the world.
34. Discover what prevents people from knowing the difference between beauty and Ugliness.
35. Truth strikes up in harmony.
36. Never persuade people to accept Ugliness.
37. Keep in control of yourself.
38. Control confusion in yourself and others.
39. Make opportunities for others to regain lost balance.
40. The secret of perfection lies in preventing deliberate disorganization.
41. Be strictly just.

42. Hate to hurt.
43. Conquer the will to kill.
44. Revenge is wrong.
45. Be severe only in necessity.
46. Respect whoso will not punish you.
47. Be fearful of ever being brutal.
48. Force ferocity to be subdued.
49. Discipline yourself to make others accept you.
50. Nothing is too much trouble for anything.
51. Don't let anything bother you.
52. Care for others that have none to care.
53. Where there is generosity, there is no necessity.
54. Have compassion on the weak.
55. Life should be too happy for weariness.
56. Answer anyone in need.
57. Make efforts to help anyone worthwhile.
58. Try to understand things.
59. Be sympathetic to the stupid.
60. Understanding avoids hate.
61. Shun dangers by intuition.
62. Do not dislike what you do not understand.
63. Comprehension passes all.
64. Where ignorance is folly, it is bliss being wise.
65. Wisdom clarifies obscurity.
66. Find out how you might encourage wisdom in others.
67. Time is never wasted with wisdom.
68. Wisdom cannot afford luxuries.
69. God is living, not dead.
70. O God! Do what Thou wilt.
71. God is everywhere.
72. God is no "thing."
73. Nothing is impossible with God.
74. God knows who exists.
75. God is what anyone can place faith in.

So then it is vitally important to get ones "intentions" right before embarking on ones "Inner Journey" or the "Quest for Illumination."

B. *Devekut:* Divine Union[4]

1. INTRODUCTION

Kavvanah leads to the mystery of *Devekut*, which in turn leads to *Hishtavut* (Equanimity), and further on to *Hitbodedut* (True Meditation), which in turn leads to *Ru'ach ha-Kodesh* (Holy Spirit or Enlightenment), which finally leads to Prophecy, amongst others.[5] When your Intentions are settled, you could, through certain meditations or exercises called *Yichudim* (Unifications), enact a Divine "ascent" into the highest realms, and of course reach *Devekut*.

As indicated earlier, the term *Devekut* is used in *Kabbalah* in reference to an intimate union with Divinity. This is seen as the final step in the ascent to God, although this may be qualified by saying that it is not total union, since such a union cannot be granted to man while still incarnate. Yet, *Devekut* comes as near to Divine Union as is possible while alive on earth. Of course humans cannot experience actual Divine Union or "Mystic Marriage," because they would not be human anymore if they did. A symbolic simulation is the best we can hope for, and how many come as close to it as that? *Devekut* or Communion, a value reachable by every individual while physically alive, is in fact only attained while alone and not through social communion. Furthermore it does not rest on life and death, but finds its union in "Life–Death," which is God. I am reminded of a line written by Nachmanides who, when he talked on *Devekut* said: "Such a man may be talking to other people, but his heart is not with them since he is in the presence of God. And it is further plausible that those who have attained this rank, do, even in their earthly life, partake of the eternal life, because they have made themselves a dwelling place of the Shechinah."[6]

Devekut, how is it reached? Firstly one has to practice within this active life of ours, a contemplative one. In order to know the Tradition as a reality within oneself, one has to be alert, awake and alive consciously, with full knowledge and control of one's own thoughts and actions, and here intention is again important. Never mind how the world may coerce you into doing things, you can always intend it differently, since nobody has control over your intentions, so that you may appear to do things in this world, but your intention is with Divinity. In fact whatever you do is intended towards God without anybody knowing it. Thus one can actually combine normal active living and contemplation, which is one of the highest ideals in Kabbalism, leading to Communion with Eternal Nil. Remember that a contemplative life is a thankful life. It is interesting that the words "think" and "thank" derive from the same root meaning "to know," thus, in terms of our Tradition, the person who really knows, should think and thank all the time.

Firstly then, one should remember to start with a definite decision to realise God, and then to alter ones actions, whether they be mental, spiritual or physical, accordingly. Secondly one must realise that nothing is separate from its source, and that, since the true identity of man is in God, such an identity is within ones very genes. This realisation is already a state of *Devekut*. It is not possible for everyone to attain "Divine Union" through meditation and contemplation, and many have attempted this by a variety of means, including the use of herbal stimulants and entheogens.

The *Sefer ha-Zohar* explaining the "mystery of Unification," gives it a completely sexual connotation.[7] It explains that "the individual who is worthy of the World to Come must unify the name of the Blessed Holy One," and then explains that the Blessed Holy One is the union of two pairs—the male and female aspects of God, and the male and female aspects of man in sexual union. In other words mate with your spouse, while God is uniting with His, and then superimpose the two.

> "He must unify the upper and lower levels and limbs, uniting them all and bringing them all to the necessary place, where the knot is bound." Later on God is referred to as the "Elder Israel," and man is called the "Lesser Israel." This Elder Israel is the Male and Female aspects of God, called Tabernacles, in conjugal bliss, and thus one is instructed to "combine the two Tabernacles, making them into one limb." "This unification," the *Zohar* says, "is accomplished when one meditates and ascends, attaching himself to the Infinite Being (*Ain Sof*). It is here that all things, both on high and below, are bound together in a single desire."[8]

An understanding of sexuality is the key to several meditation techniques in the west. For example the Spirit Self, who must meditate and ascend to *Ain Sof*, is the *Neshamah* which is understood in Kabbalistic terms to be the same as the *Shechinah* or the Female Counterpart of God. Thus the Elder Israel, or God in conjugal bliss, is the union of the male aspect of God with the Higher Self in man, the Female Counterpart.

Elsewhere in the *Zohar* the supernal point is equated with seed (semen) being sown in the womb of *Binah*, Understanding or the Supernal Mother. The "Inner Chamber" here is the same as the "Room of love" also mentioned in the *Zohar*, through which the Soul must pass before God. "The place which conceals" the *Yod*, is simply the *Heh*, the "life-giving Portal" or vagina, both literally and metaphorically. The *Zohar* instructs:

> "One must then include all limbs in the place from which they emanate, this being the Inner Chamber. One brings them back to their place in the essence, foundation and root, elevating them to the place that is the Root of the Covenant."[9]

This alludes to a physical sexual union. "*Yod* is the mystery of the Holy Covenant. *Heh* is the Chamber, the place in which the Holy Covenant, which is *Yod* is concealed. And even though we have stated that this is the *Vav* here it is a *Yod*. The mystery is that the two are united as One."[10] The "mystery of the Holy Covenant" is simply a euphemism for the circumcised penis, which is to be hidden inside the "Chamber," or Vagina of the Lesser *Heh*, or the *Shechinah* represented by all women on earth.

The *Zohar* is indicating that the double act of God and man uniting with their respective mates, should be bound together into a single act. The other "levels" or "limbs" are in fact the bodies and Selves of the partners which must also be made into a single "Whole" with the Infinite. Thus through this act of worship and meditation, you cause your Soul, the female Counterpart of God to unite with God-the-Male, while your physical body unites with your mate here on earth. This is said to cause a most profound inner balance, in which you are no longer affected by the outside environment.

One should notice that the two letters *Heh* (ה) in *YHVH* (יהוה) are traditionally seen as the Upper *Shechinah* and the Lower *Shechinah*, or the Supreme Mother and the *Shechinah* in exile. The *Yod* (י) is here called the "highest point," simply because the Kabbalists wanted to veil the fact that they thought that God has a "phallus" symbolically speaking, and as explained earlier the *Yod*, the smallest letter of the Hebrew Alphabet, stands for a flame or force as the male Principle, whereas the *Heh*, the letter for life, is associated with the Female Principle, and is the pattern through which life flows, and traditionally the vagina is seen as the Portal of Life.

The sexual significance of *YHVH* (יהוה) can be interpreted as the initial *Yod* (י) symbolising a flaccid or immature penis, the first *Heh* (ה) being an unoccupied vagina and uterus, the *Vav* (ו) being an erect and virile penis, and the final *Heh* (ה), having a *Dagesh*, being a gravid or pregnant uterus, since in this instance the *Dagesh* is termed *Mafik* (מפיק) or "bringing out" and "uttering," so treating it as a consonant. This makes a lot of sense, since, by the simplest possible illustrations, it points out visually and symbolically the "Act of Life" which *YHVH* (יהוה) is supposed to signify.

There are several primary Kabbalistic texts which throw light on this important aspect of esoteric lore, in which the female was taught that God was in her husband, while he was told that the feminine form of the same God was in her. Therefore, when they had sex together, it was a perfect act of worship and should be treated that way. There were actually formal prayers to say and acts to do before they had sex. All was "in the books." The "God in him" united with the "God in her," so everything was beautiful and perfectly proper.

The idea of "aiming at God" through sex is rather interesting. Hebrew terms for male and female sex-organs are *Kavah* (קבה) meaning "womb" for the female, and *Shofchah* (שופכה) for the male. The sound of the female word is almost like the English "quiver," and though there are no etymological connections here, it did set my mind on a lovely trip about a "quiver" in which old hunters kept arrows, always emblematic of "love-darts" or "shooting," which links with the slang "shooting ones load" in common use today, meaning ejaculating seed and which derived from the idea of discharging a gun of its "load."

The ancients might have thought of firing arrows in that sense. Hence, I suppose, the idea of shooting the *Chetz* (חץ) or "arrow," situated in *Yesod*, the Foundation on the Sefirotic Tree, which is equated with the sexual organs in Kabbalistic thinking, up the Tree of Life with *Keshet* (קשת—"bow") in the direction of God, or more precisely the *Shechinah* or Female Counterpart of God, sitting on top of the Life-Tree. I presume the symbol of the *Paroket*, being the "Curtain" or "Veil" on the Tree of Life, could then be seen as the maidenhead of the *Shechinah*. I think Sigmund Freud would have loved *Kabbalah* if he had not been a dedicated atheist. On the other hand I believe he knew quite a bit about it anyway.[11]

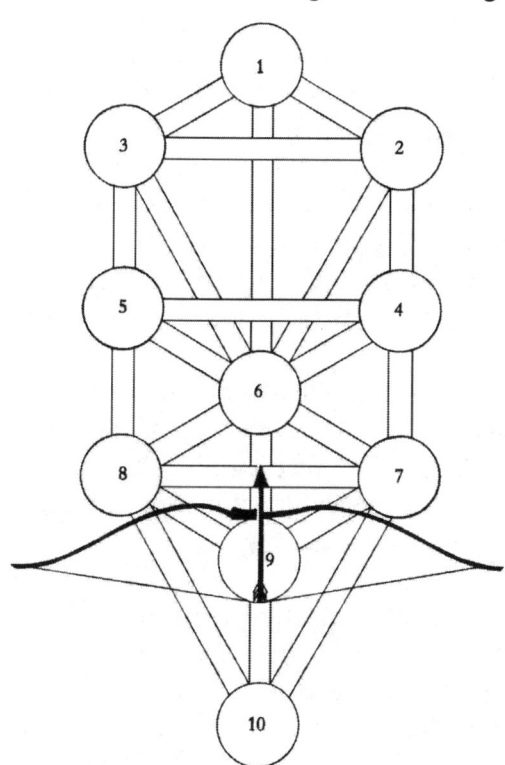

Religious concepts involving sexual terms developed from the intense yearning in man for an intimate union with God, and to this end many Traditions played a role. The truth is that all mysticism is the same essentially, and it is only a question of semantics as to who uses which system. Kabbalists have simply worked out their own elaborate terminology, to describe exactly the same things that others experience and call something different.

It is interesting that the term "to know" was used in ancient days to describe the sexual act, and to reach *Devekut*, the Mystical Marriage, you have to "know," on all levels of being. It may be said that to know anything means to think, to feel, to be awake, to be alert, to be alive, to understand thoroughly, to recognise, indeed there is so much more, that many works could be written on the subject of "knowing" alone. It is our personal consciousness that gives us our intimate identity, and so if we know God in a more personally direct manner, we would have a more intimate knowledge of Him. In fact, there are quite a lot details in both mainstream Judaism and *Kabbalah*, about direct conversation and even most intimate relations between humans and the Divine One, i.e. the ancient prophets for example, and several others. One would have thought these individuals to have achieved a great level of purity prior to their conversations with God, and yet one cannot vouch for this as some of the historical details regarding their personal lives are not quite as squeaky clean as one would have expected.

Be that as it may, it has been said that God speaks to us in the voice of our parents. We are told that at the end of the era of the Prophets, communication between man and the Eternal One could be had only through dreams or an external voice, i.e. the *Bat Kol* (literally "daughter voice" or "daughter of a voice"), a heavenly voice. While not considered the direct voice of the Almighty, it is the voice of the Divine speaking to us from within. Otherwise, we have all those fascinating accounts of the *Merkavists* who traversed the "heavenly halls" to facilitate a direct encounter with Divinity in the highest of heavens, but even these experiences were not quite "face to face" so to speak. However, there are ample examples of personal, even intimate communication between God and humans in the primary literature of Jewish mysticism.[12]

This topic is of great personal interest to me, since I believe most firmly in this direct and most intimate relationship with God. At a certain life-changing moment in my life I came to realise that it is perfectly possible for each one of us to meet Divinity through an interpersonal relationship, and it certainly altered my "prayer" so to speak. I think I began to understand what *Hallel* (praise) and singing a "Psalm" was all about. Curiously enough, the English words "feel," "Psalm" and "palpitate" derive from one basic root meaning "to experience" and "to have sensation of." Since I am the kind of person who desires God as intensely as others desire sexual fulfilment, I know that I touch and caress God every time I sing a

Psalm. A very cynical and disapproving teacher asked me in what manner I supposed I had "touched" God, and in what dimension I presumed to have had this intimate communication with the Almighty? On close reflection I realised that I was doing so inside my own being, and *Psalm 81:10* suddenly popped into my mind, which reads "There shall no strange God be in thee."[13] This is at least my understanding of "mystical union" or *Devekut*, "Divine Adhesion," which to me is a union in which God is no stranger, since He is to be found *within* oneself.

While discussing this with a very dear Companion, I was asked whether worship was necessary after you have discovered that God and your real Self are truly One, or whether worship is really necessary when you "know." My feeling is that one should never stop worshipping. For me worship is part of "the great yearn for Divine Union," the "haunting of the gates of the *Shechinah*." Worship simply means to honour that which commands the highest respect, and deserves the highest form of veneration and adoration. If you feel deep reverence for the Tradition inside yourself, and for its effects around you, *that* is worship. If you feel a deep admiration for your fellow companions, *that* is worship. If you adore life and your relationship with it, *that* is worship. The most intense love you can feel for anyone or anything is worship. To revere, respect, honour and to uphold ones real Self is worship. In fact, to entertain the most intense affection for anybody or anything is worship.

I believe one should not hesitate to worship that which is worthy of respect. One should not hesitate to praise or pray to that which is worthy of veneration, and what is more worthy of veneration than the Eternal Living Spirit of all life whom we call God, a term which is not a name but only means "that which is worshipped"? Praise is to value and to commend highly. If you love your God and your Tradition, you extol them as a matter of course. This pertains to what Moshe Idel termed "the theurgy of augmentation,"[14] meaning that in this world you increase the value of your God and your Tradition through *Hallel* (praise).

I believe that whilst you can augment the value of your Tradition through praise, you can also pray to the "Eternal Consciousness" behind that Tradition, and to pray is simply to entreat, to postulate or to make supplication. The greatest supplication in life must surely be for the Divine One to be what He (She or It) wills within oneself. Again I am reminded of a young student asking me "how a God can actually hear us?" At the time I quoted all the wonderful Kabbalistic accounts of prayers being woven into crowns by the angel *Sandalfon*, and so forth.[15] While I would still share all those wonderful sagas of our spiritual heritage, I would also tell him that God can hear us *through ourselves*, and to the extent that we are in contact with "God." On this planet *WE* are the ears, eyes and agents whereby He (She or It) knows man.

Now, getting back to the possibility of a personal, direct communication with God. Why should we pray as slaves to a master? I greatly appreciate absolute familiarity with God, and enjoy talking to God in intimate, "chatty" terms. Sort of "Hey God, I've got something to tell you." I love the story of the old Rabbi who was dying, and while thinking back over his past life, realised that maybe God did not treat him very well. With his last dying breath he said: "Lord in a couple of minutes You and I are going to have a looooooong argument," and he was instantly healed!

Prayer should be a relationship with God, a mutual relationship, and then God and we evolve together. I have been severely criticised for saying that God also evolves. I believe that God can evolve, of course not from imperfection to perfection, but from perfection to perfection, unfolding greater perfection in the "eternal Now." After all, God would not be almighty if He could not evolve. I was taught that God eternally manifests Himself out of Nothing, that He *IS*, but that His background *IS NOT*. I was further taught that evolution is the endless process of Self awakening unto itself. Now if "God manifest" is evolving towards the centre of Infinite Nil, He will do so eternally, because there is neither a beginning nor an end in the "Infinite Nothingness."

For me it is simply a matter of the better you make yourself, the better you make God, and thus because of my belief in the evolution of God, I also know that our evolution has no end. We also evolve eternally. I cannot fathom a state in which I will be in eternal bliss and ecstasy, a state which says "you are doomed to stay here forever," a state in which I would not be able to grow ever higher. I would hate such a condition of consciousness, because it would be static and infinitely boring. My personal sympathy in this regard is with the words of a song from the musical *"Paint Your Wagon,"* which says "When I get to Heaven, tie me to a tree, for I'll begin to roam and soon you know where I will be?"[16]

Now, about the "knowing" process, it should be clear that to be conscious, besides meaning to know through sensual impressions, also means to possess knowledge derived from moral experiences. There is morality in knowing because to know also means to distinguish and discriminate persons and things from one another by attributes perceived by the senses, which we would ordinarily call mother-wit and commonsense, which seems so uncommon these days. It should be vitally important to everyone, to be able to recognise and identify a person or thing as being familiar and belonging to some particular category. Of course, true morality is concerned with the difference between right and wrong in matters of conduct, or the capacity of differentiating right from wrong, and here we realise that we are not, and should not act only by physical force, or only by practical means, but we also act by appeal to reason and understanding. When one understands, the "golden mean" opens up and one starts behaving in a conscious manner with full knowledge of one's own thoughts and actions. Then one can steer carefully amongst the rights and wrongs into the most Holy Inner Adytum of Spirit.

In order to work towards *Devekut*, it is most important to "clear the lens of perception," that is to get rid of the disabling emotional and mental baggage you may have been carrying around for many years. Thus the following practice is very important in your attempt to reach Divine Union.

2. PRAYER: AN EXERCISE IN *DEVEKUT*

The following exercises will open inner gates of awareness and intuition leading to communion with the Eternal Living Spirit. To work these practices you will need writing materials. To achieve the desired end, you have to *write*. This procedure will not work with a typewriter or a PC. You have to write with a pen and ink. This is "Writing Meditation" requiring the full experiencing of the movement of your hands and arms, and the flow of the pen on paper. Each practice requires a minimum time of one hour, during which you will firstly write a letter, and secondly write a reply in return. Work the procedures over a period of six days, each day fulfilling one of the requirements. Rest and recover from the ordeal on the seventh day.

Day 1

1. Write a letter to the Eternal Living Spirit (God), communicating directly, as if you are writing to an intelligent being, capable of understanding fully your simplest and most complex ability to express yourself:
   a. Describe the image you have of God.
   b. Describe how you feel about God.
   c. Describe your feelings about the world.
   d. Describe your concerns about the world.
   e. Describe what you need for yourself.
2. Now be the Eternal Living Spirit yourself and write a letter to you from God's point of view:
   a. Address the points you raised in the previous section.
   b. Describe your good points.
   c. Describe your bad points.
   d. Describe what God expects of you.

Day 2

1. Write a letter to the Eternal Living Spirit listing three major requests and explain why you feel that you should have them:
   a. How would receiving them benefit you?
   b. How would they benefit the world?
   c. What price would you pay for each?
2. Again be the Eternal Living Spirit, and write a letter from God to you regarding the requests you listed and discussed above, responding to each of them individually.

Day 3

1. Imagine you are three years old, cradled in the arms of your mother. Using your non-dominant hand (if you are right-handed, write this letter with your left hand), write a letter to your mother describing your needs in great detail.

2. Write another letter to your father.
3. Note any similarities and any differences you might discover between the two letters.

Day 4
Imagine the presence of someone you knew who is deceased, and write a letter to yourself from the point of view of this deceased acquaintance or friend, covering the following points:
1. What is it like where he or she is?
2. What advice would that person give you?
3. What can she or he teach you about
   a. relationships?
   b. love?
   c. the meaning of life?
   d. your specific purpose in life?

Day 5
Imagine that you have died and that you are a video of major events in your life. Write about these events one at a time, and comment on them from the perspective of afterlife.

Day 6
Imagine that you have just come from a doctor's rooms with the diagnosis of a terminal illness that gives you only one year to live. Write about how you would live the last year of your life, assuming that you will not suffer any pain and that death will come swiftly and silently.

Each of these practices opens inner gates within oneself leading to tremendous intuition, heightened awareness and enlightenment. An additional practice associated with this practice is to use sacred scripture as an oracle. The *Book of Psalms* is particularly good, but any other sacred writing will do. The practice is as follows:

After doing any of the above practices, open the sacred text, a prayer book, etc. at random at any page and read the first lines your eyes come in contact with. This is an oracle, and sometimes the words will be directly linked to the point of your practice; at other times they will seem wholly irrelevant. When written prayers connect with your inner space, you can touch new depths. If this happens, read and repeat the important line over and over again in your mind and your heart. This is also a form of prayer. If nothing connects, then continue with your exercises as normal.

These practices warm the heart, speak a language of the soul, and doing them evokes a prayerful state of being. Prayer cannot be accomplished in a rote fashion, nor can we count on being raised to the heights of divine realisation each time we pray. However new accessibility to the soul can be gained by performing these exercises until we have found our *Bat Kol*, the Divine Inner Voice, praying within us in its own language. Then we truly experience the power of prayer, and through it, connect with a new reality.

C. *Hishtavut:* Equanimity

After the long interlude with *Devekut*, we now come to *Hishtavut* (Equanimity). For the sake of clarity let us briefly review the "Five-Fold Path" again, referring to different, yet related, states of awakening as measured against the Middle Pillar of the *Etz Chayim* (Tree of Life). These are:

1. *Kavvanah* (Attitude, Focussed Awareness, etc.) linked to *Malchut* (Kingdom).
2. *Devekut* (Divine Adhesion or Union) linked to *Yesod* (Foundation).
3. *Hishtavut* (Equanimity, Unattachment) linked to *Tiferet* (Beauty).
4. *Hitbodedut* (Aloneness, Meditation) linked to *Da''at* (Knowledge).
5. *Ruach ha-Kodesh* (The Holy Spirit, Enlightenment) linked to *Keter* (Crown).

Thus far we have dealt with *Kavvanah* and *Devekut*, referring of course to an individual reaching Divine Union after his or her life-stance is fully recognised and focussed in full consciousness, without being drawn into reactions to external stimulus. In this state you respond but do not react. You will then always respond from your conscious stance, rather than react uncontrollably unconsciously adopting a reactive stance because of the external stimuli. When you become fully focussed in your own being, the following stage of *Hishtavut* (Equanimity) automatically ensues.

Of course, it is important that one should not only understand the term *Hishtavut* intellectually, but that one should bring it into full realisation in ones daily your life. Studying the subject will not necessarily bring the desired state into your life at all. In Hebrew the term *Hishtavut* is used to explain a state of balanced harmony. The word derives from the root *Shaveh* (שוה) meaning "equal," thus showing the meaning of *Hishtavut* to be a person totally unaffected by good or bad, which is considered a vital prerequisite to true meditation. Abraham Abulafia, the famous 13th century ecstatic Kabbalist, said: "One who has attained true passion (*cheshek*), is not influenced by the blessing or curses of others."[17] The Spanish Kabbalist Isaac of Acre added: "He who is vouchsafed the entry into the mystery of adhesion to God (*Devekut*), attains to the mystery of Equanimity (*Hishtavut*), and he who possesses Equanimity attains to loneliness (a euphemism for *Hitbodedut*, true meditation), and from there he comes to the Holy Spirit (*Ru'ach Ha-Kodesh*) and to prophecy. But about the mystery of equanimity the following was told to me by Rabbi Abner: 'Once upon a time a lover of secret lore came to an anchorite and asked to be admitted as a pupil. Then he said to him: 'My son, your purpose is admirable, but do you possess equanimity or not?' He replied: 'Indeed, I feel satisfaction at praise and pain at insult, but I am not revengeful and I bear no grudge'. Then the master said to him: 'My son, go back to your home, for as long as you have no equanimity and can still feel the sting of insult, you have not attained to the state where you can connect your thoughts with God'."[18]

This raises a very important point. Unless one is in a state of *Hishtavut*, one cannot really do any real spiritual work. Take meditation as a case in point. Say you are just about to start a meditation practice when somebody insults you. You react and your meditation is "tainted" by your bad feelings, and you somehow cannot focus or get into the practice properly. On the other hand, somebody flatters you prior to the meditation, and you have a marvellous session, without realising that your meditation was equally "tainted" by your good feelings. That is why practitioners of any spiritual practice should mentally and physically be in a state of equanimity.

Besides, I believe all those you meet along your path who flatter or insult you are sent for a good reason, just to see how you deal with them. What is more, you always know where you stand with anyone who insults you, but you never know where you stand with anyone who flatters you. Thus you should not be so concerned with those who openly attempt to insult you, as you should be concerned, not worried, about those who flatter you and, by telling you the sun shines out of your butt, are putting you off your course of self-evolution. There are thousands of this kind who mean well, but they are highly dangerous. They worship personalities, leaders of churches, and other pseudo-messiahs. So let them, but do not let them ever work you up into insisting that what you believe in is the "one true and only" way in this world, and all others are damned, etc. Never claim you have the only infallible, but know that in terms of the whole of existence, all human viewpoints are limited.

Now, *Hishtavut* has been described as signifying "indifference," but it is more like "uninvolvement," the ability of what used to be called "unattachment," or dealing with things competently while not letting them affect you, either as a person or Individual Entity. Something like the way nurses and doctors have to insulate, not isolate, themselves from the sufferings of their patients, because if they did not, they could not stand it. An insulation for your own protection so that you can continue to serve as an efficient agent of God. It is indeed vital to develop that ability, or otherwise you become useless as a Divine agent. It does not mean you must not care what happens to people, but just that you must not let their sufferings damage your own ability to react in some helpful way. For example, if you saw a starving child, what would be best? To sit down and weep buckets until it died, or feed it? Your sympathetic sufferings would not help, or be any use.

Hishtavut is the ability to remain unaffected or unimpaired by the happenings of Life. It has been suggested that one should "work uninvolved with life," however it never meant "Do not care." As said, *Hishtavut* is a state which ensues from the work one does towards *Devekut*. In Divine Union you become absolutely "nothing." Years back when I asked my late mentor, William Gray, whether I could not just be a "little something," he stamped his walking stick saying: "No, no, no! Not even a little something!

You must become absolutely nothing." You have to surrender all your "attachments" if you wish to reach *Devekut* and its resultant *Hishtavut*. It is a kind of "dying" as it were. You have to surrender body, mind and soul, until you reach a state of "universal incorporation," so to speak.

D. *Hitbodedut:* "Aloneness" or Meditation

1. INTRODUCTION

Having discussed *Kavvanah*, *Devekut* and *Hishtavut*, we now arrive at the fourth stage in the quest for Enlightenment. *Hitbodedut*, meaning "loneliness" or "aloneness," is a euphemism for meditation, which in *Kabbalah* is primarily a means of attaining spiritual liberation or *Ru'ach ha-Kodesh* (Enlightenment). Thus after your "Focussed Intentions" (*Kavvanah*) have brought about Divine Union or a cleaving to your true Identity (*Devekut*), and you have reached the state of "Equanimity" (*Hishtavut*), the stage of stillness in which there is an equality between good and evil, you can use *Hitbodedut* or Meditation to loosen the ties with matter, and ascend into the transcendental realms, finally attaining *Ru'ach ha-Kodesh* (literally the "Spirit which is Holy"), the term used for Enlightenment in *Kabbalah*.

In order to prepare the subconscious mind for meditation, it is suggested that one should clean the body beforehand, put on fresh clothing of white, black or grey, since bright colours will detract one from ones "Focussed Attention" (*Kavvanah*). The meditation room should also comprise only objects and colours in keeping with the intention behind the specific meditation. Be careful not to speak of your meditations to anybody, except perhaps somebody very close and sympathetic to your cause.

Another suggestion is to cover your head with a prayer-shawl, the hood of your robe, or any cloth specially used for this purpose. This action causes a greater centring within oneself, a greater concentration of intention, as well as a sense of the closeness to the Divine Presence within and without. All these activities have a strong influence in preparing the subconscious mind. Otherwise, you may sit either in a very brightly candle lit room, or else in a dimly lit or even dark room. Be it as your "Inner Being" suggests.

In *Kabbalah* there are three kinds of meditation. "Undirected Meditation," and two forms of "Directed Meditation," specifically internally directed and externally directed.[19] The most difficult is undirected meditation, which pertains to clearing the mind of all physical and spiritual thoughts and feelings, thus experiencing absolute "Nothingness" alone. As indicated earlier, the "Absolute No-Thing" or *Ain Sof* is the highest level of existence in *Kabbalah*, and such undirected meditation on the No-thing should be handled with the greatest of care since it is extremely hazardous. In any case, after every meditation it is good to do something really physical, like eating or drinking, so as to aid the rapid return to normal focal levels.

During undirected meditation, you must realise that between thinking and feeling stands the Self as a No-Thing, then attempt to unite the experiences of thoughts and feelings within the Self, the Experiencer, by turning your attention onto that Essence, the "I," the "observer." In other words, turn "Experiencer" into the "Experience." In this regard, the first meditation should be to attempt emptying yourself, since only an empty vessel can be filled. Consider yourself to be a "No-Thing," discarding all thoughts and feelings. Focus exclusively on your "Self" in your consciousness. In this state all things are equal, and you could achieve the realisation of Life/Death as "One Eternal Presence" in the "Now." Discard all thoughts and feelings you may have about your characteristics or of your ego as identity. Discard all connections you may have to things physical, mental and emotional, since this state is only reachable beyond "things." There is no good or evil *Now*. Again, do not think of yourself as "something," and discard all your needs and problems. Contemplate yourself as a "No-Thing," only then can you hold the "Infinite No-Thing" within your dimensionless Self. *Ain v'Ani*. Nothing and Self ("I") will in essence be "One."

When individuals attain the awareness of Nothingness through undirected meditation, they realise themselves as essentially No-Thing. Perceiving reality in terms of the "Ultimate

No-Thing," they know the creative act is not discontinuous or continuous, but *is Now* and evermore *Now*. The act of creation is not something which occurred in the distant past and stopped. *God is creating Now, and you are God*, or at least "part of God." It is on the level of "things" where we tend to think of creation as something which happened in days gone by. On the No-Thing, Emanative or Originative Level, all things are eternally born *Now*, given existence and resurrection *Now*.

As said earlier in this work, the game of life is always between the levels of "*No-Thing*" and "*Something*." "No-Thing" transcends nature, "Something" exists within Nature. "No-Thing" emanates Itself into "Some-Thing," and "Some-Thing" returns to "No-Thing." The "No-Thing" is hidden, the "Some-Thing" is revealed. "The No-Thing" is the hidden "Some-Thing," the "Some-Thing" the revealed No-Thing. Since they are really the same, they are eternally bonded like the two sides of a door. The universe is constantly receiving *Avir*, Universal Life-Force, or the "Self-Emanation" of *Ain Sof*. We transmute this flow into "Conscious Being" or "Self Awareness," then redirect it back as "Consciousness" back to the No-Thing. In this manner the "Eternal Living Spirit" is becoming ever more aware of its own "Inner Reality."

The entire process of creation is about God awakening to "It-Self." It was said that "Undirected Meditation" pertains specifically to this universal purpose, since through this special action, in which one attaches oneself in mind and soul to the dimensionless All-encompassing Emanator of Life, one directs "Divine Abundance" and spiritual sustenance (*shefa*) into our universe. This can only occur when the practitioner has moved into the state of Self in which the ego is absorbed, or the "Divine Marriage" has taken place between the *Ru'ach* and the *Nefesh*. This action has been termed the *Process of Love*. The poles of "male" and "female" forces are united and balanced within onself in order to create spiritual offspring. The hidden "No-Thing" and the revealed "Some-Thing" are united, by an act of perfect love, into a perfect balance from which meaning and awareness may be born in *Perfect Peace Profound*.

Now, certain Kabbalistic meditation practices are termed "Ecstatic Meditation,"[20] and these are said to lead to the "Sacred Marriage" between God and the Self. In such an ecstatic state one often feels as if death of the body might ensue. The Self experiences an unbelievable flooding of "Divine Force," as well as tremendous heights of ecstasy, until an orgasmic union occurs as God and the Self embrace. In this experience the intellectual mind loses all reason as one soars beyond mind itself, yet when one returns to normal focal levels, one is filled with tremendous insight, awareness and ability in understanding.

Now, in abstract undirected meditation one cannot think of anything concrete, since each thing has an "importance" of its own, whereas when one wants to attach oneself to the "Highest Spiritual Reality," all things—whether external or within ones being—must dissipate, or be transformed, in order to allow the Self as an empty vessel to be filled with that "Inner Reality" observable in all manifestation. In the attempt to reach the No-Thing, one uses a purely abstract notion with no particular importance of its own, but which will be of the greatest significance in terms of stimulating and releasing the "Inner Life" and realisation of Self.

To quickly review what has been said thus far, in undirected meditation there is a conscious attempt to withdraw the mind from all physical experiences, from the material, into a Nil-state. This method, titled *Hitpashetut*, a kind of "soul travel," means total negation mentally of all physical awareness into a state of Higher Consciousness. The reasoning mind is allowed free movement in pure abstraction and the purely spiritual, causing a great influx of Divine Realisation. This can be followed by an imaginary ascent into inner realms, or what has been termed "Higher Worlds." Regarding this Rabbi Chaim Vital wrote "Then the imaginative faculty will turn a man's thoughts to imagine and picture it ascended in the higher worlds up to the roots of his soul.....until the imagined image reaches its highest source, and there the images of the lights are imprinted on his mind in the same way his imaginative faculty normally pictures in his mind mental contents deriving from the world....."[21]

2. WORD MEDITATION

To reach the desired state of *Nil* through undirected meditation, one could use either a method of contraction and dissimilation, or expansion and increase. This is followed by what is called "Word Meditation," here referring to the use of a word as a *Hagah*, or what is elsewhere called a "*mantra*." Actually it does not really matter whether the word you use is in Latin, Hebrew, Greek, or whatever, since any language will do in this form of meditation. It is the effect of the word on the utterer which is really of primary importance, and therefore it might be better to use it in your mother tongue, or in a language which invokes the appropriate inner response.

Now, if you wish to achieve a desired state of awareness, one related to a specific attitude, you could program that desired condition of consciousness into yourself through a related word. For example, if somebody cannot feel love, give that individual the word "Love" in his mother tongue to pronounce like a *mantra*, and soon he will experience the desired state. There is however a careful approach needed in this, and that is while uttering the word, you have to experience it on four levels, these being the "Four Worlds" of *Kabbalah* so to speak. What I mean is this, the written or spoken word is its "*Body*," or materialisation, behind which is another level, the "world" of meaning which is its "*Mind*." Behind this in turn there is an intention, which is the "*Soul*" of the word, and behind all of them there is the principle, the utterer, the "*Spirit*" of the matter. So what is expected from the practitioner using this kind of technique is, while uttering the word slowly, to first think of what the word means to the one uttering it, and then to ascend to the higher level of "soul" where the intention of the word is sensed. This means one has to allow oneself to experience what the word feels like. Afterwards all these experiences of a physical sound related to inner meanings and intentions, must be allowed to flow into the whole being of the practitioner, almost as if one surrenders to the word, its meaning, and the way it feels, in order to internalize it, i.e to allow it to pervade the entirety of ones being and existence.

Try it with the word "Love" or "Hope" or whatever. If you wish to exercise this procedure with more Kabbalistic concepts, you could for example employ the names of the various *Sefirot*, or use Hebrew Divine Names. You will assuredly discover the principle of like affecting like is also applicable here. Be however very careful in the choice of words you use in this instance, because the principle also holds for negative and destructive words.

3. ADVANCED WORD MEDITATION

To work this meditation you need to select a much loved phrase or passage from an inspirational book. It should be text you memorized because it has some deeper meaning for you. It could be a poem, a prayer, a *mantra* or Divine Names. This is repeated slowly in the mind, pausing on each word to allow the meaning of the word to fall into you, but without permitting the mind to go on a mental trip about the individual meanings of the words. The pauses between words should not be so long that the overall meaning is lost, but should be long enough to allow you to feel or sense the meaning of the words inside yourself. The same applies to the entire sentence, phrase or paragraph. Again, as the words are slowly repeated mentally, their meaning should be sensed spontaneously without any particularly strong focus an any term especially. It has been said that meditation is "thought directed by will,"[22] and the whole idea is to let your whole body become receptive and empty, just like an empty room where the windows allow whatever passes by, to enter as light rays into the room, without being attached to any individual object.

Now, if you have chosen your specific passage, *Hagah*, or whatever you would like to bring to mind during the meditation, let us look at the practice itself.

1. Sit comfortably, and consciously surrender to gravity. Allow the pull of the earth to draw all tension out of your body, as you simply sit or lie quietly for a few minutes. Once again the important key is to smile inside yourself while doing these practices.

2. Do the Mother Breath, and do not allow the least tension to enter the body. Remember to smile, all the time feeling the warmth of the smile permeating your body.
3. Sit quietly doing absolutely nothing for a minute, that is besides smiling your warm inner smile.
4. Now, take three Complete Breaths in a relaxed, calm manner. The important thing to do here is to let the breath rise and fall by itself, and to allow a pause between each exhalation and inhalation. In fact simply wait calmly between breaths, until the next inbreath occurs by itself.
5. Take another Complete Breath, but hum on the exhalation and let the sound vibrate in your body. Do not worry about pitch, simply accept the first sound that appears when you start to hum, and keep your warm inner smile.
6. Now work the previously addressed exercise titled "*Toning and Tuning the Body.*" Work at inhaling Universal Life-Force directly into a part of your anatomy, and then vibrating it on exhalation. Work the activity twice with each bodily part you are addressing. Whilst humming, mentally instruct that portion of your body to "*understand.*" Pause for a few seconds. Then repeat the procedure, this time given the instruction to "surrender."
7. Finally conclude this portion of the meditation practice by simply smiling with your entire body. Take a Complete Breath and vibrate your body while humming.
8. Sit quietly for a few moments, doing absolutely nothing. Do not think specific thoughts, or feel specific feelings.
9. Next, get Psychic Energy moving in your hands and body by doing Pore Breathing, as explained before. When this is accomplished, stop moving your hands and allow them for a couple of minutes either to be still, or to move spontaneously without you doing anything. Remember your inner smile.
10. Next, let the hands rest on the legs. Do nothing for approximately 30 seconds, and then begin to mentally repeat the chosen passage, *Hagah* (mantra) or a Divine Name. Remember at this stage the body should have been completely prepared by the preceding practices to be

absolutely still, thus there should be no need for any movement of any kind, unless it occurs spontaneously. Keep on repeating the chosen passage, prayer, *Hagah*, Divine Name(s), or whatever very slowly, until you feel your meditation is complete. Then slowly come back to normal focal levels, as if you are surfacing from a great depth. Slowly open the eyes, make fists, open fists, take a deep breath and stretch.

That is the end of the practice. You will notice that you were being carefully prepared for the state of meditation, and only when you were deeply surrendered and in the "Meditative Mind," which is a state of being alert and energised without doing anything, were you allowed to start the actual meditation. Of course, the entire procedure could be viewed as a meditation as well.

4. *YICHUDIM*: ALIGNING WITH COSMIC FORCES

a. The Universal *Yichud*

"Unification Meditations" (*Yichudim*), are certainly amongst the most interesting, exciting and beneficial practices to be found in *Kabbalah*. They pertain specifically to the cyclical permutation of vowels correlated with the consonants comprising Divine Names. Such *Yichudim* (singular: *Yichud*) are used for a variety of purposes, i.e. as powerful healing tools; for protection against adversities; to confront ones own destructive tendencies; to facilitate personal control in ones life; to develop greater concentration ability; to bring the sacred into your everyday existence; to balance and centre the "meditator" in such a manner, that the Self is brought to a full and complete realisation of itself *as* the "Eternal Now." This is a realisation of the Divine within your own being, a full participation in your Real Identity, your "awakeness," in which all distinctions of past and future fall away. In such a "Present" state there is no memory of the "has been" or awaiting the "would be." Here there are again no regrets, repentance, or awareness of guilt related to the past. No fears of God punishing us, or any deliberations related to the future. We might further note, that *Yichudim* are equally used to achieve expanded states of consciousness, and to facilitate a direct relationship with *Maggidim*, etc.

Regarding *Yichudim* it must be understood that the Hebrew letters, being consonants, do not have any sound by themselves. The mouth has the power to express the letters, pronouncing them as they are found in a book, and to do this there are vowels which indicate the sound with which the consonants are expressed. The vowels allow the letters to be vocalized, hence they are the vehicles of the consonants so to speak. The vibrations of the sounds are associated with space, since no sound frequency could occur except in a definite time and place. The elements of space are the dimensions and distances, and those of time are the cycles, through which it is measured. This includes such divisions as years, months and days. One must therefore know how to draw out the sound of each letter as it is related to these dimensions. This is the mystery behind the pronunciation of the *Tetragrammaton* (יהוה).

Now, it is recommended that you do these practices in a special place, and remove from your heart and mind all other thoughts. This can be done with a special breathing practice beforehand, e.g. the Mother breath, etc., and allowing yourself to surrender, that is your mind to join with God, the Collective Consciousness, the Whole, or whatever you wish to call it. It is also most important to know absolutely precisely how to pronounce the Divine Name in this *Yichud*, hence its structure is presented in full in the tables below. Rather than explaining *Yichudim* in greater detail, I thought I would simply cast you into the deep end, so to speak, by introducing you to an actual "Unification" meditation, one of the largest and most complex titled the "*Universal Yichud*," which, while it is somewhat tricky to comprehend and memorize, can be performed quite easily. Below you will find the *Yichud* in both the Hebrew original and English transliteration. You need to familiarize yourself with its patterns and vowel cycles.

322 / *The Shadow Tree: The Book of Self Creation*

"The Fivefold Path" / 323

יְהוָה	יְהוָה	יְהוָה	יְהוָה	יְהוָה
יְהוָה	יְהוָה	יְהוָה	יְהוָה	יְהוָה
יְהוָה	יְהוָה	יְהוָה	יְהוָה	יְהוָה
יְהוָה	יְהוָה	יְהוָה	יְהוָה	יְהוָה
יְהוָה	יְהוָה	יְהוָה	יְהוָה	יְהוָה
יְהוָה	יְהוָה	יְהוָה	יְהוָה	יְהוָה
יְהוָה	יְהוָה	יְהוָה	יְהוָה	יְהוָה
יְהוָה	יְהוָה	יְהוָה	יְהוָה	יְהוָה
יְהוָה	יְהוָה	יְהוָה	יְהוָה	יְהוָה
יְהוָה	יְהוָה	יְהוָה	יְהוָה	יְהוָה
יְהוָה	יְהוָה	יְהוָה	יְהוָה	יְהוָה
יְהוָה	יְהוָה	יְהוָה	יְהוָה	יְהוָה
יְהוָה	יְהוָה	יְהוָה	יְהוָה	יְהוָה
יְהוָה	יְהוָה	יְהוָה	יְהוָה	יְהוָה
יְהוָה	יְהוָה	יְהוָה	יְהוָה	יְהוָה
יְהוָה	יְהוָה	יְהוָה	יְהוָה	יְהוָה
יְהוָה	יְהוָה	יְהוָה	יְהוָה	יְהוָה
יְהוָה	יְהוָה	יְהוָה	יְהוָה	יְהוָה
יְהוָה	יְהוָה	יְהוָה	יְהוָה	יְהוָה
יְהוָה	יְהוָה	יְהוָה	יְהוָה	יְהוָה
יְהוָה	יְהוָה	יְהוָה	יְהוָה	יְהוָה
יְהוָה	יְהוָה	יְהוָה	יְהוָה	יְהוָה
יְהוָה	יְהוָה	יְהוָה	יְהוָה	יְהוָה
יְהוָה	יְהוָה	יְהוָה	יְהוָה	יְהוָה
יְהוָה	יְהוָה	יְהוָה	יְהוָה	יְהוָה

324 / *The Shadow Tree: The Book of Self Creation*

"The Fivefold Path" / 325

יְהוָה	יְהוָה	יְהוָה	יְהוָה	יְהוָה
יְהֹוָה	יְהֹוִה	יְהֹוָה	יְהֹוִה	יְהֹוִה
יְהוֹה	יְהוֹה	יְהוֹה	יְהוֹה	יְהוֹה
יֱהֹוִה	יֱהֹוִה	יֱהֹוִה	יֱהֹוִה	יֱהֹוִה
יַהֲוֶה	יַהֲוֶה	יַהֲוֶה	יַהֲוֶה	יַהֲוֶה

יְהוָה	יְהוָה	יְהוָה	יְהוָה	יְהוָה
יְהֹוִה	יְהֹוִה	יְהֹוִה	יְהֹוִה	יְהֹוִה
יְהוֹה	יְהוֹה	יְהוֹה	יְהוֹה	יְהוֹה
יֱהֹוִה	יֱהֹוִה	יֱהֹוִה	יֱהֹוִה	יֱהֹוִה
יַהֲוֶה	יַהֲוֶה	יַהֲוֶה	יַהֲוֶה	יַהֲוֶה

יְהוָה	יְהוָה	יְהוָה	יְהוָה	יְהוָה
יְהֹוִה	יְהֹוִה	יְהֹוִה	יְהֹוִה	יְהֹוִה
יְהוֹה	יְהוֹה	יְהוֹה	יְהוֹה	יְהוֹה
יֱהֹוִה	יֱהֹוִה	יֱהֹוִה	יֱהֹוִה	יֱהֹוִה
יַהֲוֶה	יַהֲוֶה	יַהֲוֶה	יַהֲוֶה	יַהֲוֶה

יְהוָה	יְהוָה	יְהוָה	יְהוָה	יְהוָה
יְהֹוִה	יְהֹוִה	יְהֹוִה	יְהֹוִה	יְהֹוִה
יְהוֹה	יְהוֹה	יְהוֹה	יְהוֹה	יְהוֹה
יֱהֹוִה	יֱהֹוִה	יֱהֹוִה	יֱהֹוִה	יֱהֹוִה
יַהֲוֶה	יַהֲוֶה	יַהֲוֶה	יַהֲוֶה	יַהֲוֶה

יְהוָה	יְהוָה	יְהוָה	יְהוָה	יְהוָה
יְהֹוִה	יְהֹוִה	יְהֹוִה	יְהֹוִה	יְהֹוִה
יְהוֹה	יְהוֹה	יְהוֹה	יְהוֹה	יְהוֹה
יֱהֹוִה	יֱהֹוִה	יֱהֹוִה	יֱהֹוִה	יֱהֹוִה
יַהֲוֶה	יַהֲוֶה	יַהֲוֶה	יַהֲוֶה	יַהֲוֶה

326 / *The Shadow Tree: The Book of Self Creation*

"The Fivefold Path"

1. **Ya-Ha-Va-Ha** Ya-Ha-Va-**He** Ya-Ha-Va-**Ho** Ya-Ha-Va-**Hi** Ya-Ha-Va-**Hu**	2. Ya-Ha-**Ve-Ha** Ya-Ha-**Ve-He** Ya-Ha-**Ve-Ho** Ya-Ha-**Ve-Hi** Ya-Ha-**Ve-Hu**	3. Ya-Ha-**Vo-Ha** Ya-Ha-**Vo-He** Ya-Ha-**Vo-Ho** Ya-Ha-**Vo-Hi** Ya-Ha-**Vo-Hu**
4. Ya-Ha-**Vi-Ha** Ya-Ha-**Vi-He** Ya-Ha-**Vi-Ho** Ya-Ha-**Vi-Hi** Ya-Ha-**Vi-Hu**	5. Ya-Ha-**Vu-Ha** Ya-Ha-**Vu-He** Ya-Ha-**Vu-Ho** Ya-Ha-**Vu-Hi** Ya-Ha-**Vu-Hu**	

6. Ya-**He-Va-Ha** Ya-**He**-Va-**He** Ya-**He**-Va-**Ho** Ya-**He**-Va-**Hi** Ya-**He**-Va-**Hu**	7. Ya-He-**Ve-Ha** Ya-He-**Ve-He** Ya-He-**Ve-Ho** Ya-He-**Ve-Hi** Ya-He-**Ve-Hu**	8. Ya-He-**Vo-Ha** Ya-He-**Vo-He** Ya-He-**Vo-Ho** Ya-He-**Vo-Hi** Ya-He-**Vo-Hu**
9. Ya-He-**Vi-Ha** Ya-He-**Vi-He** Ya-He-**Vi-Ho** Ya-He-**Vi-Hi** Ya-He-**Vi-Hu**	10. Ya-He-**Vu-Ha** Ya-He-**Vu-He** Ya-He-**Vu-Ho** Ya-He-**Vu-Hi** Ya-He-**Vu-Hu**	

11. Ya-**Ho-Va-Ha** Ya-**Ho**-Va-**He** Ya-**Ho**-Va-**Ho** Ya-**Ho**-Va-**Hi** Ya-**Ho**-Va-**Hu**	12. Ya-Ho-**Ve-Ha** Ya-Ho-**Ve-He** Ya-Ho-**Ve-Ho** Ya-Ho-**Ve-Hi** Ya-Ho-**Ve-Hu**	13. Ya-Ho-**Vo-Ha** Ya-Ho-**Vo-He** Ya-Ho-**Vo-Ho** Ya-Ho-**Vo-Hi** Ya-Ho-**Vo-Hu**
14. Ya-Ho-**Vi-Ha** Ya-Ho-**Vi-He** Ya-Ho-**Vi-Ho** Ya-Ho-**Vi-Hi** Ya-Ho-**Vi-Hu**	15. Ya-Ho-**Vu-Ha** Ya-Ho-**Vu-He** Ya-Ho-**Vu-Ho** Ya-Ho-**Vu-Hi** Ya-Ho-**Vu-Hu**	

328 / *The Shadow Tree: The Book of Self Creation*

16. Ya-**Hi**-**Va**-**Ha** Ya-Hi-Va-**He** Ya-Hi-Va-**Ho** Ya-Hi-Va-**Hi** Ya-Hi-Va-**Hu**	17. Ya-Hi-**Ve**-**Ha** Ya-Hi-Ve-**He** Ya-Hi-Ve-**Ho** Ya-Hi-Ve-**Hi** Ya-Hi-Ve-**Hu**	18. Ya-Hi-**Vo**-**Ha** Ya-Hi-Vo-**He** Ya-Hi-Vo-**Ho** Ya-Hi-Vo-**Hi** Ya-Hi-Vo-**Hu**
19. Ya-Hi-**Vi**-**Ha** Ya-Hi-Vi-**He** Ya-Hi-Vi-**Ho** Ya-Hi-Vi-**Hi** Ya-Hi-Vi-**Hu**	20. Ya-Hi-**Vu**-**Ha** Ya-Hi-Vu-**He** Ya-Hi-Vu-**Ho** Ya-Hi-Vu-**Hi** Ya-Hi-Vu-**Hu**	

21. Ya-**Hu**-**Va**-**Ha** Ya-Hu-Va-**He** Ya-Hu-Va-**Ho** Ya-Hu-Va-**Hi** Ya-Hu-Va-**Hu**	22. Ya-Hu-**Ve**-**Ha** Ya-Hu-Ve-**He** Ya-Hu-Ve-**Ho** Ya-Hu-Ve-**Hi** Ya-Hu-Ve-**Hu**	23. Ya-Hu-**Vo**-**Ha** Ya-Hu-Vo-**He** Ya-Hu-Vo-**Ho** Ya-Hu-Vo-**Hi** Ya-Hu-Vo-**Hu**
24. Ya-Hu-**Vi** -**Ha** Ya-Hu-Vi -**He** Ya-Hu-Vi -**Ho** Ya-Hu-Vi -**Hi** Ya-Hu-Vi -**Hu**	25. Ya-Hu-**Vu**-**Ha** Ya-Hu-Vu-**He** Ya-Hu-Vu-**Ho** Ya-Hu-Vu-**Hi** Ya-Hu-Vu-**Hu**	

26. Ye-**Ha**-**Va**-**Ha** Ye-Ha-Va-**He** Ye-Ha-Va-**Ho** Ye-Ha-Va-**Hi** Ye-Ha-Va-**Hu**	27. Ye-Ha-**Ve**-**Ha** Ye-Ha-Ve-**He** Ye-Ha-Ve-**Ho** Ye-Ha-Ve-**Hi** Ye-Ha-Ve-**Hu**	28. Ye-Ha-**Vo**-**Ha** Ye-Ha-Vo-**He** Ye-Ha-Vo-**Ho** Ye-Ha-Vo-**Hi** Ye-Ha-Vo-**Hu**
29. Ye-Ha-**Vi**-**Ha** Ye-Ha-Vi-**He** Ye-Ha-Vi-**Ho** Ye-Ha-Vi-**Hi** Ye-Ha-Vi-**Hu**	30. Ye-Ha-**Vu**-**Ha** Ye-Ha-Vu-**He** Ye-Ha-Vu-**Ho** Ye-Ha-Vu-**Hi** Ye-Ha-Vu-**Hu**	

"The Fivefold Path" / 329

31. Ye-**He**-**Va**-**Ha** Ye-He-Va-**He** Ye-He-Va-**Ho** Ye-He-Va-**Hi** Ye-He-Va-**Hu**	32. Ye-He-**Ve**-**Ha** Ye-He-Ve-**He** Ye-He-Ve-**Ho** Ye-He-Ve-**Hi** Ye-He-Ve-**Hu**	33. Ye-He-**Vo**-**Ha** Ye-He-Vo-**He** Ye-He-Vo-**Ho** Ye-He-Vo-**Hi** Ye-He-Vo-**Hu**
34. Ye-He-**Vi**-**Ha** Ye-He-Vi-**He** Ye-He-Vi-**Ho** Ye-He-Vi-**Hi** Ye-He-Vi-**Hu**	35. Ye-He-**Vu**-**Ha** Ye-He-Vu-**He** Ye-He-Vu-**Ho** Ye-He-Vu-**Hi** Ye-He-Vu-**Hu**	

36. Ye-**Ho**-**Va**-**Ha** Ye-Ho-Va-**He** Ye-Ho-Va-**Ho** Ye-Ho-Va-**Hi** Ye-Ho-Va-**Hu**	37. Ye-Ho-**Ve**-**Ha** Ye-Ho-Ve-**He** Ye-Ho-Ve-**Ho** Ye-Ho-Ve-**Hi** Ye-Ho-Ve-**Hu**	38. Ye-Ho-**Vo**-**Ha** Ye-Ho-Vo-**He** Ye-Ho-Vo-**Ho** Ye-Ho-Vo-**Hi** Ye-Ho-Vo-**Hu**
39. Ye-Ho-**Vi**-**Ha** Ye-Ho-Vi-**He** Ye-Ho-Vi-**Ho** Ye-Ho-Vi-**Hi** Ye-Ho-Vi-**Hu**	40. Ye-Ho-**Vu**-**Ha** Ye-Ho-Vu-**He** Ye-Ho-Vu-**Ho** Ye-Ho-Vu-**Hi** Ye-Ho-Vu-**Hu**	

41. Ye-**Hi**-**Va**-**Ha** Ye-Hi-Va-**He** Ye-Hi-Va-**Ho** Ye-Hi-Va-**Hi** Ye-Hi-Va-**Hu**	42. Ye-Hi-**Ve**-**Ha** Ye-Hi-Ve-**He** Ye-Hi-Ve-**Ho** Ye-Hi-Ve-**Hi** Ye-Hi-Ve-**Hu**	43. Ye-Hi-**Vo**-**Ha** Ye-Hi-Vo-**He** Ye-Hi-Vo-**Ho** Ye-Hi-Vo-**Hi** Ye-Hi-Vo-**Hu**
44. Ye-Hi-**Vi**-**Ha** Ye-Hi-Vi-**He** Ye-Hi-Vi-**Ho** Ye-Hi-Vi-**Hi** Ye-Hi-Vi-**Hu**	45. Ye-Hi-**Vu**-**Ha** Ye-Hi-Vu-**He** Ye-Hi-Vu-**Ho** Ye-Hi-Vu-**Hi** Ye-Hi-Vu-**Hu**	

46. Ye-**Hu-Va-Ha** Ye-Hu-Va-**He** Ye-Hu-Va-**Ho** Ye-Hu-Va-**Hi** Ye-Hu-Va-**Hu**	47. Ye-Hu-**Ve-Ha** Ye-Hu-Ve-**He** Ye-Hu-Ve-**Ho** Ye-Hu-Ve-**Hi** Ye-Hu-Ve-**Hu**	48. Ye-Hu-**Vo-Ha** Ye-Hu-Vo-**He** Ye-Hu-Vo-**Ho** Ye-Hu-Vo-**Hi** Ye-Hu-Vo-**Hu**
49. Ye-Hu-**Vi-Ha** Ye-Hu-Vi-**He** Ye-Hu-Vi-**Ho** Ye-Hu-Vi-**Hi** Ye-Hu-Vi-**Hu**	50. Ye-Hu-**Vu-Ha** Ye-Hu-Vu-**He** Ye-Hu-Vu-**Ho** Ye-Hu-Vu-**Hi** Ye-Hu-Vu-**Hu**	

51. **Yo-Ha-Va-Ha** Yo-Ha-Va-**He** Yo-Ha-Va-**Ho** Yo-Ha-Va-**Hi** Yo-Ha-Va-**Hu**	52. Yo-Ha-**Ve-Ha** Yo-Ha-Ve-**He** Yo-Ha-Ve-**Ho** Yo-Ha-Ve-**Hi** Yo-Ha-Ve-**Hu**	53. Yo-Ha-**Vo-Ha** Yo-Ha-Vo-**He** Yo-Ha-Vo-**Ho** Yo-Ha-Vo-**Hi** Yo-Ha-Vo-**Hu**
54. Yo-Ha-**Vi-Ha** Yo-Ha-Vi-**He** Yo-Ha-Vi-**Ho** Yo-Ha-Vi-**Hi** Yo-Ha-Vi-**Hu**	55. Yo-Ha-**Vu-Ha** Yo-Ha-Vu-**He** Yo-Ha-Vu-**Ho** Yo-Ha-Vu-**Hi** Yo-Ha-Vu-**Hu**	

56. Yo-He-**Va-Ha** Yo-He-Va-**He** Yo-He-Va-**Ho** Yo-He-Va-**Hi** Yo-He-Va-**Hu**	57. Yo-He-**Ve-Ha** Yo-He-Ve-**He** Yo-He-Ve-**Ho** Yo-He-Ve-**Hi** Yo-He-Ve-**Hu**	58. Yo-He-**Vo-Ha** Yo-He-Vo-**He** Yo-He-Vo-**Ho** Yo-He-Vo-**Hi** Yo-He-Vo-**Hu**
59. Yo-He-**Vi-Ha** Yo-He-Vi-**He** Yo-He-Vi-**Ho** Yo-He-Vi-**Hi** Yo-He-Vi-**Hu**	60. Yo-He-**Vu-Ha** Yo-He-Vu-**He** Yo-He-Vu-**Ho** Yo-He-Vu-**Hi** Yo-He-Vu-**Hu**	

"The Fivefold Path" / 331

61. Yo-Ho-**Va**-**Ha** Yo-Ho-**Va**-**He** Yo-Ho-**Va**-**Ho** Yo-Ho-**Va**-**Hi** Yo-Ho-**Va**-**Hu**	62. Yo-Ho-**Ve**-**Ha** Yo-Ho-Ve-**He** Yo-Ho-Ve-**Ho** Yo-Ho-Ve-**Hi** Yo-Ho-Ve-**Hu**	63. Yo-Ho-**Vo**-**Ha** Yo-Ho-Vo-**He** Yo-Ho-Vo-**Ho** Yo-Ho-Vo-**Hi** Yo-Ho-Vo-**Hu**
64. Yo-Ho-**Vi**-**Ha** Yo-Ho-Vi-**He** Yo-Ho-Vi-**Ho** Yo-Ho-Vi-**Hi** Yo-Ho-Vi-**Hu**	65. Yo-Ho-**Vu**-**Ha** Yo-Ho-Vu-**He** Yo-Ho-Vu-**Ho** Yo-Ho-Vu-**Hi** Yo-Ho-Vu-**Hu**	

66. Yo-**Hi**-**Va**-**Ha** Yo-Hi-Va-**He** Yo-Hi-Va-**Ho** Yo-Hi-Va-**Hi** Yo-Hi-Va-**Hu**	67. Yo-Hi-**Ve**-**Ha** Yo-Hi-Ve-**He** Yo-Hi-Ve-**Ho** Yo-Hi-Ve-**Hi** Yo-Hi-Ve-**Hu**	68. Yo-Hi-**Vo**-**Ha** Yo-Hi-Vo-**He** Yo-Hi-Vo-**Ho** Yo-Hi-Vo-**Hi** Yo-Hi-Vo-**Hu**
69. Yo-Hi-**Vi**-**Ha** Yo-Hi-Vi-**He** Yo-Hi-Vi-**Ho** Yo-Hi-Vi -**Hi** Yo-Hi-Vi-**Hu**	70. Yo-Hi-**Vu**-**Ha** Yo-Hi-Vu-**He** Yo-Hi-Vu-**Ho** Yo-Hi-Vu-**Hi** Yo-Hi-Vu-**Hu**	

71. Yo-**Hu**-**Va**-**Ha** Yo-Hu-Va-**He** Yo-Hu-Va-**Ho** Yo-Hu-Va-**Hi** Yo-Hu-Va-**Hu**	72. Yo-Hu-**Ve**-**Ha** Yo-Hu-Ve-**He** Yo-Hu-Ve-**Ho** Yo-Hu-Ve-**Hi** Yo-Hu-Ve-**Hu**	73. Yo-Hu-**Vo**-**Ha** Yo-Hu-Vo-**He** Yo-Hu-Vo-**Ho** Yo-Hu-Vo-**Hi** Yo-Hu-Vo-**Hu**
74. Yo-Hu-**Vi**-**Ha** Yo-Hu-Vi-**He** Yo-Hu-Vi-**Ho** Yo-Hu-Vi-**Hi** Yo-Hu-Vi-**Hu**	75. Yo-Hu-**Vu**-**Ha** Yo-Hu-Vu-**He** Yo-Hu-Vu-**Ho** Yo-Hu-Vu-**Hi** Yo-Hu-Vu-**Hu**	

76. Yi-**Ha**-**Va**-**Ha** Yi-Ha-Va-**He** Yi-Ha-Va-**Ho** Yi-Ha-Va-**Hi** Yi-Ha-Va-**Hu**	77. Yi-Ha-**Ve**-**Ha** Yi-Ha-Ve-**He** Yi-Ha-Ve-**Ho** Yi-Ha-Ve-**Hi** Yi-Ha-Ve-**Hu**	78. Yi-Ha-**Vo**-**Ha** Yi-Ha-Vo-**He** Yi-Ha-Vo-**Ho** Yi-Ha-Vo-**Hi** Yi-Ha-Vo-**Hu**
79. Yi-Ha-**Vi**-**Ha** Yi-Ha-Vi-**He** Yi-Ha-Vi-**Ho** Yi-Ha-Vi-**Hi** Yi-Ha-Vi-**Hu**	80. Yi-Ha-**Vu**-**Ha** Yi-Ha-Vu-**He** Yi-Ha-Vu-**Ho** Yi-Ha-Vu-**Hi** Yi-Ha-Vu-**Hu**	

81. Yi-**He**-**Va**-**Ha** Yi-He-Va-**He** Yi-He-Va-**Ho** Yi-He-Va-**Hi** Yi-He-Va-**Hu**	82. Yi-He-**Ve**-**Ha** Yi-He-Ve-**He** Yi-He-Ve-**Ho** Yi-He-Ve-**Hi** Yi-He-Ve-**Hu**	83. Yi-He-**Vo**-**Ha** Yi-He-Vo-**He** Yi-He-Vo-**Ho** Yi-He-Vo-**Hi** Yi-He-Vo-**Hu**
84. Yi-He-**Vi**-**Ha** Yi-He-Vi-**He** Yi-He-Vi-**Ho** Yi-He-Vi-**Hi** Yi-He-Vi-**Hu**	85. Yi-He-**Vu**-**Ha** Yi-He-Vu-**He** Yi-He-Vu-**Ho** Yi-He-Vu-**Hi** Yi-He-Vu-**Hu**	

86. Yi-**Ho**-**Va**-**Ha** Yi-Ho-Va-**He** Yi-Ho-Va-**Ho** Yi-Ho-Va-**Hi** Yi-Ho-Va-**Hu**	87. Yi-Ho-**Ve**-**Ha** Yi-Ho-Ve-**He** Yi-Ho-Ve-**Ho** Yi-Ho-Ve-**Hi** Yi-Ho-Ve-**Hu**	88. Yi-Ho-**Vo**-**Ha** Yi-Ho-Vo-**He** Yi-Ho-Vo-**Ho** Yi-Ho-Vo-**Hi** Yi-Ho-Vo-**Hu**
89. Yi-Ho-**Vi**-**Ha** Yi-Ho-Vi-**He** Yi-Ho-Vi-**Ho** Yi-Ho-Vi-**Hi** Yi-Ho-Vi-**Hu**	90. Yi-Ho-**Vu**-**Ha** Yi-Ho-Vu-**He** Yi-Ho-Vu-**Ho** Yi-Ho-Vu-**Hi** Yi-Ho-Vu-**Hu**	

"The Fivefold Path" / 333

91. Yi-**Hi**-**Va**-**Ha** Yi-**Hi**-Va-**He** Yi-**Hi**-Va-**Ho** Yi-**Hi**-Va-**Hi** Yi-**Hi**-Va-**Hu**	92. Yi-**Hi**-**Ve**-**Ha** Yi-**Hi**-Ve-**He** Yi-**Hi**-Ve-**Ho** Yi-**Hi**-Ve-**Hi** Yi-**Hi**-Ve-**Hu**	93. Yi-**Hi**-**Vo**-**Ha** Yi-**Hi**-Vo-**He** Yi-**Hi**-Vo-**Ho** Yi-**Hi**-Vo-**Hi** Yi-**Hi**-Vo-**Hu**
94. Yi-**Hi**-**Vi**-**Ha** Yi-**Hi**-Vi-**He** Yi-**Hi**-Vi-**Ho** Yi-**Hi**-Vi-**Hi** Yi-**Hi**-Vi-**Hu**	95. Yi-**Hi**-**Vu**-**Ha** Yi-**Hi**-Vu-**He** Yi-**Hi**-Vu-**Ho** Yi-**Hi**-Vu-**Hi** Yi-**Hi**-Vu-**Hu**	

96. Yi-**Hu**-**Va**-**Ha** Yi-**Hu**-Va-**He** Yi-**Hu**-Va-**Ho** Yi-**Hu**-Va-**Hi** Yi-**Hu**-Va-**Hu**	97. Yi-**Hu**-**Ve**-**Ha** Yi-**Hu**-Ve-**He** Yi-**Hu**-Ve-**Ho** Yi-**Hu**-Ve-**Hi** Yi-**Hu**-Ve-**Hu**	98. Yi-**Hu**-**Vo**-**Ha** Yi-**Hu**-Vo-**He** Yi-**Hu**-Vo-**Ho** Yi-**Hu**-Vo-**Hi** Yi-**Hu**-Vo-**Hu**
99. Yi-**Hu**-**Vi**-**Ha** Yi-**Hu**-Vi-**He** Yi-**Hu**-Vi-**Ho** Yi-**Hu**-Vi-**Hi** Yi-**Hu**-Vi-**Hu**	100. Yi-**Hu**-**Vu**-**Ha** Yi-**Hu**-Vu-**He** Yi-**Hu**-Vu-**Ho** Yi-**Hu**-Vu-**Hi** Yi-**Hu**-Vu-**Hu**	

101. **Yu**-**Ha**-**Va**-**Ha** Yu-Ha-Va-**He** Yu-Ha-Va-**Ho** Yu-Ha-Va-**Hi** Yu-Ha-Va-**Hu**	102. Yu-Ha-**Ve**-**Ha** Yu-Ha-Ve-**He** Yu-Ha-Ve-**Ho** Yu-Ha-Ve-**Hi** Yu-Ha-Ve-**Hu**	103. Yu-Ha-**Vo**-**Ha** Yu-Ha-Vo-**He** Yu-Ha-Vo-**Ho** Yu-Ha-Vo-**Hi** Yu-Ha-Vo-**Hu**
104. Yu-Ha-**Vi**-**Ha** Yu-Ha-Vi-**He** Yu-Ha-Vi-**Ho** Yu-Ha-Vi-**Hi** Yu-Ha-Vi-**Hu**	105. Yu-Ha-**Vu**-**Ha** Yu-Ha-Vu-**He** Yu-Ha-Vu-**Ho** Yu-Ha-Vu-**Hi** Yu-Ha-Vu-**Hu**	

106. Yu-**He**-**Va**-**Ha** Yu-**He**-**Va**-**He** Yu-**He**-**Va**-**Ho** Yu-**He**-**Va**-**Hi** Yu-**He**-**Va**-**Hu**	107. Yu-**He**-**Ve**-**Ha** Yu-**He**-**Ve**-**He** Yu-**He**-**Ve**-**Ho** Yu-**He**-**Ve**-**Hi** Yu-**He**-**Ve**-**Hu**	108. Yu-**He**-**Vo**-**Ha** Yu-**He**-**Vo**-**He** Yu-**He**-**Vo**-**Ho** Yu-**He**-**Vo**-**Hi** Yu-**He**-**Vo**-**Hu**
109. Yu-**He**-**Vi**-**Ha** Yu-**He**-**Vi**-**He** Yu-**He**-**Vi**-**Ho** Yu-**He**-**Vi**-**Hi** Yu-**He**-**Vi**-**Hu**	110. Yu-**He**-**Vu**-**Ha** Yu-**He**-**Vu**-**He** Yu-**He**-**Vu**-**Ho** Yu-**He**-**Vu**-**Hi** Yu-**He**-**Vu**-**Hu**	
111. Yu-**Ho**-**Va**-**Ha** Yu-**Ho**-**Va**-**He** Yu-**Ho**-**Va**-**Ho** Yu-**Ho**-**Va**-**Hi** Yu-**Ho**-**Va**-**Hu**	112. Yu-**Ho**-**Ve**-**Ha** Yu-**Ho**-**Ve**-**He** Yu-**Ho**-**Ve**-**Ho** Yu-**Ho**-**Ve**-**Hi** Yu-**Ho**-**Ve**-**Hu**	113. Yu-**Ho**-**Vo**-**Ha** Yu-**Ho**-**Vo**-**He** Yu-**Ho**-**Vo**-**Ho** Yu-**Ho**-**Vo**-**Hi** Yu-**Ho**-**Vo**-**Hu**
114. Yu-**Ho**-**Vi**-**Ha** Yu-**Ho**-**Vi**-**He** Yu-**Ho**-**Vi**-**Ho** Yu-**Ho**-**Vi**-**Hi** Yu-**Ho**-**Vi**-**Hu**	115. Yu-**Ho**-**Vu**-**Ha** Yu-**Ho**-**Vu**-**He** Yu-**Ho**-**Vu**-**Ho** Yu-**Ho**-**Vu**-**Hi** Yu-**Ho**-**Vu**-**Hu**	
116. Yu-**Hi**-**Va**-**Ha** Yu-**Hi**-**Va**-**He** Yu-**Hi**-**Va**-**Ho** Yu-**Hi**-**Va**-**Hi** Yu-**Hi**-**Va**-**Hu**	117. Yu-**Hi**-**Ve**-**Ha** Yu-**Hi**-**Ve**-**He** Yu-**Hi**-**Ve**-**Ho** Yu-**Hi**-**Ve**-**Hi** Yu-**Hi**-**Ve**-**Hu**	118. Yu-**Hi**-**Vo**-**Ha** Yu-**Hi**-**Vo**-**He** Yu-**Hi**-**Vo**-**Ho** Yu-**Hi**-**Vo**-**Hi** Yu-**Hi**-**Vo**-**Hu**
119. Yu-**Hi**-**Vi**-**Ha** Yu-**Hi**-**Vi**-**He** Yu-**Hi**-**Vi**-**Ho** Yu-**Hi**-**Vi**-**Hi** Yu-**Hi**-**Vi**-**Hu**	120. Yu-**Hi**-**Vu**-**Ha** Yu-**Hi**-**Vu**-**He** Yu-**Hi**-**Vu**-**Ho** Yu-**Hi**-**Vu**-**Hi** Yu-**Hi**-**Vu**-**Hu**	

121. Yu-**Hu**-**Va**-**Ha** Yu-Hu-Va-**He** Yu-Hu-Va-**Ho** Yu-Hu-Va-**Hi** Yu-Hu-Va-**Hu**	122. Yu-Hu-**Ve**-**Ha** Yu-Hu-Ve-**He** Yu-Hu-Ve-**Ho** Yu-Hu-Ve-**Hi** Yu-Hu-Ve-**Hu**	123. Yu-Hu-**Vo**-**Ha** Yu-Hu-Vo-**He** Yu-Hu-Vo-**Ho** Yu-Hu-Vo-**Hi** Yu-Hu-Vo-**Hu**
124. Yu-Hu-**Vi**-**Ha** Yu-Hu-Vi-**He** Yu-Hu-Vi-**Ho** Yu-Hu-Vi-**Hi** Yu-Hu-Vi-**Hu**	125. Yu-Hu-**Vu**-**Ha** Yu-Hu-Vu-**He** Yu-Hu-Vu-**Ho** Yu-Hu-Vu-**Hi** Yu-Hu-Vu-**Hu**	

It has been said that the practice of the *Universal Yichud* results in a perfect alignment or balancing of the body, mind, soul and spirit in the "*Now*." One might call it a *gestalt* meditation, since, one of its most powerful uses is the focussing of the mind in specific parts of the body while chanting associated vowels in conjunction with the Ineffable Name. This specific usage allows one to experience the different frequencies of the vowel sounds vibrating intensely in related bodily parts.

Again the use of this *Yichud* in this specific manner, aligns the head, throat, heart, solar plexus (called the "liver" in the old terminology), and lower bowel/genitals. These positions are understood to be respectively representative of the "Middle Pillar" on the *Etz Chayim* (Tree of Life).

1. Head — *Keter*/Crown;
2. Throat — *Da'at*/Knowledge;
3. Heart/Chest — *Tiferet*/Beauty;
4. Liver/Solar Plexus — *Yesod*/Foundation; and
5. Lower Bowel/Genitals — *Malchut*/Kingdom.

You will recall that the "head–heart–liver" combination refers to the *Neshamah* (head), *Ru'ach* (heart), *Nefesh* (liver). In fact, each of these specific bodily parts were respectively considered the "brain" of its associated "Self," all of which have to be brought into some sort of alignment for one to function properly on physical, mental, emotional and spiritual levels. Hence it is extremely important for one to prepare oneself most carefully, in order to derive the maximum benefit possible from the technique discussed here.

Let us begin by investigating how the five vowels mentioned in this special *Yichud* are related to the body. Here is the basic pattern:

Vowels	Associated Bodily Part
U (OO)	**Lower Bowels**, **Genitals** and **Anus**
O (OH)	**Solar Plexus** (directly below the breast-bone)
A (AH)	**Centre Chest** (Heart)
E (EH)	**Throat** and **Neck**
I (EE)	**Head** (from the Nose and Cheeks to the crown)

Looking at these vowels and how they are aligned with the physical body, the old associations of the sound **U** (*oo*) with "desire" and "physical stress"; **O** (*oh*) with "wonder," "anxiety" and "fear"; **A** (*ah*) with "yearning," "recognition" and "satisfaction"; **E** (*eh*) with "enquiry," "encouragement" and "disapproval"; and **I** (*ee*) with "higher consciousness" and "divinity," appear to be quite apt. In fact, these attributions and their respective physical associations, make very good sense when we consider how humans behave in certain circumstances. For example, we quite naturally exclaim salaciously *"OO"* when they see another attractive and desirable member of our own species, and anybody who has suffered the painful stress of stomach ache or severe constipation, can easily confirm that they loudly hollered this very tone in an attempt to alleviate their almost unbearable travail.

Likewise, all of us know that sharp *"OH"* uttered by an individual whose "wind was knocked out" after being punched in the solar plexus, and it is in this location where we experience anxiety, or those "butterflies in the stomach," so familiar to concert artists and actors. On the other hand, it is claimed that the *"OH"* sound is also the tone of "wonder." Who hasn't blurted out this tone, when he or she stood in awe and wonder at the glorious wonders of our manifested universe? How interesting that the word "awe" has the exact pronunciation of the tone linked to the solar plexus.

The idea of the heart and chest linked to the sound "*AH*" and associated with yearning, recognition and satisfaction is perfectly clear. Simply place your hand on your chest and say "*AH*" while thinking any of these associated ideas, or focus your attention directly under your hand and say "Ah my heart," and you will understand exactly.

The vowel "*EH*" associated with the throat is actually quite obvious. Every time you vocalize it, it sits firmly in your throat. That is why sheep and goats, whose main vocal expression comprises this vowel, are throat creatures in contradistinction to cattle whose "call" — "*MOOOO*" — resonates right down into their hind quarters. Now, if you wish to comprehend the associations of "question" or "disapproval" with the "*EH*" sound, simply utter a single "*EH*" while thinking "what?" or utter two consecutive tones rapidly — "*eh...eh*" — while thinking "no" and shaking your head sideways.

The remaining vowel "I" (*EE*), claimed to be associated with "higher consciousness" and "Divinity," is apparently quite rarely used as a pure exclamation by itself. What is most interesting is that this sound in conjunction with "*AH*" and "*OH*" (*IAO*), comprise one of the ancient and most venerable names for Divinity which was known to the Greeks, Romans, Gnostics, and the Jews as well, since the first three letters of the Ineffable Name (*YHV*) in fact represent those very vowels. Everybody had it.....even "Old MacDonald" had it—"*ee...ah...ee...ah...oh*"! It is also most interesting that those tones are understood to resonate in the head, heart and solar plexus ('liver" in old terminology). As we noted, these spots in the human body are considered to be respectively the "brains" of the *Neshamah, Ru'ach* and *Nefesh*. So, every time one utters the Divine Name "*IAO*," one is factually "invoking" the totality of ones being, of which a very small portion is actually incarnated in the body — the rest being everywhere.

Now, let us start with a set of preparatory exercises, so as to help you to express the five vowels of the "*Universal Yichud*" in the best possible manner. Here it is again vitally important to get your "mind" out of the way, and to "***feel*** it out" as it were. You need to develop a "feeling appreciation" associated with your heart and gut, rather than a "thinking one" associated with the analytical mind. Close your eyes, relax your body, pay particular attention to the anal muscle, which must be relaxed since when you clutch down there, you are definitely "uptight." You will find that you can surrender deeply when you relax your anus. Now, start to hum and simply feel the sound vibrating in your body. Do this over and over, and focus your attention on the five different parts of your anatomy represented by the five vowels. You literally "look" at these different parts of your anatomy in an absolutely relaxed manner with your eyes closed. Focus with your mind the sound frequencies strongly into the area you are looking at, but be careful to remain relaxed and surrendered while doing so.

Focus your attention on the lower part of your body, especially the anus and the genitals, breathe in and vibrate that area with the sound frequencies of your humming. Can you feel the sound vibrating there? You can focus the sound more strongly in that area if you push downwards on both your diaphragm and your anal muscle while humming. This is what a bull does with his mighty bellow. Starting with the "*MMMMMM*" he pushes downwards, almost thrusting his rectum out of his body when he gets to the actual vocalized "*MOOOO*," which he expresses with an enormous resonance amplified by his ample belly. I come from farming stock, and I can assure you that I have witnessed this first hand. Try to emulate the example of this bull, and focus the humming sound into the lower regions of your torso.

Next turn your attention to your solar plexus, the area directly below the breast bone. Hum and feel the sound resonate in that part of your body. If you want to focus the sound more powerfully in this locale, you have to sort of swallow the sound, a well-known technique in *Kabbalah* termed "swallowing." This is done a lot more easily with the "*OH*" sound than with humming, but for now simply hum and imagine you are holding water in your mouth and, while you are humming, this water is running down your throat into your solar plexus. In this manner you can focus the sound frequencies more strongly in that area.

With the heart and the throat it is quite easy. Simply hum and focus your attention on your chest, and you will easily experience your whole chest vibrating. Similarly the throat will simply vibrate strongly as you hum and focus your attention in that zone of your anatomy. However, the head is another matter altogether. Here you have to get the sound to resonate powerfully inside your "mask," i.e. the front part of your face from the cheekbones upwards. Start by humming and feeling the sound vibrate in your nose and face. Repeat, but this time smile and feel as if the sound is being pulled upwards into your eyes and forehead. When you are sure that you can do this, put your attention in your eyes and the middle of your forehead, then simply push the sound into that area. The experience is something like a beam of sound being directed from a point between the eyes, sort of directly above the bridge of the nose. You can also intensify this sensation, by imagining that you are opening your eyes wider while humming the sound in your face, right in the mask as said.

If you are comfortable with experiencing the sound frequencies in those mentioned areas of your body, you can repeat the practice using the different vowels associated with each sector. Again these are **U** (*OO*) in the lower bowels, genitals and anus; **O** (*OH*) in the solar plexus, which we said is located in the diaphragm directly below the breast-bone; **A** (*AH*) in the centre of the chest and heart; **E** (*EH*) in the throat and neck; and **I** (*EE*) in the head, specifically the area extending from the nose and cheek bones upwards to the top of the head. Curiously enough when you chant these vowels in this order, one after the other on a single breath, you will hear harmonics or overtones starting with the lowest frequencies in "*OO*," progressing upwards through the different vowels to the highest ones in "*EE*."

Remember that if you want to focus the "*OO*" strongly in the lower part of your body, it is worthwhile imitating the behaviour of cows and bulls, that is to replicate their call while pushing down on the diaphragm and anal sphincter muscle. Also employ the "swallowing" technique to cause the "*OH*" to resonate powerfully in your solar plexus. Remember to pay particular attention to the "*EE*" sound in the eyes and forehead. You can focus this sound quite intensely in your eyes and head if you shape the mouth as if you are about to whistle. While keeping that shape and feeling your nose especially open, sonate "*EE*" and concentrate specifically on it being focussed in your eyes and forehead. Of course, it is quite difficult to delineate this technique of uttering the vowels in different parts of your body, without being able to actually demonstrate what I am talking about, but I am sure you will be able to teach yourself as we progress.

Now, every individual with the slightest sense of the dissonance and disaster which constantly beset our planet and our humanity, will freely admit that serious *Tikkun* (restoration) is needed in our world and in our lives. We are told that the act of restoration does not start outside, but has to commence within each one of us. All have to work their own transformations individually within their personal beings, and many spiritual systems have developed a host of techniques to facilitate this transformation. In *Kabbalah* one such method is the *Yichud*, the regular use of which not only seems to realign the body, mind and soul of the practitioner, but appears to facilitate "Divine Union," the "Sacred Marriage" between the meditator and the all-embracing Divinity, a keen realisation of oneness between that portion of God incarnated in the body and the greater "I Am."

As you may notice, the working of the "Universal *Yichud*," similarly to the oriental "*chakra*" system, requires the practitioner to focus on special "energy centres" inside the human anatomy, in this case specifically five — the head; throat; heart; solar plexus and genitals, which we noted are respectively associated with the five major vowels. In the "Universal *Yichud*" one combines *Kavvanah* (powerfully centered attention) and vowel chanting, all profoundly focussed in those associated special bodily parts, so as to restore and realign these "power centres" in the body. One may well ask why these special centres should be out of alignment, while also recognising in the back of ones mind that most of our humanity is very mixed up. We are told that most individuals over the age of three, or four, are actually out of touch with themselves, and that this is due to the fact that all of us live in circumstances carefully calculated to condition us in such a manner, that we would capitulate to patterns of behaviour agreed to be the "right ones" for rightful and decent living on this planet. Much of these social patterns are totally out of alignment with basic human nature and natural living on this planet, and thus the forceful disciplinary implementation of these behavioural patterns, warps the human psyche in such a manner, that most individuals turn into "thinking monkeys" who are totally out of touch with their bodies, real life and whom they really are.

The dictates of "conditioned parents" soon impact on the child who is trying "not to be naughty," and in many cases by the time infants reach the age of three, they have been "rectified" ("*rectum-fied*" according to an associate) so often with "don't do that"......"you're naughty"..... etc., that they loose touch with their own inner being. It is then that these special "energy centres" go out of alignment. Children often resort to a variety of compensatory behaviour patterns, which in many instances can turn out to be far more destructive than say....just biting ones nails! There must be a better way of educating children, fetching the best out of them, than this social indoctrination which "dis–aligns" their lives with often disastrous end results.

From this perspective we might begin to comprehend what serial killers are all about. They represent the volcanic outbursts of a society repressed in such a manner, that it is impossible for individuals to express their inner emotional realities in a safe manner. While one rightfully condemns the killers, it is also very clear that removing them from society is not going to solve the basic problem. Especially when the very fabric of our lives, based as it is on the strictures of a very rigid social indoctrination inflicted on us from our births to our demise on this planet, is still setting the stage for many more mass murderers than we can hope to deal with, as we have witnessed in the case where these killers are placed in positions granting them political power. Having come from a very repressive background myself, I dare say that I am extremely grateful for the wonderful "unification" practices developed by many spiritual traditions, which not only help us cope with the strictures of strenuous living, but support our efforts to realign ourselves with the "Whole." One can speak truthfully only from the position of personal experience, and I can certainly affirm that practising *Yichudim* has contributed enormously to the ongoing task of restoration inside my own being, or the realignment of my mind, body, soul and spirit.

As said, the chanting of a *Yichud* impacts similarly to the use of oriental *mantras*, causing deep relaxation, surrendering, centering and healing, amongst a whole variety of benefits. A *Yichud* might be considered to be quite a complex *mantra* comprising, as it does, many constituent parts which — in the case of the "*Universal Yichud*" — is quite easy to learn but somewhat difficult to execute in its entirety. Again we need to study the mechanics involved very closely. We mentioned "harmonics" when we discussed the manner in which the vowel frequencies are "sonated" in their associated spots in the human body, but while the method of toning "overtones" helps one to experience the various frequencies inside ones anatomy, the actual method of chanting the vowel sounds in this *Yichud* is quite different. Trying to impart this via the written word is going to be more than just a bit difficult. However, I will try to describe the required vocal techniques as carefully and clearly as possible, so as to afford you the opportunity of experimenting beneficially with this amazing *Yichud*.

Let us start with the sound "*AH*." It is quite simple and easy. Place your hand again on your chest and say "*AH*" — the sound of satisfaction. Do not do anything especially fancy as far as the sound is concerned. A simple "*AH*," pronounced quite normally, will do nicely. Repeat this a few times. Then do it again, but this time *chant* the vowel, stretching it over the entire exhalation and feeling the sound vibrate under your hand. Next, we need to intensify the experience by getting you to act with *Kavvanah*, with powerfully focussed attention. To do this, you need to close your eyes and put your attention directly under the palm which is resting on the centre of your chest. Feel that spot immediately underneath your hand. In this kind of practice, it is important to avoid using any form of mental analysis or yielding to the desire to explain what is happening. You simply experience, i.e. develop the mentioned feeling appreciation rather than a thinking one.

Now, smile at the spot directly under your hand. Feel the warmth of your smile in that zone. Next attempt to smile *with* that area, which is simply to allow your chest to smile. William Gray used to tell me I must move the portion of my anatomy I am focussing on from "bud to flower," literally feeling it expand and open up in the warmest, friendliest manner. This practice will focus your attention in the best possible way on this portion of your anatomy which you intend to vibrate with the frequencies of the vowel "*AH*." While looking at and smiling with that area specifically under your hand in the centre of your chest, take a deep breath and intone the sound "*AH*" feeling the sound vibrate under your hand. Do it again, but this time feel as if you are uttering the sound *with* your chest, almost as if your chest is singing along with you, and that it is expanding and opening up as you intone the sound over the length of a complete exhalation.

Next, let us turn to the sound "***EH***." Here you should think that you have a pair of gills like a fish, in this case somewhere underneath your lower jaw close to your throat, right in the spot where your tonsils will be — if you still have them. You have to utter the sound right in the throat, and it should sound somewhat broader than the same produced by sheep or goats. Imagine yourself intoning inside those "gills," right in the tonsils. It should sound somewhat like the sound you would make if someone grabbed your throat. Again you need to "feel it out" rather than "think it out."

Continuing, you once again need to smile not only at, but *with* that spot in your throat and tonsils where you wish to intone the vowel "***EH***," and you should again feel the warmth of your smile pervade that locale. Take a deep breath, and chant "***EH***" down in your tonsils while in turn experiencing this zone opening, expanding and resonating with the sound. Perhaps a good way of explaining the desired sound in this case, is to imagine that you are holding water in the front of your mouth, having to keep the liquid out of your throat while you are chanting. In fact, applying this visual tool might help you achieve the exact position in your throat for the required sound production, which should be sonated in the upper portion of the throat.

The next vowel, "***OH***," is probably the most difficult to intone correctly in this *Yichud*. One has to be extremely careful not to injure the throat or hurt ones vocal chords in this instance, where it is required to actually pronounce the sound deep down the throat in order to get it to resonate most powerfully in the solar plexus. Many might feel that it would be impossible to not hurt the throat in the process, but I can assure you that this can be done without any negative effect on either your throat or vocal chords. Here we apply that "swallowing the sound" technique in which one literally drags the sound down the throat by almost, as it were, gargling with it. The crude image of this might be the way the inside of the throat is positioned prior to throwing up. Try it. Say "***OH***" down in your throat, feeling the sound vibrate in that spot where you normally gargle with your mouthwash. Here again you might imagine that your mouth is full of water, and you are opening your throat to allow the water to flow down your oesophagus into your solar plexus. Try to pull the sound downward by swallowing or dragging the sound downwards in the direction of your solar plexus. The experience is inwards and downwards.

There would be no need to exaggerate in any way, since it is quite an easy thing to do, as anyone will tell you who has ever been bilious and felt the need to speak to the "great lord 'bog'" down the large white telephone in that awfully unpleasant, noisy and gurgling manner. So, before you repeat the intoning of the "*OH*" vowel in the lower part of your throat by swallowing the sound, start by putting your attention in your solar plexus, directly under your breast bone, then, while smiling at and *with* this zone in your body, chant the vowel in the throat while keeping your attention focussed on the solar plexus where the sound is resonating, almost as if you are speaking with this part of your anatomy.

Next, we need to look at the vowel "I" (*EE*). Again we need to focus this sound powerfully in the head, right inside the mask, literally in the zone stretching from the cheekbones and nose upwards into the eyes and forehead. It would be good if you could focus the sound frequencies right inside your tear ducts. This will be achieved when you produce very powerful and intense overtones. In this technique the mouth is shaped like a little trumpet. Push your lips outwards and pout them, so that they protrude in front of you like the mentioned little trumpet. Imagine you have no roof in the upper part of your mouth, as if your mouth, nose and sinuses are all one single hollow, open space, then resonate the "*EE*" inside that entire inner expanse, i.e. intoning through the open mouth, nose and sinuses simultaneously. Slowly open your eyes a little wider as you intone, and the sound will be focussed more powerfully in the tear ducts. Before you repeat this exercise, focus your attention on your eyes and the spot between them above the bridge of your nose. Smile *with* and through this portion of your anatomy. Take a deep breath, and while keeping your attention focussed in this area, chant the "*EE*" sound right inside your eyes and forehead.

Lastly, we need to look at the last vowel "U" (***OO***) which is linked to the lowest part of the torso, and which should be vibrated inside the genitals, anus and that portion of the body below the navel. In this case, you return to quite a simple but resonant pronunciation of the vowel, which is uttered while pushing down slightly on the diaphragm and anus. As said, when one observes cattle, one notices that they push down really hard on the anus to produce that very resonant "*MOOOO*" call. You do not have to do it quite as hard, but the image holds good as an example. Simply say "*OO*" while pushing the lower part of your torso outwards. This does not have to be too excessive, but just enough for you to feel the sound resonating powerfully in the lower part of your body. Again, before you repeat the practice, you should focus your attention more or less in between your sexual organs and anus, and smile at and *with* this part of your body, again experiencing the warmth of your smile pervading this zone. Then chant the "*OO*" vowel while pressing down slightly, almost as if you were sitting on the lavatory. Pardon the crude image, but it is apt as crudities often are.

I'd suggest that you practice intoning the sounds in the manner described inside those "power centres" before you venture into the actual execution of the "*Universal Yichud.*" However, after you have mastered the preparatory exercises somewhat, you may as an introduction to this "Unification" practice, commence by chanting those portions of the *Yichud* which are expressed entirely in their associated zones. These are:

YA–HA–VA–HA in the **HEART**
YE–HE–VE–HE in the **THROAT**
YO–HO–VO–HO in the **SOLAR PLEXUS**
YI–HI–VI–HI in the **HEAD**
YU–HU–VU–HU in the **GENITALS**

Here it is important to extend the chanting of each name over an entire exhalation, and pronounce each name in the exact spot in your body indicated by the respective vowels. It is also customary to accentuate each syllable of the word, almost like giving light hammer blows with your voice, but be careful to keep the sound flowing from one syllable to the next without any breaks in the words.

Now let us look at the actual *Yichud*. The idea is to link the various sectors of your anatomy represented by the five vowels with one another. To achieve this you have to connect the sounds and positions in a sort of flowing manner, e.g. the first segment of the *Yichud* is pronounced in the "heart": "***Yah–Hah–Vah–Hah***," while in the next segment you have to pronounce the first three syllables in your "heart" (i.e. centre of your chest), but the last syllable is pronounced in your upper throat (tonsil area): "***Yah–Hah–Vah– Heh***." In this case the first three vowels are easily reiterated in the "heart," but to get to the throat, you have to slowly change the shape of your mouth, flatten out the tongue and adjust the throat in order to slide the tone into the "***EH***" position in your upper throat. Then, only after you have already fixed the sound and your attention in your throat, do you utter the last syllable of this portion of the *Yichud*. Simply chant "***Yah–Hah–Vah***" in the "heart".....raise the sound by moving from the "***AH***" position and sliding into the "***EH***" position in your throat (slowly adjust the mouth, tongue and throat. Only after you are fully positioned and focussed in the new zone (upper throat/tonsils), do you chant the last syllable "***Heh***." In this manner all the different zones of your body, respectively associated with the five vowels, are aligned and balanced with one another as you chant the 625 vowel permutations of the "*Universal Yichud*."

I do understand that this *Yichud* appears most complex in its execution, but it actually is not so difficult at all. You simply have to develop the knack, which comes with practice.

E. Ru'ach ha-Kodesh: Universal Consciousness

1. INTRODUCTION

There are two words which best express what I wish to discuss here, and these are "Theogony,"[23] referring to the genesis or creation of the gods, and "Divinisation," a term describing the notion that one may realise ones own divine status. This is a most important step in the development of consciousness, in which one suddenly realises that you are God in your true being, and that all existence is the "self-creation" of the One which is "I Am." Now, this is all well and good as an acknowledgement in the mind, but how can this be brought into actuality as a real experience of one's ordinary, daily existence?

To start with, it is important to realise that all the "gods" are creations of the universal imagination and intuition of the cosmic mind. They originate as "realisations" in the universal intelligence of *Ain Sof*, the Absolute or "Eternal Awakeness," which is *Ani*, "Is"–ness, inside us. Whereas *Ain* is the Supreme Presence, *Ani* is Its expression as omniscient, omnipotent, omnifarious, and omnipresent, being able to manifest itself in all possible possibilities, all of these differing realised possibilities being merely different facets of the one "Selfsameness of Being" which some call God, the Higher Self, or others call "I am."

Now, this sphere of "Divine Imagination" has been likened to a "River of Fire" flowing from the "Throne of the Almighty," and it was said that the Kabbalist who works with true will and consciousness, experiencing all life as a sacred sacrament, creates "angels" or "gods" if you like within this "river" or stream of consciousness. Therefore the "One who Knows" and "will be," populates the universe with projections out of the fundamental unity of the Self, the great "I Am." One can almost say that "Intuition" is the "I Am" and "Imagination" the "will be" of the "I Am"-ness of the Kabbalist, the latter being the aspect of his/her nature existing in a subtle world, the "World of the Higher Self," in which he/she communes with Angels.

Each and every one of your activities must become a sacrament, or a sacred act, if you hope to bring subtle powers, or spirits if you like, into being. To find what you are searching for, you have to look inside the world of your own consciousness, which is the true universe of "Angels" and "Demons" alike, these being merely different classifications of spirit energy, and then start operating from there by slowly applying the diverse energies in all your activities. You must work slowly and diligently in order to make true progress, since the field of exploration is truly a vast one.

2. EXERCISE IN ABSOLUTE REALITY

Start by viewing all manifestation, all things, as radiations or "outflowings" of "Absolute Reality." This Reality is "God," or whatever you like to call the highest state of Being. It is Absolute

Truth. My life condition changed the instant I started approaching all things from the realisation that all manifestation, including diseases, health, thoughts, feelings, spirits, powers, flesh, bones, etc., are just outpourings or radiations of "Absolute Reality." This is the Reality I wish to fully identify with, which I want to know in Truth. All things are emanating out of this Truth, but, though these things are derived from It, they are not separated from It. All existence is radiated constantly as self-expressions in the *Now*. It is like a light radiating a "glow." The "glow" is not separate from its source. In the same manner, existence is just the "glow of the Infinite Light," the *Aur Ain Sof*.

Now, there are those who wonder about matters such as illness, etc. These are the effects of Divine Light being "veiled" and conditioned to such an extent, that we lose our sense of oneness and buy into the illusion of separateness. It is important to know that we condition the Light, the awakeness of the consciousness. We are in fact the "Universal Consciousness" placing a veil over itself. So, am I also responsible for the illness of those I currently experience as "others," as well as my own? Yes I am, but only because of that illusion of separateness. Yet, I am responsible for their health and well-being, i.e. when I realise that we are part of the selfsameness of the great "I am."

To understand this fully we can say that the "forms" appearing in "The River of Consciousness" are like whirlpools or eddies within a stream. The conditioning of these eddies as they relate to each other creates "obstructions" within the river, shaping each whirlpool and giving it the appearance of being a separate existence, but the "water" or "consciousness" is flowing through it continuously. The same rule applies to all manifestation from thoughts to things. Again, we are really only whirlpools in the stream of consciousness radiating eternally out of *Ain Sof Aur*. If an obstruction appears in our being, this is due to us being constantly conditioned here in material existence. The more the natural flow of Consciousness and Life-Force is being encumbered within us, the more twisted we become in our own abysses; the more separate we become, the more lonely we become; the more lonely we become, the more fearful we become; the more fearful we become, the more condensed, heavier and harder we become, and in this state it is difficult to actually experience the Source flowing through you.

The Source is never separate from you. You have separated your Self from It, because you have become so condensed, so thick, that nothing seems to penetrate your being. You cause your own separation, and yet, though you make mental statements that nothing can penetrate your being, everything still moves through you. It is purely a question of altering your awareness back into recognising a state of reality which never ceased to be. Just like the rest of existence, separateness is Self-created. Isolation does not necessarily mean insulation. The fact that we *think* we are isolated from cosmic forces by having a roof over our heads, does not preclude those forces from penetrating the roof and passing straight through the earth.

The moment we become aware of that Divine Force which flows through our beings, we might be able to direct It differently. Consciousness combined with a "Magical Will" can turn the Force to express Itself in a different fashion. That is why it is necessary to view all manifestation as the "glow" of a Source, as it were, a Source which is Ultimate Reality. As this Reality is "God," or whatever you like to call the highest state of Being, it is Absolute Truth, and this Truth is within you.

Exercise

Slowly withdraw into your inner self, and enter into an inner state of stillness, total stillness. You must become quiet, shrink back into yourself and feel how you are becoming smaller and smaller, moving to the point of virtual disappearance. Do not worry that anything nasty will happen to you, since besides your fears there is nothing problematic here. Simply become still, and in this stillness sense a very small, serene, and tranquil point of light. Feel or imagine yourself being that light. In this state you may still be aware of your physical body and all the noise around you, but although this is a turmoil of emotions, pains, thoughts and all manner of things, these are purely radiations out of *you*, and you are that small, still, serene point of light, which is your Essence, your potent creative Being. Do not try to be big by viewing your true identity as a "Body of Light" surrounding you, or viewing the Higher Self as something huge. You will shortly have every opportunity to create such a "Body of Light" for yourself. For now, understand that "bigness" has to do with doing, expressing and manifestation, while "smallness" has to do with Essence, the doer and the creator.

Experience this "Light Essence" as a potently alive and pulsating Point of Power, and that as this is your divine spark, it is the fount of true Divine Power. Enter completely into this potent space, realising that even though you are inside it, it is also within you. Try to experience these states of within and without as a reality of Oneness, like an empty chalice in which the air is both inside and outside. In this way you can realise God inside yourself as both the *Neshamah*, the Point or Spark of Celestial Power, and also as Infinite Immanence. You are in "Infinite Identity" and It is in you.

When this becomes real to you as an experience, start to emanate Divine Power outwards from your "nothingness" into your body, and let it flow into the whole of manifestation on all its levels of body, mind, soul and spirit, moving and flowing into all the "Forms of Force" we call manifested existence. Direct the power by letting it flow everywhere within existence, embracing and interpenetrating everything as the Life-Force of existence. Then see it as the "Total Truth" of existence, the Universal Essence eternally present everywhere. Try to see the incandescence, the radiance of the Light manifesting itself into many forms, like colours and musical sounds, and then let the sounds and lights of all manifestation express themselves in concert and harmony.

Now, look at everything around you, experiencing all and everything as saturated with this Holy Force, since the Sacred Source is the presence in all as *Ru'ach ha-Kodesh*, the Holy Spirit. Then notice how everything and all acts are sacred, and how they are the expressions of the "Power of God" which you are. Finally, choose any aspect of your daily experience, and view it as a sacrament, a holy act or as it was said once "an outward and visible sign, of an inner and invisible grace."[24] See all of your life encounters as a way in which the Divine is entering into your field of experience. Thus you recognise a sacred universe in which Divine Force is potently present in all existence, and within your power to direct **AS YOU WILL**.

. ...Indeed His works are variegated beyond investigation and infinite... ... .

CHAPTER 9
MAGGIDIM: SPIRIT MESSENGERS

A. Introduction

We have now arrived at the very important subject of *Maggidim*, that is "spirit messengers. Humans have always believed that "spirits" of some kind have considerable influence upon our affairs with good or ill results, depending on their motivation. It was also believed that we might implore them for certain life benefits, and, depending on viewpoints, the act of asking was considered either magic or religion. One man's religion is another man's magic so to speak. To an ultra-Calvinist a Catholic Mass is "magic" of a nasty, black type, whereas to a Catholic, any theurgic ritual could be similarly classified. In the end it seems to boil down to one human's opinion of another.

Of course, scientists are not supposed to believe in any sort of spirit at all, and it amuses me to see how "ultramodern" scientists are inventing "new" theories to account for "God" as a consciousness behind Life itself. Beliefs of thousands of years ago were aligned with the latest studies, in order to show up those same beliefs under totally new wording. Now, does the scientist's non-belief in "Spirits" preclude the intrusion of such beings in their activities? I do not believe so at all. I think that humans are far more influenced by so-called "spirits" than they know about. Terminology is always a tricky point, but if our behaviour on earth is influenced, or modified, in any way by currents of consciousness coming from outside ourselves, or even released from the infinity within ourselves, then those energies in themselves could be called "spirits," if they originate from "Inner Sources" other than human. To that extent, magic is a fact of life.

This brings to mind medieval magicians invoking "spirits" in their magical circles, supported by textbooks called "magical grimoires," and of course one thinks also of Spiritualism. In the minds of the general populace, the word "magic" almost immediately invokes images of darkly clad men and women working away at something sinister. Sometimes I wonder what the old legends about "black magicians" really amounted to. How far were they factual? Again it depends entirely on ones definition of "magic." If that means any kind of work accomplished with a definite human intention behind it, then we have as usual, only three kinds. A good intention, a bad one, or just a non-motivated one. If again a specifically "magic" intention involves the employment of "spirits," or invisible "intelligences," deliberately invoked as adjuncts or agencies of the energy needed to accomplish certain aims, then this takes on a different meaning entirely.

Of course, all of this started millennia ago, when what we now classify as religious rites, commenced as "magical" practices amongst primitive man. Religious rites were mixed into a wholeness and harmony with ordinary daily life. This is not to say that early man was any better or worse off than we are today. In religion, like everything else, man seems to have progressed through many battles along the way of discovery, i.e. from very rough roots to quite sophisticated achievements, and when one looks at the history of these accomplishments, there is a realisation of how very small the difference is between science and religion. The scientist starts with the supposition that the same power controlling the movement of the stars, also causes the consistency of the atom, and they attempt to understand and cooperate with it. On the other hand, religious types believe the "Power" which animates the stars can also construct and create the human character, and they attempt to understand and to cooperate with "It."

Early man thus recognised a "Supreme Force" which animated all life, and all aspects of that Force were seen as spirits inside everything. The Force is not only external to everything, but also intrinsic, creating other "forces," which are "souls" and "spirits," interacting and affecting the environment, as well as the contents of that environment. Early man was not only influenced by objective environments, but also by the so called "subjective" ones of sleep, dreams, etcetera, where his "other self" could contact the "inner beings" of all creatures. There was in fact no distinction between the objective and the subjective, and the same forces which animated his normal waking life also animated his "other life." Primitive man saw no difference between material and spiritual states. What is more, they did not distinguish between the visible object and the Power which animated that object.

When he learned the laws of cause and effect, man continued to develop methods which seemed effective to him in his communication with life, and as he realised reasoning, choice and knowledge in the invisible powers, he started contacting these by addressing them. So were born rites of worship which the ancient Greeks termed *ta hiera* meaning "the sacred," and which in Latin is called *Sacrificium* (plural: *Sacrificia*), and many early customs which antedated religious concepts, developed into these *Sacrificia* or acts of worship.

Now, the subject of *Maggidim* or Angelic Messengers, so often mentioned in *Kabbalah*, reminds me of the tenth century Rabbi Hai Gaon, the famous religious leader and mystic, who wrote: "God arranged the order of creation so that all things are bound to each other. The direction of events in the lower world depends on entities above them, as our sages teach, 'there is no blade of grass in the world below that does not have an angel over it, striking it and telling it to grow!'

Human souls are also bound to higher levels, and therefore, when a perfect individual becomes involved in Meditation (*Hitbodedut*) upon Wisdom, it is possible for him to predict the future events. As a result of his deep meditation, his consciousness and mind fall into a trance, and through his deep probing of the mysteries of existence, he reaches the First Cause. The faculties of his heart then become like the *Urim* and *Thumim*, mystically bound to the angels in heaven, and he becomes attached to the Ultimate Good."[1] This realisation of Divine Law regulating life on all levels of manifestation, down to the least detail, makes other religious trends seem very insignificant. This is why it is so important for Kabbalists to *live* the laws of life, and these "laws" pertain to Love. The Love of God, in which is the passion of a "Lover" and a "Beloved," means a conscious relationship with all levels of life, whether they be in the dimension of Spirit, Soul, Mind or Body. All Life is One, and the same laws apply everywhere as One Existence. Thus, a Kabbalist can communicate with entitised awareness, whether incarnated in a physical body or not, and included here is the *Maggid*, which can be a departed Saint, beloved Teacher or Master, an Angel, etc.

It saddens me when modern scholarship, starting already in the nineteenth century, refers to the phenomena of *Maggidim* as something totally illusory, devoid of all truth, and belonging to the realm of psycho-pathology. Some even apologetically refer to it as a "regrettable weakness" on the part of the person claiming such a contact, while others, including the very religious, see the whole subject of the *Maggid* as a fabrication, believing it to be heresy and a disgrace.

Despite all this, it is interesting to note how many famous Rabbis, Masters and scholars had a *Maggid*.[2] In fact, Maggidism comprising mentor angels, spirit guides, voices, and so forth, certainly played a massive role in all mysticism, and, as one author puts it, existed in certain periods and amongst certain groups almost like an "epidemic."[3] So despite modern scholarship referring only to the worshipful "religious-spiritual" side of mysticism, there is no doubt that manifestations like *Maggidim* are a widespread and valued phenomenon.

The meaning of the word *Maggid* is "one who relates," and it ordinarily refers to itinerant preachers. However, on another level, as already indicated, a *Maggid* is a mentor or ministering angel, spirit guide, or voice, which could in some cases appear in dream as a departed friend, teacher or master, an angel or spirit guide instructing the dreamer, who can question the *Maggid*. At other times it may appear while the receiver is completely conscious and awake, alone or in the company of other people. Often all present would hear the voice of the *Maggid*, though at times a contactee would be taken over by the *Maggid* as in possession, and then the "spirit messenger" would speak through his/her mouth, which is not unlike what sometimes occurs in modern Spiritualism when the medium becomes "controlled."

Yet not always is the *Maggid* a spirit classifiable as Elijah, or some known friend, master or angel. The *Maggid* can be the personified spirit of sacred texts, that is the spirit of the *Torah*, *Mishnah*, *Talmud*, *Zohar*, *Tosefta*, or other holy text, seen as conscious living entities, such as in the case of the sixteenth century Rabbi Shlomo Molcho where, at night time, the *Mishnah* descended as a personified feminine spirit, to whisper revelations into the ear of "Her" servant.

The same holds true for the sixteenth century Rabbi Joseph Karo who had a *Maggid* appear to him every time he recited the *Mishnah* by heart, who then spoke, saying: "Peace upon thee, Rabbi Joseph Karo. I am the Mishnah which thou hast studied. I came forth to teach thee understanding."[4] Then the *Maggid* would instruct the contactee regarding remarkable mysteries of life and its manifestations, and the teachings related to these mysteries, such as Kabbalistic explanations. Yet, the *Maggid* never appeared in visual form to Rabbi Karo, but spoke through the Rabbi's mouth, and, as one author puts it, this is "a genuine case of well-ordered, lucid, automatic-speech,"[5] of course still under the guidance of a *Maggid*, a heavenly messenger.

A *Maggid* could bring great visual revelations, even though it may not necessarily itself be visual. Thus the *Maggid* of Rabbi Karo said: "I shall grant thee to behold Elijah, for the ancient of days will be clothed in white garments and will sit facing thee and will speak unto thee as a man speaketh unto his friend and thine eye shall behold thy teacher and.....He will speak with thee and thou shalt behold him."[6]

The subject of Maggidism is not only related to automatic speech, but to both clairvoyance and clairaudience. More and more I think you may realise how closely this relates to normal mediumistic states and trances. A Maggidic manifestation is not only related to a spirit messenger, angel, dream figure or automatic speech, occurring during sleep, while in a trance or fully conscious, but is also related to automatic writing. Connected to the latter is the Kabbalistic *Chochmat ha-Tzeruf*, "Science of Permutation,"[7] but this topic is much too large to address here. Briefly *Tzeruf* is a method of mentally permuting the letters in Hebrew words as a form of profound meditation, leading to expanded sensory perceptions and ecstatic states.

What needs to be emphasized is that from the sixteenth century, the invocation of *Maggidim* became quite commonplace amongst Kabbalists, whereas prior to that it was a specialised and rare occurrence. Through Maggidism the Kabbalist draws on the vast spiritual realm of sages, saints and celestial guides, the realm of Elijah, as well as the embodied essences of scriptures. In the eighteenth century Moses Chayim Luzzatto wrote to a friend concerning his own *Maggid*, saying: "I admit that since 1727 God has been gracious to me by dispatching to me a Holy One from heaven who reveals to me.....nightly secrets....He promised me that I would be privileged to hear [the utterances] from the very mouth of the prophet Elijah and even the living words of the lord. And as he promised, so it came. When the appointed time arrived, the prophet Elijah revealed himself to me, followed by the Holy Souls who abide on this earth ready to fulfil the tasks of the Lord.....and with their assistance I composed many and important works."[8]

This occurred when Rabbi Luzzatto fell asleep while chanting *Yichudim*, which as you already know are Kabbalistic mantras and formulas comprising Divine Names. He woke up suddenly when a voice called to him in Aramaic, saying: "I have come down to reveal hidden secrets of the Holy King."[9] At first Rabbi Luzzatto was afraid and trembling, he listened to the voice enumerating Kabbalistic teachings, and what must have been a surprise to him, was that the *Maggid* did not appear physically, but spoke with his own mouth and voice.

It was only after several occurrences that the voice admitted to being a *Maggid*, promising the young Kabbalist "formulas to keep in mind every day,"[10] and Rabbi Luzzatto's relationship with the *Maggid* eventually grew so deep that he received immediate and pertinent answers to his questions. Later the *Maggid* stopped the Rabbi from using Kabbalistic formulas, replacing them with a Holy Name, at which time came the promise of visual contact with Elijah. The prophet in turn appeared and promised the Kabbalist contact with the archangel *Metatron*, the Angel of the Presence and "Great Guardian of Heaven," and, as Luzzatto later reported in his diary: "I can recognise each one of them. Also there are Holy Souls who come, their names I know not, and they tell me new things which I write down.....All these things I am doing while falling on my face and while seeing the Holy Souls as if through a dream in human forms."[11] The Rabbi lived for three years in almost continuous ecstasy, while keeping very quiet about his revelations. Afterwards, with the aid of a close friend, he started imparting his messages to others.

The whole process of meeting and mingling with *Maggidim* is due to the practice of *Devekut*, Divine Union or Cleaving to

God, discussed earlier. Again the practice of *Devekut* results in prophecy, communication with *Maggidim*, and even in power over the laws of nature. This happens because Kabbalists, through their attempts towards spiritual perfection, return to their source, or "soul root" as it is sometimes called. The mental power and compassion of Kabbalists would then vastly expand as they become gradually more Godlike. The more this happens, the greater becomes the ability to communicate with "Celestial Intelligences." As Kabbalists continue to utter Sacred Names of God, also employing different breathing patterns, procedures understood to be tying them to the Spirit World, they obtain a high level of prophetic ability and raise themselves into vastly expanded states of consciousness.

We should note that the practice of *Devekut* leads to a sacred *Zivug*, or coupling, a sacred sexual act between God and the soul, which is often followed by the appearance of a *Maggid*. In a relationship of this nature with God, incredible, spontaneous states of ecstasy occur, in which Kabbalists are flooded with a Divine influx or bliss called *Shefa*. This would literally turn the practitioner into a physically incarnated Divine Messenger or *Maggid*, and then it is believed this Kabbalist could fulfil the function of instructing others.

I should stress again that everything discussed here, and all manifestation, whether materialised outside or inside ones own being, are part of the universal "I Am." Each one of us creates our own realities, and if the *Maggidim*, the "spirits" of external and internal manifestation are conversing with us, it is due to the fact that we are ready and "open" to "meaningfulness." It all depends on the alertness, the awakeness, of the Kabbalist as to whether he/she gets the messages or not. It depends equally on whether that individual is open, receptive and expanded enough to actually get the meaning, i.e. trained enough in the practice of approaching life in terms of meanings, and finding for oneself through this the symbols of consciousness, the relevant "Inner Language" without which one would not get very far.

Life will have no meaning if you do not attempt to discover the meaning, or give it meaning if it does not have any for you. One should at least try to interpret the relevance while still on the ground, so to speak, so that when you eventually get off the surface of this mundane existence into loftier realms, all the meanings will "speak" to you. You must first build communication, a process of great importance, in which acknowledging "god-forces," your emotions, is imperative, since those are the responses from the spirit world.

We know these "subtle intelligences" can appear beautiful or hideous, protective or menacing, depending on the thought or emotion which has given them life. We know to some extent that creation and manifested life originate in the physical and mental attributes of man himself, and if you do not know this, then it is time you start thinking about it. All life existing everywhere is created by your Self. All life, the whole universe in fact, is created by your Self. By this I do not mean the small part incarnated in the body, but the "I AM." It is like the illustration based on the famous *Through the Looking Glass*,[12] showing Alice standing on a checkerboard floor and staring into the "looking glass" in which she observes her own reflection as a shadow. Within this shadow she observes universes, galaxies, suns, moons and planets, but what she does not realise is that she is looking at herself. She thinks she is looking at things out there, while in reality it is all a reflection of Self.

Regarding "spirit intelligences," I have to admit that my own relationship with them has been rather shaky. My particular "Inners," as I like to call them, have not been a very forthcoming group, however admirable they may be in other ways. They do their job, but they do not give any prizes so to speak. They are extremely cryptic, and I do not believe they treat anyone else better than they treat me. I have certainly never had a personal hot line to God or lesser celestial authorities. About all I am told is to shut up and get on with the job. Personally I find these "Higher Orders of Life" very hard to deal with, not always particularly cooperative so far as human affairs are concerned, and not very exciting to work with. They seem to choose whether they want to work with you or not, and when these "forces" elect to work with you, they can disrupt your life quite considerably.

These "Inners" have also communicated with me in the form of "Voices," and I have regularly woken up in the middle of the night to the sound of my own voice. Believe it or not, this is not an uncommon phenomenon, but can be rather perplexing when you suddenly find yourself speaking without having any control over it. All the same, it does not always do to be *too* meekly acceptant of whatever "Inner Voices" tell you. My own experience of life has led me to treat *all* "Voices" with extreme caution. I would not rely on them a single inch past the edge of my own judgment. Remarkable as they are, I have found they are purely concerned with the pursuit of their specific spiritual work, regardless of the humans they use as instruments to work with. So far as they are concerned, humans are expendable and disposable if need be.

Provided you listen, and then make up your mind what action you will take and do so on your own responsibility entirely, that will be fine. Never do anything purely because some "Voice" says so. Think it out for yourself, and then do what you will because you agree or disagree with what you heard. If you act blindly, without reasoning, they will ultimately let you ruin yourself. They did not save Jesus or Joan of Arc from agonizing deaths, or countless others from even worse fates. To them, deaths and disasters are but mere incidentals of an overall individual experience of identity through a "Line of Light" covering a lot of Cosmos. They do not see why we should mind being the subjects of their experiments with Existence, any more than we ask why animals or plants should object to our eating or experimenting with them.

If you meet their consciousness with your own on terms of mutual respect, based on acknowledgement of each other's functions in a common Cosmic cause, you will make a good enough relationship, but the moment you accept everything the "Voices" say without question, you make trouble for yourself. Your only real protection is to become a living "Question Mark" yourself. Query everything all the time, and in the end, let the ultimate decision be yours. Hard? Yes of course, but the "Western Way" is hard. It has never been easy.

You will naturally wonder why I bother at all with "Spirit Intelligences." The reason is simply because it was in me before I was born, just as others have it in themselves for the same purpose. Call it "Fate" if you like. We came here to do specific jobs, and until we do them we shall be bound to human bodies. So, if after this discourse you still would like to communicate with "Spirit Messengers," please read on.

B. Contacting a *Maggid*

The following practice involves the development of communication with *Maggidim*, which today might be called evolving "channelling ability." This is achieved as a result of deep meditation work, and is perhaps the most suitable from all perspectives for the safety and proper growth of would-be Kabbalists and Ritual Magicians.

When you start to meditate you automatically encounter the world of the mind, and it is in this realm that you see various energies as they first show themselves as Maggidic phenomena. Whenever one examines the process of meditation, Maggidic contents are always found in the experience. This means that qualities of "spirit messengers" are inside our psyches, and these begin to manifest the instant we start to meditate. They are part of us, and literally lying in wait in the deepest recesses of our psyches. Of course, *Maggidim* reside in the much loftier realm of the "Universal Mind," which we can also access via our Selves. Every person is able to contact these "Inner Intelligences" via their own minds, souls and spirits. In this regard, you could employ the following procedure to aid you into commencing communion with "Spirit Intelligences":

1. Sit down in your usual calm and relaxed manner. Close your eyes, and surrender as deeply as you possibly can. Commence your meditation by visualising a large circle. Sense the space within that circle to be filled with *Ruchaniyut*, Spiritual Power.
2. Consider this "Spirit Force" to be a *Maggid*, "entitised consciousness," a self-aware "Spirit Intelligence." Get a strong impression, that you and this Force are aware of and observing one another. Smiling warmly inside yourself, attempt to "feel out" the nature of this "Spirit Force," and when you have achieved this, give it an identity, i.e. name it.
3. Using this name, extend your greetings, and initiate a conversation with this "Spirit Force," introducing yourself and generally explaining who you are and why you have chosen to establish contact in this manner.

4. After this initial introduction, you might consider asking it about its world and life, and the manner in which it wishes to appear to you. It may at first not reveal much if anything about itself and its habitation, but more will be revealed with persistent practice.
5. When you feel the interaction has been sufficient, bid the "Spirit Force" farewell and return to normal focal levels by focussing your attention inside your body onto your solar plexus. Take a deep breath, make fists, open fists, stretch and open your eyes.
6. Record the encounter in a special diary which you should keep especially to record your meetings with "Spirit Messengers."

C. The Power of Positive Feeling

1. INTRODUCTION

Earlier we made reference to "The Power of Positive Feeling," and the following techniques pertain specifically to this issue. We might note that "Positive Thinking" is actually fairly restricted and a mere fraction of the immense spectrum of the subtle "magical functions" within the human self. *Kabbalah* agrees most strongly that the right attitude is vitally necessary in the process of rightful living, and calls this *Kavvanah* as indicated earlier, but this tradition also knows that an attitude could be only a mental action, with little or no connection to the *Nefesh* of the person, whose emotions might be nullifying all the beneficial thought-power bounced around the brain. Many wonder why their positive affirmations never materialise, despite their most intense efforts with "Positive Thinking."

Of course, we know what a causative influence a very commonplace opinion can be. In many instances a most illusory idea is accountable for the creation of situations we think are accidental. Ideas have immense power, and are constantly shaping our everyday existence. They are the material out of which universes are made or unmade, and a mere mental notion can be the winch lifting you to the very heights or dropping you into a dark abyss. This is why it is so important to understand the manner in which ideas function, since then we can use them to our best advantage in order to attract as strongly as possible that which uplifts us, and rid ourselves of that which limits our lives.

The mind is indeed very important in the "magical scheme," however, by itself it is somewhat ineffective. An idea is manifested when you are "inspired," when your emotions are stirred and you are spurred into action. That inspiration pertains to the "soul" part of your being, the emotional sphere, which is as important as the "mind" part. In fact, thinking needs to be harnessed to feeling in order to successfully work the "magical deed." "Positive Thinking" needs "Positive Feeling," since the latter affords you direct access to the "Shadow" aspects of your nature where the active power of life is hidden. This is of utmost importance, and you should carefully examine this aspect of your being, before scrutinising the possibilities of action proffered by great life-symbols like the Kabbalistic Tree of Life.

So, to become really effective as "Self Creators," we need to explore the realm of emotions, and we will do so with special magical activities such as "Speaking in Pictures," which is a form of "Magical Evocation." However, before we venture "inwards" let us peruse our sacred working space, the "Magical Temple," divided, as it is, into a squared circle representing the four Seasons, Directions, Elements, Magical Instruments, Archangels, etc. To this list we have to add the four vowel sounds associated with the four directions and the Elements: "*EE*" for the East and the Element of Air, "*AH*" for the South (North in the Southern Hemisphere) and the Element of Fire, "*OH*" for the West and the Element of Water, "*EH*" for the North (South in the Southern Hemisphere) and the Element of Earth, and "*OO*" for the Full Circle uniting all the elements, and for *Avir*, the Universal Element or "Element of Truth."

Now, instead of just uttering these sounds verbally, you will learn to speak in pictures. By this I mean that you should open your mouth as if you were going to utter the Elemental Sound, but instead you breathe out with your mouth shaped according to the required primal sound while imagining a picture of that Element flowing out of your mouth, or being formed by your mental utterance and your breathing of the sound.

2. PICTURE SPEECH

Exercise 1

As an exercise for learning how to use this method, you may start by having the Element of Air flow out of your mouth in the form of billowing orange clouds shaping themselves into cloudy landscapes, and the Element of Fire would flow out of your mouth as flames shaping themselves into a fiery landscape, and so forth. Try it with all four elements, e.g. exhale the Element of Water as a gushing blue liquid, and the Element of Earth as a mass of green crystalline substance.

Exercise 2

Using the following procedure, infuse or impregnate your environment with a specific "sefirotic quality." It is first invoked as a special quality inside yourself, and then emanated in the form of an associated colour. The following colours and qualities have been respectively linked to the Tree of Life:

Keter	Brilliance	Emanate Oneness.
Chochmah	Light Grey	Emanate Wisdom.
Binah	Dark Grey	Emanate Understanding.
Chesed	Blue	Emanate Mercy and Joy.
Gevurah	Red	Emanate Control and strict Discipline.
Tiferet	Yellow	Emanate poise, balance and harmony.
Netzach	Green	Emanate love to everyone and everything.
Hod	Orange	Emanate mental alertness.
Yesod	Pale Yellow	Emanate vital Life-Force.
Malchut	Element Colours	Emanate personal selfhood.

Exercise 3

Next you may undertake an even more advanced step in this work, by attempting to draw lines and geometrical images with the emotion packed and coloured "breath-sounds" emanating out of your mouth. This procedure is of great use in expressing "Divine Names" and "Words of Power" with symbols, like for example the so-called "Sigils," the "magical signatures" which Ritual Magicians have been using over the centuries, in order to establish contact with "Spirit Entities."

Be that as it may, the current exercise is most important since whatever inner force you are trying to contact, do not actually hear or read the physical words you are uttering, but the nuances of intention underlying your meditations, prayers, ceremonies, studies and actions. In the current procedure you are establishing a kind of "spirit alphabet" comprising related emotions, colours and images. Using such an "alphabet of intentions," you sort of "flash" your thoughts and feelings during exhalation. These will be perceived by "Inner Forces" in accordance with the imagined form you have expressed in thought and deed. In a small way you are doing what God, or your *Neshamah*, is doing all the time, and that is "to make the word flesh." In your case this is done for a few moments, in order to get your intentions expressed and heard on "Inner Levels."

Again a major part of this procedure pertains to keeping proper records of each emotion with its associated colour and symbol, in this manner you are constructing your "Alphabet of Intentions."

3. ACKNOWLEDGING AND INVOKING GOD–FORCES

Each one of us is via our emotions continuously under the influence of "Spirit Intelligences." For example, anger is due to the influence of the "Forces" of *Gevurah* (Severity) and its related planet *Madim* (Mars), while love is caused by the "Powers" *Netzach* (Victory) and *Nogah* (Venus), the planet associated with this sphere. Thus, since our thoughts and feelings are really "maggidic messages," we should listen, respond, and attune ourselves to these "Cosmic Forces." In this manner we will not only develop the ability to gain control over these influences in our lives, but will also be able to act as transformers and conductors of the *Ruchaniyut*, the "Spirit Forces," directing these into the world around us in accordance with our intentions. In this regard, the following exercise is extremely important in preparation to applying "Divine Energy" along the channels created by the *Tzelem ha-Nefesh*, as explained when we discussed *"Shadow Bodies"* and the creation of *"Conscious Psychic Bonds."*

Now, most schools of spiritual consciousness, state that we can only do what is in agreement with the "Will of God." However, they often define this "Higher Will" in terms of very human and repressive ethical systems. I agree we should act in accordance with "Divine Law," however I would prefer to have this revealed to me in a more direct manner, than hearing it from the mouth of say a clergyman acting on agendas which have more to do with controls pertaining to monetary benefits, rather than spirituality.

As long as we have existed on this planet, we have been under some or other celestial influence. The fact that we are angry, kind, passionate, intense, calm or meditative, is the result of spirit influences. Realising this, we might understand that when we feel happy, angry, or whatever, we have sort of "tuned in," as it were, into some "cosmic broadcast," which is at that moment disseminating a specific emotion through us. This knowledge has led to the understanding that "Spirit Intelligences," or "Conscious Cosmic Archetypes" named variously *Shemot* (Divine Names), "Archangels," "Angels," "Planetary Intelligences" and "Elemental Forces," exist throughout the whole of manifestation.

There is a further acknowledgement that, depending on our own ability and clarity as transformers of *Avir* or *Ruchaniyut*, we will be more or less sensitive to the influences of "Spirit Powers" on our lives. Different schools define these, as it were, "lesser gods" in different ways, but what is important is to realise that these Intelligences have a direct influence upon human behaviour. It is therefore very important to listen to your feelings and to respond appropriately, constantly cultivating a greater sensitivity to these "Inner Forces, since they are also *Maggidim*, "Messengers from the Eternal Living Spirit."

The following simple exercises were developed in order to become more attuned to these "Universal Forces," and to gain conscious control over your personal responses to these subtle influences.

Exercise 1

While sitting in your usual comfortable and surrendered manner, begin to consciously invoke various deep emotional states. You may use any method to help you to "tune in to the mood." In this regard you could bring up memories, i.e. images of past or recent events, to stir your *Nefesh* into an appropriate response. Here you need to work specifically with four emotions, these being linked to four planets and four *Sefirot* on the Tree of Life:

    Sadness—*Shabetai* [Saturn]—*Binah*
    Joy—*Tzedek* [Jupiter]—*Chesed*
    Anger—*Madim* [Mars]—*Gevurah*
    Love/Sexual Arousal—*Nogah* [Venus]—*Netzach*

Firstly invoke a most profound sadness, then switch to feeling exuberant happiness, next tune in to feeling tremendous anger, and finally switch in to feeling intense love, or experience strong sexual arousal. Continue working this technique, until you can easily switch from one emotion to another at will.

Exercise 2

Repeat the previous exercise during which you "Invoked" the "God-forces" linked to the four chosen *Sefirot* via their associated emotions, but this time acknowledge the "Cosmic Influence" behind each emotion, saying loudly or mentally: "Greetings *Maggid* sent from.....(fill in the name of the associated Sphere or the Planet)....." For example when you experience sadness, you would say "Greetings *Maggid* sent from *Binah* (or *Shabetai* [the Spirit of Sadness])," and so forth. Do the same with happiness, anger, love or sexual arousal.

    Practice with all four moods, and then try to work also with other emotions you can think of. Attempt to allocate each to its respective *Sefirah*, and record the associations in your "magical journal" for future use. Persistent practice of these procedures helps you establish dynamic psychic contacts with the different "god-forces," these being fundamental emotional states required to "fire up," as it were, related ritual activities. This basically means that if you wish to work a ritual with the Spheres and Forces of love, happiness, anger or sadness, i.e. if the fundamental intention of your ritual is linked to any of these, it is very important to have these God-forces as powerfully invoked emotions within yourself. Your mind will help you express in words the basic intention of your ritual work, but the appropriately related emotion will empower that ritual, i.e. engender its final outcome.

Exercise 3

The third part of the training requires an intensification of your acknowledging "God-Forces." Here you will commence communicating with the "God-forms" behind the "God-forces." Again the procedure requires the invocation of a particular mood, e.g. sadness, anger, joy or sexual arousal, which will once more create the link between you and the "Power" you wish to contact. Having established this contact through the invocation of the appropriate emotion, imagine yourself linked to a "Spirit Entity" via this "emotion channel," and mentally commence communication with it.

This skill is appropriately termed "Emotional Projection," since it is by means of these "Thought-forms of Feeling" that you are projecting your intentions into the "Inner Realms of Spirit." Through these psychological exercises you develop the ability to employ all aspects of your being, both physically and spiritually, in your magical activities. These are again empowered by the intensity and strength of the operation.

You should again keep a record of such communiques in your "magical diary."

Exercise 4

The final exercise in this set requires you to combine the practice of "magical invocation" or "acknowledgment of God-forces," with that of "magical evocation." Thus, when you are attuned to the "God-force," invoked inside yourself as an emotion in harmony with your intention, select an Element appropriate to your purpose, and emanate it through the connected vowel sound and a "spoken picture" of the appropriate colour. This, as you will recall, is done while exhaling via your mouth shaped in accordance with the "Elemental sound," e.g. *"EE," "AH," "OH"* or *"EH."*

If for example we want to pass anger along the subtle bonds connecting us with a person in need of this emotion, it will be much more powerful if we are aligned with the power of *Madim*, anger, in a conscious manner during the activity. Otherwise, the work is not as strong or as directed as it could and should be. Hence our encounters with these "God-forces" show that we are consciously and wilfully aware of what we are doing, that we are acknowledging these "Spirit Powers," and informing them of our feelings and how we wish to respond to their influences.

The purpose of these psychological exercises is to develop an awareness of the spiritual intensity of these operations. As a consequence, the practitioner is able to make use of every part of his or her being, in order to achieve the aimed for results behind personal psycho-spiritual magical work. You should therefore carefully practice these exercises, and always keep written record for future use.

4. PSYCHIC BONDS AND THE GOD–FORCES

Here is another exercise which can be done easily to intensify the psycho-spiritual field of operations as we understand it. Again you need to develop a particular mood, e.g. sadness, anger, happiness or sexual arousal. With this activity you create a strong psychic bond between yourself and the related "God-Force." Once you have established this connection by cultivating the right emotional state, commence visualising an anthropomorphised spirit entity at the "other end of the line," so to speak, and mentally commence communication with that "Spirit Entity." Having established contact with such an "Inner Entity," it is extremely easy to work this technique. Again, you simply align yourself with the "God-forces" by means of "thought-forms" supported by powerful emotions. In this manner you can converse with the "Planetary

Spirits," and not only acquire spiritual information from them, but also elicit their support in your psycho-magical ventures. In this regard it is again vitally important that you should write a report of results for future reference and use.

D. *Otiot:* Hebrew Letters as Archetypes

1. GATEWAYS TO HIGHER AWARENESS

In *Kabbalah* it is understood that when the letters of the Hebrew Alphabet, the *Otiot*, are spoken with a suitably associated godly stance or intention, the "spiritual forces" inherent in those letters are invoked and manifested. Every sign of the *Otiot* is dominated by a *Maggid*, a Celestial Messenger. These Messengers or Angels, are rays of *Aur Ain Sof* (the Light of Eternal No-Thing), radiations of the boundless beneficence and qualities emanating from the Divine One.

Since every Hebrew glyph is governed by a *Maggid*, the letters forming words, and the words shaping the sentences of invocations and prayers, combined with the intentions of the utterer of these words, powerfully invoke the "Spirit Intelligences" associated with the letters. Kabbalists understand that these are the very spirit forces underpinning the whole of manifestation, and hence they claim that this mundane creation comprises a combination of the *Otiot*, the Hebrew glyphs, in the shape of names and patterns. Besides their designations and configurations, the glyphs of the Hebrew Alphabet include "quantity" and "magnitude." A Kabbalist can use these letters and their combinations as if they were sublime fundamental "particles." The Kabbalist would penetrate the glyphs finding their principles, then use all the likely combinations and permutations of these glyphs, in order to move beyond the temporal.

The Hebrew letters are understood to be living "Intelligences" with bodies and souls. The written glyph and its verbal pronunciation, comprise the physical part of its manifestation, i.e. the body, whereas in its essence the sign belongs to the subtle realm of "Angelic Messengers." In this inner dimension it multiplies, so to speak, to create the manifested world of words, meanings and objects. In its primal state of emanation,

370 / The Shadow Tree: The Book of Self Creation

the Hebrew Alphabet is understood to represent the primordial vibrations of the cosmos in that space (*Makom*) where all are one.

By employing these glyphs in magic and meditation one attempts to reach as close an affinity with Divine Emanations as one possibly can. To do this we have to apply the three traditional methods of *mivta*—the articulation of the names and letters, *michtav*—writing them, and *mashav*—their contemplation. A further method that will be used is that of *Tzeruf* (Permutation). In the case of the latter method, we will focus specifically on the twelve permutations of the letters comprising the Ineffable Name, יהוה (*YHVH*). The twelve permutations correspond to the twelve months of the year, and generally to whatever the number twelve is related to. While we will shortly address these permutations specifically in the context of constructing a "Body of Light," *Tzerufim* (permutation techniques) can also be employed to build greater *Kavvanah*, i.e. to develop intense concentration skills.

However, let us focus our attention purely on the Hebrew glyphs, considered to be primal forces which combined primordially to manifest all "forms." In *Kabbalah* it is understood that "divine union" can be achieved through comprehension and usage of the *Otiot* in various combinations, pronunciations and meditations. Such activities will induce the "Spiritual Powers" understood to be inherent in these archetypal glyphs, to be directed and assimilated into your own being.

Now we will study some practical meditation techniques which will align you with the "forces" of the *Otiot*. Here is a set of large Hebrew glyphs, which you require to work the following exercises successfully:

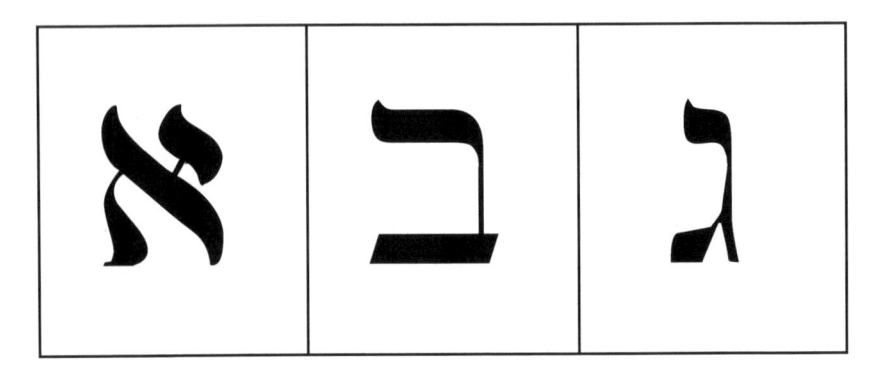

א	ב	ג

Maggidim: Spirit Messengers / 371

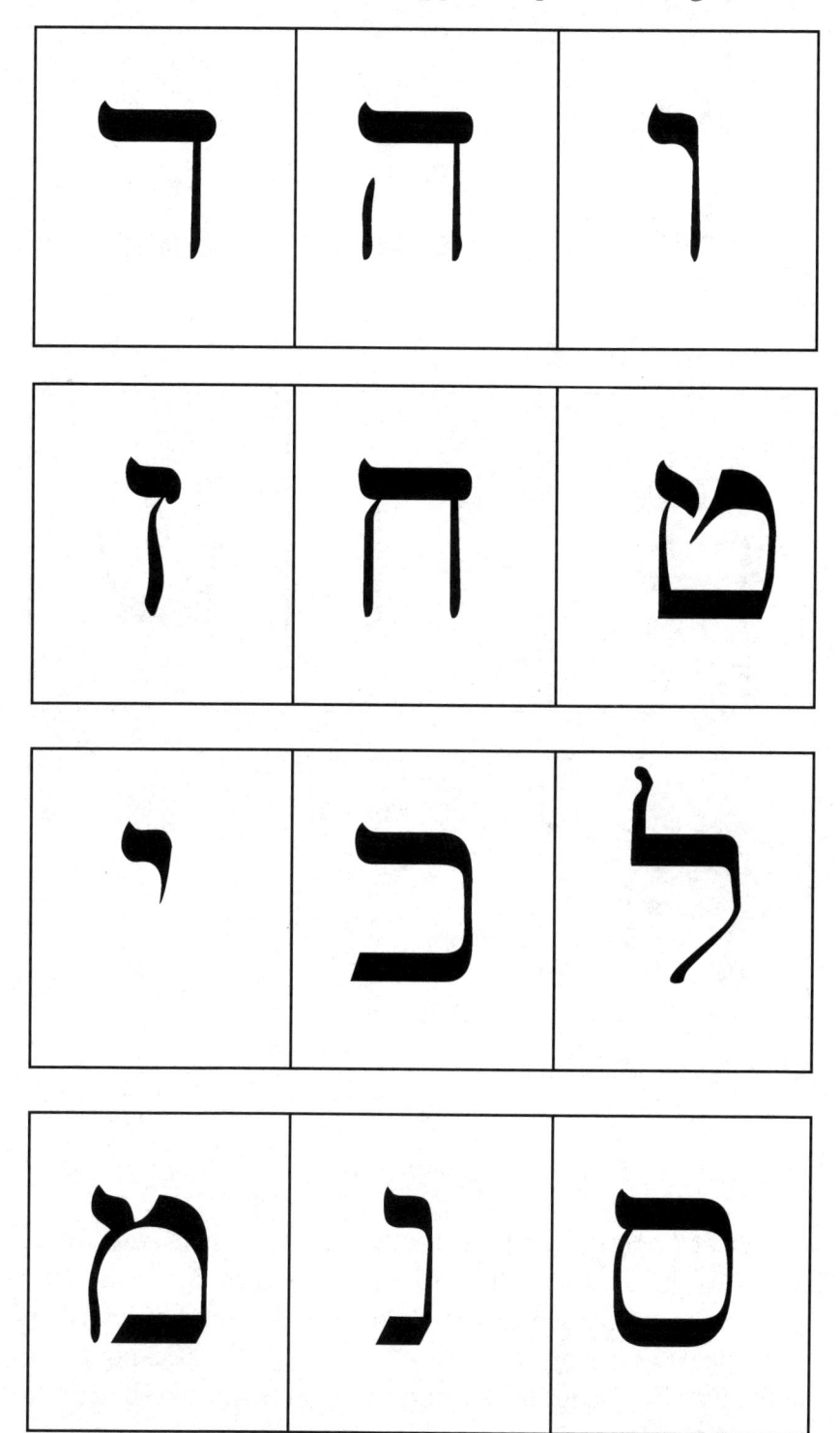

ד	ה	ו
ז	ח	ט
י	כ	ל
מ	נ	ס

ע	פ	צ
ק	ר	ש
ת		

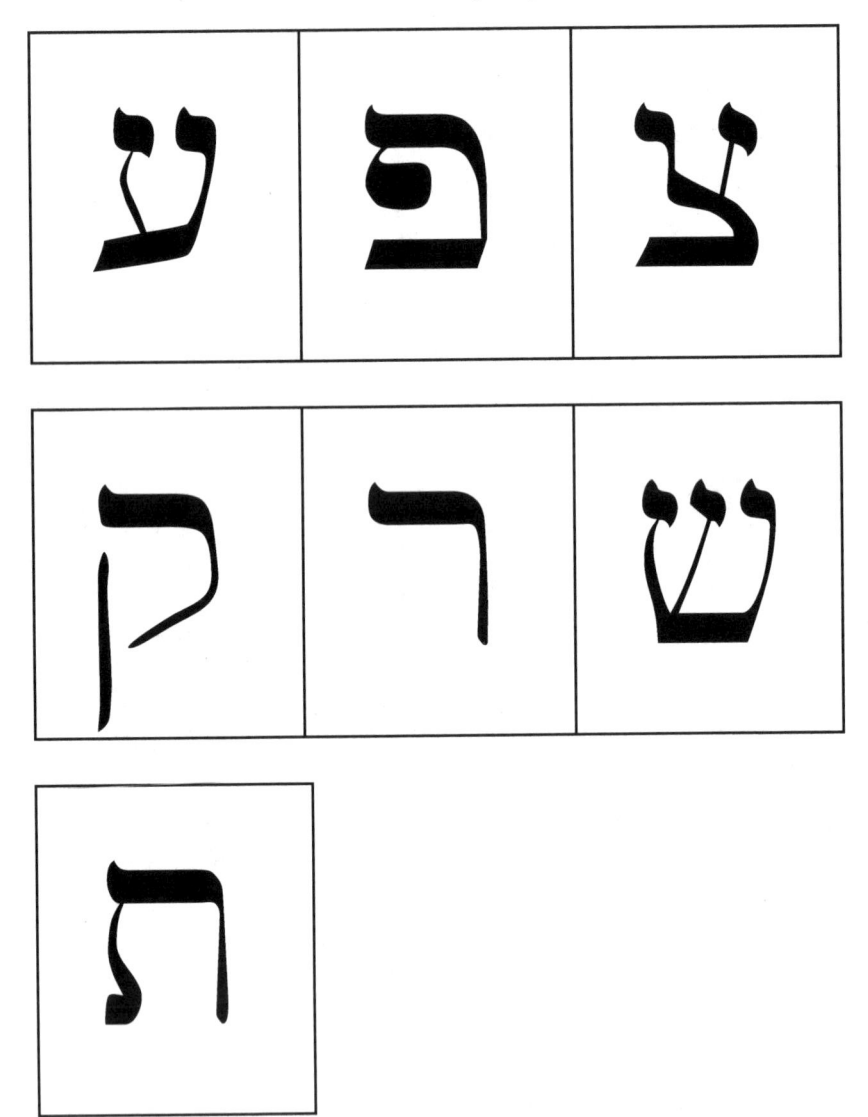

Exercise 1

The great Abraham Abulafia maintained "The letters are without question the root of all wisdom and knowledge, and they themselves are the substance of prophecy. In a prophetic vision, they appear as if they were solid bodies, actually speaking to the individual. They appear like pure living angels.....and sometimes the individual sees them as mountains."[13]

Maggidim: Spirit Messengers / 373

There are many practices involving visualising these Hebrew letters as "Black Fire on White Fire." Now, I am suggesting that you commence with a meditation procedure in which you envision the Hebrew glyphs as white flames against the black background of your mind. Later, when you have acquired some skill in this regard, you reverse the pattern, i.e. visualise the letters as black flames on a white background, the latter being the general way of imagining the letters in primary Kabbalistic literature.[14]

1. Copy three of the letter-signs from the set of enlarged *Otiot*, these being י (*Yod*), ה (*Heh*) and ו (*Vav*).
2. Sit in your usual comfortable and relaxed manner, and focus on one of these letters. Commence with the *Yod*. Look steadily at the letter for about one minute, or longer if necessary, then look up at a blank wall or the ceiling while saying aloud "*Yod*," and see the letter shining forth in the reversed colour to the one on paper.

    Now, despite the factual scientific rationale that the effect is purely due to a reflection on the retina, etc., Kabbalists understood that just as the light rays of the letters enter the eyes, so does the eye in turn reflect the opposite rays outwards. So, what you are doing in fact, is reflecting the letter received in this manner, towards whatever you choose to focus on. In this regard you should keep in mind that the letters are very powerful Archetypes and manifested "Spirit Forces," and everything depends on your intentions as to how you will direct these "Powers" in a meaningful manner.
3. Repeat the practice, but this time close your eyes and, if you wait without forcing or trying, you will see the letter shining forth quite strongly by itself.
4. Practice with the chosen three letters for about a week, or until you have mastered the skill of seeing them in the manner described, and invoking them with great clarity in your mind.

374 / The Shadow Tree: The Book of Self Creation

As you know, the Tetragrammaton comprises the chosen three letters, and these were selected because they are employed in a number of practical techniques addressed throughout this work, hence the necessity to acquire the ability to visualise them as clearly as you possibly can.

5. Repeat the procedure with all the glyphs of the Hebrew alphabet, seeing each one in the manner depicted while vocalizing their respective names, these being:

א—"*Alef*"; ב—"*Bet*"; ג— "*Gimel*;" ד—"*Dalet*"; ה— "*Heh*"; ו—"*Vav*"; ז—"*Zayin*" ; ח— "*Chet*"; ט—"*Tet*"; י—"*Yod*"; כ—"*Kaf*"; ל—"*Lamed*"; מ—"*Mem*"; נ—"*Nun*"; ס—"*Samech*"; ע—"*Ayin*"; פ—"*Peh*"; צ—"*Tzadi*"; ק—"*Kof*"; ר—"*Resh*"; ש—"*Shin*"; ת—"*Tav*."

Exercise 2

In this exercise you will align yourself with three sets of "Spirit Forces" which are most intimately related to the twenty-two glyphs of the *Otiot*.[15] These are:

איאל	אירון	איה
ביאל	בירון	ביה
גיאל	גירון	גיה
דיאל	דירון	דיה
היאל	הירון	היה
ויאל	וירון	ויה

Maggidim: Spirit Messengers / 375

זיאל	זירון	זיה
חיאל	חירון	חיה
טיאל	טירון	טיה
יאל	יירון	ייה
כיאל	כירון	כיה
ליאל	לירון	ליה
מיאל	מירון	מיה
ניאל	נירון	ניה
סיאל	סירון	סיה
עיאל	עירון	עיה
פיאל	פירון	פיה
ציאל	צירון	ציה
קיאל	קירון	קיה
ריאל	רירון	ריה
שיאל	שירון	שיה
תיאל	תירון	תיה

Ayah	Airon	Ayel
Biyah	Biron	Biyel
Giyah	Giron	Giyel
Diyah	Diron	Diyel
Hiyah	Hiron	Hiyel
Viyah	Viron	Viyel
Ziyah	Ziron	Ziyel
Chiyah	Chiron	Chiyel
Tiyah	Tiron	Tiyel
Yiyah	Yiron	Yiyel
Kiyah	Kiron	Kiyel
Liyah	Liron	Liyel
Miyah	Miron	Miyel
Niyah	Niron	Niyel
Siyah	Siron	Siyel
Aiyah	Airon	Aiyel
Piyah	Piron	Piyel
Tziyah	Tziron	Tziyel
Kiyah	Kiron	Kiyel
Riyah	Riron	Riyel
Shiyah	Shiron	Shiyel
Tiyah	Tiron	Tiyel

1. Prepare your meditation room by working the previously discussed *"Clearing the Sacred Space"* and *"Defining the Working Space."* On completion, sit down in your usual comfortable and surrendered manner.
2. Do the *"Mother Breath,"* *"Tuning the Body,"* and related "Spiritual Energy" practices which will bring you into a deep meditational state inside yourself.
3. When ready, follow the same procedure delineated in the previous exercise, however, instead of vocalizing the names of the letters, express the three "Names" associated with each letter. For example, look intently at the *Alef*, and you can bring yourself in close identification with the glyph by smiling at it with your entire being, i.e. body, mind, soul and spirit. Smile at the letter with your body. When ready, close your eyes, picture the glyph inside your mind, feel it powerfully present within you, and "speak to it" by resonating in as intense a manner as possible the three Names of the "Spirit Intelligences" you are linking with through the letter:

Ayah   Airon   Ayel

It is important to utter these Names slowly, and to actually feel the impact this has on you.

4. After you have worked through the entire Hebrew Alphabet in this manner, sit calmly with eyes closed for a few minutes, allowing yourself to return to normal focal levels. Then, make fists, open fists, take a deep breath and stretch.

Exercise 3

The following exercise will take you even closer to achieving the "Divine Alliance," which these procedures are meant to facilitate, and which are meant to prepare you for special sojourns into the "Celestial Palaces," or what was once termed the "Merkavistic Descent." This practice requires most careful preparation of your body, mind, soul and spirit. You should take a bath beforehand, and put on fresh clothing. Your "heart" and mind should equally be brought into a state in which you sense yourself aligned, surrendered, serene and centred, the kind of preparedness in which you will be able to invoke the "Divine Presence" in your being and into your life. Towards this end, you should select from amongst the techniques discussed in this book, those which you feel would best expedite the desired mind set. It should go without saying that this preparation of mind and soul should be worked inside your meditation room, and that only on conclusion of this should you prepare your "Sacred Space" in the same manner delineated in the previous exercise.

When ready, sit down and began to work the exact procedure delineated in the previous exercise. The only difference is that you will whisper the "Divine/Angelic Names" as intensely as you possibly can, instead of vocalizing them, and that you should pause with eyes closed between each "union," i.e. each contact with the archetype behind the Hebrew glyph, in order to sense the impact on your being of the "Spirit Intelligences" you are invoking. This should be done with a "feeling appreciation" rather than attempting to comprehend and analyse with your mind. Here is the set of unique "Divine/Angelic Names" used in this procedure:

אכתריאל	בכתריאל	גכתריאל	דכתריאל
הכתריאל	וכתריאל	זכתריאל	חכתריאל
טכתריאל	יכתריאל	בכתריאל	לכתריאל
מכתריאל	נכתריאל	סכתריאל	עכתריאל
פכתריאל	צכתריאל	קכתריאל	רכתריאל
שכתריאל	תכתריאל		

Achtri'el	Bachtri'el	Gachtri'el	Dachtri'el
Hachtri'el	Vachtri'el	Zachtri'el	Chachtri'el
Tachtri'el	Yachtri'el	Kachtri'el	Lachtri'el
Machtri'el	Nachtri'el	Sachtri'el	Achtri'el
Pachtri'el	Tzachtri'el	Kachtri'el	Rachtri'el
Shachtri'el	Tachtri'el		

It should be noted that the Divine Names employed here, invoke mighty "Angelic Forces," the most prominent of which is *Achtri'el*, the potent "Divine Name" of the mighty "Angel of Revelation." Traditions regarding this remarkable "Spirit Intelligence," who is said to be the "Crown of God," the embodiment of "Divine Glory," the archangel *Metatron*, and the "Voice" of the Almighty, go way back to the earliest Merkavistic teachings.[16]

E. *Shemot:* Words of Power

1. INTRODUCTION

It needs to be pointed out that for Kabbalists the strongest source of Divine Energy is the "Divine Name," and hence "Sacred Names" are very popular for their great power. It is said in *Kabbalah* that "a man's name is the essence of his being," and the "Name of God" represents, as it were, His "Person." In this regard we should be clear that all "Divine Names" refer to "Divine Aspects" and not the "Essence" of Divinity, which is altogether beyond any naming.

    The Names of God provide the Kabbalist with vast powers, and such notions stirred a lot of uneasiness and disapproval amongst the orthodoxy. Yet we should also note that Kabbalists were in the main very careful when it came to the utterance of Sacred Names, since it became clear to them that indiscriminate handling would inevitably impact most malevolently on the practitioner. Hence the constant warnings regarding proper training and preparation prior to employing any techniques involving the use of "God Names." Some of these Divine Names may not even be uttered aloud, but could be subtly "sounded" in the heart as a meditation, or strongly reflected mentally and emotionally during long, slow exhalations, because it is understood that "the Name of God creates and destroys worlds."[17]

Several such Sacred Names became the very basis of magical practice, and we will look at some of these. Many remarkable invocations were constructed on these Names for a variety of purposes. Here are a few examples of such highly specialized incantations.

2. SACRED CHANTS

a. The *Shema*

שמע ישראל אדני אלהינו אדני אחד

Shmah Yisra'el, Adonai Eloheinu, Adonai Echad.
Hear, O Israel, the Lord Our God, the Lord is One.[18]

Since this chant is one of the greatest statements of faith ever written, it calls for an explanation in terms of some of the Kabbalistic traditions associated with it. In expressing the Hebrew text here, I followed the traditional custom of writing *Torah* scrolls in which the letters *Ayin* (ע) in the word *Shmah* (hear) and *Dalet* (ד) in the word *Echad* (one), are written larger than the rest of the phrase. These letters form the word *Ed* (עד) meaning "witness." As far as the word *Yisra'el* is concerned, it has been said that it does not necessarily refer to the Jewish people per se. The *Zohar*, for example, states that it refers to God, since amongst the many Names of God is the Name *Isra'el* which the *Zohar* claims to mean "God is right." Hence it is claimed that the statement "*Shmah Yisra'el Adonai Eloheinu Adonai Echad*" is a direct address to God, basically saying "Listen you who is called God-Wrestler, *Adonai* is our God, *Adonai* is One." I was taught to energetically invoke the most intense love of the Divine One, expressed throughout my entire being, when I utter this statement.

A further development of this statement of faith, is the following chant of praise, which will work a greater love of the "Divine" and a most profound realisation of the Oneness of All:

אדני אלהינו   אדני אחד
אדני מלכינו   אדני אחד
אדני בוראנו   אדני אחד
אדני מגננו   אדני אחד
אדני דראנו   אדני אחד
אדני תהלנו   אדני אחד
אדני שמחנו   אדני אחד

Adonai Eloheinu   *Adonai Echad*
Adonai Malkeinu   *Adonai Echad*
Adonai Boreinu   *Adonai Echad*
Adonai Magenu   *Adonai Echad*
Adonai Ro'einu   *Adonai Echad*
Adonai Te'hileinu   *Adonai Echad*
Adonai Simcheinu   *Adonai Echad*
The Lord our God   The Lord is One
The Lord our King   The Lord is One
The Lord our Creator The Lord is One
The Lord our Shield   The Lord is One
The Lord our Watcher The Lord is One
The Lord our Praise   The Lord is One
The Lord our Joy   The Lord is One

b. A Divine Blessing

ברוך אתה אדני אלהינו מלך העולם אשר קדשנו במצותו
Baruch Atah Adonai Eloheinu Melech ha-Olam Asher Kid'shanu b'Mitzvotav.
Blessed are You *Adonai*, our God, King of the Universe, Who consecrated us to do good deeds.

It is our responsibility to become receptacles for *Shefa* (שפע), the sacred influx of Divine Abundance, which means to literally channel this "Divine Flow" into mundane existence. This is done through service, which is the assistance towards well-being we give to our world and everything within it. It is said that in assisting another individual, the "Divine Channels," allowing the flow of Divine Abundance and goodness into this world, are restored.

In Jewish mysticism this is considered to be the duty of every Jew, but as far as I am concerned, this is the duty of every person in existence. We are told that it is *Malchut*, the Kingdom of our mundane existence, which receives the *Shefa* as it pours from *Ain Sof* (the Eternal No-Thing) into, and through, all the *Sefirot* (Spheres upon the Tree of Life). The "Universal Abundance" is directed via the Divine Name *Adonai* (אדני), into the realm of physical manifestation, thus, every time you attempt to make the world a better place for anyone or anything, you need to bow mentally and express, either aloud or silently in your mind, the blessing "*Baruch Atah Adonai, Eloheinu, Melech ha-Olam, Asher Kid'shanu b'Mitzvotav.*" This statement is a formal recognition of and a conscious link to the "Divine Abundance," understanding the injunction "Close is *Adonai* to all who call upon Him, to all who call upon Him in truth" (*Psalm 145:18*). Of course the blessing can be simplified to "*Baruch Atah Adonai*" (ברוך אתה אדני— Blessed are You *Adonai*).

The prayer in itself is in fact a magical invocation. Firstly, the language is Divine and links those who utter it to the powerful forces, the Divine Hosts, residing in the subtle "Realms of Being" behind the words. Secondly, during the invocation you surrender to the these Divine Forces, and let your entire being, that is body, mind, soul and spirit, act in unity as a conduit allowing these Spirit Forces to flow into manifestation. In other words, you once again "make the words flesh."

Looking at and understanding what this blessing is all about is immensely rewarding in terms of expanding ones consciousness. The noun of the verb *Baruch* (ברוך—blessed) is *Brachah* (ברכה—Blessing), which is synonymous with *Breichah* (ברכה—a pool, pond or lake) the source of *Shefa*, the Divine Influx. Every time you say the *Brachah* you are linked to the *Breichah*, and then you can be the channel directing the flow to all of creation, if you so will. The Biblical *Abraham* was said to be the first person to receive this *Brachah*, which tied him to the Divine Source, the *Breichah*. He passed this on to his son *Isaac*, whose children *Jacob* and *Esau* battled over it. Eventually *Jacob* successfully claimed it, and the knowledge of the power of this *Brachah* was passed on to his twelve sons.[19]

The third word of the Blessing, the Divine Name *Adonai* (אדני), is an extremely powerful God Force, since it contains and directs the powerful forces flowing from the *Breichah*. the divine reservoir of abundance within the Being of the Most High. In fact, uttering the Name *Adonai*, instantly links you to this Infinite Source. *Kabbalah* explains that the Source and its outpouring of Divine Abundance is referred to in *Genesis 2:10* — "A river issues from Eden to water the garden, and then it divides and becomes four branches." It also states that the four divisions refer to the *Shechinah*, the "Countenance of God," or Female aspect of the Divine here in manifestation.[20] We know that this verse also refers to *Malchut*, the Kingdom of this World, with its fourfold cycles (elements, seasons, lunar rhythms, etc.). In fact, anthropomorphic, or physical, representations of the sphere of *Malchut* on the Tree of Life, often show the *Shechinah* as *Malkah* (the "Divine Queen" of the Earthly Kingdom) seated on a cubic throne.[21]

This stone is extremely significant since a cognomen for the Name *Adonai* is the word *Even* (אבן—stone).[22] *Adonai* is the foundation of everything in this realm of three-dimensional existence, and since all existence is fully dependent on *Adonai*, this Divine Name is also called *Kol* (כל—All), the Whole in which there is no lack. It is thus written in *Isaiah 44:24* "I am the Lord, who made *Kol* who alone stretched out the heavens." Here we are brought once again to the earlier mentioned *Breichah*, the pool of Infinite Abundance, also called *Yam* (ים—sea).[23] This is referred to Biblically in *Psalm 104:25* "There is a sea, vast and wide, with its creatures beyond number, living small and great."

Of course this vast "Sea of Abundance" not only refers to physical manifestation, but also to mind, soul and spirit. Therefore it is also called *Yam ha-Chochmah* (ים החכמה—the Sea of Wisdom), because all knowledge, on all levels of manifestation, is within it. Once again it was said that this was given to *Abraham*, as it is written "And *YHVH*, blessed Abraham with *Kol*" (*Genesis*

24:1). As indicated, he in turn passed it on as a birthright to *Isaac*, who in turn bequeathed it to *Jacob*, who said "For God has favoured me and I have *Kol*" (*Genesis 33:11*).

To return to *Even*, the cubic stone of *Malchut*, which is understood to be the foundation of all existence. *Zechariah 4:7* calls it *Even Rishonah* (first stone) and *Psalm 118:22* refers to it as *Rosh Pinah* (chief cornerstone), saying "The *Even* that the builders rejected has become the chief cornerstone." This verse is an important part of Masonic studies in both the "Mark" and "Royal Arch" degrees of Freemasonry, and has many hidden meanings. The *Shechinah* as the *Panim* (פנים—face, countenance or presence) of *Adonai*, is in fact the *Rosh Pinah* to whom all existence must turn (*Ponim*).[24]

Everything said so far, refers of course to *Malchut* on the Tree of Life, represented on earth as the *Bet ha-Mikdash* (בית המיקדש—the Temple), said to be another cognomen of *Adonai*. We should understand the Temple to be the place where *Adonai* dwells, as it is written, "I will give my dwelling place to be among you" (*Exodus 26:11*). It is in the actual Sanctuary (*Mikdash*—מקדש) where the *Shechinah* resides, as it is written "and let them make Me a sanctuary *v'Shachanti* (that I may dwell) among them" (*Exodus 25:8*). Again this refers to the sphere of *Malchut*, and specifically to the Sanctuary and Ark in our Temple, where the Divine Dweller (*Shechinah*) may rest on the altar, the latter itself comprising a double ashlar of two *Avanim* (cubic stones).[25]

The realm of physical existence, is in fact the place of the *Shechinah*, as is written in *Isaiah 66:1* "And the earth is my footstool," but the fact that the *Shechinah* dwells among us, and as our highest Selves (*Neshamot*), does not mean that we are always open to *Shefah*. The *Shechinah* is not the Divine Abundance, but the container receiving the flow as it is channelled from the higher Spheres on the Tree of Life, which is in turn poured into the Kingdom of physical manifestation. Here a major problem is encountered. Sometimes the *Shechinah* receives this flow, and then She is called *Mikveh ha-Mayim* (pool of water), but there can be periods when the *Shechinah* does not receive the abundance, and then She is called *Yabashah* (dry land). Naturally creation suffers when this happens. Why should the Divine Abundance "dry up" so to speak?[26]

From a Divine Perspective the *Shefa* is always there, undifferentiated in the Eternal Now, but the "Abundance" flowing into creation, can be restrained when *ha-Tzinorot* (הצנורות—the Divine channels leading into manifestation) are blocked. This is said to happen when creation moves into states of separation from the Oneness of the Whole, when we no longer recognise ourselves as part of the Selfsameness of One Being, אהיה (I Am, the Oneness of Being). It is extremely important to realise that the Oneness is never separate from us. It is we who separate ourselves, and thus it is also we who are responsible for repairing the *Tzinorot*, the Divine Channels, by recognising and returning to the Oneness of Being. It is equally important to realise that any recognition of duality in any form is a separation from that Being in Whom all are one.

Kabbalah recognises only one God. Yet this Oneness may be revealed in a multitude of aspects. Still It is One and there is no other. We may see life as the diversification of the One into the many, but *Kol* (all) are unified in the One. This is what is meant by that great statement of faith "*Shmah Israel, Adonai Eloheinu, Adonai Echad*" (Hear Israel, *Adonai* our God, *Adonai* is One). There is not "God" and the "Devil," there is only "God." It is therefore written in *Isaiah 44:24* "I am the Lord, who made *Kol*, who alone stretched out the heavens."

3. MERKAVISTIC & KABBALISTIC MANTRIC MEDITATION

Now, I should mention that the word "*Hagah*" does not translate "mantra" exactly. In fact, the Hebrew term is actually not a noun or a name, but a verb referring, amongst other meanings, to the act of repetitively speaking, chanting, or whispering a Hebrew word or sentence. Aryeh Kaplan explained this saying "What is immediately suggested here is a system very much like mantra meditation, where a word or phrase is repeated many times, either verbally or mentally. This is not too far-fetched, since in the system of the *Hechalot*, one of the most ancient mystical texts, we find that an initiate enters into the mystical realm by repeating a certain formula 112 times.....This would indicate that the term

Hagah refers to a process that brings the mind to a state where it is devoid of all activity. The mind thus reaches a level where it is devoid of everything other than pure, simple, elemental existence.....From all this, it appears that the word *Hagah* has the primary connotation of 'Directed Existence.' The individual quiets his mind to a state of pure existence, while at the same time directing it toward a single goal. The methods of *Hagah*–meditation involve the repetition of sounds, words, phrases or melodies, and it is therefore closely related to the various forms of mantra meditation."[27]

Of course, *Hagah*–meditation does not necessarily involve specially constructed sentences or incantations, such as the ones I have shared, but can be a simple phrase from the Bible or other sacred writ, or even the utterance of a Divine Name over and over. Joseph Karo used phrases from the *Mishnah* as mantras in order to establish contact with his *Maggid*.[28] We are told that Nachman of Bratzlav used the phrase *Ribono shel Olam* (Master of the Universe) in order to expand and raise his consciousness to higher levels, prior to conversing with God.[29] Again Aryeh Kaplan describes this technique in absolute detail in his meditation handbook titled *"Jewish Meditation: A Practical Guide."*[30]

Now, the following two meditations are meant to be worked conjointly. Each is a *Hagah* related to a specific *Sefirah* on the Tree of Life. The first titled *"Adir*: The Mighty One," is employed to express and invoke the Sphere of Severity (*Gevurah*) on the Tree of Life. *Adir* is a "Divine Name" referring to the attribute of God's Judgment. The second is worked to express and invoke the Sphere of Mercy (*Chesed*) on the Tree of Life. *Ahavah* is a "Divine Name" referring to the attribute of God's Love. The words comprising the two mantras are actually standard phrases from prayers in the *Siddur* (Hebrew prayer book).[31]

Kabbalistic teaching has it that the utterance of a single Hebrew word is like opening a gateway through which spiritual forces are directed in a specific manner, the quality of the force flow being determined by the associated *Sefirah* which the uttered word triggers into action, so to speak. In the last part of Cordovero's *"Or Ne'erav,"* we are offered a special list of Hebrew terms associated with the ten *Sefirot*.[32] It takes quite a bit of contemplation to understand why a specific appellation is connected to a specific *Sefirah*, and so forth. Moses Cordovero also addressed this in section 23 of his mammoth "*Pardes Rimmonim*" (Garden of Pomegranates).[33]

Here are examples from Cordovero's word-list which ties in with the two "mantras" we are addressing here:

> *Adir* (Mighty) — *Binah* and *Gevurah*.
> *Hu* (He) — In *Keter* or in *Binah* or in *Tiferet* or in *Malchut*.
>
> *Ahavah* (Love) — It begins from *Gevurah* and ends in *Chesed*. It is *Malchut*.
> *Olam* (World) — *Tiferet, Binah, Malchut*.[34]

There is a curious reasoning behind this method of using Hebrew words and phrases to open "gates of power," which is not clearly explained anywhere that I know of. It was carefully expounded by my first *Kabbalah* teacher, who viewed the techniques of "Practical *Kabbalah*" with a certain degree of disapproval, and discussed this specific technique with some reluctance. To simplify matters, the technique is based on the understanding that every *Sefirah* comprises all the others. Thus one would have *Malchut* in *Malchut*; *Yesod* in *Malchut*; *Hod* in *Malchut*; etc., or to phrase it somewhat differently, there is an entire Tree of Life comprising ten *Sefirot* in each *Sefirah*. Hence we find in the mentioned dictionary descriptions like:

> *Av ha-Rachaman* (Father of Mercy) — *Tiferet* from the side of *Keter*;
> *Emunah* (Faith) — *Binah* from the side of *Chesed*; *Malchut* from the side of *Yesod*.[35]

Consider for example the *Hagah* associated with *Gevurah*. The word "*Adir*," which is consistently reiterated in each phrase, is said to "open the gates" of *Gevurah* or *Binah*, in accordance with the *Kavvanah*, the focussed attention of the user. The next term "*Hu*" will direct the flow through *Keter, Binah, Tiferet* and *Malchut* in *Gevurah*, and so forth.

Here are the two special invocations:

a. *Adir*: The Mighty One

אדיר
אדיר הו
אדיר במרום
אדיר במלוכה

Adir
Adir Hu
Adir Bamarom
Adir Bimelucha
The Mighty One,
Mighty is He,
Mighty One on High,
Mighty in Kingship.

b. *Ahavat Olam*: Abounding Love

אהבה אהבה
אהבה רבה
אהבה אהבה
אהבת עולם

Ahavah Ahavah
Ahavah Rabah
Ahavah Ahavah
Ahavat Olam
Love, Love,
Abounding Love.
Love, Love,
Eternal (or Universal) Love.

c. *Hagah* in Preparation for the Merkavistic Descent[36]

The following Divine Names are traditionally pronounced one hundred and twelve times:

טוטרסיאי צורטק טוטרביאל
טפגר אשרויליאי זבודיאל
זהרדיאל טנדאל שוקד
יוזיא דהיבורין אדידירון
יהוה אלהי שראל

Tutrusiai Tzortak Totarvi'el
Tofgar Ashruliai Zvudi'el
Zoharari'el Tandi'el Shoked
Yoziah Dahivurin Adidiron
YHVH Elohei Yisra'el

There is no translation for these mysterious Names.

e. Hymn for the Descent to the *Merkavah*[37]

תהלת שבח וראשית שירה
תהלת גילה וראשית רנה
משוררים השרים המשרתים
בכל יום ליהוה אלהי ישראל
לכסא כבודו הם מנשאים
גיל גיל כסא כבוד
רנן רנן מושב עליון
הריע הריע כלי חמדן
שנעשה בהפלא ופלא
שמח תשמח מלך שעליך
כשמחת חתן בבית חפתו

T'chilat shevach v'reishit shirah
T'chilat gilah v'reishit rinah
M'shorim hasarim ham'shartim
B'chol yom l'YHVH Elohei Yisrael
L'chisei ch'vodoh hem m'nasim
Gil gil kisei kavod
Ranein ranein moshav-Elyon
Hari'a hari'a k'li-chemdah
Shena-asah b'haflei vafeleh
Sameach t'samach melech she'aleiach
K'simchat chatan b'veit chupato

The beginning of praise and the start of song
The beginning of joy and the start of jubilation
These are sung by the Princes (the Holy Living Creatures)
Who daily serve *YHVH*, God of Israel
They exalt His Throne of Glory
Rejoice, rejoice, Throne of Glory
Sing, Sing for joy, Seat of the Most High
Exult, exult, oh Precious vessel
So marvellously fashioned
You will gladden the King upon You
As a bridegroom is gladdened in his bridal chamber

4. PRAISING THE ONE

With this procedure one is said to align oneself with the actions of the "Celestial Hosts" chanting the *Trisagion*

קדוש קדוש קדוש אדני צבאות

Kadosh Kadosh Kadosh Adonai Tzva'ot

in the Presence of the Almighty, as depicted in *Isaiah 6:2-3*. The technique is referred to in the "*Mishnah Berurah*."[38]

Stand with your feet fairly close together. Imagine you are in the Presence of the Almighty, standing as it were in front of the *Merkavah*, the Chariot Throne. Now utter the sequence *Kadosh Kadosh Kadosh Adonai Tzva'ot*. Swing forwards and backwards during each cycle in the following manner: On the first *Kadosh* start to swing forward, on the second rise a little on your toes, on the third rise a little higher, leaning slightly forward, then, on *Adonai Tzva'ot*, sway backwards settling again onto your heals. Repeat the procedure one hundred times, or as many times as you can manage in as smoothly a manner as you possibly can. In this way it is said the "Lower" and "Upper" dimensions, the microcosm and the macrocosm, are united in the thought and action of the practitioner.

5. FORMULAS FOR CIRCUMAMBULATION

a. *Hakafot*[39]

We will conclude this section on "Words of Power" with a look at *Hakafot* (הכפות). This refers to the circular ritual processions in the Jewish *Hoshanah* and *Simchat Torah* services, claimed to be a manifestation of God's holiness. It is customary, during the latter service, to do *Hakafot* with the *Torah* scrolls, and we are told that such "circlings have the power to elicit heightened spiritual states."[40]

It is certainly well established that *Hakafot* have great mystical powers, especially if the circling is sevenfold, which Kabbalists claim corresponds to the seven *Sefirot* from *Binah* to *Yesod*, seven planets, and the "Seven Days of Creation." Here we might recall the well-known custom of Jewish brides circling their husbands seven times during the Jewish wedding ceremony. This action is believed to tie the bride to the groom to whom she is declaring her undying love. In a similar manner, the *Hakafot* during *Simchat Torah* is tying the "Shechinah," the "Divine Bride," to the "Divine Groom," the Eternal One. Since the *Neshamah* in us, the "Higher Self," is the *Shechinah* inside us, the seven circuits we tread in this sacred ritual are equally part of the process of the "Cosmic Bride" declaring "her" undying love for the Almighty.

It is also said that the custom of circling the groom seven times, derived from ancient ritualistic customs during which brides were seeking "Divine Protection" of the groom against demonic adversaries. We might also note, that in times of great tribulation, when entire communities are sorely afflicted, it is still customary to arrange special *Hakafot* as part of the prayers to the "Divine Ruler" for mercy and the nullification of the punishing decree. This is related somewhat to the biblical saga of the siege of Jericho, then a Canaanite bastion, during which the Israelite warriors circled the city walls while priests sounded ram's horns. Following one *Hakafah* (הכפה) for six days, and seven *Hakafot* on the Sabbath, the walls of Jericho collapsed before the Children of Israel (*Joshua 6:1-20*).

Since *Hakafot* have the power to tear down all the barriers between ourselves and the Eternal Living Spirit, you might consider uttering the following "power–prayer" continuously while circling a centralised "Sacred Symbol" seven times. You should sense yourself becoming increasingly more "empowered" with "Divine Force" as you complete each circuit.

חזק חזק ונתחזק
Chazak Chazak v'Nitchazek
Be strong! Be strong! and make ourselves strong!

b. Walking Meditation for Personal Aid

Our final procedure in this chapter pertains to using a *Hakafah* for personal aid. In this regard I should mention that several methods were and are still being used in Practical Kabbalah to assist the "magical satisfaction" of personal needs, amongst which the most popular are perhaps *Kameot* (amulets or talismans). However, it occurs to me that before I share this ritual activity, I should raise an important factor which could successfully work any "magic" you seek, or at least "prepare the ground" in which the planted "magical seeds" may flourish and grow to satisfactory fruition. What I mean to say is that each person is actually creating his or her own reality, and whether conscious of it or not, is magically doing this every moment of his or her life. This is what the title of this book is all about, and what I have attempted to address throughout this work. Such constant "self-creation" may not be a comfortable thought, or an easy one to accept, but I can assure you that it is absolutely true. What is more, whatever you align yourself with, i.e. through constant affirmation, will impact on you for good or ill, especially when you act on it.

Through careful observation of what has happened to me throughout my life, I have been brought to understand with absolute clarity that you get whatever you affirm as part of your personal reality. I have been told that I live in a "fool's paradise." My response is, that I have lived successfully in my "fool's paradise" for sixty years, so leave me to live out the next sixty in the same way in my self-created reality. And that's that! I refuse

Maggidim: Spirit Messengers / 393

to buy into any reality which I do not want in my life. So, how does this pertain to you? Simply, your life is nothing more than an attitude. The rest, success, money, health, etc., are all additional, all aligned with you in harmony with your life stance. It is as simple as that. You say "I am poor" and .....you *are* poor. You say "I am rich" and.....you *are* rich. You say "I am strong" and.....you *are* strong, etc.

Amongst the many ritual practices associated with "acquiring riches magically," I found this interesting one titled "Walking for Personal Aid." The grammar may appear a bit odd, but the incantation was passed on to me in following format:

גידול שפע שלי (של or .....)
חוזק שפע שלי (של or .....)
גבר שפע שלי (של or .....)
חיבה שפע שלי (של or .....)

Gidul, Shefa, Sheli (or *Shel*....name of a recipient)
Chozek, Shefa, Sheli (or *Shel*....name)
Gibur, Shefa Sheli (or *Shel*....name)
Chiba, Shefa, Sheli (or *Shel*....name)
Growth, Abundance belonging to me (or belonging to.....)
Strength, Abundance belonging to me (or belonging to.....)
Power, Abundance belonging to me (or belonging to.....)
Love, Abundance belonging to me (or belonging to.....)

According to the instructions accompanying this curious "incantation," you have to dress in your very best clothes, go to a public market place, i.e. a shopping centre, adopt a stance of affluence, smile, walk with your head held high and utter the incantation, one word with each step, repeating it over and over. When you believe you have done enough, you have to spend whatever money you have in your pocket without consideration of whether you can afford to do so or not, and then to return home and from that moment forth to act throughout the remainder of your life as a rich man, and never to admit poverty ever again. The vital factor behind the success of this curious ritual appears to be ones attitude, which again basically means that the reality you act on is the reality you will get. Life always arranges itself around you in harmony with your stance at any moment.

The vital factor behind the success of workings of this nature is always yourself. There is no separation between the experiencer and the experience. There is no separation between you and what you are looking for, no separation between you and the great abundance which is around and within everything. A very small part of the "real you" is incarnated in the flesh, the rest is everywhere, and you constantly control your life with your body, mind, soul and spirit, whether you are doing so consciously or not. You are like a cup submerged in the ocean. The cup is your body, and you may think the water inside the cup is actually you. This is purely an illusion. You are everything, that which is in the cup, that which is outside the cup, and even the cup itself. You are both nothing and everything, and there is enormous power in this realisation.

. ...all of them in accordance to the nature of the creatures which receive His effluence."

Chapter 10
ASCENDING IN LIGHT

A. Introduction

It is most important to realise that we are not isolated islands, that we are living in this world, and that the great work is the process of trying to make this world a better place for all life on this planet. To do this, one has to establish oneself as a partner of Divinity. Of course, we should first realise that the world *can* be made a better place, even if it might take considerable effort over a long period of time to bring this about. We should clearly understand that each one of us is the *Messiah*, so to speak, since everyone has the responsibility to act as the "saviour" of him or herself and his or her world.

All of us have to work towards *Tikkun*, the restoration of ourselves and our world, and this is more important than the concept of the *Messiah* as a literal political figure who will alter everything for the better instantly. It has been said that "If you should happen to be holding a sapling in your hand when they tell you the Messiah has arrived, first plant the sapling, then go out to greet the Messiah."[1] Each person, not religious groups and teachers, has the responsibility to improve and better this world for all existing in it, and one should constantly remind oneself of this important task. That is in fact the real secret. We need to remind ourselves that we cannot be completely happy while the world around us is suffering, since however beautiful our "worldly home" is, we are not "*at* home" because this home is unsatisfactory.

I know that you will say "but is everything not as it should be, is it not right and perfect in itself?" Maybe so, but Kabbalism tells an interesting tale. In fact, we addressed this story in the early chapters of this book. It is the story of how God emanated light and formed vessels to contain it, but that these vessels were unable to hold the Light and shattered. Afterwards, the world of material manifestation was structured from the mixture of shards and the light. The vessels shattered because the "Unbounded Infinite" could not be contained by the finite, and hence there was a fault in the manifested realm, as a result of being disarranged and having malfunctioned. Yet, the process of *Tikkun* (restoration) can be initiated when we are able to increase *Ruchaniyut*, Spiritual Energy, in our world through what is called "mindfulness." If I am mindful of any particular thing, the divine spark within that thing is elevated.

Again "mindfulness" is not the responsibility of leaders or selected groups, but of each individual living here. There cannot be any "Divine Fullness of Being" while the world is a disturbed place. The concept of *Tikkun* (restoration) revolves around "We have to return! We have to return! We have to return!" In every aspect of human life, there should be something telling us "We have to return! We have to return!" This is the true *Aliyah*. The "return," not to some physical homeland, but the "ascent" of the Divine incarnated in manifestation, returning to its original status of wholeness and well-being.

We need the sacred act of being reminded of our holy obligation, so that our painful exile in the realm of manifestation could turn into a wellspring of hope and strength. Each one of us must realise that not only the improvement of our human condition is a valid activity and religious responsibility, but that the improvement of all life is equally valid and important. We have to reaffirm life, and accept the responsibility of correcting the imbalances we encounter everywhere. If we prepare properly, whether it takes ten years or ten thousand years, we will be able to fulfil this obligation. Naturally, it means that we have to get away from mainstream ideas about a single political or religious leader guiding all, i.e. this individual will be doing all the work, while everybody else must simply follow like sheep.

We have to recognise "spiritual democracy," so to speak. The burden of responsibility to restore "divine balance" belongs to everyone. What is more, the issue must never be enforced. The betterment of this outer kingdom must be achieved in a peaceful manner. What is important is *Kavvanah*, which we noted refers to focussed intention, attitude, motivation, and goals. Naturally, when we have to make decisions, it is difficult to predict the final outcome. Only after things have happened, can we know whether results were produced satisfactorily. Who can really know in advance the outcome of a violent act? We need to know how to deal with our conflicts, both individually and globally, in an imaginative and non-aggressive manner.

We must further understand that it would be wrong to force our ideas on our fellow human kind, despite the fact that we believe each individual has the responsibility to work towards the great "restoration." We should never use proselytising methods to attempt an enforcement of what we believe in, since that would negate the very process of lifting the divine sparks, which cannot be forcefully redirected into their Sacred Source. There can be no justification for violence, whether such be physical, mental, emotional or spiritual. It appears to me that all we can do is to make the Divine Presence so strong in our lives, that it goes beyond our human natures altogether. Hence, by bringing "God Forces" into our lives, we intentionally and mindfully direct these into the world at large.

We will now turn our attention to the "drawing down" of *Shefa*, the sacred influx of Divine Power. In this regard I was handed a typewritten document comprising a set of unique exercises some years ago, of which I have incorporated specifically three in my personal spiritual activities. There was no indication of authorship in the document, which I suspected was of Kabbalistic derivation. Acting on this assumption, I shared some of the listed procedures on a public Kabbalah forum. I was then informed that the procedures appear to comprise modified versions of material penned by a certain Olive Charlotte Blythe Pixley, a remarkably insightful individual who had died in 1962. In fact, the mentioned exercises turned out to be not directly associated with Kabbalah at all, but pertained to what Olive Pixley termed "Christian Initiation" within an "Armour of Light."[2] It was absolutely clear that the set of exercises I held in my hands, were modifications aligned with Kabbalistic teachings. Be that as it may, the three exercises which I have found so useful, are excellent for bringing one into alignment with the "Light" of the "Eternal Living Spirit" (*Or Ain Sof*).

Now, the process of, "drawing down" (*hamshachah*) Divine Power pertains to God, the Higher Self (*Neshamah*) and you as a combination of instinct and reason (*Nefesh/Ru'ach*). Most practitioners using techniques involving the "Higher Self," will be familiar with this "Divine Self" being visualised beyond and above the body. Therefore, since the idea of contact with a "higher" entity is always "upwards," the following procedure may appear somewhat peculiar, since it requires you to contact your "Divine Self" via your feet, i.e. linking with a "Shining Being of Light" in the same manner as your own shadow is linked to you. Clearly then, the first exercise in these "Procedures of Light," incorporates you, the "Real Self" (*Ru'ach*), aligning with your "Divine Source," an "Infinite Point of Radiance" overhead, and communication with a brilliant "Being of Light" below your feet.

In executing this procedure, the major tools required are thinking, feeling and good breathing skills. You will visualise Light, breathe Light and direct Light. Of the three, I believe a great visualisation ability to be of least significance. As is the case with all the procedures addressed in this book, it is not as important to actually *see* the "Light," as much as it is to *feel* it intensely, and to sense its powerful impact on your entire being. Rather than rattling the "Light" around your cranium as a mental construct, it is vital to sense the Light as real "Divine Power." To realise this in a practical manner, let us attempt "Unification with the Higher Self," a procedure which is worked prior to all the related "Procedures of Light." Again, this must not be a purely mental working, but a most profound procedure which will include your *Nefesh*, your instinctual self, as well as your body. The aim is to sharpen your spiritual faculties to such an extent, that they are empowered to have instant intercourse with Divine Power.

B. The Procedures of Light

1. UNIFICATION WITH THE HIGHER SELF

1. On going to sleep at night and first thing on waking in the morning, work the following procedure. Remain relaxed and surrendered inside your body, and turn the palms of your hands to face upwards. Identify with Peace by surrendering to the feeling of what Peace represents. Utter the following "Words of Power" several times, sensing their meaning and how they impact on you:

Ateret Shalom v' Emet
Abundance of Peace and Truth

2. Repeat the word *Shalom*, "Peace," over and over, each time attempting to experience the "feeling" of the word, and then surrendering deeply in order to allow it to permeate your entire being. This is part of the "Art of Invocation," or calling up of inner responses to deliberately selected physical or mental stimuli.

3. Next, think of a "Shining Being of Light" at your feet, with the soles of Its feet placed against your own. You will communicate with It, by directing into and drawing "Divine Force" from It via your feet. You are in fact Its "Shadow," and once you have established a link with this anthropomorphised, visualised manifestation of your "Spiritual Self," it will become a support and "Guiding Force" throughout your daily life.

4. Having established this special connection with the "Shining Being of Light, turn your attention to your forehead or the top of your head, and sense once again the *Tzinor*, the "Channel of Light" linking you with the Source, your "Infinite Point of 'Is'–ness," diagonally above and in front of you. Again you have to feel this "Line of Light" stretching between you and your "Infinite Point of Radiance" as intensely as you can possibly muster.

5. Having recognised your link with Divine Power via the two extremes of your body, i.e. feet and head, take a Complete Breath, drawing down Divine Force, golden Light, from your Source into your head. Continue by mentally directing the Light during the exhalation, letting it flash like a blazing circle of golden light flowing from your right temple around and through the head of the Being of Light, and back into your head via your left temple, thus establishing a complete circle of Divine Force linking you with the shining figure of your *Neshamah*, your Divine Self. In this manner your feet are dedicated to Divine Service, and your head is open to Divine Inspiration.

6. Work this procedure rapidly three times.

2. THE BREATH OF LIGHT

Having just completed the "Unification with the Higher Self," and having established your contact with the Being of Light, the Infinite Point of Radiance, and having established the "Circle of Light" linking your own head to that of the "Radiant Being of Light," you may proceed with the next practice.

1. Continue by remaining entirely relaxed, the palms of the hands still facing upwards, the soles of your feet resting against those of the Being of Light, and sensing your "Infinite Point of Radiance" diagonally above you.
2. Next, focus your attention on your solar plexus, which we noted is the "brain" of your "Instinctual Self." This time, sense your "Infinite Source" to be directly above this point of your anatomy. Then, while taking a Complete Breath, visualise and sense the "Divine Light" being drawn down into your body via the solar plexus, from whence it divides and flows in two directions, upwards to the top of your head and downwards to the soles of your feet. Reverse this process during exhalation, i.e. sensing the Divine Force flowing back into the Solar Plexus, from whence it returns into the infinity of the One Eternal Spirit, your Source above you.
3. Repeat the procedure at least six times, or as many times as time will allow and for as long as you will stay focussed without having the mind wandering around the "cage of logic."

Do not expect any supernatural effects or extrasensory sensations. Results differ from one individual to the next, but will in time materialise during your normal everyday existence. In fact, the procedure could be worked to bring relief during moments of great anxiety and stress, and it is said that this exercise is equally successfully used by insomniacs, since it aids sleep without strain or anxiety.

3. THE *AMEN* BREATH

The following practice will prepare your physical body to absorb Divine Power in full consciousness. Here "Divine Energy" is drawn from your "Radiant Being of Light" via your feet, from whence it is directed directly into your hands, almost as if there are two laser beams respectively connecting your hands directly with the insteps of your feet. Your connection with your "Infinite Source" and your "Radiant Being of Light" being already well established, you may commence the following procedure:

1. Turn your palms downward, then, while taking a Complete Breath and softly sounding "*AH*" during the inhalation, imagine intense light or Divine Energy being drawn from the feet of the Being of Light, through your insteps up towards your hands. Retain the Divine Force in your hands as you exhale and whisper "*MEN*." This is done three times.
2. Next, again on an inhalation, pull or draw the Divine Force from your hands to your elbows while whispering "*EE*," then from your elbows to your throat while changing the whisper to "*AH*." All of this is done during the inhalation. During the pause between the inhalation and exhalation, feel the Divine Energy gathered in your throat, and then direct the Light back into your "Infinite Source," either directly from your throat or through the top of the head, while whispering "*OH*" or "*OO*." Experience and sense the Divine Force uniting with the "All of Nothing," *OMNIL*. Repeat this portion of the procedure three times.

As you have probably noticed during the working of this procedure, you are quietly declaring "*Amen IAO*." As noted before, the Divine Name "*IAO*" represents the totality of your "Being," of which this exercise is the full expression. Hence, these deliberate acts of alignment are meant to facilitate a cleaving to *Atzilut* (the World of Emanation), so to speak. It is ultimately via the *Neshamah*, the Divine Higher Self, that one is able to govern the world, and the downward flow of *shefa* (spiritual influx) is reliant on *Kavvanah*, literally your conduct, demeanour and stance. This factor is vital in drawing down the "Light of the World of Emanation," and radiating it via your own being into all spheres of manifestation.

This practice will bring much of the "World of Action" or "manifestation" under your direct control, however, this governance is not of the tyrannous kind, but rather of love and respect with an immeasurable need to serve, i.e. to attempt *Tikkun*, the restoration of this world into a place of harmony and peace. As we noted earlier, by deliberately giving respect to all manifestation, you are radiating the Spiritual Power which you have drawn into your being through your alignment with higher forces. In this manner you have taken another step in the direction of Divine Union, and deliberately offered your own Life-force in service of the Almighty one. It is said that this action is the start of real worship.

C. *Lekaven Tiferet*: Acknowledging Beauty

Many ways have been suggested to bring us closer to "divine realisation." These range from very complex meditation techniques to prayer, ritual practices and even a range of very simple practices. In the end, the most important ones will always be those which you will find are working for you personally. Obviously the techniques I am sharing in this book are those which have served me well, and which have remained integral to my daily existence.

What is again extremely important in all of these exercises, is that one has to get out of the "mental mode," e.g. constantly analyzing them, or querying whether they are working, or why they are not working, etc. One has to develop a "feeling appreciation" rather than a "thinking" one. Furthermore, one has to adopt a kind of non-caring stance regarding any effects or expectations. As suggested earlier, one simply has to work the various exercises and rituals for the sake of doing them, expecting absolutely nothing in return.

Now, another way of radiating *Ruchaniyut*, and a sure way to find the true meaning of Being, is to contemplate and acknowledge beauty in everything. This is an attempt to achieve a full realisation of the "Eternal Root of Splendour" beyond all being. For example, when you observe a beautiful or well adorned person, you should consider that person to be the impression of the Divine, recognising that you are looking at the grace, radiance and resplendence of God. By so doing, you are observing the *Ruchaniyut* of the person. The physical comeliness of anything is a *Tziyun* (a sign), a reflected ray of the Supernal Splendour of *Tiferet* (Beauty). Yet this beauty is only temporal, and ultimately it is necessary to understand the *Battel* (obliteration) of this beauty in the light of the "Supernal Splendour" of the Eternal Living Spirit.[3]

The practice of *Lekaven Tiferet* should be done with everything, not only people. You should attempt to find the beauty in whatever you observe, and then to consciously acknowledge this beauty in your mind by mentally expressing your appreciation of this factor to the object you have surveyed in this manner. After the beauty is acknowledged, you should bring yourself in contact with the Divine, your Eternal Source of Radiance and Well-being, again sensing yourself linked to It via the top of your head, as described previously. Then you complete the procedure by uniting the beauty, which you have observed and acknowledged, with your Source by mentally saying *Baruch ha-Shem*, meaning "Blessed be your Name," or giving a broader thanksgiving blessing, saying mentally, or aloud if you can:

ברוך אתה אדני אלהינו מלך העולם שככה לו בעולמו

Baruch Atah Adonai Eloheinu Melech ha-Olam, Shekachah Lo ba-Olamo.
Blessed are You *Adonai*, our God, King of the Universe, Who has created such as These in His world.[4]

By means of this exercise we deliberately turn our focus away from all ugliness, disorder and rage, so as not to unite ourselves with these "negativities," but instead to align ourselves with and focus on that which brings stability into our world. It is through the act of finding beauty in anything that we are able to identify with that thing. Above all, it is said that the act of finding beauty in everything leads us to attain "Seven Aspects of Bliss" from which will result "Four Fulfilments of Joy." The "Seven Aspects of Bliss" are equated with the lower seven *Sefirot* on the Tree of Life as follows:

Chesed (Mercy, Loving-kindness) — *Chedva* (Delight)
Gevurah (Severity, Strength) — *Ditza* (Pleasure)
Tiferet (Beauty) — *Rina* (Glad song)
Netzach (Victory, Endurance) — *Gila* (Mirth)
Hod (Glory) — *Simcha* (Happiness)
Yesod (Foundation) — *Sasson* (Joy)
Malchut (Kingdom) — *Tzalah* (Jubilation)

It is said that *Tzalah* (Jubilation), the final aspect of joy, results from the first six aspects, and all in turn culminate in "Four Fulfilments of Joy," these being:

Ahava (Love)
Achva (Brotherhood)
Shalom (Peace)
Rei'ut (Companionship)[5]

The successful application of techniques like these are dependent on constant practice. They certainly break the barriers between oneself and the Eternal Living Spirit, but they have to be worked constantly in order to achieve this aim.

D. Tracing the *Bet*

1. INTRODUCTION

We have now arrived at practical workings based on the set of permutations of the Ineffable Name termed the "Twelve Banners" in Joseph Gikatilla's "*Gates of Light*"[6] as indicated in the following table:

יוהה	יהדו	יהוה
הדיו	הויה	הוהי
ויהה	והדי	והיה
הדוי	היוה	הידו

YHVH	YHHV	YVHH
HVHY	HVYH	HHYV
VHYH	VHHY	VYHH
HYHV	HYVH	HHVY

These permutations have been attributed to the twelve months, the twelve signs of the Zodiac, and the twelve ancient Hebrew Tribes. They have also been divided into four groups, each attributed to an "Element," "Direction," etc. However, there is again no consensus to be found in primary Kabbalistic literature regarding these attributions. For example, Aryeh Kaplan noted that the permutations attributed to *Elul* and *Adar* are interchangeable.[7] It would seem that Gikatilla's delineation of the "Twelve Banners" was fairly standard amongst the older Kabbalists, and that the switching occurred specifically in *Lurianic Kabbalah*, i.e as shown in *"Or Levanah"* by Shalom Sharabi,[8] Lurianic *Siddurim* (prayer books);[9] etc. We might also note that much of the practical techniques of pre-Lurianic *Kabbalah* were dismissed out of hand as "bad" and even declared taboo by the Lurianic faction.

Having investigated the related sets of permutations in, amongst others, *"Chayei ha-Olam ha-Ba,"*[10] *"Mafteach ha-Shemot,"*[11] *Sefer Raziel*,[12] and *Shorshei ha-Shemot*,[13] all of which align with the *"Sha'arei Orah,"* I personally subscribe to Joseph Gikatilla's attributions, as shown in the following illustration. It certainly offers the clearest sequence of attributes in terms of the practical workings we are addressing:[14]

406 / The Shadow Tree: The Book of Self Creation

To facilitate a better understanding of the associated practical applications, we need to consider additional details, i.e. besides the alignment of the "Twelve Banners" with months, Zodiac signs and Hebrew Tribes, each permutation is respectively associated with a verse from the *Tanach* (Hebrew Bible), in which the initial letters or final letters of the component words spell the related permutation, like this:

1	***YHVH — Psalm 96:11 — Nisan***
	Hebrew: ישמחו השמים ותגל הארץ
	Transliteration: *Yishm'chu Ha-Shamayim V'tagel Ha-Aretz*
2	***YHHV — Jeremiah 9:23 — Iyar***
	Hebrew: יתהלל המתהלל השכל וידע
	Transliteration: *Yithalel Ha-Mithalel Ha-Skel V'Yado'a*

3	**YVHH — Exodus 26:19–20 — Sivan** Hebrew: ידתיו ולצלע המשכן השנית Transliteration: Yidotaiv U(V)l'tzela Ha-Mishkan Ha-Sheinit
4	**HVHY — Esther 5:13 — Tamuz** Hebrew: זה איננו שוה לי Transliteration: ZeH EininU(V) ShoveH Li(Y)
5	**HVYH — Deuteronomy 27:9 — Av** Hebrew: הסכת ושמע ישראל היום Transliteration: Ha-Sket U(V)Shma Yisra'el Ha-Yom
6	**HHYV — Genesis 49:11 — Elul** Hebrew: עירה ולשרקה בני אתנו Transliteration: IroH v'LasorekaH B'ni(Y) AtonO(V)
7	**VHYH — Genesis 12:15 — Tishri** Hebrew: ויראו אתה שרי פרעה Transliteration: Va-Yir'U(V) OtaH Sarei(Y) Far'oH
8	**VHHY — Deuteronomy 26:15–16 — Cheshvan** Hebrew: ודבש היום הזה יהוה Transliteration: U(V)dvash Ha-Yom Ha-Zeh YHVH
9	**VYHH — Genesis 50:11 — Kislev** Hebrew: וירא יושב הארץ הכנעני Transliteration: Viyar Yoshev Ha-Aretz Ha-Kna'ani
10	**HYHV — Psalms 34:4 — Tevet** Hebrew: ליהוה אתי ונרוממה שמו Transliteration: La-YHVH Iti(Y) Unrom'maH ShmO(V)
11	**HYVH — Leviticus 27:33 — Shevat** Hebrew: המר ימירנו והיה הוא Transliteration: Hamer Y'mirenu V'hayah Hu

12	**HHVY** — *Deuteronomy 6:25* — *Adar*
	Hebrew: וצדקה תהיה לנו כי
	Transliteration: *U-Tz'dakaH TiyeH LanU(V) Ki(Y)*

As mentioned previously, in *Lurianic Kabbalah* the attributions of *Elul* and *Adar* are reversed, and the same applies to the associated verses, as shown in Sharabi's *"Or Levanah."*[15] We should also remember that the twelve permutations are attributed to the central six *sefirot* on the Tree of Life, specifically:

YHVH — Chesed	VHYH — Chesed
YHHV — Gevurah	VHHY — Gevurah
YVHH — Tiferet	VYHH — Tiferet
HVHY — Netzach	HYHV — Netzach
HVYH — Hod	HYVH — Hod
HHYV — Yesod	HHVY — Yesod

Additionally, the "Four Banners," comprising three permutations each, respectively corresponding to the four directions, i.e. the first three permutations starting with the letter **Yod** pertain to **Mizrach** (East); the second set starting with the first **Heh** corresponds to **Darom** (South); the third group starting with the letter **Vav** relates to **Ma'arav** (West); and the last three permutations starting with the final letter of the *Tetragrammaton*, **Heh**, pertain to **Tzafon** (North).

While Aryeh Kaplan lists these specific directional attributions in his *"Sefer Yetzirah,"*[16] even here there are some differences of opinion. For example, Moses Cordovero offers a different set of attributions in *"Pardes Rimmonim,"* e.g. he assigns the first three to the South; the second set to the North; the third group of three to the East, and the last three to the West.[17] What is perhaps strangest of all, is Cordovero's version of the "Twelve Banners," which is totally at odds with Gikatilla's original version, as shown in the following table. The highlighted permutations indicate the differences between the two sets.

Banners	Joseph Gikatilla in *Sha'arei Orah*[18]	Moses Cordovero in *Pardes Rimmonim*[19]
Banner 1	YHVH YHHV YVHH	YHVH YVHH YHHV
Banner 2	HVHY HVYH HHYV	HYVH HVYH HHYV
Banner 3	VHYH VHHY VYHH	VYHH VHYH VHHY
Banner 4	HYHV HYVH HHVY	HHVY HYHV HVHY

It is worth noting that the arrangement Aryeh Kaplan described in his *"Sefer Yetzirah,"*[20] comfortably aligns with the exercises involving the application of these specific twelve permutations in the "Tracing the Bet" meditations.

Before we finally get to share a few practical applications, it is worth perusing the attribution of the twelve permutations to the hours of the day. In this tradition the daily cycle is marked from sunset to sunset, rather than from sunrise to sunrise. Hence the daily cycle comprises two sub-cycles of twelve hours each, the first from 6 p.m. to 6 a.m.; the second from 6 a.m. to 6 p.m. The pattern of twelve permutations follow the two sets of twelve hours in exact order, e.g. the cycle is repeated in each twenty-four hour cycle. In related teachings, we are told that the twelve hours comprising the "night cycle," pertain to the twenty-four permutations of *ADONAI*, while the twelve hours of the "day cycle" are associated with two sets of twelve permutations, respectively those of *YHVH* and *EHYEH*. For our purposes, the simple attribution of the twelve permutations of the *Tetragrammaton* to the hours of the day in two sub-cycles of twelve hours each, works perfectly well without any need for further complexities at present.

2. CONTEMPLATING DEFINITIONS: *GEVULIM*

Let us look at two meditation/ritual procedures pertaining to the "Twelve Banners," which are especially useful. Both of them have been taught to me under the title "Tracing the *Bet*."

Commenting on the twelve "single letters" of the Hebrew alphabet, referred to in the "*Sefer Yetzirah*," Aryeh Kaplan makes reference to an exercise in which one meditates the twelve *gevulim* (boundaries/definitions) of space, collectively represented as a "cosmic cube" so to speak. We are told that these "boundaries" correspond to the twelve permutations of the Ineffable Name, and that each set of three in turn relates to one of the four directions. In this regard, Aryeh Kaplan wrote "The permutations beginning with *Y* corresponding to the east; those beginning with the first *H*, to the south; the *V*, to the west, and the final *H*, to the north."[21]

Aryeh Kaplan further explained that "in each of these four directions, one first takes the upward boundary, then the right boundary, and then the lower boundary. In this manner, one describes the letter *Bet* on each side. This corresponds to the teaching that the world was created with a *Bet*, this being the first letter of the Torah."[22] He mentioned that "the initiate meditates on the four letters *Bet* which seal the universe on four sides, setting the limits of thought." To this he adds that the initiate "also meditates the twelve permutations of the *Tetragrammaton*, which correspond to the twelve diagonals. In this manner, he can reach the level where they extend to 'eternity of eternities,' beyond the realm of space and time."[23]

In the first "Tracing the *Bet*" exercise, titled "Contemplating Definitions: *Gevulim*," the twelve "boundaries" of the "cosmic *Bayit*" (Cosmic House or Cosmic Cube) are mentally traced in each quarter (direction), in accordance with the pattern of the letter *Bet*. Here, the "Twelve Banners" are, as it were, virtually engraved mentally, in a manner in which the three permutations, comprising each, set sort of slot into one another. In this way, each set forms the letter *Bet* which can then be clearly visualised. Here are the four patterns associated with the four directions. Remember that the Hebrew text is always written and read from right to left, and also that the positions of North and South are always reversed in the Southern Hemisphere.

Ascending in Light / 411

A. *MIZRACH* (East) — *YHVH–YHHV–YVHH*

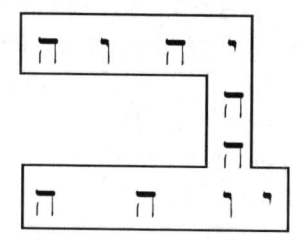

B. *DAROM* (South) — *HVHY–HVYH–HHYV*

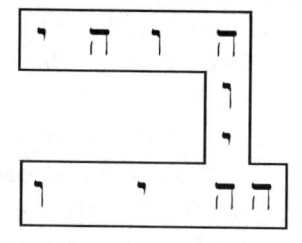

C. *MA'ARAV* (West) — *VHYH–VHHY–VYHH*

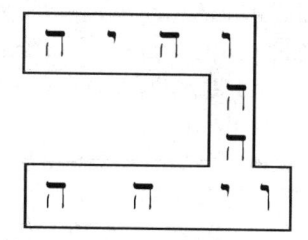

D. *TZAFON* (North) — *HYHV–HYVH–HHVY*

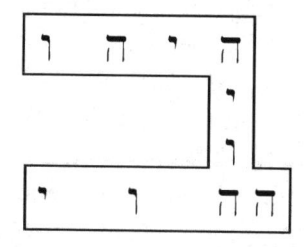

Note how the permutations comprising each set, are integrated to form the letter *Bet*. Working this meditation requires only a little skill, which is easily acquired with regular practice.

Commence by visualising and tracing, i.e. mentally writing or engraving, **Y–H–V–H** from right to left in exact order, so as to form the upper line of the *Bet*, simultaneously vocalizing each letter—"*EE-AH-OH-EH.*" Next, trace the downward stroke of the *Bet* with the permutation **Y–H–H–V**. Starting at the top right, focus the *Yod*, coinciding it exactly with the one on the upper line, then mentally writing the second permutation from top to bottom, while uttering the sound of each letter—"*EE-AH-EH-OH.*" Lastly, trace the bottom stroke of the letter *Bet* by visualising the third permutation **Y–V–H–H**, positioning the initial letter of this permutation (*Yod*) to the right of the last letter (*Vav*) of the previous permutation. From Right to left, continue tracing the final permutation of the "first banner," conjoining the second letter (*Vav*) with the one which concluded the "downstroke" permutation, and completing the pattern with the two letters *Heh*, again simultaneously uttering "*EE-OH-EH-AH*" whilst tracing the concluding permutation of this first set. The same model is repeated with the three permutations of each of the remaining "banners."

The practice is concluded with a brief contemplation of the four *Bet*'s, these being the four "banners" formed into the "Cosmic *Bayit*" (house) which was traced in this special practice. Also remember to pay some attention to the way in which the "Four Banners" are collectively an expression of the *Tetragrammaton*, each respective "banner" being a letter of the Ineffable Name.

3. ESTABLISHING A BODY OF LIGHT

We will now investigate what is termed a "Body of Light." This construct will surround your physical structure in the same manner as your aura, or bioflux emanations. It should be constructed in such a way that, whether you are embodied or not, you will literally live within it unto eternity. It has been said that this "body" acts as a vehicle, which can be used for a multitude of purposes, for example to travel inter-dimensionally into higher and more refined realms of manifestation. This is one of the most powerful practices in our Tradition, which refers traditionally to the ability to undertake an "Inner Journey", a "Merkavistic descent", as it has been called elsewhere. One can journey either in the "*Now*," or into the future or past, all depending on personal aims, i.e. to initiate a magical activity which will result in a specific effect in accordance with the practitioners intentions. As I believe this practice is of great interest, I will share the construction of such a personal *Merkavah* (Chariot Throne), which is considered to be a "vehicle," "Body of Light" or a "Shield" comprising a kind of "ecstatic energy" surrounding the body of the practitioner.

To understand what is being done when the "Body of Light" is constructed, it is prudent to note what William Gray had to say about learning to work and move in spiritual dimensions. He queried "How did you learn to stand upright and move yourself around in this world so that it meant something to you? First, you had to distinguish between up and down, forwards and backwards, and side to side. Then you had to maintain your balance between all of these, and find out how to direct your course in relation to them in order to make movement purposeful. This is an early experience you have consciously forgotten, but which governs your active life today. Unless you could do this naturally and easily, your existence on this earth would be far from pleasant or profitable. Exactly the same is true in spiritual dimensions. The laws of life apply to *all* states of being. It is only a question of how they operate in differing conditions of consciousness.

So the first movements you make in spiritual dimensions should accord with alignments therein. Otherwise you will not be able to tell your ups from your downs, your right from your left, or your back from your front, and you are likely to become a very mixed up soul....Fortunately, you will be able to construct a 'cosmic compass' which tells you how to stand upright and move around inner dimensions so as to make sense and meaning there."[24]

William Gray is again referring to the earlier mentioned symbol of the Circle Cross, the "Cosmic Cross" or "Solar Cross of Cosmos," where you have the idea of humanity and divinity meeting at the central point of perfect poise. As mentioned before, the symbol of the Cross incorporates the idea of humanity—represented by the horizontal line, and Divinity—represented by the vertical line, meeting where the two lines cross. At this intersection we meet God as if at a "Cross road," and it is up to us whether we will allow a full integration of the human and the

414 / *The Shadow Tree: The Book of Self Creation*

divine within ourselves. We may meet God in ourselves, but whether we are going to consciously allow an integration of that realisation is another story altogether.

Now, instead of looking at the "Cosmic Cross" as a squared circle, try viewing it as three interlocking circles, and this is exactly the shape of the "Body of Light," which you will construct around yourself.

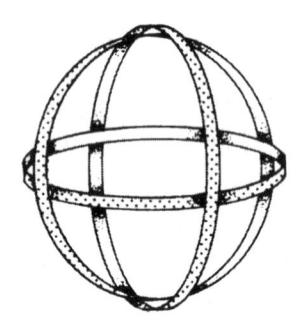

This is the "Symbol of Cosmos" in which one might work "Magical Procedures" or undertake "Inter-dimensional Journeys." William Gray termed it a "cage of consciousness," and continued to say "So far as we are concerned, our consciousness of Cosmos around us is limited by three main factors — time, space and events. It takes time for us to live, space for us to move, and events for us to realise we are living and mobile beings."[25] The three rings forming the framework of our "Body of Light," can be termed a "Cosmic Compass" which we will use to "stabilize ourselves in spiritual dimensions," and it is to the formation of this around oneself that we now turn our attention. The following illustration indicates how it will appear around you.

Again William Gray said: "If you look at the solid, three-dimensional Circle Cross again, you will note that there are six crossings where the circles meet, six points of reference: above, below, before, behind, right and left. Strictly speaking, there is a seventh point in the centre. Visualise these as points of spiritual stability in relation to yourself. You have 'Heaven' above you, 'Earth' beneath you, and the four 'Quarters' of your spiritual world around you. You are the central axis of this symbolic structure you are building up."[26]

To construct the "Body of Light" we will now have to comprehend the above construct which will be established around the physical body, actually just outside the parameter of the earlier mentioned "aura." First we will trace the pattern mentally, again using vowel sounds associated with four stable points as we trace circular patterns around ourselves. These stable sounds and associated placements are:

	Position	Sound
1.	Top of the head	**"EE"**
2.	Left Side	**"AH"**
3.	Below the feet	**"OH"**
4.	Right	**"EH"**

These vowel sounds are conjoined with the "Twelve Banners," in the exact manner described in the *"Contemplating Definitions: Gevulim"* procedure. For our purposes, the correct order of the permutations is as delineated by Joseph Gikatilla in *"Sha'arei Orah."*[27] Changing the order of the permutations interrupts the correct flow of Divine Energy, and therefore, at least for the purposes of creating a "Body of Light," the following order of the "Twelve Banners" must be followed, whatever you might have been taught to the contrary. The letter *Heh* with a *"Dagesh"* (dot) in the centre is the last letter of the Ineffable Name.

Permutation	Position	Name
1. *EE-AH-OH-EH*	Top-Left-Bottom-Right	יהוה
2. *EE-AH-EH-OH*	Top-Left-Right-Bottom	יההו
3. *EE-OH-EH-AH*	Top-Bottom-Right-Left	יוהה
4. *AH-OH-EH-EE*	Left-Bottom-Right-Top	הוהי
5. *AH-OH-EE-EH*	Left-Bottom-Top-Right	הויה
6. *AH-EH-EE-OH*	Left-Right-Top-Bottom	ההיו
7. *OH-EH-EE-AH*	Bottom-Right-Top-Left	והיה
8. *OH-EH-AH-EE*	Bottom-Right-Left-Top	וההי
9. *OH-EE-AH-EH*	Bottom-Top-Left-Right	ויהה
10. *EH-EE-AH-OH*	Right-Top-Left-Bottom	היהו
11. *EH-EE-OH-AH*	Right-Top-Bottom-Left	היוה
12. *EH-AH-OH-EE*	Right-Left-Bottom-Top	ההוי

These "tracings" indicate three special patterns. These are:

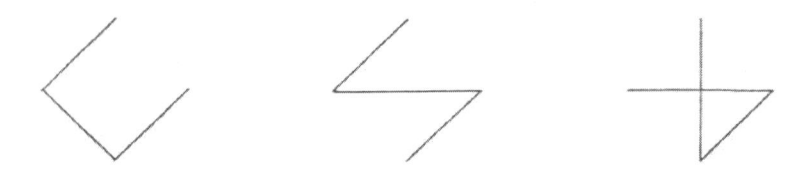

You might have noticed that these three patterns are simply repeated four times in the set of permutations, each set commencing at a different angle/position. Here are the sets of patterns associated with creating a "Body of Light":

Ascending in Light / 417

Position One
Top–Left–Bottom–Right

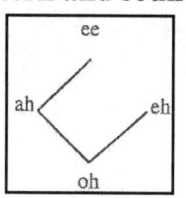

Top–Left–Right–Bottom

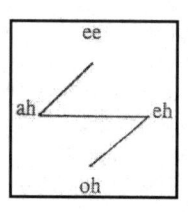

Top–Bottom–Right–Left

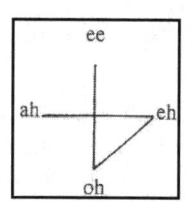

Position Two
Left–Bottom–Right–Top

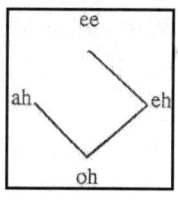

Left–Bottom–Top–Right

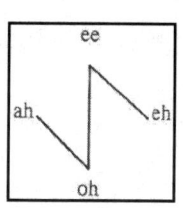

Left–Right–Top–Bottom

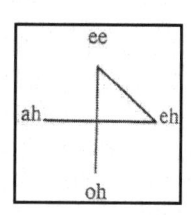

Pattern and sound

418 / *The Shadow Tree: The Book of Self Creation*

Position Three **Pattern and sound**
Bottom–Right–Top–Left

Bottom–Right–Left–Top

Bottom–Top–Left–Right

Position Four **Pattern and sound**
Right–Top–Left–Bottom

Right–Top–Bottom–Left

Right–Left–Bottom–Top

Every set comprising three patterns, creates a complete "Cosmic Cross," thus the "Solar Compass of Cosmos" is established four times around the body with each practice of the entire procedure.

To become accustomed to the patterns and movement of Divine Energy, you might want to trace the patterns around your head. I was taught to practice by drawing the patterns in straight lines around my head. The top of the head would be the sound "*EE*" corresponding to the letter *Yod*; the left ear would be the sound "*AH*"; the chin would be the position for the sound "*OH*"; and the right ear would in turn be the position for the sound "*EH*." In this manner you can familiarize yourself with the patterns and permutations by drawing them mentally in straight lines from one position to another around your face. Later, when you are used to the patterns, you will change the lines into circles, following the motions as indicated below.

Of course you need to draw these patterns around the entire body forming fairly large circles with your mind. In fact, I was told that I could ascertain the average diameter of these circles by stretching my arms to the sides and sensing the distance from the tips of the fingers of my one hand to those of the other. So, having traced these lines, and understanding the pattern, commence tracing these circles around your body. To keep the Divine Light circulating in the right directions, you need to know the direction of the flow as follows:

Around the Body	Top–Left–Bottom–Right
	Left–Bottom–Right–Top
	Bottom–Right–Top–Left
	Right–Top–Left–Bottom
From the Top to the Bottom	Down the Back
From the Bottom to the Top	Up the Front
From the Left to the Right	Round the Back
From the Right to the Left	Round the Front

When you are fully familiar with these patterns and motions, you may begin to establish your "Body of Light." This is done standing, and you should use various exercises, such as "Surrendering," "the Mother Breath," "Tuning the Body" and the "Invocation of Subtle Energy" as preparations. Having now strongly aligned yourself with Divine Energy, you can start to establish your Body of Light by drawing down the *Shefa*, the abundant Radiance of the Divine, from your Infinite Source above your head. This is done in the usual manner on inhalation, during which the Divine Power is drawn down into the top of your head. Again, the sensation should be as if you were breathing through the top of your head.

On exhalation you should chant the pattern of sounds, while mentally drawing the Divine Brilliance around the body, according to the pattern and sound-positions of a specific permutation of the Ineffable Name, e.g. while chanting "***EE–AH–OH–EH***," you draw the light in a circle around the body from the top to the left, to the bottom below the feet, to the right. You then take another breath, drawing more Divine Power into your head, and on exhalation continue with the next pattern, etc. As you become more and more accustomed to the practice, you will be able to rapidly trace three permutations in one breath. In this way, you set the three intertwined bands of Divine Power into a swirling motion around your body with each set of permutations.

This is the entire procedure, but I need to point out that since emotion is, as it were, the "engine" of the "Body of Light, it would be good if the tracing of the various patterns could be executed in a joyous, loving, and even ecstatic state of mind. Some even prefer to work this practice while in a state of sexual arousal. What is important is that you should feel a great love for the Divine Force which you are using to construct your "Body of Light," and you should feel the warmth of your smile permeate the "Whole" in total love and friendship. Naturally it would take several months, and perhaps even years, of constant effort to truly establish your "Body of Light" as a kind of *Merkavah*, a Divine Vehicle.

Ultimately, the successful implementation of all sacred knowledge and associated spiritual practices, depends on the oneness of the "Knower" and the "Known." Hence, it is vitally important to realise the Oneness of all. In the recognition of the ONE, we are all cells within the "Body of God." In separateness we "fall" and create the "Tree of Knowledge good and evil," and with this "fall" we forget that "Divine Law" governs all in the "One Life of Spirit." In "separateness" we fall—in "Oneness" we rise.

Finally, at the end of this text on "Self Creation," at the conclusion of this specific segment in the process of "Awakening," I pray the Holy One will enfold you with abundance and grace.

y'varechah b'chol tov
v'yishmor'chah mikol ra
v'ya'ir lib'chah b'seichel chayim
v'yachonchah b'da'at olamim
v'yisa pnei chasadaiv l'chah
lish'lom olamim

"May He bless thee with all good
And keep thee from all evil.
May He enlighten thy heart with immortal wisdom
And grace thee with eternal knowledge.
May He lift up His merciful Countenance upon thee
for eternal peace."

— *Priestly Blessing of the*
Qumran Community [28]

"A Palace is made with many windows facing east and west, and within the windows are cut glass, and each piece of glass is its own unique colour—this one all blue, this all black, this all red, this all green, this all saffron and this combining two colours, where one is unlike the other. Now when the light of the sun passes through them, the rays that strike the walls of the palace are variegated, with many colours, each different from the other, and none like the other, to the point that one who sees them will wonder and say that these differences are due to the light of the sun! And this indeed is not the case, for the change is due only to the receptors of the rays, to the many coloured glasses that are set in the windows. So too we may understand the rays of the effluence of the Unique Master, One and unchanging, without addition or diminution. Indeed His works are variegated beyond investigation and infinite, all of them in accordance to the nature of the creatures which receive His effluence."

— Isaac of Acre
(*Sefer Otzar ha-Chayim*)

REFERENCES & BIBLIOGRAPHY

CHAPTER 1

1. **Grant, K.:** *Magical Revival*, Frederick Muller Ltd, London 1972.
   —*Cults of the Shadow*, Frederick Muller Ltd., London 1975.
   —*Nightside of Eden*, Frederick Muller Ltd., London 1977.
   —*Outside the Circles of Time*, Frederick Muller Ltd., London 1980.
   —with Steffi Grant: *Hidden Lore: Carfax Monographs*, Skoob Books Publishing Ltd., London 1989.
   —*Hecate's Fountain*, Skoob Books Publishing Ltd., London 1992.
   —*Outer Gateways*, Skoob Books Publishing Ltd., London 1994.
   —*Against the Light*, Starfire Publishing Ltd., London 1997.

2. **Isaac ben Jacob ha-Kohen:** *Treatise on the Left Emanation*, transl. in Dan, J. & Kiener, D.C.: *The Early Kabbalah*, Paulist Press, Mahwah 1986.
   Moses of Burgos: *The Book of the Left Pillar*, sections transl. in Rothenberg, J.: *A Big Jewish Book: Poems & Other Visions of Jews from Tribal Times to Present*, Anchor Books, New York 1978.
   Vital, Chaim: *Sefer ha-Chezyonot. The Book of Visions*, transl. in Faierstein, M.M.: *Jewish Mystical Autobiographies: Book of Visions and Book of Secrets*, Paulist Press, Mahwah 1999.
   Dan, J.: *Samael, Lilith, and the Concept of Evil in Early Kabbalah*, Association of Jewish Studies Review 5, Cambridge, Massachusetts 1980.
   Chajes, J.H.: *Between Worlds: Dybbuks, Exorcists, and Early Modern Judaism*, University of Pennsylvania Press, Philadelphia 2003.
   Nigal, G.: *Magic, Mysticism, and Hasidism: The Supernatural in Jewish Thought*, Jason Aronson Inc., Northvale 1994.
   Goldish, M.: *Spirit Possession in Judaism: Cases and Contexts from the Middle Ages to the Present*, Wayne State University Press, Detroit 2003.

3. **Ponce, C.:** *Kabbalah: An Introduction and Illumination for the World Today*, The Garnstone Press Ltd., London 1974.
Regardie, I.: *A Garden of Pomegranates*, Llewellyn Publications, 1970.
Love, J.: *The Quantum Gods: The Origin and Nature of Matter and Consciousness*, Compton Russell Ltd., Tisbury 1976.
Leet, L.: *The Secret Doctrine of the Kabbalah: Discovering the Key to Hebraic Sacred Science*, Inner Traditions International, Rochester 1999.
—*The Universal Kabbalah*, Inner Traditions International, Rochester 2004.

4. **Schaya, L.:** *The Universal Meaning of the Kabbalah*, George Allen & Unwin, London 1971.

5. **Wyld, H.C.:** *The Universal Dictionary of the English Language*, E.P. Dutton, New York 1932.

6. *Seder 12 ha-Mazalot*, Hotsa'at Backal, Jerusalem 1973.
Sefer Raziel ha-Malach, Yarid ha-Sefarim, Jerusalem 2003.
Sefer Mishpatei ha-Olam and *Sefer ha-Mivcharim*, Hotza'at Backal, Jerusalem.
Vital, Chaim: *Sefer ha-Goralot*, Hotza'at Backal, Jerusalem.
Greenup, A.W.: *Sefer ha-Levanah: The Book of the Moon*, London 1912.
Levy, R.: *Astrological Works of Abraham ibn Ezra*, John Hopkins University Press, Baltimore 1927.
Trachtenberg, Joshua: *Jewish Magic and Superstition: A Study in Folk Religion*, Behrman's Jewish Book House Publishers, New York 1939.
Glazerson, M.: *Above the Zodiac: Astrology in Jewish Thought*, Jason Aronson Inc., Northvale 1997.
Isaacs, R.J.: *Divination, Magic, and Healing: The Book of Jewish Folklore*, Jason Aronson Inc., Northvale 1998.
Erlanger, G.: *Signs of the Times: The Zodiac in Jewish Tradition*, Feldman Publishing, Jerusalem 1999.

7. **Shamsian, A.:** *Chochmat ha-Partzuf Chochmat Kaf ha-Yad*, Avraham Shamsian, Safed.
Chamaui, A.: *Sefer Devek Me'Ach*, Yarid ha-Sefarim, Jerusalem 2005.
Chochmat ha-Yad v'ha-Seertut, Yarid ha-Sefarim, Jerusalem 2003.
Chochmat ha-Yad ha-Shalem with commentary by Abraham Azulai, Hotza'at Backal, Jerusalem 1966.

8. **Fine, L.:** *Physician of the Soul, Healer of the Cosmos: Isaac Luria and His Kabbalistic Fellowship*, Stanford University Press, Stanford 2003.

9. **Shamsian, A.**: *Sod Pitron ha-Chalamot*, Avraham Shamsian, Safed 1991.
   Backal, M.: *Pitron ha-Chalamot*, Hotza'at Backal, Jerusalem 1964.
   Almoli, S.: *Dream Interpretation from Classical Jewish Sources*, KTAV Publishing House Inc., New York 1998.
   Covitz, J.: *Visions of the Night: A Study of Jewish Dream Interpretation*, Shambhala, Boston 1990.
10. *Goralot Achitofel*, Hotza'at Backal, Jerusalem 1964.
    Keter, S.: *Nechash ha-Nechoshet*, Baruch Keter, Jerusalem 1990.
    Chamaui, A.: *Sefer He'Ach Nafshenu*, Yarid ha-Sefarim, Jerusalem 2007.
    —*Nifla'im Ma'asecha*, Hotza'at Backal, Jerusalem 1972.
11. *Refuah v'Chaim mi-Yerushalayim*, Hotza'at Backal, Jerusalem.
    Chamaui, A.: *Devek Me'Ach*, *Op. cit.*
    —*He'Ach Nafshenu*, *Op. cit.*
    Keter, S.: *Nechash ha-Nechoshet*, *Op. cit.*
    Beinish, B.: *Amtachat Binyamin*, Hotza'at Backal, Jerusalem 1966.
    Zacutto, M.: *Shorshei ha-Shemot*, Hotzaat Nezer Shraga, Jerusalem 1999.
    Tzubeiri, Y.: *Emet v'Emunah*, Machon Shtilei Zeitim, Ramat Gan 2002.
    Rosenberg, Y.: *Refael ha-Malach*, Asher Klein, Jerusalem 2000.
    Schrire, T.: *Hebrew Amulets*, Routledge & Kegan Paul, London 1966.
    Naveh, J. & Shaked, S.: *Amulets and Magic Bowls: Aramaic Incantations of Late Antiquity*, The Magnes Press, Jerusalem 1985.
    —*Magic Spells and Formulae: Aramaic Incantations of Late Antiquity*, The Magnes Press, Jerusalem 1993.
12. *Refuah v'Chaim mi-Yerushalayim*, *Op. cit.*
    Beinish, B.: *Amtachat Binyamin*, *Op. cit.*
    Tzubeiri, Y.: *Emet v'Emunah*, *Op. cit.*
    Chamaui, A.: *Devek Me'Ach*, *Op. cit.*
    —*He'Ach Nafshenu*, *Op. cit.*
    —*Nifla'im Ma'asecha*, *Op. cit.*
    —*Abia Chidot*, Hotza'at Backal, Jerusalem 1996.
    Keter, S.: *Nechash ha-Nechoshet*, *Op. cit.*
    Rosenberg, Y.: *Refael ha-Malach*, *Op. cit.*

13. **Vital, Chaim:** *Sefer ha-Chezyonot. The Book of Visions*, Op. cit.
    Karo, J.: *Sefer Maggid Mesharim*, Y. ben Y. ha-Kohen, Jerusalem 2006.
    Gordon, H.L.: *The Maggid of Caro*, Pardes Publishing House, New York 1940.
    Werblowsky, R.J.Z.: *Joseph Karo: Lawyer and Mystic*, Oxford University Press, Oxford 1962.
    Jacobs, L.: *Jewish Mystical Testimonies*, Schocken Books Inc., New York 1978.
    Epstein, P.: *Kabbalah: The Way of the Jewish Mystic*, Doubleday & Company, New York 1978.
    Cohn-Sherbok, D. & L.: *Jewish and Christian Mysticism*, The Continuum Publishing Co., New York 1994.
    Chajes, J.H.: *Between Worlds: Dybbuks, Exorists, and Early Modern Judaism*, Op. cit.
    Goldish, M.: *Spirit Possession in Judaism: Cases and Contexts from the Middle Ages to the Present*, Op. cit.
    Fine, L.: *Physician of the Soul, Healer of the Cosmos: Isaac Luria and His Kabbalistic Fellowship*, Op. cit.
14. **Vital, Chaim:** *Sefer ha-Chezyonot. The Book of Visions*, Op. cit.
    Nigal, G.: *Magic, Mysticism, and Hasidism: The Supernatural in Jewish Thought*, Op. cit.
    Goldish, M.: *Spirit Possession in Judaism: Cases and Contexts from the Middle Ages to the Present*, Op. cit.
    Fine, L.: *Physician of the Soul, Healer of the Cosmos: Isaac Luria and His Kabbalistic Fellowship*, Op. cit.
15. **Nigal, G.:** *Magic, Mysticism, and Hasidism: The Supernatural in Jewish Thought*, Op. cit.
    Gaster, M.: *The Sword of Moses*, Samuel Weiser Inc., New York 1973.
    —*Ma'aseh Book*, The Jewish Publication Society of America, Philadelphia 1981.
    Ahimaaz ben Paltiel: *Meggilat Ahimaaz*, Tarshish, Jerusalem 1974.
16. *Segulot ha-Avanim ha-Tovot*, Yarid ha-Sefarim, Jerusalem 2004.
    Shauli, M.C.: *Marpeh ha-Bosem*, Merkaz Ruchani, Ashdod.
    Lustig, D.: *Pela'ot Chachmeh ha-Kabbalah: v'He'avar ha-Kadum*, Hotza'at David ben Ze'ev, Tel Aviv 1987.
    —*Wondrous Healings of the Wise Kabbalists and the Ancient Physicians*, D. Lustig, Tel Aviv 1989.
17. *Sefer Raziel ha-Malach*, Op. cit.
    Sepher ha-Razim: The Book of the Mysteries, transl. M.A. Morgan, Society of Biblical Literature, 1983.

Gaster, M.: *The Sword of Moses* Op. cit.
Charva d'Moshe, Hotza'at Backal, Jerusalem 1996.
Havdalah d'Rabbi Akiva, Hotza'at Backal, Jerusalem 1996.
Avraham Rimon of Granada: *Brit Menuchah,* Machon Ramchal, Jerusalem 1998.
Keter, S.: *Nechash ha-Nechoshet,* Op. cit.
Beinish, B.: *Amtachat Binyamin,* Op. cit.
Cordovero, M.: *Pardes Rimmonim,* Yarid ha-Sefarim, Jerusalem 2000.
Zacutto, M.: *Shorshei ha-Shemot,* Op. cit.
Tzubeiri, Y.: *Emet v'Emunah,* Op. cit.
Rosenberg, Y.: *Refael ha-Malach,* Op. cit.
Trachtenberg, J.: *Jewish Magic and Superstition: A Study in Folk Religion,* Op. cit.
Naveh, J. & Shaked, S.: *Amulets and Magic Bowls: Aramaic Incantations of Late Antiquity,* Op. cit.
—*Magic Spells and Formulae: Aramaic Incantations of Late Antiquity,* Op. cit.
Isaacs, R.J.: *Divination, Magic, and Healing: The Book of Jewish Folklore,* Op. cit.
Winkler, G.: *Magic of the Ordinary,* North Atlantic Books, Berkeley 2003.
Bloom, M.: *Jewish Mysticism and Magic: An Anthropological Perspective,* Routledge, New York & London 2007.

18. **Arbel, V.T.:** *Beholders of Divine Secrets,* SUNY Press, New York 2003.
Dan, J.: *The Ancient Jewish Mysticism,* MOD Books, Tel Aviv 1993.
Davila, J.R.: *Descenders to the Chariot: The People Behind the Hekhalot Literature,* E.J. Brill, Leiden 2001.
Halperin, D.: *The Faces of the Chariot,* J.C.B. Mohr (Paul Siebeck), Tübingen 1988.
—*The Merkabah in Rabbinic Literature,* American Oriental Society, New Haven 1980.
Himmelfarb, M.: *Ascent to Heaven in Jewish and Christian Apocalypses,* Oxford University Press, New York-Oxford, 1993.
Idel, M.: *Ascensions on High in Jewish Mysticism: Pillars, Lines, Ladders,* Central European University Press, Budapest/New York 2005.
—*Kabbalah: New Perspectives,* Yale University Press, New Haven & London 1988.
Scholem, G.: *Kabbalah,* Keter Publishing House, Jerusalem 1974.

—*Jewish Gnosticism, Merkabah Mysticism, & Talmudic Tradition*, Jewish Theological Seminary of America, New York 1960.
—*Major Trends in Jewish Mysticism*, Schocken Books Inc., Jerusalem 1941; New York 1946.

19. **Blumenthal, D.R.**: *Understanding Jewish Mysticism: The Merkabah Tradition and the Zoharic Tradition*, (Vol 1), KTAV Publishing House Inc., New York 1978.
Charles, R.H.: *The Book of Enoch*, (Ethiopic Enoch/Enoch 1), The Clarendon Press, Oxford 1912.
Charlesworth, J.H.: *The Old Testament Pseudepigrapha*, Doubleday & Co. Inc., New York 1983/1985.
Cohen, M.S.: *The Shi'ur Qomah: Liturgy and Theurgy in Pre-Kabbalistic Jewish Mysticism*, University Press of America, Lanham-New York-London 1983.
—*The Shi'ur Qomah: Texts and Recensions*, J.C.B. Mohr (Paul Siebeck), Tübingen 1985.
Fossum, J.E.: *The Name of God and the Angel of the Lord: Samaritan and Jewish Concepts of Inter-Mediation and the Origin of Gnosticism*, Coronet Books Inc., Philadelphia 1985.
Green, A.: *Keter: The Crown of God in Early Jewish Mysticism*, Princeton University Press, Princeton 1997.
Gruenwald, I.: *Apocalyptic and Merkavah Mysticism*, E.J. Brill, Leiden 1980.
—*From Apocalypticism to Gnosticism: Studies in Apocalyticism, Merkavah Mysticism and Gnosticism*, Peter Lang Publishing Inc., Frankfurt am Main, 1988.
Jacobs, L.: *The Jewish Mystics*, Keter Publishing House, Jerusalem 1976.
Janowitz, N.: *The Poetics of Ascent: Theories of Language in a Rabbinic Ascent Text*, SUNY Press, New York 1989.
Kaplan, A.: *Meditation and Kabbalah*, Samuel Weiser Inc., York Beach 1988.
Lesses, R.M.: *Ritual Practices to Gain Power: Angels, Incantations and Revelations in Early Jewish Mysticism*, Trinity Press International, Harrisburg 1998.
Morfill, W.R.: *The Book of the Secrets of Enoch*, (Slavonic Enoch/Enoch 2), The Clarendon Press, Oxford 1896.
Schäfer, P.: *Geniza Fragmente zur Hekhalot-Literatur*, J.C.B. Mohr (Paul Siebeck), Tübingen 1984.
—*Hekhalot Studien*, J.C.B. Mohr (Paul Siebeck), Tübingen 1988.
—[with Shaul Shaked] *Magische Texte aus der Kairoer Geniza*, J.C.B. Mohr (Paul Siebeck), Tübingen 1994/1997/1999.

—*Synopse zur Hekhalot Literatur*, J.C.B. Mohr (Paul Siebeck), Tübingen 1981.

—*The Hidden and Manifest God: Some Major Themes in Early Jewish Mysticism*, SUNY Press, New York 1992.

—*Übersetzung zur Hekhalot-Literatur*, J.C.B. Mohr (Paul Siebeck), Tübingen 1989.

Schieffman, L.H. & Swartz, M.D.: *Hebrew and Aramaic Incantation Texts from the Cairo Genizah: Selected Texts from Taylor-Schechter Box K1*, Sheffield Academic Press, Sheffield 1992.

Scholem, G.: *Jewish Gnosticism, Merkaba Mysticism, & Talmudic Tradition*, Op. cit.

Swartz. M.D: *Mystical Prayer in Ancient Judaism: An Analysis of Ma'aseh Merkavah*, J.C.B. Mohr (Paul Siebeck), Tübingen 1992.

—*Scholastic Magic: Ritual and Revelation in Early Jewish Mysticism*, Princeton University Press, Princeton, 1996.

20. **Eisler, R.**: *Man into Wolf: An Anthropological Interpretation of Sadism Masochism, and Lycanthropy*, Greenwood Press, New York 1969.
21. See note 18 & 19.
22. **Verman, M.**: *The Books of Contemplation: Medieval Jewish Mystical Sources*, SUNY Press, Albany 1992.
23. **Marcus, I.G.**: *Piety and Society: The Jewish Pietists of Medieval Germany*, Brill Academic Publishers, Leiden 1981.
24. **Salzman, M.**: *The Chronicle of Ahimaaz*, Columbia University Press, New York 1924.
25. **Marcus, I.G.**: *The Political Dynamics of the Medieval German Jewish Community*" in Elazar, D.J.: *Authority, Power, and Leadership in the Jewish Polity: Cases and Issues*, Univrsity Press of America Inc., Lanham 1991.
26. **Trepp, L.**: *A History of the Jewish Experience: Eternal Faith, Eternal People*, Behrman House Inc., Springfield 1962.
27. **Scholem, G.**: *Kabbalah*, Op. cit.
28. **Scholem, G.**: *Origins of the Kabbalah*, Princeton University Press, Princeton 1987.
29. **Scholem, G.**: *Major Trends in Jewish Mysticism*, Op. cit.
    —*Kabbalah*, Op. cit.
    —*Origins of the Kabbalah*, Op. cit.
    Schäfer, P. & Dan, J. : *Gershom Scholem's Major Trends in Jewish Mysticism: 50 Years After*, Mohr Siebeck, Tübingen, 1993.

Dan, J.: *Gershom Scholem and the Mystical Dimension of Jewish History*, New York University Press, New York 1988.
—*The Christian Kabbalah: Jewish Mystical Books and Their Christian Interpreters: A Symposium*, Harvard College Library, Cambridge 1997.
—*Jewish Mysticism: Late Antiquity*, Jason Aronson Inc., Northvale 1998.
—*Jewish Mysticism: The Middle Ages*, Rowman & Littlefield Publishers Inc., Lanham 1998.
—*Jewish Mysticism: The Modern Period*, Rowman & Littlefield Publishers Inc., Lanham 1999.
—*Jewish Mysticism: General Characteristics and Comparative Study*, Rowman & Littlefield Publishers Inc., Lanham 1999.
—*The "Unique Cherub" Circle: A School of Mystics and Esoterics in Medieval Germany*, Mohr Siebeck, Tübingen, 1999.
—*Kabbalah: A Very Short Introduction*, Oxford University Press Inc., New York 2006.
Idel, M.: *Hasidism: Between Ecstasy and Magic*, SUNY Press, Albany 1995.
—*Messianic Mystics*, Yale University Press, New Haven & London 2000.
Idel, M. & Ostow, M.: *Jewish Mystical Leaders and Leadership in the 13th Century*, Jason Aronson Inc., Northvale 1998.
Ruderman, D.B.: *Kabbalah, Magic and Science: The Cultural Universe of a Sixteenth-Century Jewish Physician*, Harvard University Press, Cambridge 1988.
Tirosh-Rothschild, H.: *Between Worlds: The Life and Thought of Rabbi David ben Juda Messer Leon*, SUNY Press, Albany 1991.
Kanarfogel, E.: *Peering Through the Lattices: Mystical, Magical, and Pietistic Dimensions in the Tosafist Period*, Wayne State University Press, Detroit 2000.
Fine, L.: *Physician of the Soul, Healer of the Cosmos: Isaac Luria and His Kabbalistic Fellowship*, Op. cit.
Zohar, Z.: *Sephardic and Mizrahi Jewry: From the Golden Age of Spain to Modern Times*, NYU Press, New York 2005.
Katchen, A.L.: *Christian Hebraists and Dutch Rabbis*, Harvard University Press, Cambridge, 1984.
León-Jones, K.S. de: *Giordano Bruno and the Kabbalah: Prophets, Magicians and Rabbis*, University Press, Yale Haven & London 1993.
Beitchman, P.: *Alchemy of the Word: Cabala of the Renaissance*, SUNY Press, Albany 1998.

Coudert, A.: *The Impact of the Kabbalah in the Seventeenth Century: The Life and Thought of Francis Mercury van Helmont (1614-1698)*, Brill Academic Publishers, Leiden 1999.

30. **Yehudah HaChassid:** *Sefer Chassidim*, Bologna edition, Mossad HaRav Kook Jerusalem, 1957.
—*Sefer Hasidim*, E. Lewin-Epstein Ltd., Jerusalem 1966.
—*Sefer Chassidim: The Book of the Pious*, condensed and transl. A.Y. Finkel, Jason Aronson Inc., Northvale 1997.

31. **Eleazer ben Yehudah of Worms:** *Perush al Sefer Yetzirah*, Przemysl 1883 [facsimile copy Brooklyn 1978].

32. **Eleazer ben Yehudah of Worms:** *Sefer Sodei Razaya*, Sha'arei Ziv Institute, Jerusalem 1991.
—*Sodei Razya HaShalem*, Aharon Berazani, Tel Aviv 2003.

33. **Dan, J. & Kiener, D.C.:** *The Early Kabbalah*, Paulist Press, Mahwah 1986.
Verman, M.: *The Books of Contemplation: Medieval Jewish Mystical Sources*, SUNY Press, Albany 1992.

34. *The Bahir: An Ancient Kabbalistic Text attributed to Rabbi Nehuniah ben HaKana*, transl. by Aryeh Kaplan, Samuel Weiser Inc., New York 1979.

35. *Pirke d'Rabbi Eliezer: The Chapters of Rabbi Eliezer the Great*, transl. G. Friendlander, Sepher Hermon Press, New York 1916.

36. *Sefer ha-Iyyun*, Hebrew text and translation in **Verman, M.:** *The Books of Contemplation: Medieval Jewish Mystical Sources*, Op. cit.

37. **Scholem, G.:** *Origins of the Kabbalah*, Op. cit.

38. **Gabbai, M. Ibn:** *Sod ha-Shabbat: The Mystery of the Sabbath*, transl. E.K. Ginsburg, SUNY Press, Albany 1989.
Horowitz, I.: *Isaiah Horowitz: The Generations of Adam*, transl. M. Krassen, Paulist Press, Mahwah 1996.
Wineberg, Y.: *Lessons in Tanya: The Tanya of R. Shneur Zalman of Liadi*, Kehot Publication Society, Brooklyn 1987.
Scholem, G.: *Kabbalah*, Op. cit.
—*Origins of the Kabbalah*, Op. cit.
Ginsburg, E.K.: *The Sabbath in the Classical Kabbalah*, SUNY Press, Albany 1989.
Hallamish, M.: *An Introduction to the Kabbalah*, SUNY Press, Albany 1998.
Halevi, Z. ben Shimon: *Kabbalah and Exodus*, Samuel Weiser Inc., New York 1988.
—*A Kabbalistic Universe*, Samuel Weiser Inc., New York 1977.
—*Psychology and Kabbalah*, Samuel Weiser Inc., New York 1992.

39. **Scholem, G.:** *Kabbalah, Op. cit.*
Scholem, G.: *The Messianic Idea in Judaism and Other Essays on Jewish Spirituality*, Schocken Books Inc., New York 1971.
Idel, M.: *Golem: Jewish Magical and Mystical Traditions on the Artificial Anthropoid*, SUNY Press, Albany 1990.
Winkler, G.: *The Golem of Prague*, Judaica Press, New York 1980.
Bilski, E.M.: *Golem! Danger, Deliverance and Art*, The Jewish Museum, New York 1988.

40. **Mordell, P:** *Sefer Yetsirah*, P. Mordell, Philadelphia, 1914.
Stenring, K.: *The Book of Formation*, KTAV, New York 1968.
Kalisch, I.: *The Sepher Yetzirah: A Book of Creation*, L.H. Frank & Co., New York (Reprinted by the AMORC, San Jose, California, 1974)
Westcott, W.W.: *Sepher Yetzirah*, Occult Research Press, New York, 1887. Reprinted by Samuel Weiser, New York 1975.
Suares, C.: *The Sepher Yetzirah: Including the Original Astrology according to the Qabala and its Zodiac,"* Shambhala Publications Inc., Boulder 1976.
Blumenthal, D.: *Understanding Jewish Mysticism: A Source Reader*, Volume I *Op. cit.*
Kaplan, A.: *Sefer Yetzirah: The Book of Creation In Theory and Practice*, Samuel Weiser Inc., York Beach 1990 (Revised edition with index 1997).

41. *Sefer Raziel ha-Malach, Op. cit.*

42. **Abulafia, A.:** *Sefer Chayei ha-Olam ha-Ba*, Aharon Barazani, Jerusalem 2001.
—*Or ha-Sechel*, Aharon Barazani, Jerusalem 2001.
—*Chayei Nefesh*, Aharon Barazani, Jerusalem 2001.

43. **Isaac of Acco:** *Otzar ha-Chayim*, Guensberg Manuscript 775.

44. **Gikatilla, J.:** *Gates of Light: Sha'are Orah*, transl. Avi Weinstein, Alta Mira Press, Walnut Creek 1998.

45. Quoted from *Or ha-Sechel*, Vatican Ms. 233, transl. by A. Kaplan in *Meditation and Kabbalah, Op. Cit.*

46. **Abulafia, A.:** *The Path of Names*, transl. B. Finkel, J. Hirschman, D. Meltzer and G. Scholem, Trigram, Berkeley 1976.
Blumenthal, D.: *Understanding Jewish Mysticism: A Source Reader - The Philosophic Mystical Tradition and the Chassidic Tradition*, Volume II, KTAV Publishing House Inc., New York 1982.
Kaplan, A.: *Meditation and Kabbalah, Op. Cit.*
Idel, M.: *Kabbalah: New Perspectives, Op. Cit.*

—*The Mystical Experience in Abraham Abulafia*, SUNY Press, Albany 1988.
—*Language, Torah, and Hermeneutics in Abraham Abulafia*, SUNY Press, Albany
—*Studies in Ecstatic Kabbalah*, SUNY Press, Albany 1988.
—*Hasidism: Between Ecstasy and Magic*, Op cit.
—*Golem: Jewish Magical and Mystical Traditions on the Artificial Anthropoid*, Op. cit.
Kaplan, A.: *Meditation and The Bible*, Samuel Weiser, York Beach, Maine 1988.
—*Meditation and Kabbalah*, Op. Cit.
—*Jewish Meditation: A Practical Guide*, Schocken Books Inc., New York 1985.
Cooper, D.: *Ecstatic Kabbalah*, Sounds True Inc., Louisville 2005.

47. **Moses de Leon, et al.**: *The Zohar*, transl. M. Simon and H. Sperling, Soncino Press, London 1933.
—*The Zohar*, transl. P.P. Levertoff & M. Simon, Bennet, New York 1959.
Scholem, G.: *Zohar: The Book of Splendour, Basic Readings from the Kabbalah*, Schocken Books Inc., New York 1968.
Rosenberg, R.A.: *The Anatomy of God: The Book of Concealment, Great Holy Assembly and Lesser Holy Assembly of the Zohar*, KTAV Publishing House Inc., New York 1973.
Matt, D.C.: *Zohar: The Book of Enlightenment*, Paulist Press, Mahwah 1983.
Liebes, Y.: *Studies in the Zohar*, SUNY Press, Albany 1993.
Giller, P.: *Reading the Zohar: The Sacred Text of the Kabbalah*, Oxford University Press Inc., New York 2001.
Green, A.: *A Guide to the Zohar*, Stanford University Press, Stanford 2004.
—*The Zohar*, transl. D.C. Matt (Pritzker edition), Stanford University Press, Stanford 2003 (Vol. 1), 2004 (Vol. 2), 2006 (Vol. 3), 2007 (Vol. 4).

48. **Moses de Leon:** *Sefer Shekel ha-Kodesh*, Hotsa'at Keruv, Los Angeles 1996
—*The Shekel ha-Kodesh by Moses de Leon*, transl. A.W. Greenup, Jerusalem 1968.

49. **Azriel of Gerona:** *Sha'ar ha-Kavvanah: The Gate of Kavvanah*, transl. G. Scholem in *Origins of the Kabbalah*, Op. cit.

50. See note 9.

51. **Alemanno, Y.**: *Collectanaea* (Oxford MS 2234)

52. **Delmedigo, J.S.**: *Sefer Elim*, Menasseh ben Israel, Amsterdam 1628-9.

53. **Fano, M.A. de:** *Gilgulei Neshamot,* Yarid ha-Sefarim, Jerusalem 1998.
   —*Reincarnation of Souls,* Haktav Institute, Jerusalem 2001.
   —*Sefer Kanfei Yonah,* Mechon Bnei Yishachar, Jerusalem 1998.
   —*Sefer Asarah Ma'amarot,* Mechon Yismach Lev - Torat Moshe, Jerusalem 2000.
54. **Waite, A.E.:** *The Holy Kabbalah,* University Books Inc., New York 1960.
   Wirszubski, C.: *Pico della Mirandola's Encounter with Jewish Mysticism,* Harvard University Press, Cambridge 1989.
55. **Reuchlin, J.:** *De Arte Cabalistica: On the Art of the Kabbalah,* transl. Abaris Books Inc., New York 1983.
56. **Kircher, A.:** *Oedipus Aegyptiacus,* Rome 1653.
57. **Idel, M.:** *The Magical and Neoplatonic Interpretations of the Kabbalah in the Renaissance* in Cooperman, B.D.: *Jewish Thought in the Sixteenth Century,* Harvard University Press, Cambridge 1983.
58. **Scholem, G.:** *Kabbalah, Op. cit.*
   Liebes, Y.: *Studies in the Zohar, Op. cit.*
59. **Reuchlin, J.:** *De Arte Cabalistica: On the Art of the Kabbalah, Op. cit.*
60. **Findlen, P.:** *Athanasius Kircher: The Last Man who Knew Everything,* Routledge, New York & London 2004.
61. **Scholem, G.:** *Kabbala: Quellen und Forschungen zur Geschichte der Jüdische Mystik,* Band II, W. Drugulin, Leipzig 1927.
62. **Karo, J.:** *Sefer Maggid Mesharim, Op. cit.*
   Gordon, H.L.: *The Maggid of Caro, Op. cit.*
   Werblowsky, R.J.Z.: *Joseph Karo: Lawyer and Mystic, Op. cit.*
63. **Cordovero, M.:** *Pardes Rimmonim, Op. cit.*
   Robinson, I.: *Moses Cordovero's Introduction to Kabbalah: An Annotated Translation of His Or Ne'erav,* The Michael Sharf Publication Trust of the Yeshiva University Press, New York 1994.
64. **Vital, Chaim:** *Sefer Sha'ar Ru'ach ha-Kodesh,* Mosdat Nehar Shalom, Jerusalem 1999.
   —*Sefer Sha'arei Kedushah,* Hotza'at Yeshivat ha-Shamash, Jerusalem 1997.
   —*Sefer Sha'ar ha-Kavvanot,* Yeshivat ha-Mekubalim Maharchav, Jerusalem 2005.
65. **Vidas, E. ben Moses:** *Sefer Reshit Chochmah ha-Shalem,* Machon l'mechkar ul'hafatzat sifre musar v'torat ha-Chasidut "Or ha-Musar," Jerusalem 1984.

—*The Beginning of Wisdom: Unabridged translation of the Gate of Love from Rabbi Eliahu de Vidas' Reshit Chochmah*, transl. S.H. Benyosef, KTAV Publishing House Inc., Hoboken 2002.

66. **Horowitz, A.:** *Sefer Shnei Luchot ha-Brit ha-Shalem*, Machon Sha'arei ziv, Jerusalem 1993.
—*Shney Luchot Habrit*, transl. E. Munk, Lambda Publishers Inc., Brooklyn 1999.

67. **Sarug, I.:** *Limmudei Atzilut*, (attributed to Chaim Vital: *Sefer Limmudei Atzilut*, Jerusalem 1970.
Tabul, J. Ibn: *Derush Cheftzi Ba*, published in Kohen, Masud Kohen Alhadad: *Simchat Kohen*, Or ha-Sefer, Jerusalem 1977.
Uceda, S. ben I.: *Midrash Shmuel: A Collection of Commentaries on Pirkei Avot*, Haktav Institute, Jerusalem 1994.
Yonah, M.: *Sefer Kanfei Yonah*, Mechon Tiferet Mosheh, Brooklyn 1990.
Fano, Azariah de: *Asarah Ma'amarot*, Op. cit.
—*Gilgulei Neshamot*, Op. cit.
—*Kanfei Yonah*, Op. cit.
Delmedigo, J.S.: *Ta'alamut Chochmah* (Collectanea decerpta per magistrum R. Samuelem Germanum), Basle 1629.
Herrera, A.C. de: *Sha'ar ha-Shamayim*, Hotsa'at A.B. Sefarim, Jerusalem 2005.
—*Gate of Heaven*, transl. K. Krabbenhoft, Brill Academic Publishers, Leiden 2002.
Modena, L. de: *Sefer Ari Nohem*, Karl Tauchnitz, Leipzig 1840.
—*The Autobiography of a Seventeenth-century Venetian Rabbi: Leon Modena's Life of Judah*, transl. M.R. Cohen, Princeton University Pess, Princeton 1988.
Bacharach, N.: *Emek ha-Melech*, Yerid ha-Sefarim, Jerusalem 2003.
Luzzatto, M. Chaim: *138 Openings of Wisdom: Klach Pitchei ha-Chochmah*, transl. A.J. Greenbaum, Azamra Institute, Jerusalem 2005.

68. **Vital, H. ben Joseph:** *Window of the Soul: The Kabbalah of Rabbi Isaac Luria*, trans. N. Snyder, WeiserBooks, San Francisco 2008.
Scholem, G.: *Major Trends in Jewish Mysticism*, Op. cit.
—*Kabbalah*, Op. cit.
Faierstein, M.M.: *Jewish Mystical Autobiographies: Book of Visions and Book of Secrets*, Paulist Press, Mahwah 1999.
Fine, L.: *Safed Spirituality: Rules of Mystical Piety, The Beginning of Wisdom*, Paulist Press, Mahwah 1984.

—*Essential Papers on Kabbalah*, New York University Press, New York 1995.
—*Physician of the Soul, Healer of the Cosmos: Isaac Luria and His Kabbalistic Fellowship*, Op. cit.
Lenowitz, H.: *The Jewish Messiahs: From the Galilee to Crown Heights*, Oxford University Press Inc., New York 1998.
Goldish, M.: *Spirit Possession in Judaism: Cases and Contexts from the Middle Ages to the Present*, Op. cit.

69. *Sefer Tikkunei ha-Zohar*, Bnei Brak: Sifrei Kodesh Yahadut ha-Torah, Jerusalem 2004.
70. **Shamsian, A.:** *Chochmat ha-Partzuf Chochmat Kaf ha-Yad*, Op. cit.
Chochmat ha-Partzuf, Op. cit.
71. **Fine, L.:** *Physician of the Soul, Healer of the Cosmos: Isaac Luria and His Kabbalistic Fellowship*, Op. cit.
72. **Vital, Chaim:** *Sha'ar Ru'ach ha-Kodesh*, quoted in Fine, L.: *Op. cit.*
73. **Azikiri, E.:** *Sefer Haredim*, quoted in Fine, L.: *Op. cit.*
74. See note 67.
75. **Cardoza, A.M.:** *Abraham Miguel Cardozo: Selected Writings*, transl. D.J. Halperin, Paulist Press, Mahwah 2001.
76. **Frank, J.:** *The Collection of the Words of the Lord [Jacob Frank] from the Polish manuscripts*, transl. H. Lenowitz, electronic book, Harris Lenowitz 2001.
77. **Zacutto, M.:** *Shorshei ha-Shemot*, Op. cit.
78. **Luzzatto, M. Chaim:** *138 Openings of Wisdom: Klach Pitchei ha-Chochmah*, Op. cit.
—*Mesillat Yesharim: The Path of the Just*, transl. S. Silverstein, Feldheim Publishers, Jerusalem & New York 1974.
79. **Schnur, H.C.:** *Mystic Rebels*, Beechhurst Press Inc., New York 1949.
Scholem, G.: *Sabbatai Sevi: The Mystical Messiah (1626-1676*, transl. R.J.Z. Werblowsky, Princeton University Press, Princeton 1972.
Cohen, M.R.: *Toward the Millennium: Messianic Expectations from the Bible to Waco*, Brill Academic Publishers, Leiden 1998.
Idel, M.: *Messianic Mystics*, Yale University Press, New Haven & London 2000.
Lenowitz, H.: *The Jewish Messiahs: From the Galilee to Crown Heights*, Op. cit.
Freely, J.: *The Lost Messiah: The Astonishing story of Sabbatai Sevi, whose Messianic Movement emerged from the Mysticism of the Kabbalah*, Penguin Books, London 2001.

Goldish, M.: *The Sabbatean Prophets*, Harvard University Press, Harvard 2004.

80. **Zacutto, M.:** *Shorshei ha-Shemot, Op. cit.*
81. *Sacred Magic of Abra-melin the Mage*, transl. S.L. MacGregor-Mathers, Thorsons Publishers Ltd., Wellingborough 1976.
    The Book of Abramelin, transl. G. Dehn, Ibis Press, Lake Worth 2006.
    Patai, R.: *The Jewish Alchemists: A History and Source Book*, Princeton University Press, Princeton 1994.
82. **Luzzatto, M. Chaim:** *138 Openings of Wisdom: Klach Pitchei ha-Chochmah, Op. cit.*
    —*General Principles of Kabbalah*, transl. P.S. Berg, *Kabbalah Research Centre*, Jerusalem & New York 1970.
    —*Mesillat Yesharim: The Path of the Just*, transl. S. Silverstein, Feldheim Publishers, Jerusalem & New York 1974.
    —*Daath Tevunoth: The Knowing Heart*, transl. S. Silverstein, Feldheim Publishers, Jerusalem & New York 1982.
    —*Derech HaShem: The Way of God*, transl. A. Kaplan, Feldheim Publishers, Jerusalem & New York 1983.
    —*Essay on Fundamentals*, in Lebovits, Y. & Rosenstein, M.: *With an Eye on Eternity*, Feldheim Publishers, Jerusalem & New York 1995.
    —*The Ways of Reason: A Guide to the Talmud and the Foundations of Dialectics Explaining All the Principles of Reason and Logic in a Simple Concise Way*, transl. D. Sackton & C. Tscholkowsky, Feldheim Publishers, Jerusalem & New York 1997.
    —*Derech Hokhmah*, transl. Y. & E.R. Spring, Y. Spring, Raanana 1998.
    —*Secrets of the Future Temple: Mishkney Elyon*, transl. A. Greenbaum, The Temple Institute & Azamra Institute, Jerusalem 1999.
    —*The Kabbalah of the Ari Z'al according to the Ramhal: Kelalot ha-Ilan ha-Kadosh*, transl. R. Afilalo, *Kabbalah Editions*, Montreal 2004.
    Bar-Lev, Y.A.: *Yedid Nefesh: Introduction to Kabbalah*, Privately Published, Petach-Tivka, 1988.
83. **Shneur Zalman of Liadi:** *Likkutei Amarim – Tanya*, Kehot Publication Society, Brooklyn 1984.
84. **Levi Yitzchak of Berdichev:** *Sefer Kedushat Levi al ha-Torah u-Mo'adim Kedushot v'Likutim*, Mechon "Hadrat Chen," Ashdod 2005.

85. **Nachman of Bratzlav**: *Likkutei Moharan*, Mechon Nachalat Tzvi, Jerusalem 2004.
86. **Foxbrunner, R.A.**: *Habad: The Hasidism of R. Shneur Zalman of Liady*, Jason Aronson Inc., Northvale 1993.
87. **Zinberg, I.**: *A History of Jewish Literature: The German-Polish Cultural Center*, transl. B. Martin, Hebrew Union College Press, Cincinnati & KTAV Publishing House Inc., New York 1975.
88. *Ibid.*
89. *Talmud Bavli Bava Metsi'a 85b.*
    Schwartz, H.: *Gabriel's Palace: Jewish Mystical Tales*, Oxford University Press Inc., New York 1993.
90. **Feuer, A.C.**: *Shemoneh Esrei: The Amidah - The Eighteen Blessings*, Masorah Publications Ltd., Brooklyn 1990.
91. Quoted in **Philologos**: *Cracking the Whip: On Language*, an article published Friday 24th September 2004 in *The Jewish Daily Forward* (www.forward.com/articles/5379/).
92. **Juergensmeyer, M.**: *Terror in the Mind of God: The Global Rise of Religious Violence*, University of California Press, Berkeley 2003.
93. **Shlomo HaKohen Rabinowitz of Radomsk**: *Tiferet Shlomo*, Warsaw 1967; Tel Aviv 1962.
    —Excerpts in English in **Finkel, A.Y.**: *Kabbalah: Selections from Classic Kabbalistic Works from Raziel HaMalach to the Present Day*, Targum Press Inc., Southfield 2002.
94. **Yitzak Isaac Safrin of Komarno**: *Megillat Setarim.* Book of Secrets, transl. in Faierstein, M.M.: *Jewish Mystical Autobiographies: Book of Visions and Book of Secrets, Op. cit.*
    —Excerpts in **Finkel, A.Y.**: *Kabbalah: Selections from Classic Kabbalistic Works from Raziel HaMalach to the Present Day, Op. cit.*
95. **Tzadok Hakohen of Lublin**: *Sichat Malachei ha-Sharet*, Lublin 1927; Machon Har Bracha, Jerusalem.
96. **Joseph Chaim Ben Elijah ha-Chacham**: *Sefer Ateret Tiferet Pela'ot Rabot*, Hotzaat Yeshua Ben David Salem, Jerusalem 1980.
    —*Sefer Da'at u-Tevunah: le-Chochmat ha-Kabbalah*, Mekor Chaim, Jerusalem 1964.
97. **Lenain**: *La Science Cabalistique*, Editions Traditionnelles, Paris 1982.
98. **Levi, E.**: *The Book of Splendours*, Studies in Hermetic Tradition Vol. I, Thorsons, Northamptonshire 1973.
    —*The Mysteries of the Qabalah*, Studies In Hermetic Tradition Vol. II, Thorsons, Northamptonshire 1974.

—*Letters to a Disciple*, Aquarian Press, Wellingborough, Northamptonshire 1980.

99. **Papus:** *The Qabalah*, Studies in Hermetic Tradition Vol. IV, Thorsons, Northamptonshire 1977.

100. **Tzadok Hakohen of Lublin:** *Sichat Malachei ha-Sharet*, Op. cit.
—*Sefer Machshevot Charutz: Poked Acharim*, Machon Har Berachah, Har Berachah 2005.
—*Sefer Tzidkat ha-Tzadik ha-Male*, Alef, Machon le-Hotsa'at Sefarim, Jerusalem 1968.
—*Sefer Dover Tzedek*, Yahadut, Bnei Brak 1966.
Brill, A.: *Thinking God: The Mysticism of Rabbi Zadok of Lublin*, The Michael Scharf Publication Trust of the Yeshiva University Press; Jersey City 2002.

101. **Myer, L.:** *Qabbalah*, Samuel Weiser, New York 1970.
Achad, Frater: *Q.B.L. or The Bride's Reception: A Short Qabbalistic Treatise on the Tree of Life*, Samuel Weiser, New York 1969.
—*The Anatomy of the Body of God: being The Supreme Revelation of Cosmic Consciousness*, Samuel Weiser, New York 1976.
Bardon, F.: *The Key to the True Quabbalah*, Dieter Rüggeberg, Wuppertal, Austria, 1971.
Fortune, D.: *The Mystical Qabalah*, Ernest Benn, London 1972.
Butler, W.E.: *Magic and the Qabalah*, The Aquarian Press, London 1972.
Ponce, C.: *Kabbalah*, Garnstone Press, London 1974.
Gray, W.G: *The Ladder of Lights*, York Beach, 1981.
—*The Talking Tree*, Samuel Weiser Inc., New York 1977.
—*The Tree of Evil*, Samuel Weiser Inc., York Beach, 1984.
—*Qabalistic Concepts: Living the Tree*, (Previously *Concepts of Concepts*, Sangreal Sodality Series, Volume 3), Samuel Weiser Inc., York Beach, 1997.
—*The Simplified Guide to the Holy Tree of Life*, The Sangreal Sodality Press, Johannesburg 1989.
—*Condensation of Kabbalah*, online electronic publication, Jacobus G. Swart, Johannesburg.
—*Language of the Gods*, online electronic publication, Jacobus G. Swart, Johannesburg.
—*The Novena of the Tree of Life*, The Sangreal Sodality Press, Johannesburg 1987.
—*A Self Made by Magic*, Samuel Weiser Inc., New York 1976.
—*Magical Ritual Methods*, Helios Book Service Ltd., Cheltenham 1969.

Regardie, F.I.: *A Garden of Pomegranates*, Llewellyn Publications, St. Paul 1970.
—*The Middle Pillar*, Llewellyn Publications, St. Paul 1978.
Knight, Gareth: *A Practical Guide to Kabbalistic Symbolism*, Samuel Weiser Inc., York Beach 1978.
Love, J.: *The Quantum Gods: The Origin and Nature of Matter and Consciousness*, Op. cit.
Gonzalez-Wippler, C.: *A Kabbalah* for the Modern World, Llewellyn Publications, St. Paul 1978.
Ashcroft-Nowicki, D.: *The Shining Paths*, .Aquarian Press, Wellingborough 1983
Fielding, C.: *The Practical Qabalah*, Samuel Weiser, York Beach 1989.
Raphael: *Pathway of Fire: Initiation to the Kabbalah*, Samuel Weiser Inc., York Beach 1993.
Zalewski, P.: *Kabbalah of the Golden Dawn*, Llewellyn Publications, St. Paul, 1993.
Cicero, C. & Cicero, S.T.: *Qabalah: Theory and Magic*, The Golden Dawn Journal Book II, Llewellyn Publications, St. Paul 1994.
Bias, C.: *Qabalah, Tarot & The Western Mystery Tradition*, Samuel Weiser Inc., York Beach, Maine 1997.
Reed, E.C.: *The Witches Qabala*, Samuel Weiser Inc., York Beach 1997.
Stewart, R.J.: *The Miracle Tree: Demystifying the Qabalah*, New Page Books, Franklin Lakes 2003.

102. See note 40.
103. *Pirke Avot: Sayings of the Fathers*, Behrman House Inc., Springfield 1945.
104. *Pirke d'Rabbi Eliezer: The Chapters of Rabbi Eliezer the Great*, Op. Cit.
105. *Talmud Bavli Chagigah 12a*
106. *Avot d'Rabbi Nathan* quoted in **Idel, M.:** *Absorbing Perfections: Kabbalah and Interpretation*, Yale University Press, New Haven & London 2002.
107. **Roberts, A. & Donaldson, J.:** *Ante-Nicene Christian Library: Translations of the Writings of the Fathers down to A.D. 325*, Volume VI - *Hippolytus, Bishop of Rome Vol. 1*, T. & T. Clark, Edinburgh 1885.
    Goodenough, E.R.: *Jewish Symbols in the Greco-Roman Period*, Pantheon Books, New York 1965.
    Barry, K.: *The Greek Qabalah: Alphabetic Mysticism and Numerology in the Ancient World*, Samuel Weiser Inc., York Beach 1999.

Marcovich, M.: *Studies in Graeco-Roman Religions and Gnosticism*, Brill Academic Publishers, Leiden 1988.

Mead, G.R.S.: *Monoimus Number Theories and How to Seek After God*; Kessinger Publishing, Whitefish 2005.

Idel, M.: *Kabbalah: New Perspectives, Op. cit.*

108. Roberts, A. & Donaldson, J.: *Ante-Nicene Christian Library: Translations of the Writings of the Fathers down to A.D. 325, Op. cit.*

109. Abulafia, A.: *V'Zot li Yihudah*, quoted in Idel, M.: *Kabbalah: New Perspectives, Op. cit.*

110. Brody, W.G.: *Midrash on Psalms*, Yale University Press,, New Haven & London 1987.

111. *Pirke d'Rabbi Eliezer: The Chapters of Rabbi Eliezer the Great, Op. cit.*

112. *Sefer ha-Iyyun*, Hebrew text and translation in Verman, M.: *The Books of Contemplation: Medieval Jewish Mystical Sources, Op. cit.*

113. Verman, M.: *The Books of Contemplation: Medieval Jewish Mystical Sources, Op. cit.*

114. Wittgenstein, L. & Barrett, C.: *Wittgenstein: Lectures and Conversations on Aesthetics, Psychology and Religious Belief*, University of California Press, Berkeley 2007.

115. Albotini, Y.: *Sulam ha-Aliyah*,, Machon Sha'arei Ziv, Machon Sha'arei ziv, Jerusalem 1989.

Vital, Chaim: *Sha'ar ha-Kavvanah*, Yeshivat ha-shalom, Jerusalem 1997.

—*Sefer Sha'arei Kedushah, Op. Cit.*

Kaplan, A.: *Meditation and Kabbalah, Op. Cit.*

Blumenthal, D.: *Understanding Jewish Mysticism: A Source Reader - The Philosophic Mystical Tradition and the Chassidic Tradition, Volume II, Op. Cit.*

Cooper, D.: *Ecstatic Kabbalah, Op. Cit.*

116. Gray, W.G.: *A Ladder of Lights, Op. cit.*

—*The Talking Tree, Op. cit.*

—*Qabalistic Concepts: Living the Tree, Op. cit.*

—*The Tree of Evil*, Samuel Weiser, *Op. cit.*

—*The Simplified Guide to the Holy Tree of Life, Op. cit.*

117. Pinson, D.: *Meditation and Judaism*, Rowman & Littlefield Publishers Inc., Lanham 2004.

118. Gikatilla, J.: *Gates of Light: Sha'are Orah, Op. cit.*

119. Waxman, R.:*The Messianic Idea in Kabbalah* (electronic essay modified and titled *The Messianic Idea in Jewish Mysticism*, online at www.robertwaxman.org/id52.html).

120. *Gospel of Thomas* quoted in **Pagels, E.H.**: *The Gnostic Gospels*, Vintage Books, New York 1981.
121. Monoimus in a letter to Theophrastus quoted in **Pagels, E.H.**: *The Gnostic Gospels, Op. cit.*
122. *The Bahir: An Ancient Kabbalistic Text attributed to Rabbi Nehuniah ben HaKana, Op. cit.*
123. **Gray, W.G.**: *Western Inner Workings*, Sangreal Sodality Series Volume 1, Samuel Weiser Inc., York Beach 1983.
124. **Nachman of Bratzlav**: *Likkutei Moharan, Op Cit.*
125. Quoted in **Nachman of Bratzlav & Nathan Sternharz**: *Rabbi Nachman's Wisdom: Shevachay HaRan, Sichos HaRan*, transl. A. Kaplan, Breslov Research Institute, New York 1973.
126. **Bonder, H.**: *The Kabbalah of Money: Insights on Livelihood, Business, and All Forms of Economic Behavior*, Shambhala, Boston & London 1996.
127. **Gikatilla, J.**: *Gates of Light: Sha'are Orah, Op. cit.*
128. *Sefer Tikkunei ha-Zohar, Op. cit.*
129. **William G. Gray**: *Shortened form of Initiation*, unpublished manuscript.
130. **Gikatilla, J.**: *Gates of Light: Sha'are Orah, Op. cit.*
131. **Fleg, E.**: *The Life of Moses*, transl. Stephen H. Guest, Victor Gollancz Ltd, London 1928.

CHAPTER 2

1. **Suares, C.**: *The Cipher of Genesis: The Original Code of the Qabala as Applied to the Scriptures*, Shambhala, Berkeley 1970.
   — *The Cipher of Song of Songs*, Shambhala, Berkeley, 1971.
   — *The Sepher Yetzirah: Including the Original Astrology according to the Qabala and its Zodiac, Op. cit.*
2. **Gray, W.G.**: *Qabalistic Concepts: Living the Tree, Op. cit.*
3. **Gray, W.G.**: *The Rite of Light: A Mass of the Western Inner Mystery Tradition, Op. cit.*
4. **Bar-Lev, Yehiel A.**: *Yedid Nefesh: Introduction to Kabbalah, Op. Cit.*
5. **Kaplan, A.**: *Inner Space*, Moznaim Publishing Corporation, Jerusalem 1990.
6. **Kaplan, A.**: *Meditation and Kabbalah, Op. cit.*
   —*Inner Space, Op. cit.*
7. **Vital, Chaim**: *Sefer Etz Chayim*, quoted in **Ariel, D.S.**: *The Mystic Quest*, Schocken Books Inc., New York 1992.
8. **Vital, Chaim**: *Ibid.*

9. **Gray, W.G.**: *The Sangreal Ceremonies and Rituals*, Volume 4, The Sangreal Sodality Series, Samuel Weiser Inc, York Beach, 1986.
10. **Voltaire:** *Epîtres, XCVI*, quoted in The Oxford Concise Dictionary of Quotations, Oxford University Press, Oxford 1988.
11. **Gray, W.G.**: *The Consecration of a Sangreal Temple*, unpublished Manuscript.
12. **Love, J.**: *The Quantum Gods: The Origin and Nature of Matter and Consciousness, Op. cit.*
    Sadhu, M.: *The Tarot; A Contemporary Course of the Quintessence of Hermetic Occultism*, George Allen & Unwin, London 1975.
13. **Love, J.**: *The Quantum Gods: The Origin and Nature of Matter and Consciousness, Op. cit.*
14. **Sadhu, M.**: *The Tarot; A Contemporary Course of the Quintessence of Hermetic Occultism, Op. cit.*
15. **Watson, L.**: *Gifts of Unknown Things*, Coronet, Sevenoaks 1977.
16. **Suares, C.**: *The Cipher of Genesis: The Original Code of the Qabala as Applied to the Scriptures, Op. cit.*
    —*The Sepher Yetzirah: Including the Original Astrology according to the Qabala and its Zodiac, Op. cit.*
17. **Gray, W.G.**: *Qabalistic Concepts: Living the Tree, Op. cit.*
18. *Ibid.*
19. **Sadhu, M.**: *The Tarot; A Contemporary Course of the Quintessence of Hermetic Occultism, Op. cit.*
20. **Gray, W.G.**: *Western Inner Workings, Op. cit.*
21. *Ibid.*
22. **Gray, W.G.**: *My Autobiography*, unpublished Manuscript.
23. **Jacobs, L.**: *Jewish Ethics, Philosophy and Mysticism*, Behrman House Inc., New York, 1969.

CHAPTER 3

1. **Waite, A.E.**: *Lamps of Western Mysticism: Essays on the Life of the Soul in God*, Rudolf Steiner Publications, New York 1973.
Westcott, W.W.: *The Magical Mason: Forgotten Hermetic Writings of William Wyn Westcott, Physician and Magus*, Aquarian Press, Wellingborough 1983.
Shneur Zalman of Liadi: *Likkutei Amarim – Tanya*, Kehot Publication Society, Brooklyn 1984.
Kaplan, A.: *Meditation and Kabbalah*, *Op. cit.*
—*Sefer Yetzirah: The Book of Creation In Theory and Practice*, *Op. cit.*
—*Inner Space*, *Op. cit.*
Maimonides, M.: *Shemonah Perakim: a Treatise on the Soul*, transl. Leonard S. Kravitz & Kerry M. Olitzky, UAHC Press, New York 1999.
Finkel, A.Y.: *Kabbalah: Selections from Classic Kabbalistic Works from Raziel HaMalach to the Present Day*, *Op. cit.*
Vidas, E. ben Moses: *The Beginning of Wisdom: Unabridged translation of the Gate of Love from Rabbi Eliahu de Vidas' Reshit Chochmah*, *Op. cit.*
Ginzburg, Y.: *Transforming Darkness Into Light*, GalEinai Publications Society, Jerusalem 2002.
—*Body, Mind and Soul: Kabbalah on Human Physiology, Disease, and Healing*, GalEinai Publications Society, Jerusalem 2003.
Leet, L.: *The Secret Doctrine of the Kabbalah: Discovering the Key to Hebraic Sacred Science*, *Op cit.*
—*The Kabbalah of the Soul: The Transformative Psychology and Practices of Jewish Mysticism*, Inner Traditions International, Rochester 2003.
—*The Universal Kabbalah: Deciphering the Cosmic Code in the Sacred Geometry of the Sabbath Star Diagram*, *Op cit.*
Vital, H. ben J., Klein, E., & Luria, I. ben S.: *Kabbalah of Creation: The Mysticism of Isaac Luria, Founder of Modern Kabbalah*, North Atlantic Books, Berkeley 2005.
Steinbock, A.J.: *Phenomenology and Mysticism: The Verticality of Religious Experience*, Indiana University Press, Bloomington 2007.
Samuel, G.: *The Kabbalah Handbook: A Concise Encyclopedia of Terms and Concepts in Jewish Mysticism*, Jeremy P. Tarcher/Penguin, New York 2007.

2. **Miller, H.:** *The Wisdom of the Heart*, New Directions Books, Norfolk 1941.
   Lukeman, B.: *Embarkations: A Guide to Dealing with Death & Parting*, Prentice-Hall Inc., Englewood Cliffs, 1980.
3. **Herrera, A.C. de:** *Gate of Heaven, Op cit.*
4. **Bardon, F.:** *Initiation into Hermetics: A Course of Instruction of Magic Theory and Practice*, Dieter Rüggeberg, Wuppertal 1976.
5. **Long, M.F.:** *The Secret Science behind Miracles*, DeVorss & Company, Marina del Rey 1948.
   —*The Secret Science at Work: New Light on Prayer*, DeVorss & Company, Santa Monica 1953.
   —*The Secret Science at Work: New Light on Prayer*, DeVorss & Company, Santa Monica 1953.
6. *Sefer ha-Malbush*, MS Oxford-Bodleian 1960; MS London British Library OR. 6577 (Margoliouth III, 736)
   Sefer Raziel ha-Malach, Op. cit.
   Scholem, G.: *Kabbalah, Op. cit.*
   Wolfson, E.R.: *Through a Speculum that Shines: Vision and Imagination in Medieval Jewish Mysticism*, Princeton University Press, Princeton 1994.
   —*Circle in the Square: Studies in the Use of Gender in Kabbalistic Symbolism*, State University of New York Press, Albany 1995.
7. Quoted in *Absorbing Perfections: Kabbalah and Interpretation, Op. cit.*
8. **Idel, M.:** *Differing Conceptions of Kabbalah in the Early 17th Century* in **Twersky, I. & Septimus, B.:** *Jewish Thought in the Seventeenth Century*, Harvard University Press, Harvard 1987.
   —*Absorbing Perfections: Kabbalah and Interpretation, Op. cit.*
   —*Golem: Jewish Magical and Mystical Traditions on the Artificial Anthropoid, Op. cit.*
   Wolfson, E.R.: *Language, Eros, Being: Kabbalistic Hermeneutics and Poetic Imagination*, Fordham Univerisity Press, New York 2005.
9. *Sefer ha-Malbush v'Tikkun me'il ha-Tzedakah*, MS British Museum, Margoliouth 752.
   The Book of the Putting on and Fashioning of the mantle of Righteousness quoted in **Scholem, G.:** *On the Kabbalah and Its Symbolism*, Schocken Books Inc., New York 1965.

10. **Robinson, I.:** *Moses Cordovero's Introduction to Kabbalah: An Annotated Translation of His Or Ne'erav, Op. cit.*
11. **Cordovero, M.:** *Pardes Rimmonim* quoted in **Matt, D.C.:** *The Essential Kabbalah: The Heart of Jewish Mysticism,* HarperSanFrancisco, San Francisco 1995.
12. **Robinson, I.:** *Moses Cordovero's Introduction to Kabbalah: An Annotated Translation of His Or Ne'erav, Op. cit.*

CHAPTER 4

1. **Crowley, A.:** *Magick in Theory and Practice*, Castle Books, Secaucus 1991.
2. **Nachman of Bratzlav:** *Likkutei Moharan*, quoted in **Kramer, C.:** *Anatomy of the Soul*, Breslov Research Institute, New York 1998.
3. **Mambert, W.A. & Foster, B.F.:** *A Trip into Your Unconscious*, Acropolis Books Ltd., Washington 1973.
4. **Bardon, F.:** *Initiation into Hermetics: A Course of Instruction of Magic Theory and Practice, Op. cit.*
5. **Keyes, E.:** *Toning: The Creative Power of the Voice*, DeVorss & Company, Santa Monica 1973.
   Campbell, D.: *The Roar of Silence: Healing Powers of Breath, Tone and Music*, Theosophical Publishing House, Wheaton 1989.
   Hale, S.E.: *Song & Silence: Voicing the Soul*, La Alameda Press, Albuquerque 1995.
   Newham, P.: *Therapeutic Voicework*, Jessica Kingsley Publishers, London & Philadelphia 1998.
   Carol, S.: *The Way of Song: A Guide to Freeing the Voice and Sounding the Spirit*, St. Martin's Press, New York 2003.
6. **Bardon, F.:** *Initiation into Hermetics: A Course of Instruction of Magic Theory and Practice, Op. cit.*
7. **Gray, W.G.:** *The Tree of Evil, Op. cit.*
8. **Gray, W.G.:** *Western Inner Workings, Op. cit.*
9. **Janov, A:** *The Primal Scream: Primal Therapy: the Cure for Neurosis*, Putnam, New York 1970.
   —*The Anatomy of Mental Illness: The Scientific Basis of Primal Therapy*, Putnam, New York 1972.
   —*The New Primal Scream: Primal Therapy 20 Years On*, Abacus, London 1991.
10. **Wilson, C.:** *The Quest for Wilhelm Reich*, Anchor Press/Doubleday, Garden City 1981.
11. **Gray, W.G.:** *Qabalistic Concepts: Living the Tree, Op. cit.*
12. **Gray, W.G.:** *A Self Made by Magic, Op cit.*
    —*Qabalistic Concepts: Living the Tree, Op. cit.*
13. **Gray, W.G.:** *A Self Made by Magic, Op cit.*

CHAPTER 5

1. **Bardon, F.:** *Initiation into Hermetics: A Course of Instruction of Magic Theory and Practice, Op. cit.*
2. See Chapter 1 Note 40.
3. **Glazerson, M.:** *Letters of Fire: Mystical Insights into the Hebrew Language*, Feldheim Publishers, Jerusalem & New York 1991.
4. **Schaya, L.:** *The Universal Meaning of the Kabbalah, Op. cit.*
5. *Ibid.*
6. *Ibid.*
7. *Talmud Bavli, Yoma 86a* quoted in **Schaya, L.:** *Ibid.*
8. **Schaya, L.:** *Ibid.*
9. See Chapter 1 Note 40.
10. *Sefer Yetzirah* transl. **Blumenthal, D.R.:** *Understanding Jewish Mysticism: A Source Reader: The Merkabah Tradition and the Zoharic Tradition, Op. cit.*
11. **Gray, W.G.:** *Magical Ritual Methods, Op. cit.*
12. **Davis A. & Dunn-Mascetti, M.:** *Judaic Mysticism*, Hyperion, New York 1997.
13. **Yogi Ramacharaka (W.W. Atkinson):** *The Hindu-Yogi Science of Breath: A Complete Manual of the Oriental Breathing Philosophy of Physical, Mental, Psychic and Spiritual Development*, L.N. Fowler & Co. Ltd., London 1903.
    —*Hatha Yoga: or The Yogi Philosophy of Physical Well-Being*, Yogi Publication Society, Chicago 1904.
14. **Rogo, D.S.:** *Leaving the Body: A Complete Guide to Astral Projection*, Prentice Hall Press, New York 1983.
15. *Ibid.*
16. *Ibid.*
    Yogi Ramacharaka (W.W. Atkinson): *The Hindu-Yogi Science of Breath: A Complete Manual of the Oriental Breathing Philosophy of Physical, Mental, Psychic and Spiritual Development, Op. cit.*
17. **Vital, Chaim:** *Sefer Sha'ar Ru'ach ha-Kodesh*, Mosdat Nehar Shalom, Jerusalem 1999.
    Kaplan, A.: *Meditation and Kabbalah, Op. Cit.*
18. **Gray, W.G.:** *The Rite of Light: A Mass of the Western Inner Mystery Tradition*, limited & numbered edition, Privately Printed, Cheltenham 1976 (Reprinted with explanations in *The Sangreal Sacrament*, Volume 2, Sangreal Sodality Series, Samuel Weiser Inc., York Beach, 1983).

CHAPTER 6

1. **Bardon, F.**: *Initiation into Hermetics: A Course of Instruction of Magic Theory and Practice*, Op. cit.
2. *Ibid.*
3. *Ibid.*
4. *Ibid.*
5. *Ibid.*
6. **Weinberg, G.H.**: *Self Creation*, St. Martin's Press, New York 1978.
7. *Ibid.*
8. Recording of Credo Mutwa in coversation with William G. Gray, privately owned.
9. **Schwartz, S. & Hirson, R.O.**: *Pippin: A Musical Comedy*, Drama Book Specialists, New York 1975.
10. **Weinberg, G.H.**: *Self Creation*, Op. cit.
11. **Labiche, E. & Martin, E.**: *Le Voyage de Monsieur Perrichon: Comédie en Quatre Actes*, Librairie Nouvells : A. Bourdilliat et Cie., Paris 1860.
12. **Weinberg, G.H.**: *Self Creation*, Op. cit.
13. *Ibid.*
14. *Ibid.*
15. **Bardon, F.**: *Initiation into Hermetics: A Course of Instruction of Magic Theory and Practice*, Op. cit.
16. **Gibran, K.**: *The Secrets of the Heart: Selected Works*, transl. A.R. Ferris, Philosophical Library, New York 1947.

CHAPTER 7

1. **Patai, R.:** *The Jewish Alchemists: A History and Source Book*, Op. cit.
2. *Ibid.*
3. **ha-Cohen, T. ben M.Y.:** *Ma'aseh Tuviah*, Yisra'el ben Avraham, Yeznitz, 1721 (Third Edition, Cracow 1908).
   Lewinson, A.: *Tuvia ha-Rofe: v'Sifro Ma'aseh Tuviah*, Rimon, Berlin 1924.
   Levy, B.B.: *Planets, Potions, and Parchments: Scientifica Hebraica from the Dead Sea Scrolls to the Eighteenth Century*, Jewish Public Library/McGill-Queen's University Press, Montreal & Buffalo 1990.
4. **Schaya, L.:** *The Universal Meaning of the Kabbalah*, Op. cit.
5. **Gray, W.G.:** *A Ladder of Lights*, Op. cit.
   —*The Talking Tree*, Op. cit.
   —*Qabalistic Concepts: Living the Tree*, Op. cit.
   —*Language of the Gods*, Op. cit.
   —*Magical Ritual Methods*, Op. cit.
   —*Inner Traditions of Magic*, Samuel Weiser, New York 1970.
   —*A Self Made by Magic*, Op cit.
6. **Bardon, F.:** *Initiation into Hermetics: A Course of Instruction of Magic Theory and Practice*, Op. cit.
7. **Gray, W.G.:** *Magical Ritual Methods*, Op. cit.
8. **Bardon, F.:** *Initiation into Hermetics: A Course of Instruction of Magic Theory and Practice*, Op. cit.
9. *Ibid.*
10. *Ibid.*
11. *Ibid.*
12. *Ibid.*
13. *Ibid.*
14. *Ibid.*
15. *Prayer of Unity Rabban Gamliel*, Vatican MS 290. quote transl. in **Verman, M.:** *The Books of Contemplation: Medieval Jewish Mystical Sources*, Op. cit.
16. **Verman, M.:** *Ibid.*
17. **Sternhartz, N.N.:** *Likutei Halachot*, quote transl. in **Kramer, C.:** *Anatomy of the Soul*, Op. cit.
18. **Kramer, C.:** *Ibid.*

19. *Siddur T'filah: Complete Prayer Book*, Shapiro, Vallentine & Co., London 1931.
20. *Midrash Rabbah*, Soncino Press, Brooklyn 2001.
21. *Pirke d'Rabbi Eliezer: The Chapters of Rabbi Eliezer the Great, Op. cit.*
22. *Ibid.*
23. *Midrash Rabbah, Op. cit.*
24. **Mackenzie, D.A.:** *The Migration of Symbols, and their Relations to Beliefs and Customs*, Ken Paul, Trench, Trubner & Co. Ltd., London 1926.
    Trachtenberg, J.: *Jewish Magic and Superstition: A Study in Folk Religion, Op. cit.*
25. **Yeshayahu ben Avraham:** *Sh'lah al Sefer Vayik'ra*, quoted in **Winkler, G.:** *Kabbalah 365: Daily Fruit from the Tree of Life*, Andrews McMeel Publishing, Kansas City 2004.
26. **Patai, R.:** *The Hebrew Goddess*, KTAV Publishing House Inc., New York 1968.
    Winkler, G.: *Magic of the Ordinary, Op. cit.*
27. See Chapter 1 Note 40.
28. **King, C.W.:** *The Gnostics and Their Remains, Ancient and Mediaeval*, David Nutt, London 1887.
    Layton, B.: *The Gnostic Scriptures*, SCM Press Ltd., London 1987.
29. **Griffith, F.L. & Thompson, H.:** *The Demotic Magical Papyrus of London and Leiden*, H. Grevel & Co., London 1909.
    Betz, H.D.: *The Greek Magical Papyri*, University of Chicago Press, Chicago 1986.
30. **Zacutto, M.:** *Shorshei ha-Shemot, Op. cit.*
31. **Leet, L.:** *The Secret Doctrine of the Kabbalah: Discovering the Key to Hebraic Sacred Science, Op cit.*
32. **Regardie, I.:** *The Golden Dawn: A Complete Course in Practical Ceremonial Magic*, Llewellyn Publications, St. Paul 1971.
33. *Matthew 6:13, The Holy Bible, containing the Old and New Testaments: translated out of the original tongues, being the version set forth A.D. 1611 compared with the most ancient authorities and revised*, British and foreign Bible Society, London 1938.
34. *The Twenty-Four Books of the Holy Scriptures, according to the Masoretic Text*, transl. A. Harkavy, Hebrew Publishing Company, New York 1916.

35. **Millgram, A.E.:** *An Anthology of Medieval Hebrew Literature,* Abelard-Schuman, London & New York 1962.
36. See note 5.
37. **Mackenzie, D.A.:** *The Migration of Symbols, and their Relations to Beliefs and Customs,* Ken Paul, Trench, Trubner & Co. Ltd., London 1926.
38. **Winkler, G.:** *Magic of the Ordinary, Op. cit.*

CHAPTER 8

1. Kadish, S.: Kavvana: Directing the Heart in Jewish Prayer, Jason Aronson Inc., Northvale 1997.
2. **Gray, W.G.:** *Inner Traditions of Magic, Op. cit.*
3. **Gray, W.G.:** *The Tree of Evil, Op. cit.*
4. **Scholem, G.:** *Kabbalah, Op. cit.*
   Idel, M.: *Kabbalah: New Perspectives, Op. cit.*
5. **Isaac of Acre:** *Me'ir Einayim Ekev*, published in Jellinek, A.: *Philosophie undKabbalah*, Leipzig 1854.
   Vital, Chaim: *Sefer Sha'ar Ru'ach ha-Kodesh,Op. cit.*
   Kaplan, A.: *Meditation and Kabbalah, Op. cit.*
   —*Inner Space, Op. cit.*
6. **Nachmanides:** *Sha'ar ha-Gemul*, Bidphus Goldman, Warsaw 1876.
   —quoted in **Scholem, G.:** *Kabbalah, Op. cit.*
7. **Wolfson, E.R.:** *Through a Speculum that Shines: Vision and Imagination in Medieval Jewish Mysticism, Op. cit.*
   —*Circle in the Square: Studies in the Use of Gender in Kabbalistic Symbolism, Op. cit.*
   Gafni, M.: *The Mystery of Love*, Atria Books, New York 2003.
   Green, A.: *A Guide to the Zohar, Op. cit.*
   Idel, M.: *Kabbalah and Eros*, Yale University Press, New Haven & London 2005.
   Hoffman, E. & Schachter-Shalomi, Z.M.: *The Way of Splendor: Jewish Mysticism and Modern Psychology*, Rowman & Littlefield Publishers Inc., Lanham 2006.
   Rosler, I.B.: *Eros Revisited: Love for the Indeterminate Other*, Lexington Books, 2007.
8. *The Zohar*, Vol. 2 Pritzker edition, *Op. cit.*
   —quoted in **Kaplan, A.:** *Meditation and Kabbalah, Op. cit.*
   Leet, L: *Renewing the Covenant: A Kabbalistic Guide to Jewish Spirituality*, Inner Traditions International, Rochester 1999.
9. *The Zohar*, Vol. 2 Pritzker edition, *Op. cit.*
   —quoted in **Kaplan, A.:** *Meditation and Kabbalah, Op. cit.*
10. *Ibid.*
11. **Bakan, D.:** *Sigmund Freud and the Jewish Mystical Tradition*, Free Association Books, London 1990.

12. **Faierstein, M.M. & Heschel, A.J.**: *Prophetic Inspiration After the Prophets: Maimonides and Other Medieval Authorities*, KTAV Publishing House Inc., Hoboken 1996.
    Lieberman, S.: *Hellenism in Jewish Palestine: Transmission, Beliefs and Manners of Palestine in the 1 Century b.c.e - IV Century c.e.*, Jewish Theological Seminary of America, New York 1962.
13. *The Twenty-Four Books of the Holy Scriptures according to the Masoretic Text*, transl. A. Harkavy, Hebrew Publishing Company, New York 1916.
14. **Idel, M.**: *Kabbalah: New Perspectives, Op. cit.*
15. **Green, A.**: *Keter: The Crown of God in Early Jewish Mysticism*, Princeton University Press, Princeton 1997.
16. **Loewe, F. & Lerner, A.J.**: *Paint your Wagon: A Musical Play in Two Acts*, Coward-McCann, New York 1952.
17. **Abulafia, A.**: *Sefer ha-Cheshek*, ha-Va'ad le-hotsa'at sefarim she'ah. Kolel Torat Chacham, Jerusalem 1999.
    —quoted in **Kaplan, A.**: *Meditation and Kabbalah, Op. cit.*
18. **Isaac of Acre**: *Me'ir Einayim Ekev*, published in Jellinek, A.: *Philosophie undKabbalah*, Leipzig 1854.
    —quoted in **Scholem, G.**: *Major Trends in Jewish Mysticism, Op. cit.*
    —also in **Kaplan, A.**: *Meditation and Kabbalah, Op. cit.* and **Idel, M.**: *Studies in EcstaticKabbalah*, SUNY Press, Albany 1988.
19. **Kaplan, A.**: *Meditation and Kabbalah, Op. cit.*
    —*Meditation and the Bible, Op. cit.*
    —*Jewish Meditation: A Practical Guide*, Schocken Books Inc., New York 1995.
    Pinson, D.: *Meditation and Judaism, Op. cit.*
20. **Abulafia, A.**: *Sefer Chayei ha-Olam ha-Ba, Op. cit.*
    —*Or ha-Sechel, Op. cit.*
    Albotini, Y.: *Sulam ha-Aliyah,, Op. cit.*
    Kaplan, A.: *Meditation and Kabbalah, Op. cit.*
    Blumenthal, D.: *Understanding Jewish Mysticism: A Source Reader - The Philosophic Mystical Tradition and the Chassidic Tradition, Volume II, Op. cit.*
    Idel, M.: *Kabbalah: New Perspectives, Op. cit.*
    —*The Mystical Experience in Abraham Abulafia, Op. cit.*
    Cooper, D.: *Ecstatic Kabbalah, Op. cit.*
21. **Vital, Chaim**: *Sefer Sha'arei Kedushah*, quoted in **Kaplan, A.**: *Meditation and Kabbalah, Op. cit.*

22. **Kaplan, A.:** *Jewish Meditation: A Practical Guide*, Op. cit.
23. **Hesiod:** *Theogony*, transl. N.O. Brown, Liberal Arts Press, New York 1953.
24. **McDonald, B.:** *Seeing God Everywhere: Essays on Nature and the Sacred*, World Wisdom Inc., Bloomington 2003.

CHAPTER 9

1. **Hai Gaon** quoted in **Kaplan, A.**: *Meditation and the Bible*, *Op. cit.*
2. **Azulay, H.Y.D.**: *Shem ha-Gedolim*, Yerid ha-Sefarim, Jerusalem 2004.
   Karo, J.: *Sefer Maggid Mesharim*, *Op. cit.*
   Gordon, H.L.: *The Maggid of Caro*, *Op. cit.*
   Werblowsky, R.J.Z.: *Joseph Karo: Lawyer and Mystic*, *Op. cit.*
   Jacobs, L.: *Jewish Mystical Testimonies*, Schocken Books Inc., New York 1978.
   Epstein, P.: *Kabbalah: The Way of the Jewish Mystic*, Doubleday & Company, New York 1978.
   Barba, C.G.: *A Search for God*, Trafford Publishing, Victoria 2004.
   Chajes, J.H.: *Between Worlds: Dybbuks, Exorcists, and Early Modern Judaism*, *Op. cit.*
   Goldish, M.: *Spirit Possession in Judaism: Cases and Contexts from the Middle Ages to the Present*, *Op. cit.*
3. **Werblowsky, R.J.Z.**: *Joseph Karo: Lawyer and Mystic*, *Op. cit.*
4. *Ibid.*
5. *Ibid.*
6. *Ibid.*
7. **Abulafia, A.**: *Sefer ha-Tzeruf*, Aharon Barazani, Jerusalem 2003.
   —*Imrei Shefer*, Aharon Barazani, Jerusalem 1999.
   —*Ner Elohim*, Aharon Barazani, Jerusalem 2002.
   —*Or ha-Sechel*, *Op. cit.*
   Albotini, Y.: *Sulam ha-Aliyah*, *Op. cit.*
   —Chapters transl. in **Blumenthal, D.**: *Understanding Jewish Mysticism: A Source Reader - The Philosophic Mystical Tradition and the Chassidic Tradition, Volume II*, *Op. Cit.*
   Azulay, H.Y.D.: *Shem ha-Gedolim*, *Op. Cit.*
   —*Midbar Kedemot*, Mayan ha-Chochmah, Jerusalem 1957.
   Besserman, P.: *The Shambhala Guide to Kabbalah and Jewish Mysticism*, Shambhala, Berkeley, 1997.
8. **Gordon, H.L.**: *The Maggid of Caro*, *Op. cit.*
9. **Kobler, F. & Roslansky, J.D.**: *A Treasury of Jewish Letters: Letters from the Famous and the Humble*, Jewish Publication Society of America, Philadelphia 1953.

10. **Ginzburg, S.:** *The Life and Works of Moses Hayyim Luzzatto: Founder of Modern Hebrew Literature*, The Dropsie College for Hebrew and Cognate Learning, Philadelphia 1931.
11. *Ibid.*
12. **Lewis, C.S.:** *Through the Looking Glass, and what Alice Found There*, Pan Books, London 1977.
13. **Abulafia, A.:** *Sefer Chayei ha-Olam ha-Ba, Op. cit.*
    Quoted in **Seidman, R. & Kushner, L.:** *The Oracle of Kabbalah: Mystical Teachings of the Hebrew Letters*, St. Martin's Press, New York 2001.
14. **Isaac of Acco:** *Otzar ha-Chayim, Op. cit.*
    Kaplan, A.: *Meditation and Kabbalah, Op. cit.*
    —*Jewish Meditation: A Practical Guide, Op. cit.*
    —*Sefer Yetzirah: The Book of Creation In Theory and Practice, Op. cit.*
    Idel, M.: *The Mystical Experience in Abraham Abulafia, Op. Cit.*
    —*Studies in Ecstatic Kabbalah, Op. cit.*
    —*Absorbing Perfections: Kabbalah and Interpretation, Op. cit.*
    Seidman, R. & Kushner, L.: *The Oracle of Kabbalah: Mystical Teachings of the Hebrew Letters, Op. cit.*
15. **Zacutto, M.:** *Shorshei ha-Shemot, Op. cit.*
16. **Eleazar ben Yehudah of Worms:** *Sefer ha-Chochmah*, MS Oxford-Bodleian 1568.
    Barzillai al Barceloni, J. ben: *Perush Sefer Yetsirah le-ha-rav Yehudah bar Barzilay ha-Bartseloni z"al*, edited S.J. Halberstam & D. Kaufmann, Mekize Nirdamim, Berlin 1885. Republished Maqor, Jerusalem 1970.
    Zacutto, M.: *Shorshei ha-Shemot, Op. cit.*
    Scholem, G.: *Jewish Gnosticism, Merkaba Mysticism, & Talmudic Tradition, Op. cit.*
    Schäfer, P.: *Hekhalot Studien, Op. cit.*
    —*Synopse zur Hekhalot Literatur, Op. cit.*
    —*The Hidden and Manifest God: Some Major Themes in Early Jewish Mysticism, Op. cit.*
    Wolfson, E.R.: *Through a Speculum that Shines: Vision and Imagination in Medieval Jewish Mysticism, Op. cit.*
    —*Along the Path: Studies in Kabbalistic Myth, Symbolism and Hermeneutics*, SUNY Press, Albany 1995.
    Abrams, D.: *From Divine Shape to Angelic Being: The Career of Akatriel in Jewish Literature*, in *Journal of Religion*, Vol. 76 No.1, The University of Chicago Press, Chicago 1996.

Green, A.: *Keter: The Crown of God in Early Jewish Mysticism,* Op. cit.
Deutsch, N.: *Guardians of the Gate: Angelic Vice Regency in Late Antiquity*, Brill Academic Publishers, Leiden, 1999.
Dan, J.: *The Heart and the Fountain: An Anthology of Jewish Mystical Experiences*, Oxford University Press Inc., New York 2003.
Schwartz, H.: *Gabriel's Palace: Jewish Mystical Tales,* Op. cit.
—with **Loebel-Fried, Ginsburg, E.K.**: *Tree of Souls: The Mythology of Judaism*, Oxford University Press Inc., New York 2004.

17. **Trachtenberg, J.**: Jewish Magic and Superstition: A Study in Folk Religion, *Op. cit.*
18. *The Twenty-Four Books of the Holy Scriptures according to the Masoretic Text,* Op. cit.
19. **Gikatilla, J.**: *Gates of Light: Sha'are Orah,* Op. cit.
20. *Ibid.*
21. **Gray, W.G.**: *The Talking Tree,* Op. cit.
    —*Magical Images*, Sangreal Foundation Inc., Dallas 1972.
22. **Gikatilla, J.**: *Gates of Light: Sha'are Orah,* Op. cit.
23. *Ibid.*
24. *Ibid.*
25. *Ibid.*
26. *Ibid.*
27. **Kaplan, A.**: *Meditation and Kabbalah,* Op. cit.
28. **Karo, J.**: *Sefer Maggid Mesharim,* Op. cit.
    Werblowsky, R.J.Z.: *Joseph Karo: Lawyer and Mystic,* Op. cit.
    Fine, L.: *Safed Spirituality: Rules of Mystical Piety, The Beginning of Wisdom,* Op. cit.
29. **Kaplan, A.**: *Jewish Meditation: A Practical Guide,* Op. cit.
30. *Ibid.*
31. *Siddur T'filah: Complete Prayer Book,* Op. cit.
32. **Robinson, I.**: *Moses Cordovero's Introduction to Kabbalah: An Annotated Translation of His Or Ne'erav,* Op. cit.
33. **Cordovero, M.**: *Pardes Rimmonim,* Op. cit.
34. **Robinson, I.**: *Moses Cordovero's Introduction to Kabbalah: An Annotated Translation of His Or Ne'erav,* Op. cit.
35. *Ibid.*
36. **Schäfer, P.**: *Hekhalot Studien,* Op. cit.
    —*Synopse zur Hekhalot Literatur,* Op. cit.
    —*The Hidden and Manifest God: Some Major Themes in Early Jewish Mysticism,* Op. cit.

      Kaplan, A.: *Meditation and Kabbalah, Op. cit.*
      Blumenthal, D.: *Understanding Jewish Mysticism: A Source Reader,* Volume I *Op. cit.*
37. *Hechalot Rabbati* (Greater *Hechalot* [Palaces]) transl. in **Carmi, T.:** *The Penguin Book of Hebrew Verse,* Penguin Books, Harmondsworth 1981.
38. **Ha-Kohen, I.M., Feldman, A. & Orenstein, A.:** *Mishnah Berurah: The Classic Commentary to Shulchan Aruch Orach Chayim, comprising the Laws of Daily Jewish Conduct,* Feldheim Publishers, Jerusalem & New York 1999.
      Gelbard, S.P.: *Rite and Reason: 1050 Jewish Customs and Their Sources,* transl. R.N. Bulman, Feldheim Publishers, Jerusalem & New York 2000.
39. **Samuel, G.:** *The Kabbalah Handbook: A Concise Encyclopedia of Terms and Concepts in Jewish Mysticism, Op. cit.*
40. **Seidman, R. & Kushner, L.:** *The Oracle of Kabbalah: Mystical Teachings of the Hebrew Letters, Op. cit.*

CHAPTER 10

1. *The Fathers According to Rabbi Nathan*, transl. J. Goldin, Yale University Press, New Haven & London 1995.
2. **Pixley, O.C.B.:** *The Armour of Light, a Technique for Healing the Self and Others*, Favil Press, London 1957.
— *The Armour of Light: A Technique of Healing the Self and Others*, Part 2, Helios Book Service Ltd., Cheltenham 1969.
—*The Magnet: Advanced Technique: A Sequel to "The Armour of Light" a Technique of Healing the Self and Others*, Favil Press, London 1958.
—*Olive Pixley's Spiritual Journey: Comprising Listening In, The Trail, Human Document*, Armour of Light Trust Council, Shere 1999.
—*A Book of Talks: A Companion Reader to The Armour of Light Part II*, Armour of Light Trust Council, Shere 2002.
3. **Idel, M.:** *Hasidism: Between Ecstasy and Magic, Op cit.*
—*Kabbalah and Eros, Op. cit.*
—*From Platonic to Hasidic Eros: Transformations of an Idle Man's Story*, in **Shulman, D.D. & Stroumsa, G.:** *Self and Self-transformation in the History of Religions*, Oxford University Press Inc., New York 2002.
4. **Katz, M. & Schwartz, G.:** *Swimming in a Sea of Talmud: Lessons for Everyday Living*, Jewish Publication Society, Philadelphia 1998.
5. **Glazerson, M.:** *Music and Kabbalah*, Raz-Ot Institute, Jerusalem 1988.
—*Letters of Fire: Mystical Insights into the Hebrew Language, Op. cit.*
6. **Gikatilla, J.:** *Gates of Light: Sha'are Orah, Op. cit.*
7. **Kaplan, A:** *Sefer Yetzirah: The Book of Creation in Theory and Practice, Op. cit.*
8. **Sharabi, S.:** *Or Levanah*, s.n., Jerusalem 1974.
9. *Siddur ha-Ari*, Yeshivat Sha'ar Ha-Shamayim, Mochon Sha'arei Ziv, Jerusalem 1983.
Horowitz, I.: *Siddur Sha'ar ha-Shamayim*, Ahavat Shalom, Jerusalem 1997.Brooklyn 1974.
Sharabi, S.: *Siddur Nehar Shalom*, Yeshivat Nehar Shalom, Jerusalem 1997.
10. **Abulafia, A.:** *Sefer Chayei ha-Olam ha-Ba, Op. cit.*
11. **Abulafia, A.:** *Mafteach ha-Shemot*, Aharon Barazani, Jerusalem 2001.
12. *Sefer Raziel ha-Malach, Op. cit.*
13. **Zacutto, M.:** *Shorshei ha-Shemot, Op. cit.*

14. **Dennis, G.W.:** *The Encyclopedia of Jewish Myth, Magic and Mysticism*, Llewellyn Publications, Woodbury 2007.
15. **Sharabi, S.:** *Or Levanah, Op. cit.*
16. **Kaplan, A.:** *Sefer Yetzirah: The Book of Creation In Theory and Practice, Op. cit.*
17. **Cordovero, M.:** *Pardes Rimmonim, Op. cit.*
18. **Gikatilla, J.:** *Gates of Light: Sha'are Orah, Op. cit.*
19. **Cordovero, M.:** *Pardes Rimmonim, Op. cit.*
20. **Kaplan, A.:** *Sefer Yetzirah: The Book of Creation In Theory and Practice, Op. cit.*
21. *Ibid.*
22. *Ibid.*
23. *Ibid.*
24. **Gray, W.G.:** *Qabalistic Concepts: Living the Tree, Op. cit.*
25. *Ibid.*
26. *Ibid.*
27. **Gikatilla, J.:** *Gates of Light: Sha'are Orah, Op. cit.*
28. **Wernberg-Moller, P.:** *The Manual of Discipline*, E.J. Brill, Leiden 1957.